"Here is a modern reader's editi   thor. It is a powerful Trinitarian with God is and must ever be the inside story of the real Christian's life. The editing is excellent, and the twenty-seven-page introduction and the thirty-page analytical outline make the treatise accessible, even inviting, to any who, with Richard Baxter, see "heart-work" as the essence of Christianity. John Owen is a profound teacher on all aspects of spiritual life, and it is a joy to welcome this reappearance of one of his finest achievements."

—J. I. Packer, the Board of Governors' professor of theology, Regent College

"Among English-speaking theologians and pastors, John Owen and Jonathan Edwards run neck and neck for the first place in profound, faithful, fruitful displays of the glory of God in the salvation of sinners. Not only that, they are both running for first among the ranks of those who show practically how that glory is experienced here and now. Owen may have the edge here. And *Communion with God* is his most extraordinary effort. No one else has laid open the paths of personal fellowship with the three persons of the Trinity the way Owen does. It is simply extraordinary. What an honor it would be to God if more of his children knew how to enjoy him the way Owen does."

—John Piper, pastor for preaching and vision,
Bethlehem Baptist Church, Minneapolis, Minnesota

"Owen is not for the faint of heart or for the impatient or for the lazy. But for those who want to deepen their understanding of God's greatness and how we walk with him, this book will repay, many times over, the effort its reading requires."

—David F. Wells, Andrew Mutch distinguished professor of historical
and systematic theology, Gordon-Conwell Theological Seminary

"This is just the right time for a republishing of John Owen's great work. There is renewed interest in the Trinity these days, and there is also a deep hungering for genuine spirituality. Owen combines the two in a powerful manner, pointing the way to a vital relationship with the triune God. It good to have this classic available again—and to have it introduced by gifted interpreters of Owen's life and thought."

—Richard J. Mouw, president;
professor of Christian philosophy, Fuller Seminary

"John Owen's treatise is remarkable in many ways. It is one of the finest examples of Owen's massive output. It is a landmark in Western Trinitarian thought, uniquely wedding profound theology to Christian piety. It vividly thrusts before us the Holy Trinity as the one object of our worship. Kapic and Taylor have removed many of the difficulties of seventeenth-century writing in this edition, making accessible an old classic to a new audience. This book could revolutionize your thoughts of God, your worship of him, and how you live in today's world."

—Robert Letham, senior tutor in systematic and historical theology,
Wales Evangelical School of Theology

"Union and communion with God the Holy Trinity lies at the heart of reformation theology. John Owen was one of the greatest expositors of this, and a new edition of his classic work on the subject, updated for modern readers, is long overdue. This is exactly the kind of teaching we need to revitalize the church in our generation. As Owen's experience of the living God becomes ours we shall be set on fire with longing to know God more deeply and serve him more faithfully in a world which needs him as much now as it did in Owen's day."

—Gerald L. Bray, research professor of Beeson Divinity School,
Samford University

"John Owen's *Communion with God* is the best thing there is on "relational theology." In a nuanced and biblically rich way, Owen develops the believer's responsive engagement with God the Holy Trinity through study, worship, and meditation. This is a remarkable book that will surprise and challenge. Kelly Kapic and Justin Taylor have nicely rewrapped it, making it accessible to a new generation."

—Paul Helm, Regent College

"Owen's exceptional work is partly a biblical and dogmatic treatise, partly a searching reflection on the practice of fellowship with the triune God. This new edition deserves to claim many new readers for a classic of Protestant practical divinity."

—John Webster, chair of systematic theology,
King's College, University of Aberdeen

"John Owen was perhaps the greatest of the Puritan theologians and this new edition of his classic study of Trinitarian spirituality will be a blessing to all who read it. God's self-revelation as the Father, the Son, and the Holy Spirit is not a teaching to be checked off and shelved away for doctrinal safekeeping. It is rather the ultimate basis of prayer, ethics, worship, and Christian life itself. No one presents this truth more powerfully than the great Owen, and Kelly Kapic and Justin Taylor's new edition of *Communion with God* gives us fresh access to his mind and heart."

—Timothy George, dean, Beeson Divinity School,
Samford University; senior editor, *Christianity Today*

COMMUNION WITH THE TRIUNE GOD

COMMUNION WITH THE TRIUNE GOD

JOHN OWEN

EDITED BY
KELLY M. KAPIC AND JUSTIN TAYLOR

FOREWORD BY
KEVIN J. VANHOOZER

CROSSWAY BOOKS
WHEATON, ILLINOIS

Communion with the Triune God
Copyright © 2007 by Kelly M. Kapic and Justin Taylor
Published by Crossway Books
        a publishing ministry of Good News Publishers
        1300 Crescent Street
        Wheaton, Illinois 60187

Cover design: Josh Dennis
Cover illustration: Bridgeman Art Library
First printing 2007
Printed in the United States of America

Library of Congress Cataloging-in-Publication Data

Owen, John, 1616–1683.
    Communion with the Triune God / by John Owen; edited by Kelly M. Kapic and Justin Taylor; foreword by Kevin J. Vanhoozer.
        p. cm.
    Rev. ed. of: Of communion with God the Father, Son, and Holy Ghost, each person distinctly in love, grace, and consolation.
    Includes indexes.
    ISBN 978-1-58134-831-6 (tpb)
    1. Spirituality. I. Kapic, Kelly M., 1972– II. Taylor, Justin, 1976– III. Owen, John, 1616–1683. Of communion with God the Father, Son, and Holy Ghost, each person distinctly in love, grace, and consolation. IV. Title.
BV4501.3.O93   2007
231.7—dc22

                                      2007020762

DP	15	14	13	12	11	10	09	08	07
	9	8	7	6	5	4	3	2	1

With gratitude and love to our parents:

Gary and Linda Kapic
Gerald and Diane Taylor

O F

Communion with God

The Father, Sonne, and Holy Ghoft,
Each Perfon Diftinctly;

I N

Love, Grace, and Confolation:

O R

THE SAINTS FELLOWSHIP

With the Father, Sonne, and Holy Ghoft,

UNFOLDED.

By *JOHN OWEN* D.D.

A Servant of *JESUS CHRIST*
in the Work of the Gofpell.

God is Love. 1 Joh. 4. 8.
Tell me O thou whom my Soule Loveth where thou Feedeft. Cant. 1.7.
Make haft my Beloved, Cant. 8. 14.
Grieve not the Holy Spirit of God whereby ye are Sealed to the day of Redemp-
tion. Ephef. 4. 30.
Now there are diverfities of Gifts but the fame fpirit. And there are differences
of Adminiftrations, but the fame Lord, and there are diverfities of opera-
tions but it is the fame God. 1 Cor. 12. 4, 5, 6.

OXFORD,
Printed by A. LICHFIELD Printer to the Vniverfity,
for *THO: ROBINSON. Anno Dm.* 1657.

CONTENTS

Part 3: Of Communion with the Holy Ghost

LIST OF ABBREVIATIONS

ANF	The Ante-Nicene Fathers
LXX	Septuagint
NPNF	*The Nicene and Post-Nicene Fathers*
NPNF[1]	*The Nicene and Post-Nicene Fathers*, Series 1
NPNF[2]	*The Nicene and Post-Nicene Fathers*, Series 2
PCG	*Poetae Comici Graeci*
PG	*Patrologia Graeca*
PL	*Patrologia Latina*

Foreword

As one who has ploughed postmodern fields and cleared deconstructive hermeneutical thickets, it gives me particular pleasure to introduce and commend the work of a seventeenth-century theologian that takes us to the very heart of Puritan faith, hope, and love. Despite my extended forays into various kinds of postliberal and postconservative theology—or perhaps because of them—John Owen's study of communion with the triune God strikes me as especially significant, even contemporary, and this for three, maybe four, reasons.

In the first place, much has been made of late concerning the "renaissance" of Trinitarian theology that began with Karl Barth and picked up steam throughout the twentieth century until it achieved "bandwagon" status around 1980. One of the most important present-day litmus tests for theologians pertains to how far one accepts (or understands!) Rahner's Rule: "the economic Trinity is the immanent Trinity and vice versa."

Read against the backdrop of the current discussion, Owen's approach to the doctrine of the Trinity is impressive indeed. Owen walks a fine line that balances the oneness and the threeness, emphasizing our communion "with each person distinctly" while at the same time insisting that to commune with each person is to commune with the one God. Perhaps one advantage of Owen's approach over more than a few contemporary approaches is that he is able to preserve the distinctness of the Father's love while simultaneously focusing on Christ as the one alone who makes it known.

A second point. Christianity, it has been said, is not a religion but a personal relation. Owen agrees that theology is relational, but his account of our relation with God bears little resemblance either to the casual way in which it sometimes gets played out in dumbed-down theology and worship or to the reductionistic way it gets worked out in wised-up theology that defines persons as "nothing but" relations and which views the God-humanity relation in terms of a flattened out mutuality. Owen's *Communion with the Triune God* is indispensable reading for all those who want to go deeper into the meaning of relationality than one typically goes in the pop-theology boats that float only on the psychological surface of the matter.

The gospel is the good news that in Christ there is union and communion with God. According to Owen, communion involves "mutual relations" between God and humankind—a giving and receiving—but it does not follow that God and humankind are equal partners. Only God can bring about the union that establishes and enables the subsequent communion. Humans enjoy fellowship with God, therefore, only by actively participating in what God has unilaterally done for them in Christ through the Spirit. Owen may here have something to teach contemporary theology concerning the nature of human participation in God's triune life, namely, that participation, like communion itself, is neither a legal fiction nor idle piety but rather the meat and drink of the Christian life. We appropriate the friendship God offers through the workings of his Word and Spirit in and through our natural human faculties.

The third significant feature is Owen's emphasis on theology for right worship and faithful practice. Here too, twenty-first-century theology is playing catch-up with the Puritans as it seeks ways of coordinating theory and practice, both informally, in everyday life, and formally, in theological education. Owen's work provides just the right balance, tempering spiritual experience with biblical exegesis, and argumentative rigor with pastoral application.

"I pray God with all my heart that I may be weary of every thing else but converse and communion with him" (letter to Sir John Hartopp). This prayer signals for me a fourth way in which Owen's *Communion with the Triune God* has something to contribute, in this case to my own work in progress. As one who has seen great potential in the notion of Scripture as made up of God's speech acts, I am encouraged and intrigued by Owen's way of relating communion and communication: "Our communion . . . with God consisteth in his *communication of himself unto us, with our return unto him* of that which he requireth and accepteth, flowing from that *union* which in Jesus Christ we have with him. . . ." To be sure, by "communication" Owen has in mind every kind of divine self-giving, not only the verbal and the cognitive. In this regard, Owen's emphasis, some three hundred years before Barth, on Christ as the "medium of all communication" between God and us is particularly noteworthy.

Though Owen was born the year Shakespeare died, his writing is somewhat less accessible. Yet what we have in Owen is ultimately a holy sonnet with an extended introduction and a protracted analysis: "Let me not to the marriage of true minds / Admit impediments." Communion with the Father, Son, and Spirit begins with God's love for us and ends in our love to God. Communion with the triune God is sweeter yet more profound than human friendship or any human relationship.

In sum: Owen's work anticipates key modern and postmodern developments without falling into some of the traps to which these later movements are prone. While John Bunyan probably did not have John Owen in mind when he wrote about the House of the Interpreter in *Pilgrim's Progress*, Christians today may nevertheless find Owen to be a reliable guide to the triune way of the Word.

Kevin J. Vanhoozer
Research Professor of Systematic Theology
Trinity Evangelical Divinity School, Deerfield, Illinois

ACKNOWLEDGMENTS

Few things are more pleasurable to authors and editors than when they reach the end of an exhausting project and finally have the opportunity to write acknowledgments. Sometimes people have the impression that editing books is less time consuming than writing them. While there is some truth to that, we have found that the amount of work that goes into preparing a volume like this is substantial, and consequently the help and encouragement of many people is just as vital. With that in mind, here are some of the people for whom we are so thankful, for without their partnership in this process, the present volume and our lives would have been impoverished.

Two of Kelly's former students and research assistants deserve special mention: Cameron Moran and Brian Hecker. They worked hard, put in countless hours, and were willing to go beyond the call of duty on many occasions. We also benefited from the Latin expertise of Casey Carmichael, Daniel Hill, and Jonathan Rockey, whose assistance certainly made this volume better. Others who provided support of various kinds, including much-needed encouragement, include: Tim Cooper, Jay Green, John Holberg, Jeff and Lynn Hall, Scott Jones, Danny Kapic, Ryan Kelly, John and Lynn Malley, Tad Mindemann, Susan Hardman Moore, Jeff Morton, Paul Morton, Joy Muether, J. I. Packer, Joshua Sowin (who helped Justin create www.johnowen.org), and Carl Trueman.

We would like to acknowledge the generous support received from the Kaleo Center at Covenant College, which is funded through Lilly Endowment Inc.

Kevin Vanhoozer is worthy of many thanks for his willingness to take time away from his many other projects to pen a foreword for this volume.

We are thankful to Allan Fisher of Crossway Books for endlessly supporting and believing in this project and to Lydia Brownback for editing it and offering encouragement along the way.

Our families have been incredibly gracious, and we wish to recognize our wives, Tabitha Kapic and Lea Taylor, for their tremendous support and love. You two are truly amazing; thank you for filling our lives with color and perspective. Our children, Jonathan and Margot Kapic, and Claira and Malachi Taylor, have been a constant source of joy, reminding us of the important things in life: trucks, stickers, sand, and giggling.

Finally, we dedicate this work to our parents: Gary and Linda Kapic, and Gerald and Diane Taylor. We are thankful for your consistent love and for the sacrifices you have made through the years. May you know and ever increase in your love of the triune God in whom we find rest and communion.

INTRODUCTION

Worshiping the Triune God:
The Shape of John Owen's Trinitarian Spirituality

KELLY M. KAPIC

"So much as we see of the love of God,
so much shall we delight in him, and no more."[1]

"No sooner do I conceive of the One
than I am illumined by the Splendour of the Three;
no sooner do I distinguish Them
than I am carried back to the One."[2]

Since 1942 there has been an incredibly popular BBC radio program entitled *Desert Island Discs*. During this show the host asks a guest to select just eight "must-have" recordings they would take to the island. Similar programs turn the focus from music to books. If you had just eight books, what would they include?

---

1. John Owen, "Communion with God," in *The Works of John Owen*, ed. William H. Goold, 24 vols. (Edinburgh: Johnson & Hunter; 1850–1855; reprint by Banner of Truth, 1965) (hereafter, *Works*), 2:36.

2. *Ou phthanō to hen noēsai, kai tois trisi perilampomai, ou phthanō ta tria dielein, kai eis to hen anapheromai.* Gregory of Nazianzus, *Oration 40: The Oration on Holy Baptism*, NPNF[2] 7:375; PG 36, col. 417B. Cited by Owen in *Works*, 2:10.

When I am occasionally asked such a question, there is always one book that makes my personal short list: John Owen's *Of Communion with God the Father, Son, and Holy Ghost, Each Person Distinctly, in Love, Grace, and Consolation.*[3] What surprises me, however, is how few people are aware of this particular classic. The good news is that Owen's writings are being rediscovered and appreciated by pastors, theologians, historians, and lay readers alike.[4] The reason is simple: his work has relevance for people in all of these categories.

Owen's writings are theologically rich, pastorally wise, and exegetically stimulating. One need not agree with everything this Puritan wrote in order to greatly profit from wrestling with his thinking. Because Owen's methodology consistently unites—rather than divides—knowledge about God and human nature, his work can have a fresh quality to it. His devotional reflection does not divorce spirituality from a robust theological infrastructure. Sadly, due to the barriers presented by Owen's difficult writing style, language, and cultural distance, his insights are often underappreciated by contemporary readers. It is our hope that through this new edition of an Owen classic, we can reintroduce a wider audience to John Owen and his approach to Trinitarian spirituality.

Brief Biography

John Owen (1616–1683) lived through an extraordinarily turbulent time in British history.[5] During his lifetime he personally witnessed the severity of a civil war, the beheading of a king, a parliament that consistently flirted with chaos, the return of an exiled king, deep religious strife, and even persecution at the hands of protestant and catholic alike. He even suffered the anguish of the death of his first wife and all of his children. Such experiences shaped this Puritan divine as he fluidly moved among the spheres of academic, political, and pastoral life.

---

3. This is the title from 1657, although even this title leaves out Owen's alternative title, which reads, *Or, The Saints Fellowship with the Father, Son, and Holy Ghost Unfolded*.

4. Those who have interacted with Owen in recent times demonstrate the growing recognition that this seventeenth-century author is receiving. Theologians include Colin Gunton, J. I. Packer, Sinclair Ferguson, Thomas Oden, Francis Watson, Alan Spence, Paul Helm, and Graham McFarlane. Church historians such as Carl Trueman, Sebastian Rehnman, Peter Toon, Joel Beeke, and Richard Muller have also given Owen renewed attention. Other authors who have drawn pastoral wisdom from Owen include John Piper, Jerry Bridges, Kris Lundgaard, and Larry Crabb.

5. The best biography on Owen remains Peter Toon, *God's Statesman: The Life and Work of John Owen: Pastor, Educator, Theologian* (Exeter: Paternoster, 1971).

Well trained at Oxford, Owen's career included not only working as an army chaplain at the personal request of Oliver Cromwell, but also serving as the vice chancellor of Oxford University (1652–1657) and dean of Christ Church, Oxford (1651–1660). When he was not serving in the academy, he was normally assisting in some kind of pastoral work, which continued until the very end of his life. Through all of this, Owen was able to produce a massive amount of literature: ultimately his writings in the authoritative nineteenth-century edition include twenty-four tightly packed volumes.[6] Through these thousands of pages, Owen covers everything from church government to justification by faith, from toleration to the nature of the atonement.[7] In the study before us, we find him delving into what it means for believers to commune with the triune God.

Communion with God: The Book

Communion with God was first published in 1657, but the material in the book grew out of sermons preached some years earlier.[8] Apparently there were many who, upon first hearing him preach through this material, were eager for it to get into print and were frustrated at the delay.[9] Remembering that the original context was primarily pastoral and not an exercise in academic polemics helps explain the tone of much of the discourse. While it is clear that he modified, revised, and added various

---

6. See n. 1. The Banner edition leaves out the Latin writings, but additional translations have recently made these volumes accessible to a wider audience: John Owen, *Biblical Theology, or, the Nature, Origin, Development, and Study of Theological Truth, in Six Books . . .* , trans. Stephen Wescott (Morgan, PA: Soli Deo Gloria, 1994). For other primary sources, see Peter Toon, ed., *The Correspondence of John Owen* (Cambridge: James Clarke, 1970); Peter Toon, ed., *The Oxford Orations of Dr. John Owen* (Cornwall: Gospel Communications, 1971).

7. Thankfully, the secondary literature on Owen is growing. For full bibliographical information, see johnowen.org/bibliography. Some good places to begin include Sinclair B. Ferguson, *John Owen on the Christian Life* (Edinburgh: Banner of Truth, 1987); Kelly M. Kapic, *Communion with God: The Divine and the Human in the Theology of John Owen* (Grand Rapids, MI: Baker Academic, 2007); Sebastian Rehnman, *Divine Discourse: The Theological Methodology of John Owen*, Texts and Studies in Reformation and Post-Reformation Thought (Grand Rapids, MI: Baker, 2002); Carl R. Trueman, *The Claims of Truth: John Owen's Trinitarian Theology* (Carlisle, PA: Paternoster, 1998); idem., *John Owen* (Aldershot: Ashgate, 2007).

8. For a detailed treatment of the history, subsequent debates, and theology of this volume, see Kapic, *Communion with God*, 147–205.

9. Owen writes in the preface: "It is now six years past since I was brought under an engagement of promise for the publishing of some meditations on the subject which you will find handled in the ensuing treatise. The reasons of this delay, being not of public concern, I shall not need to mention." He also refers to "those who have been in expectation of this duty from me."

details to this work before it was published, the heart of the material points back to the pulpit.

Convinced that believers need to know their God in order to be faithful worshipers, Owen framed his approach to Christian spirituality in a Trinitarian manner; for only in the divine persons did Owen believe we can rightly know God. Owen's contribution lies not merely in what is said but in how and when he says it, for he was a master of theological creativity and expression. The very structure of this work—with his emphasis on the Three as the way to understand the One—makes even this book's design significant in the history of Western theology. We discover a work that is intentionally and consistently *Trinitarian in structure* and *Christocentric in emphasis*.[10] In order to appreciate his method and content, let us turn to the work itself.

Overview of This Essay

Brief highlights of what will be covered in the work may prove helpful. We begin by exploring the general idea of communion with the eternal triune God; this includes reflections on Owen's distinction between union and communion, as well as his stress on the importance that the one God is eternally three. From there we turn our attention to the Father, of whom Owen believes we often have a distorted view which makes us hesitant to commune with him. When Owen's focus turns to the Son we will discover what it means to rightly know God by fixing our eyes on Christ, the great Lover of the church. Finally we briefly survey Owen's extensive work on the Holy Spirit. Special attention is paid to how, in this particular treatise, Owen encourages us to identify and worship the Spirit of God. In the end we will have a panoramic view of Owen's approach to communion with the triune God.

Communion with God: A Triune Approach

Union and Communion: Spiritual Security without Neglecting Human Activity

Central to Owen's thesis is the idea that *communion* requires "mutual relations" between God and us. Before turning to examine the relations

---

10. Owen spends more pages on his exposition on Christ (part 2, 40–222) than he does on the sections of the Father (part 1, 17–40) and Spirit (part 3, 222–74) combined. Page numbers here refer to the Goold edition.

among the divine persons, we will begin by considering our relationship with God. To experience communion there needs to be fellowship and communication—e.g., shared affections, response, delight, and satisfaction. In other words, when Owen speaks of our communion with God, he really means active communion, and not merely a state of passivity. "Communion consists in giving and receiving."[11]

But to appreciate how this informs his view of spirituality, it is important to note that Owen maintains an essential distinction between union and communion. Believers are united to Christ in God by the Spirit. This *union* is a unilateral action by God, in which those who were dead are made alive, those who lived in darkness begin to see the light, and those who were enslaved to sin are set free to be loved and to love. When one speaks of "union," it must be clear that the human person is merely receptive, being the object of God's gracious action. This is the state and condition of all true saints.

Communion with God, however, is distinct from union. Those who are united to Christ are called to *respond* to God's loving embrace. While union with Christ is something that does not ebb and flow, one's experience of communion with Christ can fluctuate. This is an important theological and experiential distinction, for it protects the biblical truth that we are saved by radical and free divine grace. Furthermore, this distinction also protects the biblical truth that the children of God have a relationship with their Lord, and that there are things they can do that either help or hinder it. When a believer grows comfortable with sin (whether sins of commission or sins of omission) this invariably affects the level of intimacy this person feels with God. It is not that the Father's love grows and diminishes for his children in accordance with their actions, for his love is unflinching. It is not that God turns from us, but that we run from him. Sin tends to isolate the believer, making him feel distant from God. Then come the accusations—both from Satan and self—which can make the believer worry that he is under God's wrath. In truth, however, saints stand not under wrath but in the safe shadow of the cross.

While a saint's consistency in prayer, corporate worship, and biblical meditation are not things that make God love him more or less, such activities tend to foster the beautiful experience of communion with God. Giving in to temptations and neglecting devotion to God threaten the

---

11. *Works*, 2:22.

communion but not the union.[12] And it is this union which encourages the believer to turn from sin and to the God who is quick to forgive, abounding in compassion, and faithful in his unending love. Let there be no misunderstanding—for Owen, Christian obedience was of utmost importance, but it was always understood to flow out of this union and never seen as the ground for it.[13] In harmony with Bunyan and other dissenters like him, Owen "insisted upon a very personal and emotional experience of union with Christ and the Holy Spirit," and out of this union naturally flowed active communion.[14]

Along these lines, when Owen unpacks the work of the Spirit, he makes a distinction between the Spirit being received in terms of "sanctification" and the Spirit's work of "consolation."[15] When he refers to *sanctification* in this context he means the work whereby the Spirit sets us apart, uniting us to Christ and making us alive. This is "a mere passive reception, as a vessel receives water."[16] This is the movement from being outside the kingdom of God to becoming a child of the King.

When Owen speaks of the Spirit's work of *consolation*, he has in mind the comforting activity of the Spirit in the life of the believer. Christians need not be passive in the hope that the Spirit will bring comfort; rather, they should (1) seek his comfort by focusing on the promises of God realized in the Spirit, (2) call out to the Spirit of supplication to bring consolation, and (3) attend "to his motions," which take us to the Father and Son. In all of this we rightly and actively receive him who freely comes to bring comfort and grace. Again, our union with God in Christ is never in jeopardy, but our sense of fellowship with God does necessitate appropriate human agency and response. "The Comforter may always abide with us, though not always comfort us; he who is the Comforter may abide, though he do not always that work."[17] Believers have the Spirit of God in them, without question, but that does not mean they should view their actions as irrelevant. Along these lines, sometimes the Spirit "tenders [i.e., offers] consolation to us" but we do not receive it

---

12. *Works*, 2:126.

13. The contemporary idea of accepting Jesus as "Savior" but not as "Lord" would make little sense to Owen, and that is not what he is arguing for here. The call to Christian holiness is never optional in Owen's view. Nonetheless, if the cart is moved before the horse, all kinds of theological and pastoral problems arise, and this is what he is aiming to avoid.

14. Dewey D. Wallace, *Puritans and Predestination: Grace in English Protestant Theology, 1525–1695* (Chapel Hill: University of North Carolina, 1982), 183.

15. For this discussion, see esp. *Works*, 2:231–33.

16. *Works*, 2:231.

17. *Works*, 2:233.

and thus do not enjoy the full fruit of his activity in us. Christian living, for Owen, neither divides the labor between the divine and human nor neglects the activity of both: we work because God works in us.[18]

Any true relation requires what Owen elsewhere calls *mutuality*, and we should not shy away from the fact that we are invited, by the Spirit, to actively commune with God.[19] This communion assumes the security of the union. Keeping in mind Owen's distinction between union and communion, one is better able to make sense of his conclusion: "*The Spirit as a sanctifier* comes with *power*, to conquer an unbelieving heart; *the Spirit as a comforter* comes with *sweetness*, to be received in a believing heart."[20] Though the Spirit will never abandon a believer, it should not surprise us that neglecting such receptivity to the Spirit's movement compromises our sense of intimacy. For Owen, grace must be understood as the ground of this relationship, from first to last, from justification to preservation of the saints, from God's acceptance of us to his glorifying the saints—grace is the bottom of the entire understanding of the saints' security and privilege before God.[21] This grace, however, demands rather than denies human response. But if we are to respond rightly, we must know to whom we are responding.

The One God Who Is Eternally Three

Who is God? To whom do I pray, trust, and cry out in times of confusion and pain? Can God really be known, or do we just have signposts to God that have little correspondence with who he really is? What does it mean for me to *know* God? Such questions *should* cut to the heart of Christian faith and experience. What could be more fundamental than making sure that one's praise is directed toward the true God and that one's view of that God is not mere fancy but correspondent with *his* reality?

Drawing from Scripture, Owen shows us that the one true God is, from all eternity, Father, Son, and Spirit; and in light of his self-manifestation,

---

18. For more on this discussion, see Kelly M. Kapic, "Life in the Midst of Battle: John Owen's Approach to Sin, Temptation, and the Christian Life," in *Overcoming Sin and Temptation: Three Classic Works by John Owen*, ed. Kelly M. Kapic and Justin Taylor (Wheaton, IL: Crossway, 2006), 23–35, esp. 32–35.

19. Owen defines communion in this way: "Our communion, then, with God consisteth in his *communication of himself unto us, with our returnal unto him* of that which he requireth and accepteth, flowing from that *union*" (*Works*, 2:81; emphasis in original).

20. *Works*, 2:233; emphasis mine.

21. Cf. *Works*, 2:155, 169–222.

we are to know, love, and respond to him as such. It is crucial here to recognize that God is and always has been triune: he does not become triune at some point in history. While such a distinction may seem unduly technical, in truth the eternality of the Trinity is pivotal to rightly grounding all manner of key doctrines (such as God's love). Without this eternal triune reality, we end up with God needing something outside himself before he can be loving. We can also end up misunderstanding the triune persons, whether pitting the persons against one another or creating an inappropriate hierarchy in God.

Owen always views the *eternal distinction* within the Godhead in light of its *unbreakable unity*.[22] Accordingly, the Father, Son, and Spirit "know each other, love each other, delight in each other, must needs be distinct; and so are they represented unto our faith." Their distinction "lies in their mutual relation one to another," and thus we are to understand that the "distinct actings and operations" of the persons grow out of this eternal mutual relation.[23] In other words, the Father is eternally the Father and not the Son, and the Son is always the Son and not the Father, while the Spirit is distinct from the Father and the Son, though proceeding from them both.[24] So when the triune God acts, he acts as he is—in perfect triunity.

Human communion with God presupposes the eternal communion of the divine persons in perfect unity and eternal distinction. Unity and distinction are crucial themes in Owen's approach to communion with God, for they tell us something about God and, consequently, something about how we are to approach him. First of all, Owen stresses the fact that *God* is free, and his freedom is framed in a Trinitarian manner:

> [S]o the love of the Father in sending the Son is free, and his sending doth no ways prejudice the liberty and love of the Son, but that he lays down his life freely also; so the satisfaction and purchase made by the Son doth no way prejudice the freedom of the Father's grace in pardoning and accepting us thereupon; so the Father's and Son's sending of the Spirit doth not derogate from his freedom in his workings, but he gives freely what he gives. And the reason of this is, because the will of the Father, Son, and Holy Ghost, is essentially the same; so that in the acting of one there is the counsel of all and each freely therein.[25]

---

22. *Works*, 2:10.

23. Both quotes are from *A Brief Declaration and Vindication of the Trinity*, in *Works*, 2:406.

24. Cf. *Works*, 2:337, 405.

25. *Works*, 2:235. Cf. *Works*, 2:238–39. While beyond our focus here, it is noteworthy that Owen often defends divine freedom first, believing that human freedom can only make sense in light of divine freedom.

Such comments point back to Owen's underlying belief in the covenant of redemption—an idea that had growing significance in the seventeenth century.[26] Scripture passages that emphasize the sending of the Son and Spirit, as well as the Father's love for the world, are all taken as indications of the eternal Trinity. Thus, in perfect oneness the three persons willed and desired the redemption of the elect. Hundreds of times throughout his writings Owen employs such language as "the counsels of God," "eternal counsels," the "divine counsel," and "counsels of his will." Such references often (though not always) point to the communion of the divine persons. Here is divine freedom, knowledge, and perfect unity—here is the One God upon whom our salvation rests.

An example of this type of approach is seen in Owen's book *Pneumatologia*. Here he exegetes John 16:13–15, which describes the Spirit speaking "whatever he shall hear." Creatively unpacking the idea of "hearing," Owen argues that this indicates a *distinction* among the persons, but not a *devaluation* of the Spirit. "Being the Spirit of the Father and Son, proceeding from both, he is equally participant of their counsels," and thus such texts point to the Spirit's "infinite knowledge of the eternal counsels of the Father and Son; he is no stranger unto them."[27]

Building on the eternal counsels, it is clear that the whole Trinity is active and exalted in redemption.[28] While Christ is at the center of the history of redemption, this divine movement of grace is triune and occurs accordingly. Owen even affirms, through use of a classic maxim, that what might be taken as "inequality of office" among the persons should in no way "prejudice the equality of nature."[29] We do not have

---

26. Cf. J. I. Packer, "A Puritan Perspective: Trinitarian Godliness according to John Owen," in *God the Holy Trinity: Reflections on Christian Faith and Practice*, ed. Timothy George (Grand Rapids, MI: Baker Academic, 2006), 101. Packer, 163, rightly highlights how John's Gospel was key in forming such views, and he gives a sampling of Johannine texts the interested reader could explore: John 3:16–17; 6:35–46; 10:1–18; chap. 17 passim. For background literature on sixteenth- and seventeenth-century approaches to various aspects of covenant theology, see, e.g., John von Rohr, *The Covenant of Grace in Puritan Thought*, ed. Charley Harkwick and James O. Duke, AAR Studies in Religion, vol. 45 (Atlanta: Scholars Press, 1986); David Wai-Sing Wong, "The Covenant Theology of John Owen" (Ph.D. diss., Westminster Theological Seminary, 1998); Peter A. Lillback, *The Binding of God: Calvin's Role in the Development of Covenant Theology*, Texts and Studies in Reformation and Post-Reformation Thought (Grand Rapids, MI: Baker Academic, 2001); W. J. van Asselt, *The Federal Theology of Johannes Cocceius (1603–1669)*, Studies in the History of Christian Thought, 100 (Leiden; Boston: Brill, 2001).

27. *Works*, 3:195–96.

28. E.g., *Works*, 2:179.

29. Here he uses the classic maxim: "inaequalitas officii non tollit aequalitatem naturae," [("Inequality of office does not remove equality of nature.")] *Works*, 2:229.

competing gods, but rather one God in three persons, free and united, wise and deliberate—One God, yet having distinction in himself.

While distinctions among the persons can be made, God always works in perfect harmony and is worshiped in light of that. Three examples may prove helpful. First, consider the example of *faith*—it is given by the Father as the source, directed toward the Son who secures and increases faith, and empowered by the Spirit of life.[30] Second, Owen employs the model of God giving diverse *gifts*: different gifts come from the same Spirit, and varieties of service from the same Lord, and various empowerments come from the same God: "so graces and gifts are bestowed, and so are they received."[31] They come from the divine persons, and thus from God, and we respond to the persons, and thus to God himself. Third, *holiness* for the saints is the will of the triune God for his people. Thus, the Father has "appointed it" (Eph. 2:10), the Son also ordains or appoints it "as the mediator" (John 15:16), and the Spirit "appoints and ordains" this holiness in believers (Acts 13:2). Christian obedience is placed in the context of the desire and empowerment of the triune God: "Our holiness, our obedience, work of righteousness, is one eminent and especial end of the peculiar dispensation of Father, Son, and Spirit, in the business of exalting the glory of God in our salvation—of the electing love of the Father, the purchasing love of the Son, and the operative love of the Spirit."[32] Our response and "gospel" obedience lights up the glory of the Father, Son, and Spirit—distinctly, yet in perfect unity.[33]

The point is that a believer's encounter with God is *always* an encounter with a divine person, not an abstraction. Building on Ephesians 2:18, Owen recognizes that when we approach the Father we come through the Son and by the Spirit: "the persons [are] being here considered as engaged *distinctly* unto the accomplishment of the counsel of the will of God revealed in the gospel."[34] In other words, distinction does not obliterate divine unity, nor does divine unity undercut distinction. Rather, unity governs distinction, and distinction must inform conceptions of unity.

Owen concludes that our communion with God is always communion with the divine persons, for *there is no God other than the persons*. His

---

30. *Works*, 2:18.
31. *Works*, 2:10. He bases this on 1 Cor. 12:4–6; cf. Eph. 4:6, which has a similar list of "one Spirit . . . one Lord . . . one God and Father of all."
32. *Works*, 2:182.
33. *Works*, 2:183–84.
34. *Works*, 2:10; emphasis in original.

thesis is fairly clear: "There is no grace whereby our souls go forth unto God, no act of divine worship yielded unto him, no duty or obedience performed, but they are distinctly directed unto Father, Son, and Spirit."[35] Later he adds, "There being such a distinct communication of grace from the several persons of the Deity, the saints must needs have distinct communion with them."[36] We worship this one God, but to rightly worship him, we approach the persons, not an abstract force. In this way, he echoes the claim of Gregory of Nazianzus that the "three are a single whole in their Godhead and the single whole is three in personalities."[37] Owen is very sympathetic with this early Cappadocian formulation of the Trinity, believing it positively influences our view of worship.

Worship That Is Trinitarian

Worship is always and only directed to the triune God. Thus, we worship the distinct persons, and yet "the person, as the person, of any one of them [i.e., the three divine persons], is not the prime *object* of divine worship, but as it is *identified* with the nature or essence of God."[38] In other words, God's essence is the object of worship. Nevertheless, you can never separate or extract the "essence" by moving beyond the persons. There is no "God behind the gods."

Consequently, when one of the divine *persons* works, *God* works, and thus is praised as God himself. According to Owen, there is always a "concurrence of the actings and operations of the whole Deity in that *dispensation*, wherein each person concurs to the work of our salvation, unto every act of our communion with each singular person."[39] To illustrate: while the Father is commonly associated with *creation*, the Son and Spirit are not absent or passive. Similarly, while one commonly looks to the Son in terms of *redemption*, in truth the Father and Spirit are essential to this work; likewise, a believer's *sanctification* cannot be understood apart from the Father and Son, despite this doctrine's common link to the Spirit.[40]

---

35. *Works*, 2:15.

36. *Works*, 2:16.

37. *Or.* 31.9. St Gregory of Nazianzus, *On God and Christ: The Five Theological Orations and Two Letters to Cledonius*, trans. Frederick Williams and Lionel R. Wickham (Crestwood, NY: St. Vladimir's Seminary Press, 2002), 123. It should be kept in mind that in a post-Descartes and post-Freud world, "person" and "personalities" can carry connotations (e.g., automony, independence, etc.) very different from originally intended.

38. *Works*, 2:18.

39. Ibid.

40. Cf. *Works*, 2:228.

Communion is with God. To commune with a divine person is nothing short of communion with God himself—not a part of God, not God
behind a mask, but God himself. Christians practice distinct communion
with the Father, Son, and Spirit, but they do not worship three gods;
rather, they bow down before the one God who is triune, in perfect
unity. Here is the drama, beauty, and vibrancy of worship. In this light
we can now appreciate Owen's significant use of Gregory of Nazianzus's
statement: "No sooner do I conceive of the One than I am illumined by
the Splendour of the Three; no sooner do I distinguish Them than I am
carried back to the One."[41]

In his own way, Owen explores the relationship between worship and
the Trinity. "The *divine nature* is the reason and cause of all worship;
so that it is impossible to *worship any one* person, and not worship the
whole Trinity."[42] He goes on to explain:

> Our access in our worship is said to be "to the Father"; and this "through
> Christ," or his mediation; "by the Spirit," or his assistance. *Here is a
> distinction of the persons, as to their operations, but not at all as to their
> being the object of our worship.* For the Son and the Holy Ghost are no
> less worshipped in our access to God than the Father himself; only, the
> grace of the Father, which we obtain by the mediation of the Son and
> the assistance of the Spirit, is that which we draw nigh to God for. So
> that *when, by the distinct dispensation of the Trinity, and every person,
> we are led to worship . . . any person, we do herein worship the whole
> Trinity*; and *every person,* by what name soever, of Father, Son, or Holy
> Ghost, *we invocate him.*[43]

Our worship is always directed toward the divine persons, but in doing
so, it is rightly given to God himself. To worship the Son is not to worship a part or portion of God, but rather it is to praise the One God

---

41. Op. cit., see n. 2 above.

42. *Works*, 2:268. Cf. *Works*, 12:380.

43. *Works*, 2:269; emphases mine. In his work *Christologia* (*The Person of Christ*) Owen makes
a similar observation: "1. That the divine nature, which is individually the same in each person
of the holy Trinity, is the proper formal object of all divine worship, in adoration and invocation;
wherefore, no one person is or can be worshipped, but in the same individual act of worship each
person is equally worshipped and adored. 2. That it is lawful to direct divine honour, worship, and
invocation unto any person, in the use of his peculiar name—the Father, Son, or Spirit—or unto them
altogether; but to make any request unto one person, and immediately the same unto another, is not
exemplified in the Scripture, nor among the ancient writers of the church" (*Works*, 1:20–21). Owen
sees this rule in many of the Fathers, including Augustine in *Enchirid.* xxxviii: "*Quando unus trium
in aliquo opere nominatur, universa operari trinitas intelligitur*" ("When one person of the three is
named in any work, the whole Trinity is to be understood to be working"), cited in *Works*, 1:21.

in three persons. And in this way, we are reminded that in the end, "the distinction, of the persons in the Trinity is not to be fancied, but believed."[44]

Knowing the Father: Overcoming Common Distortions

Unfortunately, many Christians often have a distorted view of the heavenly Father. We tend to view him as angry and full of wrath toward us. While we imagine Jesus as the one who loves us, the Father is portrayed as full of hesitation toward us—distant at best, furious at worst. It is as if Jesus pleads with the Father to put up with us and to let us live, perhaps even against the Father's desire. We often view Jesus as the "kind" person of the Trinity, with the Father only wanting us punished. Is the Father, in fact, really reluctant to show tenderness toward people?

According to Owen, the whole movement of the biblical drama of redemption points in a different direction. Jesus is not the one who convinces the Father to love us, but, rather, the Son of God becomes incarnate *in light* of the Father's eternal and free love toward us. The Father is not at odds with the Son, but rather, God the Father is love, and *out of his love* he sent his Son to die for our sins—"this love [of the Father] . . . is antecedent to the purchase of Christ."[45] In other words, while the work of Christ is all-important for redemption, it does not *make* the Father love us but is rather the *outgrowth* of God's love.[46]

Out of the Father's love the Son is sent as the embodiment of love, and the Spirit pours this love into the hearts of his children. Here the distinct actions among the divine persons are united by the same love of God. It makes sense that the test of authenticity for those who claim to know God is love—for this God is love, and those who have encountered the Son and are enlivened by the Spirit will surely show signs of love. And yet our love is always understood as a *response* to God's love, not that which generates God's love toward us.[47] Put simply, we love because God first loved us (1 John 4:19). This is what it means to discover freedom, for (in Christ and by the Spirit) saints are those who have been freed to love God and others. All of this points back to the love of the Father.

---

44. *Works*, 2:270.
45. *Works*, 2:20.
46. Cf. *Works*, 2:198–99.
47. *Works*, 2:26–31.

If the antecedent love of the Father is lost, then we might mistakenly believe that God's love for us is contingent upon our human efforts. This is not merely the mistake of ancient Pelagianism, which reduced the gospel to mere moralism, but it is also the danger of evangelical Christians who, in practice, live as if God's love for them ebbs and flows according to their actions. So when we have our quiet times for the day, or when we have given a tithe, we are confident of God's love toward us. But when our days become crowded and personal devotions end up neglected, we start to avoid God, sensing that we are under his wrath and anger. We imagine that God is waiting for us to get ourselves together before we again enter his presence. Such thinking betrays our failure to grasp the security of our union and the depth of God's love and consequently disrupts our communion with him.

Making God's love contingent on our action is a sad but common misunderstanding in the church. Remember, a believer's union is never in jeopardy. For God's love "is an eternal love, that had no beginning, that shall have no ending; that cannot be heightened by any act of ours, that cannot be lessened by any thing in us."[48] While our sense of communion with God may fluctuate, his love does not grow and diminish. The wrath of God against the sin of saints was exhausted on the cross.[49] Thus, while it is true that God sometimes disciplines his children in their sin and disobedience (cf. Heb. 12:6), he is not wrathful toward them. His disposition toward his children is always one of love. This love can bring forth the kind discipline of the loving Father, but it is just that—*an expression of love, not vengeful wrath*.[50] In fact, Owen estimates that nothing is "more grievous to the Lord, nor more subservient to the design of Satan" than for believers to have such "hard thoughts" of God.[51]

Because Owen was familiar with common Christian struggles, he knew all too well that believers often view the Father in a negative light. Instead of worshiping a compassionate God, they envision him as distant, lacking sweetness, "always angry, yea, implacable," a consuming fire with "everlasting burnings" and thus inapproachable.[52] Owen notes that some believers "are afraid to have good thoughts of God. They

---

48. *Works*, 2:30.
49. This is assumed in Owen's understanding of propitiation, an idea that appears often in his works, e.g., *Works*, 1:152; 6:381.
50. Cf. *Works*, 2:30–31.
51. *Works*, 2:34–35.
52. *Works*, 2:22, 32, 34, 36.

think it a boldness to eye God as good, gracious, tender, kind, loving. . . . And [they] think herein they do well."[53] Such a misunderstanding can quickly sap the life out of God's people. While such distortions may delight Satan, "it is exceeding[ly] grievous to the Spirit of God to be so slandered in the hearts of those whom he dearly loves."[54] Elsewhere when talking about the believer's struggles with sin, Owen powerfully reminds his readers of the great difference between their sad expectations and the Father's reality: "I *mourn* in secret under the power of my lusts and sin, where no eyes see me; but the Father sees me, and is full of compassion."[55] We need not run from the Father, but rather to his open arms of love, for by his Son and Spirit he can renew and strengthen us. He stands not over us in judgmental silence, but he sends his Word and Wisdom, that we might know the power and degree of his redeeming love. Run from him? That is the last thing he desires. Run to him—this is to understand the glory of the gospel: "Assure thyself, then, there is nothing more acceptable unto the Father, than for us to keep up our hearts unto him as the eternal fountain of all that rich grace which flows out to sinners in the blood of Jesus."[56]

To have communion with the Father—since communion consists in *mutual* relations—means that we must respond to his love. This is done, according to Owen, by receiving his love, and then by returning love to him. The order is essential: our love is always "consequential" to God's love—he does not love us based on a contingent condition that we love him, but we only and always love him based on his prior love for us.[57]

The great revelation of Christ to us is that of "God as a Father," and this matters greatly, "for the love of the Father is the only rest of the soul."[58] Elsewhere Owen proclaims, "the souls of believers exceedingly magnify Jesus Christ, that they can behold the face of God with boldness, confidence, peace, joy, assurance—that they can call him Father, bear themselves on his love, walk up and down in quietness, and without fear."[59] This statement comes in the context of Owen's noting that before we are brought into the faith, our thoughts of God are full of fear,

---

53. *Works*, 2:35.
54. Ibid.
55. *Works*, 2:262.
56. *Works*, 2:35.
57. *Works*, 2:29.
58. *Works*, 2:23.
59. *Works*, 2:191.

uncertainty, and disquiet. But to encounter the heavenly Father in his love, grace, and fellowship, we are transformed, and that transformation is understood in the context of relationship. The redeemed stand in the surety of God's full love, acceptance, mercy, and empowering grace. We need not run from God but, rather, rest in him.

Embraced by the Son

While Owen's theological approach is unapologetically Trinitarian, he is not shy about being Christ-centered—Jesus Christ is the mediator between God and man who grounds our knowledge and communion in God. To know God, we are called to look to Christ. We are often tempted to formulate views of God without reference to Christ, and in this way we run the risk of constructing a philosophical rather than biblical conception of the divine. In truth, Scripture in general and Christ in particular must govern our notion of God.

To Know God, Look to the Son

Divine attributes, or truths about God, should always be viewed through the lens of Christ. Owen argues that we will never understand "some of the most eminent and glorious properties of God" unless we see them as revealed in "the Lord Christ, but only by and in him."[60] For example, our knowledge of God's love and pardoning grace must be located in Christ and him alone. In fact, regarding some divine attributes, we have comparatively "no light of but in him; and of all the rest no true light but by him."[61] A person who claims to know God apart from these truths in Christ "knows him not at all. They know an idol, and not the only true God." For the Son is the great revelation of the Father (Heb. 1:3), and the Spirit always draws believers to the Son, who is the perfect image of God. By Jesus Christ "alone we have our understanding to know him that is true."[62] Elsewhere he writes: "There is no acquaintance with God, as love, and full of kindness, patience, grace, and pardoning mercy . . . but only in Christ."[63]

To appreciate Owen's Christ-centered approach we must recognize that for him, the incarnate Lord is the *"medium of all communication*

---

60. *Works*, 2:81.
61. Ibid.
62. *Works*, 2:83.
63. *Works*, 2:109.

between God and us. In him we meet, in him we walk. All influences of love, kindness, mercy, from God to us, are through him; all our returns of love, delight, faith, obedience unto God, are all through him."[64] While we have already noted that communion with God is fellowship with the Trinity, Owen's Trinitarian structure has a christocentric focus. "From him [Christ] have we the Spirit of life and power, whereby he bears, as on eagles' wings, swiftly, safely, in the paths of walking with God. Any step that is taken in any way, by strength that is not immediately from Christ, is one step towards hell."[65] Notice that Christ provides the strength through his Spirit. By emphasizing Christ, Owen is not meaning to pit the divine persons against one another but is aiming to maintain the biblical pattern and method for framing our communion with God. We come to the Father through the Son in the Spirit.

In addition to the divine attributes of love and mercy, Owen argues that other attributes are more fully appreciated in light of the incarnation. Here he includes such attributes as divine justice, patience, wisdom, and all-sufficiency—each of these truths about God are known at a whole different level in Jesus Christ.[66] So discussions about the attributes of God are best viewed, not vaguely, but clearly through a christological lens. To speak of these attributes as philosophical abstractions, and not in light of the incarnation, is to risk opening up all kinds of sub-Christian conceptions of God. On the other hand, Owen argues that discussing God's attributes in light of Christ yields not just greater understanding but also strong comfort for God's people. These attributes apart from Christ bring only feelings of terror, misery, and uncertainty. "There is no *saving knowledge of any property of God*, nor such as brings *consolation*, but what alone is to be had in Christ Jesus, being laid up in him, and manifested by him."[67] Going even further, Owen concludes that not only must our knowledge of God be christologically formed, but also our knowledge of *ourselves*! We cannot rightly know ourselves apart from Christ, and thus a crucial aspect of the Spirit's work is to reshape our understanding of self as illumined by the incarnate Son.[68] Finally, he connects the dots and concludes that our conception of what it means to "walk with God" must grow out of the revelation of God

64. Ibid.
65. *Works*, 2:110.
66. See *Works*, 2:83–94.
67. *Works*, 2:91.
68. Cf. *Works*, 2:94–106.

in Jesus Christ.[69] These are the keys of understanding any communion with God.

When Owen writes of the empowering love of Christ, which is the very love of God, he notes that this love actually makes things happen. "He *loves* life, grace, and holiness *into* us; he *loves* us also *into* covenant, *loves* us *into* heaven."[70] Notice that Owen frames this discussion in terms of love, and not in abstract philosophical speculation about predestination. How are we made alive and holy? By the love of Christ. How do we enjoy eternal communion with God? Because God in Christ loves us into his holy presence. "How many millions of sins, in every one of the elect, every one whereof were enough to condemn them all, hath this love overcome! [W]hat mountains of unbelief doth it remove!"[71]

The redeeming love of God is not something that can be found in contemplating the glorious stars and moon, or the regularity of the seasons. Only in Christ Jesus do we discover with utter clarity that we are not dealing with a distant deity, but the Creator God whose love becomes incarnate. Divine love cannot be put into a category of vague spirituality that can be equally understood in all religions. Rather, according to Owen, the full revelation and anchor of our understanding of God's love must be found in the incarnation.

The Lover Appears: Drawing from the Song of Songs

Following a long tradition in Western theology, Owen draws heavily from the imagery of the Song of Songs to describe the love between Christ and his bride. While allegorical interpretations of this great biblical poem can be highly suspect and problematic, we should nevertheless avoid throwing the baby out with the bath water. Certainly it seems that this Song was originally about the celebration of human love and sexuality—we should not let a neo-platonic fear of the physical lead us to neglect this natural reading of the text. On the other hand, we should also not allow modernist notions of a "scientific hermeneutic" to blind us from recognizing fascinating biblical parallels. Elsewhere in Scripture God is described as in a marital relationship with Israel, and Christ is the groom of his church, the bride. In fact, one day there will be a great wedding celebration when this relationship will be consummated in its

---

69. *Works*, 2:106–17.

70. *Works*, 2:63; my emphasis.

71. *Works*, 2:63.

fullness![72] Given such imagery, it is not unreasonable for theologians to speak of the believer's intimate communion, communication, and even what Owen calls "conjugal relations" with the Son. To draw this all from the Song of Songs would be problematic; to recognize this general motif in Scripture seems wholly appropriate.[73]

While Owen and many before him have been guilty of problematic exegesis of the particulars from Song of Songs, the general use of the imagery and idea of Christ's love for his bride is clearly (as mentioned above) a biblical motif.[74] It makes sense that a biblically saturated imagination would turn to the rich pictures and language found in the Song of Songs to unpack the imagery of Christ's love for his bride. J. I. Packer thus believes that Owen's christological reading of Canticles (i.e., Song of Songs)[75] might best be described as parable rather than allegory.[76] For in this love poem we find many idealized images of human love between a man and a woman, and if God is comfortable describing his relationship to his people in marital terms, then this Song helps guide the church's view, not merely of human love, but of God's love for his bride. This need not require a fanciful allegorical interpretation, because the historical and original intent could be preserved, serving as the guide for the multiple applications drawn from the texts. One could legitimately utilize the imagery and theological implications of this love poem as a way to help the church better know how her Heavenly Lover views her.

When Owen, especially in his commentary on Hebrews, develops principles for rightly handling biblical typology, he consistently warns against fanciful and ungrounded interpretations that can come from

---

72. See Tremper Longman, "Song of Songs," in *Dictionary for Theological Interpretation of the Bible*, ed. Kevin J. Vanhoozer, et al. (Grand Rapids, MI: Baker Academic, 2005), 760–61.

73. Interestingly, Robert W. Jenson has recently argued that the Song should be read "as a solicitation of theological allegory"; thus, this conversation is not dead. See Robert W. Jenson, *Song of Songs* (Louisville: John Knox Press, 2005), 13 (esp. 1–14); cf. Christos Yannaras, *Variations on the Song of Songs* (Brookline, MA: Holy Cross Orthodox Press, 2005).

74. It should be noted that, biblically, this marriage metaphor is used not merely in positive ways but often in negative ones, as exemplified in faithless Israel often described as a harlot. See Raymond C. Ortlund Jr., *God's Unfaithful Wife: A Biblical Theology of Spiritual Adultery* (Downers Grove, IL: InterVarsity Press, 2003). Cf. esp. Ezekiel 16. Similarly, such material appears to be the most appropriate background for making sense of God's righteous jealousy—he is not a passive lover, indifferent to his beloved's wandering eye; cf. John M. Frame, *The Doctrine of God*, A Theology of Lordship (Phillipsburg, NJ: P&R, 2002), 458–59.

75. The historic title "Canticles" is derived from the Latin Vulgate translation *Canticum Canticorum* (Song of Songs).

76. Packer, "A Puritan Perspective," 104.

unguarded allegorical readings.[77] In practice, however, Owen does not always maintain his own careful guidelines in his reading of Canticles. At times he stretches the actual text to the breaking point (e.g., seeing the Beloved as white for his deity and ruddy for his humanity, or reading into the ornaments of the Lover's head).[78] Despite this, it still seems overly hasty to dismiss the way in which many interpreters, both in the East and the West, drew insight about human communion with God from this beautiful love poem.[79]

Owen's interpretive language for the Song is intimate, at times almost uncomfortable for the reader who remembers that he is speaking of our relationship to Jesus.[80] But his point should not be missed: Jesus seeks his people as a lover seeks his beloved. This relationship includes pursuit and response. Christ's disposition toward his beloved is one of delight, finding great joy in her presence and wanting to protect her in the power of his love and grace. "And let our souls be persuaded of his sincerity and willingness in giving himself, in all that he is, as mediator unto us, to be ours; and let our hearts give up themselves unto him. Let us tell him that we will be for him, and not for another: let him know it from us; he delights to hear it."[81] This is the language of the Lover to the beloved, and this is his portrait of communion.

Here we move beyond a mere cognitive grasp of God's love to an experience of it, as found in Christ. As with his discussion of our inappropriate views of the Father, so Owen believes we tend not to really grasp Christ's love for us. Building on the imagery of Canticles, Owen voices what he believes are common thoughts among the saints concerning Christ's love: "I fear thou dost not love me, that thou hast forsaken

---

77. For the best treatment of this material in Owen, see Henry M. Knapp, "Understanding the Mind of God: John Owen and Seventeenth-Century Exegetical Methodology" (Ph.D. diss., Calvin Theological Seminary, 2002), 262–334, esp. 329–34.

78. *Works*, 2:49–50, 72–73.

79. For helpful resources with examples of how this worked in the history of interpretation, see esp. Richard A. Norris, *The Song of Songs: Interpreted by Early Christian and Medieval Commentators*, The Church's Bible (Grand Rapids, MI: Eerdmans, 2003). Other useful literature includes Richard Frederick Littledale, *A Commentary on the Song of Songs: From Ancient and Mediaeval Sources* (New York: Pott and Amery, 1869); E. Ann Matter, *The Voice of My Beloved: The Song of Songs in Western Medieval Christianity* (Philadelphia: University of Pennsylvania Press, 1990); George Louis Scheper, "The Spiritual Marriage: The Exegetic History and Literary Impact of the Song of Songs in the Middle Ages" (Ph.D. diss., Princeton University, 1971); Denys Turner, *Eros and Allegory: Medieval Exegesis of the Song of Songs* (Kalamazoo, MI: Cistercian, 1995).

80. Owen uses vivid imagery to describe this relationship: sweetness, delight, honor, safety, comfort, tenderness, purity, glory, beauty, discerning, and rejoicing; e.g., *Works*, 2:44–46, 55, 73–75.

81. *Works*, 2:59.

me; because I know I deserve not to be beloved. These thoughts are hard as hell; they give no rest to my soul."[82] Therefore, the soul will never be satisfied with mere "thoughts of Christ's love to it," but must experience and know this love which is "inconceivable, and cannot be increased" because it is full and complete.[83] Looking at our sins makes us despair that we could be loved by God, but in the embrace of Christ we discover the great Lover who does not abandon the beloved.

Responding to Christ

The reason we can delight in God is because the Son delights in us. "Christ will sup with believers: he refreshes himself with his own graces in them, by his Spirit bestowed on them. The Lord Christ is exceedingly delighted in tasting of the sweet fruits of the Spirit in the saints."[84] Christ displays a wonder of affections toward his people, and by his Spirit he will awaken anew the right affections of his people. We love, because he first delighted to love us. So Owen freely speaks of the Son's delighting in his saints, just as a groom delights in the presence of his bride without reserve or a mixture of emotion. "His heart is glad in us, without sorrow. And every day whilst we live is his *wedding-day.*"[85] In fact, building on such texts as Zephaniah 3:17 and John 1:14, he claims that "the thoughts of communion with the saints were the joy of his heart from eternity."[86] This is the background for understanding the Son's willingness, even joy (Heb. 12:2), in going to the cross on behalf of his beloved ones.[87] Christ will be the great revealer of God's mystery and secrets to the saints. But such revelation is not merely about the words on the pages of sacred Scripture, but also about embracing the fullness of the gospel embodied in Jesus Christ. "There is a wide difference between understanding *the doctrine of the Scripture* as in the letter, and a true knowing the mind of Christ."[88] The former is merely cognitive, while the latter assumes a relational character of intimacy that is only possible by the Spirit of Christ, who opens the eyes, softens the heart, and awakens the affections of his people.

---

82. *Works,* 2:128.
83. *Works,* 2:127.
84. *Works,* 2:40.
85. *Works,* 2:118.
86. *Works,* 2:118.
87. *Works,* 2:139.
88. *Works,* 2:120.

To commune with the Son we must know him and abandon our inaccurate distortions. "There are none who despise Christ, but only they that know him not; whose eyes the god of this world hath blinded, that they should not behold his glory."[89] Consequently, Owen encourages his readers to "study him a little; you love him not, because you know him not."[90] Our sin is that we do not know the bounty of Christ's mercy, and thus we do not receive from him what he is ready to supply.[91]

Enlivened and Kept by the Spirit

How are believers to know Christ so that they may love him? How can Christians bask in the love of the Father and the grace of the Son? According to Owen, only by the Spirit can anyone truly know God and enjoy his love and grace. And thus, while the Spirit is sometimes referred to as the "quiet" person of the Trinity, Owen believes that he is no less to be worshiped and glorified than the Father and Son, for he is no less God.

The Puritan Theologian of the Holy Spirit

While it may surprise many contemporary readers, the truth is that Puritanism was often known as a movement that spent considerable time exploring the person and work of the Spirit.[92] As one author comments, "It is only the truth to say that Puritan thought was almost entirely occupied with loving study of the work of the Holy Spirit."[93] Only when the Puritans' emphasis on the Spirit is appreciated can we make sense of their common concerns about certain kinds of rituals, prayer books, and the dangers of formalism.[94] While it is true that some Puritans were

---

89. *Works,* 2:52.

90. *Works,* 2:53.

91. *Works,* 1:152.

92. For a tiny sampling of seventeenth-century writings on the Spirit, often from different perspectives, see John Forbes, *A Letter . . . How a Christian Man May Discerne the Testimonie of Gods Spirit from the Testimonie of His Own Spirit* (R. Schilder: Middelburgh, 1616); Thomas Goodwin, *The Work of the Holy Ghost in Our Salvation,* ed. John C. Miller, vol. 6, *The Works of Thomas Goodwin* (Edinburgh: James Nichol, 1861–1866); Richard M. A. Hollingworth, *The Holy Ghost on the Bench, Other Spirits at the Bar* (L. Fawn: London, 1656), Samuel Petto, *The Voice of the Spirit* (London, 1654); Peter Sterry, *The Spirit Convincing of Sinne* (London, 1645).

93. B. B. Warfield, "Introduction," in *The Work of the Holy Spirit,* by Abraham Kuyper (New York: Funk & Wagnalls, 1900), xxviii, cf. xxxviii. Along similar lines, see, e.g., J. I. Packer, *A Quest for Godliness: The Puritan Vision of the Christian Life* (Wheaton, IL: Crossway, 1990), 179–89; Howard Watkin-Jones, *The Holy Spirit from Arminius to Wesley* (London: Epworth Press, 1929).

94. For a fairly nuanced handling of the background of such debates, see Horton Davies, *From Cranmer to Baxter and Fox, 1534–1690,* Worship and Theology in England, 5 vols. (Grand Rapids, MI: Eerdmans, 1996), 1:40–75, 255–324.

weary of oft-repeated ceremonies, their main concern was that such observances might become a substitute for enjoying the presence of the living Spirit. Without this pneumatological understanding, it is far too tempting to view the Puritans as merely uptight pastors ignorant about the benefit of repetition. It may be argued that many of them went too far, but it should be recognized that they did so out of a concern to make space for the ongoing work of the Spirit. They did urge their people to learn catechisms, partake of the sacraments, be active in Christian fellowship, and even to use certain kinds of prayer books, but it was always with an eye toward creating sensitivity to the Spirit's work.

Central to Puritan thinking was an effort to make sure their activities held together two realities—Word and Spirit. Thus, even when Puritans spoke of the vital importance of the Word—whether preached or read—they always linked this with the Spirit.[95] For them, Spirit and Word should always be united; when they are separated, problems quickly arise.

John Owen self-consciously viewed himself as a theologian of the Spirit, and as such he poured more time and energy into exploring questions related to the third person of the Trinity than anyone else in his day, and possibly even before him. His most exhaustive studies are found in volumes three and four of his collected works. In these tomes there are five main treaties. *Pneumatologia: A Discourse Concerning the Holy Spirit* was published in 1674. In this massive volume of 651 pages, Owen discusses all manner of things related to the Spirit. Not only does he unpack the names and titles of the Spirit, he also draws biblical insight about the Spirit's nature and personality. He looks at the Spirit's work in creation throughout the Old Testament and into the New.

As Owen explores the Spirit's work in the incarnate Christ, the reader discovers one of Owen's most brilliant and challenging insights. He believes one can make sense of Jesus' full humanity and divinity, without compromising either, only by highlighting the Spirit's work "in and on" the human nature of Christ.[96] After this, Owen unfolds the implications

---

95. Geoffrey F. Nuttall, *The Holy Spirit in Puritan Faith and Experience*, 2nd ed. (Chicago: University of Chicago Press, 1992), 20–47.

96. See esp. *Works*, 3:159–88. A stimulating discussion of this aspect of Owen's thought can be found in Alan J. Spence, *Incarnation and Inspiration: John Owen and the Coherence of Christology* (London: T. & T. Clark, 2007); Alan J. Spence, "Christ's Humanity and Ours: John Owen," in *Persons, Divine and Human*, ed. C. Schwöbel and Colin E. Gunton (Edinburgh: T. & T. Clark, 1991), 74–97. Cf. Kapic, *Communion with God*, 84–88.

of the Spirit's applying the work of Christ to the church, spending considerable time on the idea of sanctification.

Four shorter works also came from his pen, focusing on more narrow aspects of the Spirit's work. In 1677 Owen's *The Reason of Faith* was printed. Here he concentrates on the Spirit's work that enables us to know Scripture as the very Word of God. His volume *The Causes, Ways, and Means of Understanding the Mind of God* (1678) builds on this idea, arguing that all believers can interpret the Scriptures because they have the Spirit within them. The Spirit was not only active in the composition of Holy Writ, but also in the continuing illumination of the saints as they meditate on it. *The Work of the Holy Spirit in Prayer* (1682) examines not just the theology of the Spirit's activity in prayer, but also includes practical suggestions for how these truths should inform our exercises in this devotional practice. The final two treatises were published after Owen's death. In *A Discourse on the Holy Spirit as Comforter* (1693), Owen describes in detail the Spirit's role as advocate and comforter for the church, inhabiting God's people and serving as their anointing, seal, and guarantee of what is to come. Finally, in *A Discourse of Spiritual Gifts* (1693), Owen carefully distinguishes between gifts and "saving grace," as well as basic differences between "extraordinary" and "ordinary" gifts. Owen is certainly not opposed to the Spirit's giving of gifts to God's people, but he parses such gifting in the context of redemptive history and the ongoing ministry of the Church.[97]

After reading Owen's work on the Spirit, one can appreciate his claim that his research was "increased" because "I know not any who ever went before me in this design of representing the whole economy of the Holy Spirit."[98] He was well aware of the early Fathers, medieval authors, and Reformers who had written on the Spirit, and he draws heavily from them. Yet Owen's extensiveness and intensiveness set him apart. For Owen, discussion of the Spirit cannot help but be personal. Geoffrey Nuttall puts it well:

> What is new [about Owen's work on the Spirit], and what justifies Owen in his claim to be among the pioneers, is the place given in Puritan exposition to experience, and its acceptance as a primary authority. . . . The

---

97. For a contemporary example of someone trying to follow Owen's basic lead on related questions, see Sinclair B. Ferguson, *The Holy Spirit*, Contours of Christian Theology (Downers Grove, IL: InterVarsity Press, 1996), 207–39.

98. *Works*, 3:7.

interest is primarily not dogmatic, at least not in any theoretic sense, it is experimental.[99]

Not only must Word and Spirit be held together, but Christian experience must be incorporated into the discussion as well. Again, Owen's academic and pastoral concerns come together to form his method, and we discover this clearly in his earlier book on *Communion with God*.

Appreciating how much Owen wrote elsewhere on the Spirit is necessary, lest anyone misunderstand Owen's limited discussion of the Spirit in *Communion with God*. While it is a relatively short section of his book, his other writings make it clear this is not because his theology downplays the Spirit. But in this context, his aims are fairly narrow. He wants his readers to know the Spirit and then to respond to him rightly.

Worshiping the Spirit

As we have already noted, since the application of our salvation is a triune act, this action should inform our worship, and that includes rightly exalting the Spirit. The Spirit, "together with the Father and the Son, may be known, adored, worshipped, according unto his own will."[100] The Spirit is none other than the Spirit of God, and thus we are invited to commune with him. To encounter the Spirit is to encounter the triune God:

> . . . in this asking and receiving of the Holy Ghost, we have communion with the Father in his love, whence he is sent; and with the Son in his grace, whereby he is obtained for us; so with himself, on the account of his voluntary condescension to this dispensation. Every request for the Holy Ghost implies our closing with all these. O the riches of the grace of God![101]

Owen will not hesitate to encourage believers to pray to the Spirit, just as they call out to the Father and Son,[102] for our prayers are offered to the triune God. "In that person [the Holy Spirit] do we meet him [God], his love, grace, and authority, by our prayers and supplications."[103]

---

99. Nuttall, *The Holy Spirit in Puritan Faith and Experience*, 7.
100. *Works*, 3:190.
101. *Works*, 2:272.
102. *Works*, 2:229–30.
103. *Works*, 2:272.

Testing the Spirits: Knowing the Spirit of Christ

There is no hesitation in Owen's voice when he speaks of the glory of
the Spirit, and yet he believed that many during his day who claimed
to worship the Spirit were treading on dangerous ground. A group
pejoratively called the "Enthusiasts" was often lumped together in this
seventeenth-century setting. Among those who received this title, the
Quakers are the most well known.[104] Such groups tended to highlight
immediate experiences of the Spirit, and they often warned against academic learning, tradition, and certain forms of formality—all of which
they believed hindered one's openness to the Spirit.[105] While Owen was
deeply concerned about the Rationalism he saw growing on the right in
the form of Socinianism, he was equally worried about the Enthusiasts
on the left. One side seemed to deny the Spirit, while the other appeared
confused about identifying the true Spirit. For a taste of Owen's maneu-
verings through the doctrine of the Spirit, we will focus on his particular
concerns with the growing movement of Enthusiasts of his day. Since
they had experiences that they linked to the Spirit, how could one judge
the validity of such experiences? There was plenty of religious zeal, but
how could one know if it was from God?[106]

To identify the Spirit, we need to recognize that he is always the *Spirit
of Christ*. "Testing the spirits" is really about discovering the Spirit's
relation to the Son. The Spirit of God and the Spirit of Christ are one and
the same.[107] For Owen, the Spirit's activity is always viewed in light of
Christ and never apart from him. Building on 1 Peter 1:11, Owen makes
it clear that even before the incarnation, the Spirit was sent by the Son

---

104. See Geoffrey F. Nuttall, *Studies in Christian Enthusiasm: Illustrated from Early Quakerism*
(Wallingford, PA: Pendle Hill, 1948); E. Glenn Hinson, "Baptist and Quaker Spirituality," in *Chris-
tian Spirituality: Post-Reformation and Modern*, ed. Louis Depré and Don Saliers (London: SCM
Press, 1990), 324–38; Hugh Barbour, *The Quakers in Puritan England* (New Haven: Yale University
Press, 1964); Barry Reay, *The Quakers and the English Revolution* (London: Temple Smith, 1985);
Douglas Van Steere, *Quaker Spirituality: Selected Writings*, Classics of Western Spirituality (New
York: Paulist Press, 1984), esp. 3–157.

105. E.g., Samuel How, *The Sufficiency of the Spirit's Teaching without Humane Learning*
(London: William & Joseph Marshall, 1640).

106. Jonathan Edwards later found himself similarly engaged in this type of exploration, trying to maintain the importance of experience while also attempting to ground it within a biblical
framework. He ends up with his own kind of "tests." See Jonathan Edwards, *Religious Affections,*
in *The Works of Jonathan Edwards*, vol. 2, ed. John E. Smith (New Haven: Yale University Press,
1959). In this work, one of the few sources Edwards explicitly cites is John Owen's *Pneumatologia.*
The relationship of Owen's (direct or indirect) influence upon Edwards's theology has never been
fully studied.

107. *Works*, 3:60.

to testify of him.[108] It should not surprise us, therefore, to discover how he frames the Spirit's work of bringing joy and comfort: it comes as the Spirit leads the mind and heart to the reality of the person and work of Christ.[109] "The life and soul of all our comforts lie treasured up in the promises of Christ. They are the breasts of all our consolation."[110] We receive peace, hope, and encouragement through Christ, and when such experiences come, we can be confident they are coming by the working of the Comforter who draws us to the Son. "No sooner doth the soul begin to feel the life of a promise warming his heart, relieving, cherishing, supporting, delivering from fear, entanglements, or troubles, but it may, it ought, to know that the Holy Ghost is there; which will add to his joy, and lead him into fellowship with him."[111]

Experience is important for Owen, as it reminds us of the Spirit's presence, and such recognition promotes communion. Remember that we love, delight in, and enjoy God to the degree that we know him. Understanding that such experiences point to the presence of the Spirit fosters relational intimacy, not detached intellectual assent.[112] Along similar lines, the Spirit comforts as he convinces us of the Father's love—which, as a matter of fact, is best understood by looking to the Son who was sent to be the full revelation of the love and will of the Father. But notice, the Spirit brings comfort to believers, "not with an increase of corn, and wine, and oil, but with the shining of the countenance of God upon us, that he comforts our souls."[113]

One can, therefore, "test the spirits" by asking: Does this Spirit draw me toward Christ? Does the Spirit glorify the incarnate Lord? If the Spirit seems to bring "new revelations" which point toward himself rather than toward the Son, then we should be cautious, for the Spirit never draws worship away from Christ. When some in the seventeenth century claimed to have personal experiences of the Spirit, but those experiences seemed to result in a diminished significance for Christ, then Owen believed they had abandoned the biblical norm: "We may see how far that spirit is from being the Comforter who sets up himself

---

108. *Works*, 12:339.

109. *Works*, 2:237.

110. *Works*, 2:239.

111. Ibid.

112. "The fellowship we have with him [the Spirit] consists, in no small portion of it, in the consolation we receive from him." *Works*, 2:251.

113. *Works*, 2:262.

in the room of Christ."[114] Here he draws from various texts, but especially from elements in John's Upper Room Discourse. In this context the disciples learn of the Spirit's activity of bringing to mind the work of Jesus (John 14:26), glorifying him (John 16:14), and thus being the very peace which Christ can offer them (John 14:27). These strong associations make the identity of the Spirit inseparably linked to Christ, and, consequently, Owen sides with the common Western tradition that claims the Spirit is sent from the Father *and* the Son, and not only from the Father.[115] The practical implications of this are significant, for this is what allows him to frame things, such as sanctification, in a Trinitarian manner; he avoids unduly dividing—though he does distinguish—these divine activities. So it makes perfect sense for Owen to claim that Christ "sends his Holy Spirit into our hearts; which is the efficient cause of all holiness and sanctification,—quickening, enlightening, purifying the souls of his saints. . . . [O]ur union with him [i.e., Christ], with all the benefit thereon depending, floweth from this communication of the Spirit unto us, to abide with us, and to dwell in us."[116]

In his work *Perseverance of the Saints*, Owen spends a great deal of time working through material related to the indwelling of the Spirit.[117] One of his key points in that context is that we are united to Christ by his Spirit, and thus the same Spirit in him is in us.[118] Only in this way can we make sense of Peter's claim that we are "partakers of the divine nature" (2 Pet. 1:4), without somehow thinking that we become gods ourselves. But we do enjoy the Spirit of God, the same Spirit that filled Jesus beyond measure, and this Spirit is sent by Christ into our hearts. This is our confidence as we face death—for the Spirit that raised Christ from the dead now dwells in us, and thus we will be kept and even raised in and through the Spirit of the resurrected Christ. Ultimately our security rests in the Spirit of the faithful Savior who is sent into our hearts.

In *Communion with God* Owen provides some practical suggestions for how one could "test the Spirits" beyond merely the Spirit's connection to the Son. Yet, all of these tests must be viewed in light of that more fundamental one. As a quick preview, here are some other examples which are peppered throughout this volume. First, the Spirit is the *Spirit of freedom*, not bondage. When a person claims he is expe-

---

114. *Works*, 3:239.
115. Cf., e.g., *Works*, 3:60–364.
116. *Works*, 2:199.
117. See *Works*, 11:329–65.
118. For the following discussion see esp. *Works*, 11:336–42.

riencing the Spirit, but such intense experiences leave him exhausted, burdened, and without love, then this does not appear to be the Spirit. God's Spirit brings spiritual freedom, love, and rest. This freedom is a freedom *for* obedience, not a freedom from it. "*Slaves* take liberty *from* duty; children have liberty *in* duty."[119] By the Spirit the children of God freely love and obey him, and this is true freedom, grace, and love. They work not to gain approval, but in light of it: "Love is the bottom of all their duties."[120]

Second, the Spirit of God *tends to work in and through natural human faculties* (i.e., mind, will, affections, and body), rather than against or outside of them.[121] This point was important to him as many "enthusiasts" of his day were claiming the Spirit's special presence, but during such experiences they would lose control of their bodies, their minds, and their affections. It is from witnessing such experiences that the pejorative titles "Shakers" and "Quakers" evolved. From Owen's perspective, these experiences simply didn't make sense, for the true Spirit affirms creation—including human nature—rather than undermining it. By this Spirit we are renewed in God's image as he enlightens our minds, renews our wills, and redirects our affections toward God. When people claimed the Spirit made them act more like beasts than like humans, Owen would scratch his head with real skepticism about whether this was the true Spirit of God—he was fairly confident it wasn't.

Third, the Spirit is the *Spirit of prayer*. If one claimed special movements of the Spirit, but such experiences made him belittle the ordinary Christian experience of prayer, then certainly something was wrong. There is no higher avenue than prayer, for this is personal communion with God. "The soul is never more raised with the love of God than when by the Spirit taken into intimate communion with him" in prayer.[122] Other "tests" can be found in Owen's writings, but these sufficiently show his approach.

Conclusion

As a way to conclude our reflections on Owen's view of communion with the triune God, it may prove helpful to briefly mention John Calvin's defi-

---

119. *Works,* 2:214.

120. *Works,* 2:214; cf. 215.

121. For a discussion of how Owen employs faculty psychology to make sense of human communion with God, see Kapic, *Communion with God,* 35–66.

122. *Works,* 2:249; cf. 258.

nition of faith. His brief description captures much of the heart of what we find in Owen's extended discussion.

Calvin writes that faith is "a firm and certain knowledge of God's benevolence toward us, founded upon the truth of the freely given promise in Christ, both revealed to our minds and sealed upon our hearts through the Holy Spirit."[123] For Calvin, faith is not about believing that God exists—it is much more than that. Faith scandalously believes that the holy and transcendent God is "benevolent toward us." How can this be? Given our sin and the chaos of this world, how could we ever believe such a thing? Answer: this truth is known and established in Christ, who is freely given by the Father. That is the gospel. To fully grasp the Father's love toward us, we must gaze upon the Son. How can such a vision be possible in light of our sin and doubt? Only through the powerful work of the Spirit, who reveals these gospel realities to us and then seals our heart with this truth. This Spirit consistently draws us to the Son who is the perfect mediator between God and man.

For Owen, and Calvin before him, true faith was understood relationally, as we discover the Father's love through the Son's incarnation and the Spirit's illumination. In light of this revelation and embrace by God, we are to respond to him in love and trust—that is what we call faith. And the God we respond to is none other than the Father, Son, and Spirit. May you find Owen's classic work *Communion with God* pointing you in the direction of an ever-increasing enjoyment of the love, grace, and fellowship of God.

---

123. John Calvin, *Institutes of the Christian Religion*, 2 vols., The Library of Christian Classics (Philadelphia: Westminster Press, 1960), 1:3.2.7. Cf. the Heidelberg Catechism, q. 21.

A NOTE ON THIS EDITION

JUSTIN TAYLOR

Our goal in this volume has been to produce an unabridged but updated and accessible edition of Owen's *Communion with God*. This work, therefore, is neither an abridgement nor a paraphrase.[1] Instead, our goal has been to retain the original content, making adjustments and adding helps for the sake of the modern reader. Our base text has been that of the 1850s edition of Owen's *Works*, edited by William Goold,[2] though we have also consulted the original 1657 edition as necessary.

What changes have we made to the original edition of Owen's works? We have:

- broken some of Owen's large paragraphs into smaller units;
- footnoted difficult vocabulary words or phrases (at their first occurrence) and collected them into a glossary;
- Americanized the British spelling (e.g., behaviour to behavior);
- updated archaic pronouns (e.g., thou to you);

---

1. For an example of such, see John Owen, *Communion with God*, Puritan Paperbacks, ed. R. K. Law (Edinburgh: Banner of Truth, 1991).

2. We gratefully acknowledge the work of Christian Classics Ethereal Library (http://www.ccel.org/ccel/owen/communion.html) and AGES Software ("The Works of John Owen" [Rio, WI: Ages Software, 2000]) for producing digitized versions of Goold's edition.

- updated other archaic spellings (e.g., hath to have; requireth to requires);
- corrected the text in places where the nineteenth-century edition incorrectly deviated from the original;
- modernized some of the punctuation;
- placed Owen's Scripture references in parentheses and modernized the citation method;
- added our own Scripture references in brackets when Owen quotes or alludes to a passage but does not provide a reference;
- transliterated all Hebrew and Greek words, and provided a translation if Owen doesn't provide one;
- translated all Latin phrases and quotes that Owen leaves untranslated;
- provided sources for quotations and allusions where possible;
- removed Owen's intricate numbering system, which functioned as an extensive outline embedded in the body of his work;
- added headings and italics throughout this volume, and extensive outlines of our own at the beginning, to aid the reader in following the flow of Owen's thought.

An example of our limited modernizing can be seen in examining a reproduction of an original paragraph from the 1657 edition:

I. The love of God is fo. Zeph. chap. 3. v. 17. *The Lord thy God in the middeft of thee is mighty: he will fave; he will rejoyce over thee with Joy, he will R E S T in his love, he will joy over thee with Singing.* Both thefe things are here assigned unto God in his Love; R E S T and D E L I G H T. The words are בְּאַהֲבָתוֹ יַחֲרִישׁ: he fhall be *filent becaufe of his love.* To reft with contentment is expreffed by being *filent*; that is, without repining, without complaint. This God doth upon the *account* of his own *love.* fo full, fo every way compleat & abfolute, that it will not allow him to complaine of any thing in them whom he loves, but is *filent* on the account thereof. Or *reft* in his Love, that is, he will not *remove* it; he will not feek farther for another Object.

Using our editorial principles, the paragraph has been rendered in this edition as follows:

The love of God is so. "The LORD your God in the midst of you is mighty; he will save, he will rejoice over you with joy, he will rest in his love; he will joy over you with singing" (Zeph. 3:17). Both these things are here assigned unto God in his love—*rest and delight*. The words are, *yacharish* *be'ahabato* —"He shall be silent because of his love." To rest with contentment is expressed by being silent; that is, without repining, without complaint. This God does upon the account of his own love, so full, so every way complete and absolute, that it will not allow him to complain of any thing in them whom he loves, but he is silent on the account thereof. Or, "Rest in his love"; that is, he will not remove it—he will not seek further for another object.

Outline and Sources

Two features merit additional comment. First, readers familiar with the 1850s Goold edition will note that Owen's detailed numbering system— whereby virtually every paragraph is assigned an outline mark—has been removed. Adapting this system we have produced a detailed outline at the beginning of this book. We highly recommend consulting this outline while reading the book in order to achieve the fullest understanding of Owen's structure and argumentation. Each point of the outline is cross-referenced with the page in the main text for maximal convenience.

Owen's footnotes are often rather cryptic for modern researchers and readers. They are filled with Latin quotes, often from obscure sources or with no source cited at all. Furthermore, the standards have changed since Owen's time with regard to the necessity of reproducing exact quotations. These factors combine to make the task of perfectly conforming Owen's citations to modern practice all but impossible. We have sought whenever possible to locate an original source,[3] as well as a published English translation[4]—though there are times when we have been unable to locate either.[5] When a published translation is less than accurate to Owen's quoted material, we have edited the translation and prefaced the citation with the notation "cf."

---

3. Citations of PL and PG refer respectively to *Patrologia Latina* and *Patrologia Graeca*.

4. Citations of ANF and NPNF refer respectively to *The Ante-Nicene Fathers* and *The Nicene and Post-Nicene Fathers*. Superscript numerals after NPNF indicate whether it is the first or second series.

5. For future editions of this work, further bibliographic suggestions are welcome and may be directed to johnowen.org@gmail.com.

OUTLINE

---

1. Note that this point on the outline properly follows (Chapter 3), II.B. from chapter 3.

(Chapter 7)

(Chapter 8)

II. Communion with Christ in purchased grace (295)
  A. As unto acceptation with God, from the obedience of his
     life and efficacy of his death (295)
    1. The requirements of Christ for this communion (295)
       a. What he did, he did for us and not for himself (295)
       b. In what he suffered (296)
    2. The requirements of Christ to complete this communion
       (296)
       a. He offers the gospel (296)
          1) Declaratory, in the conditional promises of the
             gospel (296)
          2) A law is established, that whosoever receives it
             shall be so accepted (297)
       b. He sends them his Holy Spirit (297)
    3. Objection and answer 1 (298)
       a. Objection: If the elect are absolved by the death of
          Christ, why are they not immediately freed and rec-
          onciled upon the payment of the price? (298)
       b. Answer (299)
          1) Jesus Christ was constituted and considered as a
             common, public person in the stead of them for
             whose reconciliation to God he suffered (299)
          2) His being a common person arose chiefly from
             these things (299)
             a) In general, from the covenant entered into by
                himself with his Father to this purpose (299)
             b) In the sovereign grant, appointment, and de-
                sign of the Father, giving and delivering the
                elect to Jesus Christ in this covenant, to be
                redeemed and reconciled to himself (299)
             c) In his undertaking to suffer what was due to
                them, and to do what was to be done by them,
                that they might be delivered, reconciled, and
                accepted with God (299)
             d) He received, on their behalf and for them, all
                the promises of all the mercies, grace, good
                things, and privileges, which they were to re-

ceive upon the account of his undertaking for
them (300)

e) He was acquitted, absolved, justified, and
freed, from all and every thing that, on the behalf of the elect, as due to them, was charged
upon him, or could so be (300)

f) It became righteous with God that those in
whose stead he was, should obtain, and have
bestowed on them, all the fruits of his death in
reconciliation with God (301)

g) It was determined by Father, Son, and Holy
Ghost that the way of their actual personal
deliverance from the sentence and curse of
the law should be in and by such a way and
dispensation as might lead to the praise of the
glorious grace of God (301)

h) That until the full time of their actual deliverance, determined and appointed to them in
their several generations, be accomplished,
they are personally under the curse of the law;
and, on that account, are legally obnoxious to
the wrath of God, from which they shall certainly be delivered (301)

i) The end of the dispensation of grace being to
glorify the whole Trinity, the order fixed on
and appointed wherein this is to be done, is
by ascending to the Father's love through the
work of the Spirit and blood of the Son (302)

[1] That the Spirit may be glorified, he is
given unto us, to quicken us, convert us,
work faith in us (302)

[2] This being wrought in us, for the glory
of the Son, we are actually interested, according to the tenor of the covenant, at
the same instant of time, in the blood of
Christ, as to the benefits which he has
procured for us thereby (302)

[3] To the glory of the Father, we are accepted with him, justified, freed from

2) They gather up in their thoughts the sins for
   which they have not made a particular reckoning
   with God in Christ (317)
3) They make this commutation I speak of with
   Jesus Christ (317)
   a) Jesus Christ, by the will and appointment of
      the Father, has really undergone the punish-
      ment that was due to those sins that lie now
      under his eye and consideration (317)
   b) They hearken to the voice of Christ calling
      them to him with their burden, "Come unto
      me, all you that are weary and heavy laden"
      (317)
   c) They lay down their sins at the cross of Christ,
      upon his shoulders (318)
   d) Having thus by faith given up their sins to
      Christ, and seen God laying them all on him,
      they draw nigh, and take from him that righ-
      teousness which he has wrought out for them
      (318)

6. Objection and answer 1 (318)
   a. Objection: "Surely this course of procedure can
      never be acceptable to Jesus Christ" (318)
   b. Answer: There is not any thing that Jesus Christ is
      more delighted with than that his saints should al-
      ways hold communion with him as to this business
      of giving and receiving (318)
      1) This exceedingly honors him and gives him the
         glory that is his due (318)
      2) This exceedingly endears the souls of the saints to
         him and constrains them to put a due valuation
         upon him, his love, his righteousness, and grace
         (319)

7. Objection and answer 2 (319)
   a. Objection. "If this be so, what need is there to repent
      or amend our ways?" (319)
   b. Answer: This communion in itself produces quite
      other effects than those supposed (319)
      1) For gospel repentance (320)
      2) For obedience (320)

1. The expiating, purging, purifying efficacy of his blood
   (330)
2. The blood of Christ as the blood of sprinkling (331)
3. Him as the only dispenser of the Spirit and of all grace
   of sanctification and holiness (332)

(Chapter 10)

III. Communion with Christ in the grace of privilege (335)
   A. That which is required for the complete adoption of any
      person (336)
      1. That he be actually, and of his own right, of another
         family than that whereinto he is adopted. He must be
         the son of one family or other, in his own right, as all
         persons are (336)
      2. That there be a family unto which of himself he has no
         right, whereinto he is to be grafted (336)
      3. That there be an authoritative, legal translation of him,
         by some that have power thereinto, from one family
         into another. It was not, by the law of old, in the power
         of particular persons to adopt when and whom they
         would. It was to be done by the authority of the sover-
         eign power (336)
      4. That the adopted person be freed from all the obliga-
         tions that be upon him unto the family from whence he
         is translated; otherwise he can be no way useful or ser-
         viceable unto the family whereinto he is engrafted (336)
      5. That, by virtue of his adoption, he be invested in all
         the rights, privileges, advantages, and title to the whole
         inheritance, of the family into which he is adopted, in
         as full and ample manner as if he had been born a son
         therein (336)
   B. That which is found in the adoption of believers (337)
      1. They are, by their own original right, of another family
         than that whereinto they are adopted (337)
      2. There is another family whereinto they are to be trans-
         lated, and whereunto of themselves they have neither
         right nor title (337)
      3. They have an authoritative translation from one of these
         families to another (338)

a. An effectual proclamation and declaration of such a person's immunity from all obligations to the former family, to which by nature he was related. And this declaration has a threefold object (338)
   1) Angels (338)
      a) Generally, by the doctrine of the gospel (338)
      b) In particular, by immediate revelation (339)
   2) It is denounced in a judicial way unto Satan, the great master of the family whereunto they were in subjection (339)
   3) Unto the conscience of the person adopted (339)
b. There is an authoritative engrafting of a believer actually into the family of God, and investing him with the whole right of sonship (339)
   1) The giving a believer a new name in a white stone (339)
   2) An enrolling of his name in the catalogue of the household of God, admitting him thereby into fellowship therein (340)
   3) Testifying to his conscience his acceptance with God, enabling him to behave himself as a child (340)
4. The adopted person be freed from all obligations to the family from whence he is translated, and invested with the rights and privileges of the family he is translated into, with respect to the following (340)
a. Liberty (340)
   1) The family from whence the adopted person is translated (341)
      a) That which is real respects a twofold issue of law and sin (341)
         [1] An economical institution of a new law of ordinances, keeping in bondage those to whom it was given (341)
         [2] A natural pressing of those persons with its power and efficacy against sin (341)
            [a] Its rigor and terror in commanding (341)

        [b] Its impossibility for accomplishment,
and so insufficiency for its primitively
appointed end (341)

        [c] The issues of its transgression (341)

  b) That which is pretended, is the power of any
whatever over the conscience, when once
made free by Christ (341)

    [1] Believers are freed from the instituted law
of ordinances (341)

    [2] In reference to the moral law (341)

        [a] Liberty from its rigor and terror in
commanding (341)

        [b] Liberty from the law as the instru-
ment of righteousness (341)

        [c] Liberty from the issue of its transgres-
sion (341)

           (1) Curse (342)

           (2) Death (342)

2) There is a liberty in the family of God, as well as
a liberty from the family of Satan (342)

  a) In the principles of all spiritual service; which
are life and love (343)

    [1] It is from life; that gives them power as to
the matter of obedience (343)

        [a] Slaves take liberty from duty; children
have liberty in duty (343)

        [b] The liberty of slaves or servants is
from mistaken, deceiving conclusions;
the liberty of sons is from the power
of the indwelling Spirit of grace (343)

    [2] Love, as to the manner of their obedience,
gives them delight and joy (344)

  b) The object of their obedience is represented to
them as desirable, whereas to others it is terrible (344)

  c) Their motive unto obedience is love (344)

  d) The manner of their obedience is willingness
(345)

  e) The rule of their walking with God is the law
of liberty (345)

b. Title (345)
    1) A proper and direct right and title unto spiritual
        things (345)
        a) Unto a present place, name, and room, in the
            house of God, and all the privileges and ad-
            ministrations thereof (345)
        b) To a future fullness of the great inheritance of
            glory (345)
            [1] Unto the whole administration of the
                 family of God here (345)
                 [a] The nature of that house (347)
                 [b] The privileges of the house are such
                      as they will not suit nor profit any
                      other (347)
            [2] They have a title to the future fullness of
                 the inheritance that is purchased for this
                 whole family by Jesus Christ (347)
                 [a] The children of God are heirs of the
                      promise (348)
                 [b] The children of God are heirs of righ-
                      teousness (348)
                 [c] The children of God are heirs of sal-
                      vation (348)
    2) A consequential right unto the things of this
        world (349)
        a) The right they have is not as the right that
            Christ has; theirs is subordinate (349)
        b) That the whole number of the children of God
            have a right unto the whole earth (349)
            [1] He who is the sovereign Lord of it does
                 preserve it merely for their use, and upon
                 their account (349)
            [2] The government of the earth shall be ex-
                 ercised to their advantage (350)
        c) This right is a spiritual right, which does not
            give a civil interest, but only sanctifies the
            right and interest bestowed (350)
        d) No one particular adopted person has any
            right, by virtue thereof, to any portion of
            earthly things whereunto he has not right and

PREFACE

Christian Reader,

It is now six years past since I was brought under an engagement of promise for the publishing of some meditations on the subject which you will find handled in the ensuing treatise. The reasons of this delay, being not of public concern, I shall not need to mention. Those who have been in expectation of this duty from me, have, for the most part, been so far acquainted with my condition and employments, as to be able to satisfy themselves as to the deferring of their desires. That which I have to add at present is only this: having had many opportunities, since the time I first delivered anything in public on this subject (which was the means of bringing me under the engagements mentioned), to reassume the consideration of what I had first fixed on, I have been enabled to give it that improvement,[1] and to make those additions to the main of the design and matter treated on, that my first debt is come at length to be only the occasion of what is now tendered[2] to the saints of God. I shall speak nothing of the subject here handled; it may, I hope, speak for itself, in that spiritual savor and relish which it will yield to them whose hearts are not so filled with other things as to render the sweet things of the gospel bitter to them. The design of the whole treatise you will find, Christian reader, in the first chapters of the first part; and I shall not detain you here with the perusal of any thing which in its proper place will offer itself

---

1. good or profitable enhancement, completion.
2. offered

unto you: know only that the whole of it has been recommended to the grace of God in many supplications, for its usefulness unto them that are interested in the good things mentioned therein.

J. O.
Oxon.[3] Christ Church College
July 10, 1657

---

3. Oxford (Lat. Oxonia)

PART I

Of Communion with Each Person Distinctly—

Of Communion with the Father

Chapter 1

I n the First Epistle of John, the apostle assures them to whom he wrote that the fellowship of believers "is with the Father and with his Son Jesus Christ" (1:3),[1] and this he does with such an unusual kind of expression as bears the force of an asseveration[2]—whence we have rendered it, "Truly our fellowship is with the Father and with his Son Jesus Christ."

The outward appearance and condition of the saints in those days being very mean[3] and contemptible—their leaders being accounted as the filth of this world and as the offscouring[4] of all things[5]—the inviting [of] others into fellowship with them and a participation of the precious things which they did enjoy, seem to be exposed to many contrary reasonings and objections: "What benefit is there in *communion* with them? Is it anything else but to be sharers in troubles, reproaches, scorns, and all manner of evils?" To prevent or remove these and the like exceptions, the apostle gives them to whom he wrote to know (and that with some earnestness of expression), that notwithstanding all the disadvantages their fellowship lay under, unto

---

1. Gk. *kai hē koinōnia de hē hēmetera*, etc.
2. solemn and emphatic assertion, declaration.
3. despicable, vile, lowly.
4. refuse, filth scoured off and cast away.
5. Gk. *hōs perikatharmata tou kosmou*. Cf. 1 Cor. 4:8–13; Rom. 8:35–36; Heb. 10:32–34. *Christianos ad leones. Et puto, nos Deus apostolos novissimos elegit veluti bestiarios.* ["To the lions with the Christians!" Tertullian, *Apology*, ANF 3:47; PL 1, col. 825B; "And, '(I think) God hath selected us the apostles (as) hindmost, like men appointed to fight with wild beasts.'" Tertullian, *On Modesty*, ANF 4:88; PL 2, col. 1006B.] Acts 17:18; Gal. 6:12. *Semper casuris similes, nunquamque cadentes.* ["[we are] always like those about to fall, and never falling."]

a carnal view, yet in truth it was, and would be found to be (in reference to *some* with whom they held it), very honorable, glorious, and
desirable. For "truly," says he, "our fellowship is with the Father and
with his Son Jesus Christ."

The Saints Have Communion with God

This being so earnestly and directly asserted by the apostle, we may
boldly follow him with our affirmation, namely, "*That the saints
of God have communion with him.*" And *a holy and spiritual* communion it is, as shall be declared. How this is spoken *distinctly* in
reference to the Father and the Son, must afterward be fully opened
and carried on.

By nature, since the entrance of sin, no man has any communion
with God. He is *light*,[6] we *darkness*; and what communion has light
with darkness [2 Cor. 6:14]? He is *life*, we are *dead*—he is *love*, and
we are *enmity*; and what agreement can there be between us? Men in
such a condition have neither Christ,[7] nor hope, nor God in the world
(Eph. 2:12), "being alienated from the life of God through the ignorance
that is in them" (Eph. 4:18). Now two cannot walk together unless
they be agreed (Amos 3:3). While there is this *distance* between God
and man, there is no *walking together* for them in any fellowship or
communion. Our first *interest*[8] in God was so lost by sin,[9] as that there
was left unto us (in ourselves) no possibility of a recovery. As we had
deprived ourselves of all *power* for a return, so God had not revealed any
way of *access* unto himself, or that he could, under any consideration,
be approached unto by sinners in peace. Not any *work* that God had
made, not any *attribute* that he had revealed, could give the least light
into such a dispensation.[10]

The manifestation of grace and pardoning mercy, which is the only
door of entrance into any such communion, is not committed unto any
but unto him alone[11] *in* whom it is, *by* whom that grace and mercy was

---

6. 1 John 1:5; 2 Cor. 6:14; Eph. 5:8; John 5:21; Matt. 22:32; Eph. 2:1; 1 John 4:8; Rom. 8:7.

7. *Magna hominis miseria est cum illo non esse, sine quo non potest esse.* ["And so it is the
especial wretchedness of man not to be with Him, without whom he cannot be." Augustine, *On
the Holy Trinity*, NPNF[1] 3:192; PL 42, col. 1049.]

8. share in, claim of.

9. Eccles. 7:29; Jer. 13:23; Acts 4:12; Isa. 33:14.

10. arrangement, provision, ordering.

11. John 1:18; Heb. 10:19–21. *Unus verusque Mediator per sacrificium pacis reconcilians nos
Deo; unum cum illo manebat cui offerebat; unum in se fecit, pro quibus offerebat; unus ipse fuit,*

purchased, *through* whom it is dispensed, who reveals it from the bosom of the Father. Hence this communion and fellowship with God is not in express terms mentioned in the Old Testament. The thing itself is found there; but the clear light of it, and the boldness of faith in it, is discovered in the gospel, and by the Spirit administered therein. By that Spirit we have this liberty (2 Cor. 3:17–18). Abraham was the *friend* of God (Isa. 41:8); David, a man after his own *heart* [1 Sam. 13:14; Acts 13:22]; Enoch *walked* with him (Gen. 5:22)—all enjoying this communion and fellowship for the substance of it. But the way into the holiest was not yet made manifest while the first tabernacle was standing (Heb. 9:8). Though they had communion with God, yet they had not *parrēsian*—a boldness and confidence in that communion. This follows the entrance of our High Priest into the Most Holy Place (Heb. 4:16; 10:19). The veil also was upon them, that they had not *eleutherian*—freedom and liberty in their access to God (2 Cor. 3:15–16, etc.). But now in Christ we have boldness and access with confidence to God (Eph. 3:12).[12] This boldness and access with confidence the saints of old were not acquainted with. By Jesus Christ alone, then, on all considerations as to being and full manifestation, is this distance taken away. He has consecrated for us a new and living way (the old being quite shut up), "through the veil, that is to say, his flesh" (Heb. 10:20); and "through him we have access by one Spirit unto the Father" (Eph. 2:18). "You who sometimes were far off, are made nigh[13] by the blood of Christ, for he is our peace," etc. (Eph. 2:13–14). Of this foundation of all our communion with God, more afterward, and at large. Upon this new bottom[14] and foundation, by this new and living way, are sinners admitted into communion with God, and have fellowship with him. And truly, for sinners to have fellowship with God, the infinitely holy God, is an astonishing dispensation.[15]

---

qui offerabat, et quod offerebat. ["The same One and true Mediator Himself, reconciling us to God by the sacrifice of peace, might remain one with Him to whom He offered, might make those one in Himself for whom He offered, Himself might be in one both the offerer and the offering." Augustine, *On the Holy Trinity*, NPNF¹ 3:79; PL 42, col. 901.]

12. Gk. *Parrēsian kai tēn prosagōgēn en pepoithēsei.*

13. near

14. basis

15. *Philōn men ontōn, ouden dei dikaiosunēs dikaioi de ontes prosdeontai philias.* ["If men are friends there is no need of justice between them; whereas merely to be just is not enough—a feeling of friendship also is necessary."Aristotle, *The Nicomachean Ethics*, Loeb Classical Library (Cambridge, MA: Harvard University Press, 1962), 453.]

Communion in General

To speak a little of it in general: Communion relates to *things* and *persons*. A joint participation in any thing whatever, good or evil,[16] duty or enjoyment, nature or actions, gives this denomination[17] to them so partaking of it. A common interest in the same *nature* gives all men a fellowship or communion therein. Of the elect it is said, *Ta paidia kekoinōnēke sarkos kai aimatos*,[18] "Those children partook of" (or had fellowship in, with the rest of the world) "flesh and blood"—the same common nature with the rest of mankind; and, therefore, Christ also came into the same fellowship (*kai autos paraplēsiōs metesche tōn autōn*).

There is also a communion as to *state* and *condition*, whether it be good or evil; and this, either in things *internal* and spiritual—such as is the communion of saints among themselves; or in respect of *outward* things. So was it with Christ and the two thieves, as to one condition, and to one of them in respect of another. They were *en tō autō krimati*—under the same sentence to the cross (Luke 23:40, *ejusdem doloris socii*[19]). They had communion as to that evil condition whereunto they were adjudged,[20] and one of them requested (which he also obtained) a participation in that blessed condition whereupon our Savior was immediately to enter.

There is also a communion or fellowship in *actions*, whether *good* or *evil*. In *good*, is that communion and fellowship in the gospel, or in the performance and celebration of that worship of God which in the gospel is instituted, which the saints do enjoy (Phil. 1:5), which, as to the general kind of it, David so rejoices in (Ps. 42:4). In *evil*, was that wherein Simeon and Levi were brethren (Gen. 49:5). They had communion in that cruel act of revenge and murder. Our communion with God is not comprised in any one of these kinds; of some of them it is *exclusive*. It cannot be natural; it must be *voluntary* and by consent. It cannot be of state and conditions; but in actions. It cannot be in the same actions upon a third party; but in a return from one to another. The infinite disparity that is

---

16. *Quemadmodum enim nobis arrhabonem Spiritus reliquit, ita et a nobis arrhabonem carnis accepit, et vexit in cœlum, pignus totius summæ illuc quandoque redigendæ.* ["For as 'He has given us the earnest of the Spirit,' so has He received from us the earnest of the flesh, and has carried it with Him into heaven as a pledge of that complete entirety which is one day to be restored." Tertullian, *On the Resurrection of the Flesh*, ANF 3:584; PL 2, col. 869A.]

17. name, designation.

18. Owen has reversed the terms *aimatos* and *sarkos*.

19. Lat. "Sorrows of the same thing [i.e., condemnation] [were] shared."

20. sentenced, judged, settled judicially.

between God and man made the great philosopher conclude that there could be no friendship between them.[21] Some distance in the persons holding friendship he could allow, nor could exactly determine the bounds and extent thereof; but that between God and man, in his apprehension, left no place for it. Another says, indeed, that there is *communitas homini cum Deo*[22]—a certain fellowship between God and man—but the general intercourse[23] of providence is all he apprehended. Some arose to higher expressions; but they understood nothing whereof they spoke. This knowledge is hid in Christ; as will afterward be made to appear. It is too wonderful for nature, as sinful and corrupted. Terror and apprehensions of death at the presence of God is all that it guides unto. But we have, as was said, a *new* foundation and a *new* discovery[24] of this privilege.

Now, communion is the mutual communication of such good things as wherein the persons holding that communion are delighted, bottomed[25] upon some union between them. So it was with Jonathan and David; their souls clave to one another (1 Sam. 20:17) *in love.*[26] There was the *union* of love between them; and then they really communicated all issues[27] of love mutually.[28] In spiritual things this is more eminent: those who enjoy this communion have the most excellent union for the foundation of it; and the issues of that union, which they mutually communicate, are the most precious and eminent.

Of the union which is the foundation of all that communion we have with God I have spoken largely elsewhere, and have nothing further to add thereunto.

---

21. *Akribēs men oun en toioutois ouk estin horismos, heōs tinos hoi philon pollōn gar aphairoumenōn, eti menei, polu de chōristhentos, hoion tou theou ouk eti.* ["It is true that we cannot fix a precise limit on such cases, up to which two men can still be friends; the gap may go on widening and the friendship still remain; but when one becomes very remote from the other, as God is remote from man, it can go on no longer." Aristotle, *The Nicomachean Ethics*, Loeb Classical Library (Cambridge, MA: Harvard University Press, 1962), 478.]

22. Perhaps an oblique reference to Cicero's complaint to Epicurus concerning how man is to relate to the gods if the gods have no regard for humans: *cum homini nulla cum deo sit communitas?* ["If god and man have nothing in common?" Cicero, *De natura deorum*, trans. H. Rackham, Loeb Classical Library (Cambridge, MA: Harvard University Press, 1972), 110–13.]

23. communication

24. revelation

25. grounded

26. *Panta ta tōn philōn koina.* ["Friends hold everything in common."]

27. proceedings

28. *Kai hē paroimia, koina ta philōn, orthōs, en koinōnia gar hē philia.* ["Again, the proverb says 'Friends' goods are common property,' and this is correct, since community is the essence of friendship." Aristotle, *The Nicomachean Ethics*, 485.]

Communion with God Defined

Our communion, then, with God consists in

> his *communication of himself unto us,*
> *with our return unto him* of that which he requires and accepts,
> flowing from that *union*[29] which in Jesus Christ we have with him.

And it is twofold: (1) *perfect and complete*, in the full fruition of his glory and total giving up of ourselves to him, resting in him as our utmost end; which we shall enjoy when we see him as he is; and (2) *initial and incomplete*, in the firstfruits and dawnings of that perfection which we have here in grace; which [is the] only [aspect] I shall handle.

It is, then, I say, of that mutual communication[30] in giving and receiving, after a most holy and spiritual manner, which is between God and the saints while they walk together in a covenant of peace, ratified in the blood of Jesus, whereof we are to treat. And this we shall do, if God permit; in the meantime praying the God and Father of our Lord and Savior Jesus Christ—who has, of the riches of his grace, recovered us from a state of enmity into a condition of communion and fellowship with himself—that both he that writes, and they that read the words of his mercy, may have such a taste of his sweetness and excellencies therein, as to be stirred up to a further longing after the fullness of his salvation and the eternal fruition of him in glory.

---

29. *Nostra quippe et ipsius conjunctio, nec miscet personas, nec unit substantias, sed affectus consociat, et confœderat voluntates.* ["And certainly our union and his neither mixes our persons, nor unites our substances but joins our affections and binds our wills together." Owen attributes this quote to Cyprian, *De Coena Domini.* Though formerly attributed to Cyprian, it is (chap. 6) in a work by the twelfth-century abbot Arold of Boneval entitled *De cardinalibus operibus Christi usque ad ascensum ejus ad Patrem ad Adrium IV Pontificem Maximum*; PL 189, cols. 1609–1678A. For the quote in Cyprian's writing, see *Sancti Caecilii Cypriani opera* (Luteiae Parisiorum: Apud Viduam Mathurini Du Puis, viâ Iacobæâ, sub signo Caoronæ, 1648), 425.]

30. *Magna etiam illa communitas est, quæ conficitur ex beneficiis ultro citro, datis acceptis.* ["Another strong bond of fellowship is effected by mutual interchange of kind services." Cicero, *De Officiis*, Loeb Classical Library, trans. Walter Miller (Cambridge, MA: Harvard University Press, 1956), 58.]

Chapter 2

That the saints have communion with God, and what communion in general is, was declared in the first chapter. The *manner* how this communion is carried on, and the *matter* wherein it does consist, comes next under consideration.

The Manner of Communion with God

Distinct Communion with Each Person of the Trinity

For the *first*, in respect of the distinct persons of the Godhead with whom they have this fellowship, it is either *distinct* and peculiar,[1] or else obtained and exercised *jointly* and in common. That the saints have distinct communion with the Father, and the Son, and the Holy Spirit (that is, distinctly with the Father, and distinctly with the Son, and distinctly with the Holy Spirit), and in what the peculiar *appropriation* of this distinct communion unto the several persons does consist, must, in the first place, be made manifest.[2]

---

1. particular, characteristic, in its own way.

2. *Ecce dico alium esse patrem, et alium filium, non divisione alium, sed distinctione.* ["Now, observe, my assertion that the Father is one, and the Son one, and the Spirit one, and that They are distinct from Each Other." Tertullian, *Against Praxeas*, ANF 3:603; PL 2, Cols. 164a–b.] *Ou phthanō to hen noēsai, kai tois trisi perilampomai, ou phthanō ta tria dielein, kai eis to hen anapheromai.* ["No sooner do I conceive of the One than I am illumined by the Splendor of the Three; no sooner do I distinguish Them than I am carried back to the One." Gregory of Nazianzus, *Oration 40: The Oration on Holy Baptism*, NPNF[2] 7:375; PG 36, col. 417B.]

[In] 1 John 5:7 the apostle tells us, "There are three that bear record in heaven, the Father, the Word, and the Holy Ghost."[3] In heaven they are, and bear witness to us. And what is it that they bear witness unto? Unto the sonship of Christ, and the salvation of believers in his blood. Of the carrying on of that, both by blood and water, justification and sanctification, is he there treating. Now, how do they bear witness hereunto? Even as three, as three distinct witnesses. When God witnesses concerning our salvation, surely it is incumbent[4] on us to receive his testimony. And as he bears witness, so are we to receive it. Now this is done distinctly. The Father bears witness, the Son bears witness, and the Holy Spirit bears witness; for they are three distinct witnesses. So, then, are we to receive their several testimonies: and in doing so we have communion with them severally; for in *this giving and receiving* of testimony consists no small part of our fellowship with God. Wherein their distinct witnessing consists will be afterward declared.

[In] 1 Corinthians 12:4–6, the apostle, speaking of the distribution of gifts and graces unto the saints, ascribes them distinctly, in respect of the fountain of their communication, unto the distinct persons. "There are diversities of gifts (*charismata*), but the same Spirit" [v. 4]—"that one and the self-same Spirit," that is, the Holy Ghost (v. 11). "And there are differences of administrations (*diakonia*), but the same Lord," the same Lord Jesus (v. 5). "And there are diversities of operations (*energēmata*), but it is the same God," etc., even the Father (Eph. 4:6). So graces and gifts are bestowed, and so are they received.

And not only in the *emanation* of grace from God, and the *illapses*[5] of the Spirit on us, but also in all our approaches unto God, is the same distinction observed.[6] "For through Christ we have access by one Spirit unto the Father" (Eph. 2:18). Our access unto God (wherein we have communion with him) is *dia Christou* ("through Christ"), *en Pneumati* ("in the Spirit"), and *pros ton Patera* ("unto the Father")—the persons being here considered as engaged *distinctly* unto the accomplishment of the counsel of the will of God revealed in the gospel.

---

3. Most modern translations omit this clause, known as the Comma Johanneum, because it is not found in the earliest manuscripts and was never quoted by the church fathers.

4. obligatory

5. permeations, descents.

6. *Pasan men gar deēsin kai proseuchēn kai enteuxin, kai eucharistian anapempteon tō epi pasi theō, dia tou epi pantōn aggelōn archiereōs empsuchou logou kai theou.* ["For every prayer, and supplication, and intercession, and thanksgiving, is to be sent up to the Supreme God through the High Priest, who is above all the angels, the living Word and God." Origen, *Origen Against Celsus*, ANF 4:544; PG 11, col. 1185b.]

Sometimes, indeed, there is express mention made only of the Father and the Son: "Our fellowship is with the Father, and with his Son Jesus Christ" (1 John 1:3). The particle "and" is both distinguishing and uniting. Also John 14:23, "If a man love me, he will keep my words: and my Father will love him, and we will come unto him, and make our abode with him." It is in this communion wherein Father and Son do make their abode with the soul.

Sometimes the Son only is spoken of, as to this purpose. "God is faithful, by whom you were called unto the fellowship of his Son Jesus Christ our Lord" (1 Cor. 1:9). And Revelation 3:20, "If any man hear my voice, and open the door, I will come in to him, and will sup[7] with him, and he with me"—of which place afterward.

Sometimes the Spirit alone is mentioned. "The grace of the Lord Jesus Christ, and the love of God, and the communion of the Holy Ghost be with you all" (2 Cor. 13:14). This distinct communion, then, of the saints with the Father, Son, and Spirit, is very plain in the Scripture; but yet it may admit of further demonstration. Only this caution I must lay in beforehand: whatever is affirmed in the pursuit of this truth, it is done with relation to the explanation ensuing, in the beginning of the next chapter.

The way and means, then, on the part of the saints, whereby in Christ they enjoy communion with God, are all the spiritual and holy actings[8] and outgoings of their souls in those graces, and by those ways, wherein both the *moral* and *instituted* worship of God does consist. Faith, love, trust, joy, etc., are the natural or moral worship of God, whereby those in whom they are have communion with him. Now, these are either *immediately* acted on God, and not tied to any ways or means outwardly manifesting themselves; or else they are further drawn forth, in solemn prayer and praises, according unto that way which he has appointed. That the Scripture does distinctly assign all these unto the Father, Son, and Spirit—manifesting that the saints do, in all of them, both as they are purely and nakedly moral, and as further clothed with instituted worship, respect each person respectively—is that which, to give light to the assertion in hand, I shall further declare by particular instances.

---

7. eat, have supper.

8. *Hic tibi præcipuè sit purâ mente colendus.* ["This one must especially be worshiped by you with a pure mind."]

COMMUNION WITH THE FATHER

For the *Father*. Faith, love, obedience, etc., are peculiarly and distinctly yielded by the saints unto him; and he is peculiarly manifested in those ways as acting *peculiarly* toward them: which should draw them forth and stir them up thereunto. He gives *testimony* unto, and bears witness of, his Son: "This is the witness of God which he has testified of his Son" (1 John 5:9). In his bearing witness he is an object of belief. When he gives testimony (which he does as the Father, because he does it of the Son) he is to be received in it by faith. And this is affirmed, "He that believes on the Son of God, has the witness in himself" (1 John 5:10). To believe on the Son of God in this place is to receive the Lord Christ as the Son, the Son given unto us,[9] for all the ends of the Father's love, upon the credit of the Father's testimony; and, therefore, therein is faith immediately acted on the Father. So it follows in the next words, "he that believes not God" (that is, the Father, who bears witness to the Son) "has made him a liar" [1 John 5:10]. "You believe in God," says our Savior (John 14:1); that is, the Father as such, for he adds, "Believe also in me"; or, "Believe you in God; believe also in me." God, as the *prima Veritas*[10] upon whose authority is founded and whereunto all divine faith is ultimately resolved, is not to be considered *hupostatikōs*,[11] as peculiarly expressive of any person, but *ousiōdōs*,[12] comprehending the whole Deity; which undividedly is the prime object thereof. But in this particular it is the testimony and authority of the Father (as such) therein, of which we speak, and whereupon faith is distinctly fixed on him—which, if it were not so, the Son could not add, "Believe also in me."

The like also is said of love. "If any man love the world, the love of the Father is not in him" (1 John 2:15); that is, the love which we bear to him, not that which we receive from him. The Father is here placed as the object of our love, in opposition to the world, which takes up our affections *hē agapē tou Patros* [the love of our Father]. The Father denotes the matter and object, not the efficient cause,[13] of the love inquired after. And this love of him as a Father is that which he calls his "honor" (Mal. 1:6).

---

9. Isa. 9:6; 1 Cor. 1:30; Matt. 5:16, 45; 6:1, 4, 6, 8; 7:21; 12:50; Luke 24:49; John 4:23; 6:45; 12:26; 14:6, 21, 23; 15:1; 16:25, 27; 20:17; Gal. 1:1, 3; Eph. 2:18; 5:20; 1 Thess. 1:1; James 1:17; 1 Pet. 1:17; 1 John 2:13, etc.

10. Lat. first Truth.

11. Gk. hypostatically, personally.

12. Gk. essentially.

13. Aristotle's term for the means or agency by which something comes into being.

Further: these graces as acted in prayer and praises, and as clothed with instituted worship, are peculiarly directed unto him. "You call on the Father" (1 Pet. 1:17); "For this cause I bow my knees unto the Father of our Lord Jesus Christ, of whom the whole family in heaven and earth is named" (Eph. 3:14–15). Bowing the knee comprises the whole worship of God, both that which is moral, in the universal obedience he requires, and those peculiar ways of carrying it on which are by him appointed: "Unto me," says the Lord, "every knee shall bow, every tongue shall swear" (Isa. 45:23)—which he declares to consist in their acknowledging of him for righteousness and strength (vv. 24–25). Yea, it seems sometimes to comprehend the *orderly* subjection of the whole creation unto his sovereignty.[14] In this place of the apostle it has a far more restrained acceptation, and is but a figurative expression of prayer, taken from the most expressive *bodily* posture to be used in that duty. This he further manifests [in] Ephesians 3:16–17, declaring at large what his aim was, and whereabout his thoughts were exercised, in that bowing of his knees. The workings, then, of the Spirit of grace in that duty are distinctly directed to the Father as such, as the fountain of the Deity, and of all good things in Christ—as the "Father of our Lord Jesus Christ." And therefore the same apostle does, in another place, expressly *conjoin*,[15] and yet as expressly *distinguish*, the Father and the Son in directing his supplications, "God himself even our Father, and our Lord Jesus Christ, direct our way unto you" (1 Thess. 3:11). The like precedent, also, have you of thanksgiving, "Blessed be the God and Father of our Lord Jesus Christ," etc. (Eph. 1:3–4). I shall not add those very *many places* wherein the several particulars that do concur unto that whole divine worship (not to be communicated unto any, by nature not God, without idolatry) wherein the saints do hold communion with God, are distinctly directed to the person of the Father.[16]

Communion with the Son

It is so also in reference unto the Son. "You believe in God," says Christ, "believe also in me" (John 14:1)—"Believe also, act faith distinctly on me; faith divine, supernatural, that faith whereby you believe in God, that is, the Father." There is a believing of Christ, namely, that he is the Son of God, the Savior of the world. That is that whose neglect our Savior so

---

14. Rom. 14:10–11; Phil. 2:10.
15. join together, unite.
16. Jer. 10:10; 17:5–6; Gal. 4:8.

threatened unto the Pharisees, "If you believe not that I am he, you shall die in your sins" (John 8:24). In this sense faith is not immediately fixed on the Son, being only an owning[17] of him (that is, the Christ to be the Son), by closing with the testimony of the Father concerning him. But there is also a believing on him, called "believing on the name of the Son of God" (1 John 5:13; so also John 9:36)—yea, the distinct affixing of faith, affiance,[18] and confidence on the Lord Jesus Christ the Son of God, as the Son of God, is most frequently pressed. John 3:16, "God" (that is, the Father) "so loved the world . . . that whosoever believes in him" (that is, the Son) "should not perish." The Son, who is given of the Father, is believed on. "He that believes on him is not condemned" (v. 18). "He that believes on the Son has everlasting life" (v. 36). "This is the work of God, that you believe on him whom he has sent" (John 6:29, 40; 1 John 5:10). The foundation of the whole is laid: "That all men should honor the Son, even as they honor the Father. He that honors not the Son honors not the Father which has sent him" (John 5:23). But of this honor and worship of the Son I have treated at large elsewhere[19] and shall not in general insist upon it again. For love, I shall only add that solemn apostolical benediction, Ephesians 6:24, "Grace be with all them that love our Lord Jesus Christ in sincerity"—that is, with divine love, the love of religious worship; which is the only *incorrupt* love of the Lord Jesus.

Further: that faith, hope, and love, acting themselves in all manner of obedience and appointed worship, are peculiarly due from the saints,[20] and distinctly directed unto the Son, is abundantly manifest from that solemn doxology: "Unto him that loved us, and washed us from our sins in his own blood, and has made us kings and priests unto God and his Father; to him be glory and dominion forever and ever. Amen" (Rev. 1:5–6). Which yet is set forth with more glory: "The four living creatures, and the four and twenty elders fell down before the Lamb, having every one of them harps, and golden vials full of odors, which are the prayers of saints" (Rev. 5:8), and, "Every creature which is in heaven, and on the earth, and under the earth, and such as are in the sea, and all that are in them heard I, saying, blessing, and honor, and glory, and power be unto him that sits upon the throne, and unto the Lamb forever and ever" (Rev.

---

17. admitting, acknowledging, confessing to be true.

18. trust

19. See John Owen, *Vindiciae Evangelicae* [*Mystery of the Gospel Vindicated* (1655), in *Works*, 12:248–65.]

20. Ps. 2:7, 12; Dan. 3:25; Matt. 3:17; 17:5; 22:45; John 3:36; 5:19–26; 8:36; 1 Cor. 1:9; Gal. 1:16; 4:6; 1 John 2:22–24; 5:10–13; Heb. 1:6; Phil. 2:10; John 5:23.

5:13–14). The Father and the Son (he that sits upon the throne, and the Lamb) are held out jointly, yet distinctly, as the adequate object of all divine worship and honor, forever and ever. And therefore Stephen, in his solemn dying invocation, fixes his faith and hope distinctly on him, "Lord Jesus, receive my spirit"; and, "Lord, lay not this sin to their charge" (Acts 7:59–60)—for he knew that the Son of man had power to forgive sins also. And this worship of the Lord Jesus the apostle makes the discriminating character of the saints, "With all," says he, "that in every place call upon the name of Jesus Christ our Lord, both theirs and ours" (1 Cor. 1:2); that is, with all the saints of God. And invocation generally comprises the whole worship of God.[21] This, then, is the due of our Mediator, though as God, as the Son—not as Mediator.

COMMUNION WITH THE HOLY SPIRIT

Thus also is it in reference unto the Holy Spirit of grace. The closing of the great sin of unbelief is still described as an opposition unto and a resisting of that Holy Spirit.[22] And you have distinct mention of the love of the Spirit (Rom. 15:30). The apostle also peculiarly directs his supplication to him in that solemn benediction, "The grace of the Lord Jesus Christ, and the love of God, and the communion of the Holy Ghost, be with you all" (2 Cor. 13:14). And such benedictions are originally supplications. He is likewise entitled unto all instituted worship, from the appointment of the administration of baptism in his name (Matt. 28:19). Of which things more afterward.

Now, of the things which have been delivered this is the sum:

> there is no grace whereby our souls go forth unto God,
> no act of divine worship yielded unto him,
> [no act of] duty or obedience performed,
> but they are distinctly directed unto Father, Son, and Spirit.

Now, by these and such like ways as these, do we hold communion with God; and therefore we have that communion distinctly, as has been described.

Distinct Communication from Each Person of the Trinity

This also may further appear, if we consider how distinctly the persons of the Deity are revealed to act in the *communication* of those good

---

21. Isa. 56:7; Rom. 10:12–14.
22. Acts 7:51.

things, wherein the saints have communion with God.[23] As all the spiritual *ascendings* of their souls are assigned unto them respectively, so all their internal receiving of the communications of God unto them are held out in such a distribution as points at distinct rises and fountains (though not of being in themselves, yet) of dispensations unto us. Now this is declared two ways.

WHERE WE SEE THE DISTINCTIONS

First, when the *same* thing is, at the *same* time, ascribed *jointly* and yet *distinctly* to all the persons in the Deity, and *respectively* to each of them. So are grace and peace: "Grace be unto you, and peace, from him which is, and which was, and which is to come; and from the seven Spirits which are before his throne; and from Jesus Christ, who is the faithful witness," etc. (Rev. 1:4–5). The seven Spirits before the throne are the Holy Spirit of God, considered as the perfect fountain of every perfect gift and dispensation. All are here joined together, and yet all mentioned as distinguished in their communication of grace and peace unto the saints. "Grace and peace be unto you, from the Father, and from," etc.

Second, when the *same* thing is attributed *severally* and singly unto each person. There is, indeed, no gracious influence from above, no illapse of light, life, love, or grace upon our hearts, but proceeds in such a dispensation. I shall give only one instance, which is very comprehensive, and may be thought to comprise all other particulars; and this is *teaching*. The teaching of God is the real communication of all and every particular emanation from himself unto the saints whereof they are made partakers. That promise, "They shall be all taught of God" [John 6:45], enwraps in itself the whole mystery of grace, as to its actual dispensation unto us, so far as we may be made real possessors of it. Now this is assigned—

UNIQUE COMMUNICATIONS WITHIN THE TRINITY

Unto the Father. The accomplishment of that promise is peculiarly referred to him, "It is written in the prophets, 'And they shall be all taught of God.' Every man therefore that has heard, and has learned

---

23. *Tametsi omnia unus idemque Deus efficit, ut dicitur—opera Trinitatis ad extra sunt indivisa, distinguuntur tamen personæ discrimine in istis operibus.* ["Although one and the same God made all things, as it is said—the external works of the Trinity are undivided, nevertheless, the persons are distinguished with difference in their works."] Cf. Matt. 3:16; Acts 3:13; Gen. 19:24; 1:26; Matt. 28:19; 2 Cor. 13:14.

of the Father, comes unto me" (John 6:45). This teaching, whereby we are translated from death unto life, brought [us] unto Christ, unto a participation of life and love in him—it is of and from the Father: him we hear, of him we learn,[24] by him are we brought unto union and communion with the Lord Jesus. This is his drawing us, his begetting us anew of his own will, by his Spirit; and in which work he employs the ministers of the gospel (Acts 26:17–18).

Unto the Son. The Father proclaims him from heaven to be the great teacher, in that solemn charge to hear him, which came once [and] again from the excellent glory: "This is my beloved Son; hear him." The whole of his prophetical, and no small part of his kingly office, consists in this teaching; herein is he said to draw men unto him, as the Father is said to do in his teaching (John 12:32); which he does with such efficacy that "the dead hear his voice and live."[25] The teaching of the Son is a life-giving, a spirit-breathing, teaching—an effectual influence of light, whereby he shines into darkness; a communication of life, quickening[26] the dead; an opening of blind eyes, and changing of hard hearts; a pouring out of the Spirit, with all the fruits thereof. Hence he claims it as his privilege to be the sole master: "One is your Master, even Christ" (Matt. 23:10).

To the Spirit. "The Comforter, he shall teach you all things" (John 14:26). "But the anointing which you have received," says the apostle, "abides in you, and you need not that any man teach you: but as the same anointing teaches you of all things, and is truth, and is no lie, and even as it has taught you, you shall abide in him" (1 John 2:27). That teaching unction[27] which is not only true, but truth itself, is only the Holy Spirit of God: so that he teaches also; being given unto us "that we might know the things that are freely given to us of God" (1 Cor. 2:12). I have chosen this special instance because, as I told you, it is comprehensive, and comprises in itself most of the particulars that might be enumerated—quickening, preserving, etc.

This, then, further drives on the truth that lies under demonstration; there being such a distinct communication of grace from the several persons of the Deity, the saints must needs have distinct communion with them.

---

24. Matt. 11:25; John 1:13; James 1:18.
25. Matt. 3:17; 17:5; 2 Pet. 1:17; Deut. 18:15–20, etc.; Acts 3:22–23; John 5:25; Isa. 61:1–3; Luke 4:18–19.
26. giving life to
27. anointing

WHERE THE DISTINCTIONS LIE

It remains only to intimate,[28] in a word, *wherein this distinction lies* and what is the ground thereof. Now, this is that the Father does it by the way of *original authority*; the Son by the way of communicating from a *purchased treasury*; the Holy Spirit by the way of *immediate efficacy*.

The Father communicates all grace by the way of original authority: He quickens whom he will (John 5:21). "Of his own will begat he us" (James 1:18). Life-giving power is, in respect of original authority, invested in the Father by the way of eminency; and therefore, in sending of the quickening Spirit, Christ is said to do it from the Father, or the Father himself to do it. "But the Comforter, which is the Holy Ghost, whom the Father will send" (John 14:26). "But when the Comforter is come, whom I will send unto you from the Father" (John 15:26)—though he be also said to send him himself, on another account (John 16:7).

The Son, by the way of making out a purchased treasury: "Of his fullness have all we received, and grace for grace" (John 1:16). And whence is this fullness? "It pleased the Father that in him should all fullness dwell" (Col. 1:19). And upon what account he has the dispensation of that fullness to him committed you may see (Phil. 2:8–11). "When you shall make his soul an offering for sin, he shall prolong his days, and the pleasure of the LORD shall prosper in his hand. He shall see of the travail of his soul, and shall be satisfied: by his knowledge shall my righteous servant justify many; for he shall bear their iniquities" (Isa. 53:10–11). And with this fullness he has also authority for the communication of it (John 5:25–27; Matt. 28:18).

The Spirit does it by the way of immediate efficacy: "But if the Spirit of him that raised up Jesus from the dead dwell in you, he that raised up Christ from the dead shall also quicken your mortal bodies by his Spirit that dwells in you" (Rom. 8:11). Here are all three comprised, with their distinct concurrence unto our quickening. Here is the Father's authoritative quickening ("He raised Christ from the dead, and he shall quicken you"), and the Son's mediatory quickening (for it is done in "the death of Christ"), and the Spirit's immediate efficacy ("He shall do it by the Spirit that dwells in you"). He that desires to see this whole matter further explained may consult what I have elsewhere written on this subject. And thus is the distinct communion whereof we treat both proved and demonstrated.

---

28. communicate, make known.

Chapter 3

Having proved that there is such a distinct communion in respect of Father, Son, and Spirit, as whereof we speak, it remains that it be further cleared up by an induction of instances, to manifest what [it is], and wherein the saints peculiarly hold this communion with the *several* persons respectively: which also I shall do, after the premising [of] some observations, necessary to be previously considered, as was promised, for the clearing of what has been spoken. And they are these that follow.

Clarifying Observations

First, when I assign any thing as *peculiar* wherein we distinctly hold communion with any person, I do not exclude the other persons from communion with the soul in the very same thing. Only this, I say, *principally*, immediately, and by the way of eminency, we have, in such a thing, or in such a way, communion with some one person; and therein with the others *secondarily*, and by the way of consequence on that foundation; for the person, as the person, of any one of them, is not the prime *object* of divine worship, but as it is *identified* with the nature or essence of God. Now, the works that outwardly are of God (called "*Trinitatis ad extra*"[1]), which are commonly said to be *common and undivided*,[2] are either wholly so, and in all respects, as all works of common providence; or else, being common in respect of their acts, they are distinguished in respect of that principle, or next and immediate rise in the manner of

---

1. externally directed works of the Trinity
2. *Opera ad extra sunt indivisa* ["externally directed works are undivided"].

operation: so creation is *appropriated* to the Father, redemption to the Son. In which sense we speak of these things.

Second, there is a concurrence of the *actings* and operations of the whole Deity[3] in that *dispensation*, wherein each person concurs to the work of our salvation, unto every *act* of our communion with each singular person. Look, by whatsoever act we hold communion with any person, there is an influence from every person to the putting forth of that act.[4] As, suppose it to be the act of faith: It is bestowed on us by the Father: "It is not of yourselves: it is the gift of God" (Eph. 2:8). It is the Father that reveals the gospel, and Christ therein (Matt. 11:25). And it is purchased for us by the Son: "Unto you it is given in the behalf of Christ, to believe on him" (Phil. 1:29). In him are we "blessed with spiritual blessings" (Eph. 1:3). He bestows on us, and increases faith in us (Luke 17:5). And it is wrought in us by the Spirit; he administers that "exceeding greatness of his power," which he exercises toward them who believe, "according to the working of his mighty power, which he wrought in Christ, when he raised him from the dead" (Eph. 1:19–20; Rom. 8:11).

Third, when I assign any *particular* thing wherein we hold communion with any person, I do not do it *exclusively* unto other mediums of communion; but only by the way of inducing a special and eminent instance for the proof and manifestation of the former general assertion: otherwise there is no grace or duty wherein we have not communion with God in the way described. In every thing wherein we are made partakers of the divine nature [2 Pet. 1:4], there is a communication and receiving between God and us; so near are we unto him in Christ.

Fourth, by asserting this distinct communion, which merely respects that order in the dispensation of grace which God is pleased to hold out in the gospel, I intend not in the least to shut up all communion with God under these precincts (his ways being exceeding broad, containing a perfection whereof there is no end [Ps. 119:96]), nor to prejudice that holy

---

3. *Patēr sun huiō kai panagnō penumati / Trias prosōpois eukrinēs, monas phusei. / Mēt oun arithmō sugcheēs hupostaseis, / Mēt an theon su proskunōn timas phusin / Mia trias gar, eis theos pantokratōr.* ["The Father with the Son and all-hallowed Spirit: May you distinguish [them as] three in persons, one in nature. And so neither mingle their essences in number, nor bow down to worship the divine nature; for One [is] Three, one All-mighty God."] This quote is from the work *Iambics for Seleucus* by Amphilochius of Iconium, which has been found among the works of Gregory of Nazianzus: PG 37, col. 1590A lines 194–98.

4. *Proskunōmen tēn mian en tois trisi theotēta.* ["Let us bow before the one divinity in three." Gregory of Nazianzus, *Oration 34: On the Arrival of the Egyptians*, NPNF[2] 7:336; PG 36, col. 249B.] See Aquinas, *Summa Theologica* 22, q. 84, a. 3, q. 84, a. 1; Alexander Alensis, *Summa Universæ Theologicæ*, p. 3, q. 30, m. 1, a. 3.

fellowship we have with the whole Deity, in our walking before him in covenant-obedience; which also, God assisting, I shall handle hereafter.

The Matter of Communion with God

Communion with the Father Consists in Love

These few observations being premised, I come now to declare what it is wherein peculiarly and eminently the saints have communion with the Father; and this is *love*—free, undeserved, and eternal love. This the Father peculiarly fixes upon the saints; this they are immediately to eye[5] in him, to receive of him, and to make such returns thereof as he is delighted withal. This is the great *discovery* of the gospel: for whereas the Father, as the fountain of the Deity, is not known any other way but as full of wrath, anger, and indignation against sin, nor can the sons of men have any other thoughts of him (Rom. 1:18; Isa. 33:13–14; Hab. 1:13; Ps. 5:4–6; Eph. 2:3)—here he is now revealed peculiarly as love, as full of it unto us; the manifestation whereof is the peculiar work of the gospel (Titus 3:4).

GOD IS LOVE

"God is love" (1 John 4:8). That the name of God is here taken personally,[6] and for the person of the Father, not essentially, is evident from v. 9, where he is distinguished from his only begotten Son whom he sends into the world. Now, says he, "The Father is love"; that is, not only of an infinitely gracious, tender, compassionate, and loving nature, according as he has proclaimed himself (Ex. 34:6–7), but also one that "eminently and peculiarly dispenses himself unto us in free love." So the apostle sets it forth in the following verses: "This is love" (v. 10)—"This is that which I would have you take notice of in him, that he makes out love unto you, in 'sending his only begotten Son into the world, that we might live through him.'" So also verse 10, "He loved us, and sent his Son to be the propitiation for our sins." And that this is peculiarly

---

5. to look at, to gaze upon.

6. Deut. 33:3; Jer. 31:3; John 3:16; 5:42; 14:21; Rom. 5:5; 8:39; Eph. 2:4; 1 John 2:15; 4:10–11; Heb. 12:6. *Multo emphatikōteron loquitur quam si Deum diceret summopere, atque adeo infinite nos amare, cum Deum dicit erga nos ipsam charitatem esse, cujus latissimum tekmērion profert.* ["He speaks much more emphatically than if he were to say that God loves us exceedingly and even boundlessly, when he says that God is charity itself toward us, the most extensive proof of which he brings forth." Theodore Beza, *Jesu Christi Domini Nostri Novum Testamentum, sive Novum Foedus* (Cantabrigiae: Ex Officina Rogeri Danielis, 1642), 733.]

to be eyed in him, the Holy Ghost plainly declares, in making it antecedent to the sending of Christ, and all mercies and benefits whatever
by him received. This love, I say, in itself, is antecedent to the purchase
of Christ, although the whole fruit thereof be made out alone thereby
(Eph. 1:4–6).

Love Is Particularly Assigned to the Father

So in that distribution made by the apostle in his solemn parting benediction, "The grace of the Lord Jesus Christ, *the love of God*, and the
fellowship of the Holy Ghost, be with you all" (2 Cor. 13:14). Ascribing
sundry[7] things unto the distinct persons, it is *love* that he peculiarly as-
signs to the Father. And the fellowship of the Spirit is mentioned with
the grace of Christ and the love of God, because it is by the Spirit alone
that we have fellowship with Christ in grace, and with the Father in
love, although we have also peculiar fellowship with him; as shall be
declared.

Jesus Prays to the Father for Us, for the Father Loves Us

Says our Savior, "I say not unto you, that I will pray the Father for
you; for the Father himself loves you" (John 16:26–27).[8] But how is
this, that our Savior says, "I say not that I will pray the Father for
you," when he says plainly, "I will pray the Father for you" (14:16)?
The disciples—with all the gracious words, comfortable and faithful
promises of their Master, with most heavenly discoveries of his heart
unto them—were even fully convinced of *his* dear and tender affec-

---

7. various, particular, distinct.

8. *Quomodo igitur negat? negat secundum quid; hoc est, negat se ideo rogaturum patrem, ut
patrem illis conciliet, et ad illos amandos et exaudiendos flectat; quasi non sit suapte sponte erga
illos propensus. Voluit ergo Christus his verbis persuadere apostolis, non solum se, sed etiam ipsum
patrem illos complecti amore maximo. Et ita patrem eos amare, ac promptum habere animum illis
gratificandi, et benefaciendi, ut nullius, neque ipsius filii opus habeat tali intercessione, qua solent
placari, et flecti homines non admodum erga aliquem bene affecti.* ["How then does he deny it?
He denies by a distinction; that is, he says that he will not pray the Father to reconcile the Father
to them, to turn [him] to love and hear them; as if he were not inclined to them by his own will.
Therefore, with these words Christ wanted to persuade the apostles that not only he himself, but also
the Father as well was embracing them with the greatest love. And that the Father so loved them,
and had a mind so disposed to graciously bless them, that he had no need for anyone—not even
the Son himself—to offer the intercession by which men are usually appeased and turned toward
someone to whom they are not well-disposed." Jerome Zanchi, *De tribus Elohim*, lib. vi cap. 9,
De tribus Elohim aeterno Patre, Filio, et Spiritu Sancto, vno eode mque Iohoua, vol. 1 of *Operum
theologicorum D. Hieronymi* (Geneva: Excudebat Stephanus Gamonetus, 1605), col. 154. *Vid.
Hilary De Trinitate*, lib. vi. p. 97, ed. Eras.]

tions toward them; as also of his continued care and kindness, that he would not forget them when bodily he was gone from them, as he was now upon his departure: but now all their thoughts are concerning the Father, how they should be accepted with him, what respect he had toward them. Says our Savior:

> Take no care of that, nay, impose not that upon me, of procuring the Father's love for you; but know that this is his peculiar respect toward you, and which you are in him: "He himself loves you." It is true, indeed (and as I told you), that I will pray the Father to send you the Spirit, the Comforter, and with him all the gracious fruits of his love; but yet in the point of *love itself*, free love, eternal love, there is no need of any intercession for that: for eminently the Father himself loves you. Resolve of that, that you may hold communion with him in it, and be no more troubled about it. Yea, as your great trouble is about the Father's love, so you can no way more trouble or burden him, than by your unkindness in not believing of it.

So it must needs be[9] where sincere love is questioned.

The Holy Spirit Sheds Abroad in Our Hearts the Love of God

The apostle teaches the same, "The love of God is shed[10] abroad in our hearts by the Holy Ghost, which is given unto us" (Rom. 5:5). God, whose love this is, is plainly distinguished from the Holy Ghost, who sheds abroad that love of his; and in verse 8, he is also distinguished from the Son, for it is from that love of his that the Son is sent: and therefore it is the Father of whom the apostle here specially speaks. And what is it that he ascribes to him? Even love; which also, v. 8, he commends to us—sets it forth in such a signal[11] and eminent expression, that we may take notice of it, and close[12] with him in it. To carry this business to its height, there is not only most frequent peculiar mention of the love of God, where the Father is eminently intended, and of the love of the Father expressly, but he is also called "the God of love" (2 Cor. 13:11), and is said to be "love"—so that whoever will know him (1 John 4:8), or dwell in him by fellowship or communion (v. 16), must do it as he is love.

---

9. is of necessity
10. poured forth
11. significant, striking, remarkable, notably out of the ordinary.
12. unite, settle, consummate.

Twofold Divine Love of the Father

Nay, whereas there is a twofold divine love, *beneplaciti* (a love of good pleasure and destination) and *amicitiæ* (a love of friendship and approbation[13]), they are both peculiarly assigned to the Father in an eminent manner:

John 3:16, "God so loved the world, that he gave," etc.; that is, with the love of his purpose and good pleasure, his determinate[14] will of doing good. This is distinctly ascribed to him, being laid down as the cause of sending his Son. (So Rom. 9:11–12; Eph. 1:4–5; 2 Thess. 2:13–14; 1 John 4:8–9.)

John 14:23, there is mention of that other kind of love whereof we speak.[15] "If a man love me," says Christ, "he will keep my words: and my Father will love him, and we will come unto him, and make our abode with him." The love of friendship and approbation is here eminently ascribed to him. Says Christ, "We will come," even Father and Son, "to such a one, and dwell with him"; that is, by the Spirit: but yet he would have us take notice that, in point of love, the Father has a peculiar prerogative: "My Father will love him."

The Love of the Father Is the Fountain of All Gracious Dispensations

Yea, and as this love is peculiarly to be eyed in him, so it is to be looked on as the *fountain* of all following gracious dispensations. Christians walk oftentimes with exceedingly troubled hearts, concerning the thoughts of the Father toward them. They are well persuaded of the Lord Christ and his goodwill; the difficulty lies in what is their acceptance with the Father—what is his heart toward them?[16] "Show us the Father, and it suffices[17] us" (John 14:8). Now, this ought to be so far away, that his love ought to be looked on as the fountain from whence all other sweetnesses flow. Thus the apostle sets it out: "After that the kindness and love of God our Savior toward man appeared"

---

13. praise, approval, commendation.

14. determined, resolved, settled.

15. *Diligi a patre, recipi in amicitiam summi Dei; a Deo foveri, adeoque Deo esse in deliciis.* ["To be loved by the Father, to be received into the friendship of the most high God; to be favored by God, and even to be among the delights of God." Martin Bucer.]

16. *Te quod attinet non sumus solliciti—illud modo desideramus, ut patrem nobis vel semel intueri concedatur.* ["We are not concerned about what belongs to you—we only desire that it be granted us even once that the Father gaze upon us." Thomas Cartwright on John 14:8 in *Harmonia Evangelica* (Amsterdam, 1627), 420.]

17. satisfies, is enough for.

(Titus 3:4). It is of the Father of whom he speaks; for he tells us that "he makes out unto us," or "sheds that love upon us abundantly, through Jesus Christ our Savior" (v. 6). And this love he makes the hinge upon which the great alteration and translation of the saints does turn; for, says he, "We ourselves also were sometimes foolish, disobedient, deceived, serving diverse lusts and pleasures, living in malice and envy, hateful, and hating one another" (v. 3). All naught, all out of order, and vile. Whence, then, is our recovery? The whole rise of it is from this love of God, flowing out by the ways there described. For when the kindness and love of God appeared—that is, in the fruits of it—then did this alteration ensue.[18] To secure us hereof, there is not any thing that has a loving and tender nature in the world, and does act suitably whereunto, which God has not compared himself unto. Separate all weakness and imperfection which is in them, yet great impressions of love must abide. He is as a father, a mother, a shepherd, a hen over chickens, and the like (Ps. 103:13; Isa. 63:16; Matt. 6:6; Isa. 66:13; Ps. 23:1; Isa. 40:11; Matt. 23:37).

I shall not need to add any more proofs. This is that which is demonstrated: *There is love in the person of the Father peculiarly held out unto the saints, as wherein he will and does hold communion with them.*

The Requirements of Believers to Complete Communion with the Father in Love

Now, to complete communion with the Father *in love*, two things are required of believers: (1) *that they receive it of him;* and (2) *that they make suitable returns unto him.*

BELIEVERS MUST RECEIVE THE LOVE OF THE FATHER

That *they do receive it.* Communion consists in *giving* and *receiving.* Until the love of the Father be received, we have no communion with him therein. How, then, is this love of the Father to be received, so as to hold fellowship with him? I answer: By *faith.* The receiving of it is the believing of it. God has so fully, so eminently revealed his love, that it may be received by faith. "You believe in God" (John 14:1); that is, the Father. And what is to be believe in him? His love; for he is "love" (1 John 4:8).

---

18. follow

It is true, there is not an *immediate* acting of faith upon the Father,
but by the Son. "He is the way, the truth, and the life: no man comes
unto the Father but by him" (John 14:6). He is the merciful high priest
over the house of God, by whom we have access to the throne of grace
(Eph. 2:18): by him is our manuduction[19] unto the Father; by him we
believe in God (1 Pet. 1:21). But this is that I say—when by and through
Christ we have an access unto the Father, we then behold his glory also,
and see his love that he peculiarly bears unto us, and act faith thereon.
We are then, I say, to eye it, to believe it, to receive it, as in him; the
issues and fruits thereof being made out unto us through Christ alone.
Though there be no light for us but in the beams, yet we may by beams
see the sun, which is the fountain of it. Though all our refreshment
actually lie in the *streams*, yet by them we are led up unto the *fountain*.
Jesus Christ, in respect of the love of the Father, is but the beam, the
stream; wherein though actually all our light, our refreshment lies, yet
by him we are led to the fountain, the sun of eternal love itself. Would
believers exercise themselves herein, they would find it a matter of no
small *spiritual* improvement in their walking with God.

This is that which is aimed at. Many dark and disturbing thoughts
are apt to arise in this thing. Few can carry up their hearts and minds to
this height by faith, as to rest their souls in the love of the Father; they
live below it, in the troublesome region of hopes and fears, storms and
clouds. All here is serene and quiet. But how to attain to this pitch[20] they
know not. This is the will of God, that he may always be eyed as benign,
kind, tender, loving, and unchangeable therein; and that peculiarly as the
Father, as the great fountain and spring of all gracious communications
and fruits of love. This is that which Christ came to reveal—God as a
Father (John 1:18); that name which he declares to those who are given
him out of the world (John 17:6). And this is that which he effectually
leads us to by himself, as he is the only way of going to God as a Father
(John 14:5–6); that is, as love: and by doing so, gives us the rest which
he promises; for the love of the Father is the only rest of the soul. It is
true, as was said, we do not [have] this *formally* in the first instant of
believing. We believe in God through Christ (1 Pet. 1:21); faith seeks
out rest for the soul. This is presented to it by Christ, the mediator, as
the only procuring cause.[21] Here it abides not, but by Christ it has an

19. guidance (by the hand)
20. level, degree.
21. action or person who brings about the desired result

access to the Father (Eph. 2:18)—into his love; finds out that he is love, as having a design, a purpose of love, a good pleasure toward us from eternity—a delight, a complacency, a goodwill in Christ—all cause of anger and aversation[22] being taken away. The soul being thus, by faith through Christ, and by him, brought into the bosom of God, into a comfortable persuasion and spiritual perception and sense of his love, there reposes[23] and rests itself. And this is the first thing the saints do, in their communion with the Father; of the due improvement whereof, more afterward.

Believers Must Return Love to God

For that suitable *return* which is required, this also (in a main part of it, beyond which I shall not now extend it) consists in love (Deut. 6:4–5). God loves, that he may be beloved.[24] When he comes to command the return of his received love, to complete communion with him, he says, "My son, give me your heart" (Prov. 23:26)—your affections, your love. "You shall love the Lord your God with all your heart, and with all your soul, and with all your strength, and with all your mind" (Luke 10:27); this is the return that he demands. When the soul sees God, in his dispensation of love, to be love, to be infinitely lovely and loving, rests upon and delights in him as such, then has its communion with him in love. This is love: that God loves us first, and then we love him again. I shall not now go forth into a description of divine love. Generally, love is an affection of union and nearness, with complacency therein.[25] So long as the Father is looked on under any other apprehension, but only as acting love upon the soul, it breeds in the soul a dread and aversation.[26] Hence the flying and hiding of sinners in the Scriptures. But when he who is the Father is considered as a father, acting love on the soul, this raises it

---

22. a moral turning away; estrangement.

23. brings relief, respite.

24. *Amor superne descendens ad divinam pulchritudinem omnia convocat.* ["Love descending from above summons all things to the divine beauty." Our translation of Owen's truncated quote of Proclus. For a translation of the original, see Proclus, *Proclus: Alcibiades I*, 2nd ed., trans. William O'Neill (The Hague, 1971), 34; *Procli Commentarium in Platonis Alcibiadem* in *Procli Philosophi Platonica Opera Inedita* (Frankfurtam Main: Minerva G.m.b.H., 1962); col. 358.]

25. *Unio substantialis est causa amoris sui ipsius; similitudinis, est causa amoris alterius; sed unio realis quam amans quærit de re amata, est effectus amoris.* ["The union of substance is the cause of the love of oneself; that of likeness, is the cause of the love of another; but the real union which a lover seeks from the thing beloved, is the effect of love." Aquinas, *Summa Theologiæ* I–II.28.1.2, 61 vols., trans. Eric D'Arcy (London: Blackfriars, 1964–1981), 19:91 (Latin text on p. 90).]

26. Josh. 22:5; 23:11; Neh. 1:5.

to love again.[27] This is, in faith, the ground of all acceptable obedience (Deut. 5:10; Ex. 20:6; Deut. 10:12; 11:1, 13; 13:3).

Thus is this whole business stated by the apostle, "According as he has chosen us in him before the foundation of the world, that we should be holy and without blame before him in love" (Eph. 1:4). It begins in the *love of God*, and ends in *our love to him*. That is it which the eternal love of God aims at in us, and works us up unto. It is true, our universal obedience falls within the compass[28] of our communion with God; but that is with him as God, our blessed sovereign, lawgiver, and rewarder: as he is the Father, our Father in Christ, as revealed unto us to be love, above and contrary to all the expectations of the natural man; so it is in love that we have this intercourse with him. Nor do I intend only that love which is as the life and form of all moral obedience; but a peculiar delight and acquiescing in the Father, revealed effectually as love unto the soul.

That this communion with the Father in love may be made the more clear and evident, I shall show two things: (1) Wherein *this love of God unto us and our love to him do agree*, as to some manner of analogy and likeness. (2) *Wherein they differ*;[29] which will further discover[30] the nature of each of them.

Wherein God's Love and Our Love Agree

They agree in two things:

First, that they are each a love of *rest and complacency*.

The love of God is so. "The LORD your God in the midst of you is mighty; he will save, he will rejoice over you with joy, he will rest in his love; he will joy over you with singing" (Zeph. 3:17). Both these things are here assigned unto God in his love—*rest and delight*.[31] The words are, *yakharish be'ahabato*—"He shall be silent because of his love." To rest with contentment is expressed by being silent; that is, without

---

27. Ps. 18:1; 31:23; 97:10, 116:1; 1 Cor. 2:9; James 1:12; Isa. 56:6; Matt. 22:37; Rom. 8:28.

28. delimitation, measure.

29. *Analogon d 'en hapasais tais kath huperochēn ousais philiais, kai tēn philēsin dei ginesthai*, etc. ["The affection rendered in these various unequal friendships should also be proportionate." Aristotle, *The Nicomachean Ethics*, trans. H. Rackham (Cambridge, MA: Harvard University Press, 1962), 478.]

30. reveal, uncover.

31. *Effectus amoris quando habetur amatum, est delectatio.* ["But the effect of love, when the object loved is possessed, is pleasure." Aquinas, *Summa Theologiæ* I–II.25.2.1, 61 vols., trans. Eric D'Arcy (London: Blackfriars, 1964–1981), 19:51 (Latin text on p. 50).] *Amor est complacentia amantis in amato. Amor est motus cordis, delectantis se in aliquo.* ["Love is the lover's delight in his beloved. Love is an affection of the heart delighting itself in someone (or something)." Augustine.]

repining,[32] without complaint. This God does upon the account of his own love, so full, so every way complete and absolute, that it will not allow him to complain of any thing in them whom he loves, but he is silent on the account thereof. Or, "Rest in his love"; that is, he will not remove it—he will not seek further for another object. It shall make its abode upon the soul where it is once fixed, forever. And *complacency* or *delight*: "He rejoices with singing," as one that is fully satisfied in that object he has fixed his love on. Here are two words used to express the delight and joy that God has in his love—*yasîs* and *yagîl*. The first denotes the inward affection of the mind, joy of heart; and to set out the intenseness hereof, it is said he shall do it *besimekha*—in gladness, or with joy. To have joy of heart in gladness is the highest expression of delight in love. The latter word denotes not the inward affection, but the outward demonstration of it:[33] *agallian* seems to be formed of it. It is to exult in outward demonstration of internal delight and joy—"Tripudiare," [Latin for] to leap, as men overcome with some joyful surprise. And therefore God is said to do this *berinnah*—with a joyful sound, or singing. To rejoice with gladness of heart, to exult with singing and praise, argues [for] the greatest delight and complacency possible. When he would express the contrary of this love, he says *ouch eudokēse*—"he was not well pleased" (1 Cor. 10:5); he fixed not his delight nor rest on them. And, "If any man draw back, the Lord's soul has no pleasure in him" (Heb. 10:38; Jer. 22:28; Hos. 8:8; Mal. 1:10). He takes pleasure in those that abide with him. He sings to his church, "A vineyard of red wine: I the LORD do keep it" (Isa. 27:2–3; Ps. 147:11; 149:4). There is rest and complacency in his love. There is in the Hebrew but a metathesis[34] of a letter between the word that signifies a love of will and desire ('*ahab* is so to love), and that which denotes a love of rest and acquiescence (which is, '*abah*); and both are applied to God. He wills good to us, that he may rest in that will. Some say, *agapan*, "to love," is from *agan pothesthai*, perfectly to acquiesce in the thing loved. And

---

32. discontentment, fretting, grumbling.

33. *Externum magis gaudii gestum, quam internam animi lætitiam significat, cum velut tripudiis et volutationibus gaudere se quis ostendit.* [It signifies an outward expression of joy rather than the inner happiness of the spirit when someone shows that he is rejoicing as by leapings and tumblings–Santes Pagninus.] *gul; lætitiâ gestiit, animi lætitiam gestu corporis expressit, exilivit gaudio.* ["*gul*; He exulted in happiness, he expressed the happiness of his soul in the movement of his body, he sprang forth in joy." Mario de Calasio, *Concordantiæ Sacrorum Bibliorum Hebraicorum*, vol. 1 (Londini: Typis J. Ilive: Apud Jacobum Hodges, 1747–1749), col. 1079. Originally published in 1622.]

34. transposition of letters, sounds, or syllables within a word.

when God calls his Son *agapēton*, "beloved" (Matt. 3:17), he adds, as an exposition of it, *en ho eudokēsa*, "in whom I rest well pleased."

The return that the saints make unto him, to complete communion with him herein, holds some analogy with his love in this; for it is a love also of rest and delight.[35] "Return unto your rest, my soul," says David (Ps. 116:7). He makes God his *rest*; that is, he in whom his soul does rest, without seeking further for a more suitable and desirable object. "Whom have I," says he, "in heaven but you and there is none upon earth that I desire beside you" (Ps. 73:25).[36] Thus the soul gathers itself from all its wanderings, from all other beloveds, to rest in God alone—to satiate and content itself in him; choosing the Father for his present and eternal rest. And this also with *delight*. "Your lovingkindness," says the psalmist, "is better than life; therefore will I praise you" (Ps. 63:3). "Than life," *mekhayyim*—before lives. I will not deny but life in a single consideration sometimes is so expressed, but always emphatically; so that the whole life, with all the concernments of it, which may render it considerable, are thereby intended. Augustine, on this place, reading it *super vitas*,[37] extends it to the several courses of life that men engage themselves in.[38] Life, in the whole continuance of it, with all its *advantages* whatever, is at least intended. Supposing himself in the jaws of death, rolling into the grave through innumerable troubles, yet he found more sweetness in God than in a long life, under its best and most noble considerations, attended with all enjoyments that make it pleasant and comfortable. From both these is that of the church: "Asshur shall not save us; we will not ride upon horses: neither will we say any more to the work of our hands, you are our gods: for in you the fatherless finds mercy" (Hos. 14:3). They reject the most goodly appearances of rest and contentment, to make up all in God, on whom they cast themselves, as otherwise helpless orphans.

---

35. *Fecisti nos ad te, domine, et irrequietum est cor nostrum donec veniat ad te.* [You have made us for yourself, O Lord, and our heart is restless until it comes to you. Augustine, *The Confessions of Saint Augustin*, NPNF[1] 1:45; PL 32, col. 661.]

36. Ps. 37:7; Isa. 28:12; Heb. 4:9.

37. Latin Vulgate translation: "better than lives."

38. *Super vitas; quas vitas? Quas sibi homines eligunt; alius elegit sibi vitam negociandi, alius vitam rusticandi; alius vitam fœnerandi, alius vitam militandi, alius illam, alius illam. Diversæ sunt vitæ, sed melior est misericordia tua super vitas nostras.* ["Better than lives." What lives? Those which men have chosen for themselves. One hath chosen for himself a life of business, another a country life, another a life of usury, another a military life; one this, another that. Divers are the lives, but better is your mercy than our lives." Augustine, *Exposition on the Book of the Psalms*, NPNF[1] 8:261; PL 36, col. 0755h.]

Second, the mutual love of God and the saints agrees in this—that the way of communicating the issues and fruits of these loves is *only in Christ*. The Father communicates no issue of his love unto us but through Christ; and we make no return of love unto him but through Christ. He is the *treasury* wherein the Father disposes all the riches of his grace, taken from the bottomless mine of his eternal love; and he is the *priest* into whose hand we put all the offerings that we return unto the Father. Thence he is first, and by way of eminency, said to love the Son; not only as his eternal Son—as he was the delight of his soul before the foundation of the world (Prov. 8:30)—but also as our mediator, and the means of conveying his love to us (Matt. 3:17; John 3:35; 5:20; 10:17; 15:9; 17:24). And we are said through him to believe in and to have access to God.

The Father loves us and "chose us before the foundation of the world"; but in the pursuit of that love, he "blesses us with all spiritual blessings in heavenly places in Christ" (Eph. 1:3–4). From his love, he sheds or pours out the Holy Spirit richly upon us, through Jesus Christ our Savior (Titus 3:6). In the pouring out of his love, there is not one drop falls besides the Lord Christ. The holy anointing oil was all poured on the head of Aaron (Ps. 133:2); and thence went down to the skirts of his clothing. Love is first poured out on Christ; and from him it drops as the dew of Hermon [Ps. 133:3] upon the souls of his saints. The Father will have him to have "in all things the preeminence" (Col. 1:18); "it pleased him that in him all fullness should dwell" (v. 19); that "of his fullness we might receive, and grace for grace" (John 1:16). Though the love of the Father's purpose and good pleasure have its rise and foundation in his mere grace and will, yet the design of its accomplishment is only in Christ. All the fruits of it are first given to him; and it is in him only that they are dispensed to us. So that though the saints may, nay, *do* see an infinite ocean of love unto them in the bosom of the Father, yet they are not to look for one drop from him but what comes through Christ. He is the only means of communication. Love in the Father is like *honey in the flower*—it must be in the comb before it be for our use. Christ must extract and prepare this honey for us. He draws this water from the fountain through union and dispensation of fullness—we by faith, from the wells of salvation that are in him. This was in part before discovered.

Our returns are all *in him*, and *by him* also. And well is it with us that it is so. What lame and blind sacrifices should we otherwise present unto God! He bears the iniquity of our offerings, and he adds incense unto our prayers.[39] Our love is fixed on the Father; but it is conveyed to him through the Son of his love. He is the only way for our *graces* as well as our *persons* to go unto God; through him passes all our desire, our delight, our complacency, our obedience. Of which more afterward.

Now, in these two things there is some resemblance between that mutual love of the Father and the saints wherein they hold communion.

Wherein God's Love and Our Love Differ

There are sundry things wherein they differ:

First, the love of God is a love of *bounty*; our love unto him is a love of *duty*.

The love of the Father is a love of *bounty*—a descending love; such a love as carries him out to do good things to us, great things for us. His love lies at the bottom of all dispensations toward us; and we scarce anywhere find any mention of it, but it is held out as the cause and fountain of some free gift flowing from it. He loves us, and sends his Son to die for us—he loves us and blesses us with all spiritual blessings.[40] Loving is choosing (Rom. 9:11–12). He loves us and chastises us. [It is] a love like that of the heavens to the earth, when, being full of rain, they pour forth showers to make it fruitful;[41] as the sea communicates its waters to the rivers by the way of bounty, out of its own fullness—they return unto it only what they receive from it. It is the love of a spring, of a fountain—always communicating—a love from whence proceeds everything that is lovely in its object.[42] It infuses into, and creates goodness in, the persons beloved. And this answers the description of love given by the philosopher [Aristotle]. "To love," says he, "*Esti boulesthai tini ha oietai agatha kai kata dunamin praktikon einai toutōn.*"[43] (He that loves works out good to them he loves, as he is able.) God's power and will are commensurate—what he wills he works.

---

39. Exod. 28:38; Rev. 8:3; John 14:6; Heb. 10:19–22.

40. John 3:16; Rom. 5:8; Eph. 1:3–4; 1 John 4:9–10; Heb. 12:6; Rev. 3:19.

41. *Eran de semnon ouranon plēroumenon ombrou, pesein eis gaian.* ["And the majestic Heaven when filled with rain Yearneth to fall to Earth." Euripides, as quoted by Aristotle, *The Nicomachean Ethics*, Loeb Classical Library, trans. H. Rackham (Cambridge, MA: Harvard University Press, 1962), 455. Cf. Euripides, *Incertarum Fabularum Fragmenta*, frag. 898, lines 9–10 *Tragicorum Graecorum Fragmenta*, ed. Augustus Nauck and Bruno Snell (Hildesheim, Georg Olms Verlagsbuchhandlung, 1964), 648.]

42. *Amor Dei est infundens et creans bonitatem in amatis.* [The love of God fills and creates goodness in the beloved ones. Aquinas, *Summa Theologiæ* I.20, 61 vols., trans. Thomas Gilby (London: Blackfriars, 1964–1981), 5:61 (Latin text on p. 60).]

43. Aristotle, *Rhetoric* 2.4.1380b36.

Our love unto God is a love of *duty*, the love of a child. His love descends upon us in bounty and fruitfulness;[44] our love ascends unto him in duty and thankfulness. He adds to us by his love; we [add] nothing to him by ours. Our goodness extends not unto him. Though our love be fixed on him immediately,[45] yet no fruit of our love reaches him immediately; though he requires our love, he is not benefited by it (Job 35:5–8; Rom. 11:35; Job 22:2–3). It is indeed made up of these four things: (1) *rest*; (2) *delight*; (3) *reverence*; (4) *obedience*. By these do we hold communion with the Father in his love. Hence God calls that love which is due to him as a father, "honor": "If I be a father, where is mine honor?" (Mal. 1:6). It is a deserved act of duty.

Second, they differ in this: The love of the Father unto us is an *antecedent* love; our love unto him is a *consequent* love.

The love of the Father unto us is an *antecedent* love, and that in two respects:

It is antecedent in respect of our *love*: "Herein is love, not that we loved God, but that he loved us" (1 John 4:10). His love goes before ours. The father loves the child, when the child knows not the father, much less loves him. Yea, we are by nature *theostugeis* (Rom. 1:30)—haters of God. He is in his own nature *philanthrōpos*—a lover of men; and surely all mutual love between him and us must begin on his hand.

[It is also antecedent] in respect of all other *causes* of love whatever. It goes not only before our love, but also [before] anything in us that is lovely.[46] "God commends his love toward us, in that while we were yet sinners Christ died for us" (Rom. 5:8). Not only his love, but the eminent fruit thereof, is made out toward us as sinners. Sin holds out all of unloveliness and undesirableness that can be in a creature. The very mention of that removes all causes, all moving occasions of love whatever. Yet, as such, have we the commendation of the Father's love unto us, by a most signal testimony. Not only when we have done no good, but when we are in our blood, does he love us—not because we are better than others, but because [he] himself is infinitely good. His kindness appears when we are foolish and disobedient.

---

44. *Amor Dei causat bonitatem in rebus, sed amor noster causatur ab ea.* ["The love of God causes the goodness in things, and indeed our love is caused by it." Owen appears to be borrowing ideas and language from Aquinas, but we have been unable to find an exact location or even paraphrase of a particular relevant sentence from Aquinas.]

45. *Dilectio quæ est appetitivæ virtutis actus, etiam in statum viæ tendit in Deum primo et immediate.* ["Love, which is an act of an appetitive virtue, even in our present state tends first to God without an intermediary." Aquinas, *Summa Theologiæ* II–II.27.4, 61 vols., trans. R.J. Batten (London: Blackfriars, 1964–1981), 34:171 (Latin text on p. 170).]

46. Ezek. 16:1–14, etc.; Rom. 9:11–12; Titus 3:3–6; Deut. 7:6–8; Matt. 11:25–26; John 3:16.

Hence he is said to "love the world"; that is, those who have nothing but what is in and of the world, whose whole [portion] lies in evil.

Our love is *consequential* in both these regards:

In respect of the *love of God*. Never did[47] [a] creature turn his affections toward God, if the heart of God were not first set upon him.

In respect of *sufficient causes of love*. God must be revealed unto us as lovely and desirable, as a fit and suitable object unto the soul to set up its rest upon, before we can bear any love unto him. The saints (in this sense) do not love God for nothing, but for that excellency, loveliness, and desirableness that is in him. As the psalmist says, in one particular, "I love the LORD, *because!*" (Ps. 116:1), so may we in general; we love the Lord, *because!* Or, as David in another case [says], "What have I now done? Is there not a cause?" [1 Sam. 17:29]. If any man inquire about our love to God, we may say, "What have we now done? Is there not a *cause?*"

Third, they differ in this also: *The love of God is like himself—equal, constant, not capable of augmentation or diminution; our love is like ourselves—unequal, increasing, waning, growing, declining.* His, like the *sun,* [is] always the same in its light, though a cloud may sometimes interpose; ours, as the *moon,* has its enlargements and straitenings.[48]

The love of the Father is *equal*, etc.; whom he loves, he loves unto the end, and he loves them always alike.[49] "The Strength of Israel is not a man, that he should repent" [1 Sam. 15:29]. On whom he fixes his love, it is immutable; it does not grow to eternity, it is not diminished at any time. It is an eternal love, that had no beginning, that shall have no ending; that cannot be heightened by any act of ours, that cannot be lessened by anything in us. I say, in itself it is thus; otherwise, in a twofold regard, it may admit of change:

In respect of its *fruits*. It is, as I said, a fruitful love, a love of bounty. In reference unto those fruits, it may sometimes be greater, sometimes less; its communications are various. Who among the saints finds it not [so]? What life, what light, what strength, sometimes! and again, how dead, how dark, how weak! as God is pleased to let out or to restrain the fruits of his love. All the graces of the Spirit in us, all sanctified enjoyments whatever, are fruits of his love. How variously these are dispensed,

---

47. i.e., would.
48. constrictions
49. 1 Sam. 15:29; Isa. 46:10; Jer. 31:3; Mal. 3:6; James 1:17; 2 Tim. 2:19.

how differently at sundry seasons to the same persons, experience will abundantly testify.

In respect of its *discoveries and manifestations*. He "sheds abroad his love in our hearts by the Holy Ghost" (Rom. 5:5)—gives us a sense of it, manifests it unto us.[50] Now, this is various and changeable, sometimes more, sometimes less; now he shines, anon[51] hides his face, as it may be for our profit. Our Father will not always *chide*, lest we be cast down; he does not always *smile*, lest we be full and neglect him: but yet, still his love in itself is the same. When for a little moment he hides his face, yet he gathers us with everlasting kindness.

Objection and Answer

Objection. But you will say, "This comes nigh to that blasphemy, *that God loves his people in their sinning* as well as in their strictest obedience; and, if so, who will care to serve him more, or to walk with him unto well-pleasing?"

Answer. There are few truths of Christ which, from some or other, have not received like entertainment[52] with this. Terms and appellations[53] are at the will of every imposer; things are not at all varied by them. The love of God in itself is the eternal purpose and act of his will. This is no more changeable than God himself: if it were, no flesh could be saved; but it changes not (Mal. 3:6), and we are not consumed. What then? Loves he his people in their sinning? Yes; his people—not their sinning. Alters he not his love toward them?[54] Not the *purpose* of his will, but the *dispensations* of his grace. He *rebukes* them, he *chastens* them, he *hides* his face from them, he *smites* them, he *fills* them with a sense of [his] indignation; but woe, woe would it be to us, should he change in his love, or take away his kindness from us! Those very things which seem to be demonstrations of the change of his affections toward his [people], do as clearly proceed from love as those which seem to be the most genuine issues thereof. "But will not this encourage to sin?" He never tasted of the love of God that can seriously make this objection. The *doctrine* of grace may be turned into wantonness;[55] the *principle* cannot. I shall not wrong the saints by giving another answer

---

50. Ps. 31:16; 67:1; 119:135; 13:1; 27:9; 30:7; 88:14; Isa. 8:17.
51. presently, soon.
52. Act of upholding, maintaining, receiving; providing for; spending time with.
53. names, designations.
54. Ps. 39:11; Heb. 12:7–8; Rev. 3:19; Isa. 8:17; 57:17; Job 6:4; Ps. 6:6; 38:3–5, etc.
55. unrestrained rebelliousness

to this objection: Detestation of sin in any may well consist with the acceptation of their persons, and their designation to life eternal.

But now our love to God is ebbing and flowing, waning and increasing. We lose our first love, and we grow again in love[56]—scarce a day at a stand. What poor creatures are we! How unlike the Lord and his love! "Unstable as water, we cannot excel" [Gen. 49:4]. Now it is, "Though all men forsake you, I will not"; anon,[57] "I know not the man" [Matt. 26:33, 72, 74]. One day, "I shall never be moved [cf. Ps. 10:6], my hill is so strong"; the next, "All men are liars, I shall perish [cf. Ps. 116:11]." Whenever was the time, wherever was the place, that our love was one day equal toward God?

And thus, these agreements and discrepancies do further describe that mutual love of the Father and the saints, wherein they hold communion. Other instances as to the person of the Father I shall not give, but endeavor to make some improvement of this in the next chapter.

---

56. Rev. 2:4; 3:2; Eph. 3:16–19.
57. again

Chapter 4

Having thus discovered the nature of that distinct communion which we have with the Father, it remains that we give some *exhortations* unto it, *directions* in it, and take some *observations* from it.

Exhortations unto Communion with the Father

IT IS A DUTY FOR CHRISTIANS TO HOLD IMMEDIATE COMMUNION WITH THE FATHER IN LOVE

First, then, this is a duty wherein it is most evident that Christians are but little exercised—namely, in holding immediate communion with the Father in love. Unacquaintedness with our mercies, our privileges, is our sin as well as our trouble. We hearken not to the voice of the Spirit which is given unto us, "that we may know the things that are freely bestowed on us of God" (1 Cor. 2:12). This makes us go heavily, when we might rejoice; and to be weak, where we might be strong in the Lord. How few of the saints are experimentally acquainted with this privilege of holding immediate communion with the Father in love! With what anxious, doubtful thoughts do they look upon him! What fears, what questionings are there, of his goodwill and kindness! At the best, many think there is no sweetness at all in him towards us, but what is purchased at the high price of the blood of Jesus. It is true: that alone is the way of communication; but the free fountain and spring of all is in the bosom of the Father. "Eternal life was with the Father, and is manifested unto us" (1 John 1:2).[1] Let us, then—

---

1. "zōe hētis ēn pros tov Patera, kai ephanerōthē hēmin."

Eye the Father as love; look not on him as an always lowering father, but as one most kind and tender.[2] Let us look on him by faith, as one that has had thoughts of kindness towards us from everlasting. It is misapprehension of God that makes any [to] run from him, who have the least breathing wrought in them after him. "They that know you will put their trust in you" [Ps. 9:10]. Men cannot abide with God in spiritual meditations. He loses *soul's company* by their want[3] of this insight into his love. They fix their thoughts only on his terrible majesty, severity, and greatness; and so their spirits are not endeared. Would a soul continually eye his everlasting tenderness and compassion, his thoughts of kindness that have been from of old, his present gracious acceptance, [then] it could not bear an hour's absence from him; whereas now, perhaps, it cannot watch with him one hour. Let, then, this be the saints' first notion of the Father—as one full of eternal, free love toward them: let their hearts and thoughts be filled with breaking through all discouragements that lie in the way. To raise them hereunto, let them consider—

Whose love it is. It is the love of him who is in himself all sufficient, infinitely satiated[4] with himself and his own glorious excellencies and perfections; who has no need to go forth with his love unto others, nor to seek an object of it without[5] himself. There might he rest with delight and complacency to eternity. He is sufficient unto his own love. He had his Son, also, his eternal[6] Wisdom, to rejoice and delight himself in from all eternity (Prov. 8:30). This might take up and satiate the whole delight of the Father; but he will love his saints also. And it is such a love, as wherein he seeks not his own satisfaction only, but our good therein also—the love of a God, the love of a Father, whose proper outgoings are *kindness* and *bounty*.

What kind of love it is. And it is—

Eternal. It was fixed on us before the foundation of the world.[7] Before we were, or had done the least good, then were his thoughts upon us—then was his delight in us—then did the Son rejoice in the thoughts of fulfilling his Father's delight in him (Prov. 8:30). Yea, the delight of

---

2. Ps. 103:9; Mic. 7:18.

3. lack

4. satisfied

5. outside of, external to.

6. *sha'ashu'im yom yom* [his daily wisdom]. *Optime in Dei Filium quadrat patris delicias.* ["The best in the Son of God agrees with the delights of the Father." Jean Mercier.]

7. Rom. 9:11–12; Acts 15:18; 2 Tim. 1:9; 2:19; Prov. 8:31; Jer. 31:3.

the Father in the Son, there mentioned, is not so much his absolute delight in him as the express image of his person and the brightness of his glory, wherein he might behold all his own excellencies and perfections; as with respect unto his love and his delight in the sons of men. So the order of the words require us to understand it: "I was daily his delight," and, "My delights were with the sons of men"—that is, in the thoughts of kindness and redemption for them: and in that respect, also, was he his Father's delight. It was from eternity that he laid in his own bosom a design for our happiness. The very thought of this is enough to make all that is within us, like the babe in the womb of Elizabeth, to leap for joy [Luke 1:41]. A sense of it cannot but prostrate our souls to the lowest abasement of a humble, holy reverence, and make us rejoice before him with trembling.

Free. He loves us because he *will*;[8] there *was*, there *is*, nothing in us for which we should be beloved. Did we deserve his love, it must go less in its valuation. Things of due debt are seldom the matter of thankfulness; but that which is *eternally antecedent* to our being, must needs be *absolutely free* in its respects to our well-being. This gives it life and being, is the reason of it, and sets a price upon it (Rom. 9:11; Eph. 1:3–4; Titus 3:5; James 1:18).

Unchangeable.[9] Though we change every day, yet his love changes not. Could any kind of provocation turn it away, it had long since ceased. Its unchangeableness is that which carries out the Father unto that infiniteness of patience and forbearance (without which we die, we perish), which he exercises toward us (2 Pet. 3:9). And it is—

Distinguishing.[10] He has not thus loved all the world: "Jacob have I loved, but Esau have I hated" [Mal. 1:2–3; Rom. 9:13]. Why should he fix his love on us, and pass by millions from whom we differ not by nature (Eph. 2:3)—that he should make us sharers in that, and all the fruits of it, which most of the great and wise men of the world are ex-

---

8. Matt. 11:25–26. *Hoc tanto et tam ineffabili bono, nemo inventus est dignus; sordet natura sine gratia.* [No one has been found worthy of this great and unutterable good; nature without glare is filthy. Prosper of Aquitaine, *Letter to Rufinus* in *Ancient Christian Writers*, trans. and ann. P. De Letter (Westminster, PA: Newman Press, 1963), 32:27–28.]

9. Mal. 3:6; James 1:17; Hos. 11:9.

10. Rom. 9:12. *Omnia diligit Deus, quæ fecit; et inter ea magis diligit creaturas rationales; et de illis eas amplius quæ sunt membra unigeniti sui. Et multo magis ipsum unigenitum.* ["God loves all things that He has made, and amongst them rational creatures more, and of these especially those who are members of His only-begotten Son and the only-begotten himself much more." Augustine, *Tract. in Joan*, cx, cited in Aquinas, *Summa Theologia*, q. 20).]

cluded from?[11] I name but the heads of things. Let them enlarge whose hearts are touched.

Let, I say, the soul frequently eye the love of the Father, and that under these considerations—they are all soul-conquering and endearing.

So eye it as to receive it. Unless this be added, all is in vain as to any communion with God. We do not hold communion with him in any thing, until it be received by faith. This, then, is that which I would provoke the saints of God unto, even to believe this love of God for themselves and their own part (1 John 4:16)—believe that such is the heart of the Father toward them—accept of his witness herein. His love is not ours in the sweetness of it until it be so received. Continually, then, act thoughts of faith on God, as love to you—as embracing you with the eternal free love before described. When the Lord is, by his word, presented as such unto you, let your mind know it, and assent that it is so; and your will embrace it, in its being so; and all your affections be filled with it. Set your whole heart to it; let it be bound with the cords of this love. If the King be bound in the galleries[12] with your love (Song 7:5), should you not be bound in heaven with his?

Let it have its proper fruit and efficacy upon your heart, in return of love to him again. So shall we walk in the light of God's countenance, and hold holy communion with our Father all the day long. Let us not deal unkindly with him, and return him slighting for his goodwill. Let there not be such a heart in us as to deal so unthankfully with our God.

Considerations to Further Us in This Duty and the Daily Practice of It

Now, to further us in this duty, and the daily constant practice of it, I shall add one or two considerations that may be of importance whereunto; as—

It is exceeding acceptable unto God, even our Father, that we should thus hold communion with him in his love—that he may be received into our souls as one full of love, tenderness, and kindness toward us. Flesh and blood is apt to have very hard thoughts of him—to think he is always angry, yea, implacable; that it is not for poor creatures to draw nigh to him; that nothing in the world is more desirable than never to come into his presence, or, as they say, where he has anything to do. "Who among us shall dwell with the devouring fire? Who among us shall

---

11. Matt. 11:25–26; 1 Cor. 1:20.
12. tresses, long hair.

dwell with everlasting burnings?" say the sinners in Zion (Isa. 33:14). And, "I knew you were an austere man," says the evil servant in the gospels (Luke 19:21). Now, there is not anything more grievous to the Lord, nor more subservient[13] to the design of Satan upon the soul, than such thoughts as these. Satan claps his hands (if I may so say) when he can take up the soul with such thoughts of God: he has enough—all that he does desire. This has been his design and way from the beginning. The first blood that murderer shed was by this means (Gen. 3:5). He leads our first parents into hard thoughts of God: "Has God said so? Has he threatened you with death? He knows well enough it will be better with you"—with this engine did he batter and overthrow all mankind in one;[14] and being mindful of his ancient conquest, he readily uses the same weapons wherewith then he so successfully contended. Now, it is exceeding grievous to the Spirit of God to be so slandered in the hearts of those whom he dearly loves. How does he expostulate[15] this with Zion! "What iniquity have you seen in me?" says he (Jer. 2:5, 21); "have I been a wilderness unto you, or a land of darkness?" [Jer. 2:31]. "Zion said, The Lord has forsaken me, and my Lord has forgotten me. Can a woman," etc. [Isa. 49:14–15]. The Lord takes nothing worse at the hands of his, than such hard thoughts of him, knowing full well what fruit this bitter root is like to bear—what alienations of heart—what drawings back—what unbelief and tergiversations[16] in our walking with him. How unwilling is a child to come into the presence of an angry father! Consider, then, this in the first place—receiving of the Father as he holds out love to the soul, gives him the honor he aims at and is exceeding acceptable unto him. He often sets it out in an eminent manner, that it may be so received: "He commends his love toward us" (Rom. 5:8). "Behold, what manner of love the Father has bestowed upon us!" (1 John 3:1). Whence, then, is this folly? Men are afraid to have good thoughts of God. They think it a boldness to eye God as good, gracious, tender, kind, loving: I speak of saints; but for the other side, they can judge him hard, austere, severe, almost implacable, and fierce (the very worst affections of the very worst of men, and most hated of him—Rom. 1:31; 2 Tim. 3:3), and think herein they do well. Is not this soul-deceit from Satan? Was it not his design from the beginning to inject such thoughts of God? Assure yourself, then, there is nothing

---

13. subject

14. *Eph hō pantes hēmarton*, Rom. 5:12.

15. reason earnestly with someone so as to dissuade them

16. evasions, falsifications.

more acceptable unto the Father than for us to keep up our hearts unto
him as the eternal fountain of all that rich grace which flows out to
sinners in the blood of Jesus. And—

*This will be exceeding effectual to endear your soul unto God, to cause
you to delight in him, and to make your abode with him.* Many saints
have no greater burden in their lives than that their hearts do not come
clearly and fully up, constantly to delight and rejoice in God—that there
is still an indisposedness[17] of spirit unto close walking with him. What
is at the bottom of this distemper? Is it not their unskillfulness in or neglect of this duty, even of holding communion with the Father in love?
So much as we see of the love of God, so much shall we delight in him,
and no more. Every other discovery of God, without this, will but make
the soul fly from him; but if the heart be once much taken up with this
the eminency of the Father's love, it cannot choose but be overpowered,
conquered, and endeared unto him. This, if anything, will work upon
us to make our abode with him. If the love of a father will not make a
child delight in him, what will? Put, then, this to the venture: exercise
your thoughts upon this very thing, the eternal, free, and fruitful love
of the Father, and see if your hearts be not wrought upon to delight in
him. I dare boldly say: believers will find it as thriving a course as ever
they pitched on in their lives. Sit down a little at the fountain, and you
will quickly have a further discovery of the sweetness of the streams.
You who have run from him, will not be able, after a while, to keep at
a distance for a moment.

Objections and Answers

OBJECTION AND ANSWER I

But some may say, "Alas! how shall I hold communion with the Father
in love? I know not at all whether he loves me or no; and shall I venture
to cast myself upon it? How if I should not be accepted? Should I not
rather perish for my presumption, than find sweetness in his bosom?
God seems to me only as a consuming fire and everlasting burnings; so
that I dread to look up unto him."

I know not what may be understood by knowing of the love of
God; though it be carried on by spiritual sense and experience, yet it
is received purely by believing. Our knowing of it is our believing of
it as revealed. "We have known and believed the love that God has to

---

17. disinclination, unwillingness.

us. God is love" (1 John 4:16). This is the assurance which, at the very entrance of walking with God, you may have of this love. He who is truth has said it; and whatever your heart says, or Satan says, unless you will take it up on this account, you do your endeavor to make him a liar who has spoken it (1 John 5:10).

Objection and Answer 2

"I can believe that God is love to others, for he has said he is love; but that he will be so to me, I see no ground of persuasion; there is no cause, no reason in the world, why he should turn one thought of love or kindness toward me: and therefore I dare not cast myself upon it, to hold communion with him in his special love."

He has spoken it as particularly to you as to anyone in the world. And for cause of love, he has as much to fix it on you as on any of the children of men; that is, none at all without himself. So that I shall make speedy work with this objection. Never anyone from the foundation of the world, who believed such love in the Father, and made returns of love to him again, was deceived; neither shall ever any to the world's end be so, in so doing. You are, then, in this, upon a most sure bottom. If you believe and receive the Father as love, he will infallibly be so to you, though others may fall under his severity. But—

Objection and Answer 3

"I cannot find my heart making returns of love unto God. Could I find my soul set upon him, I could then believe his soul delighted in me."

This is the most *preposterous* course that possibly your thoughts can pitch upon, a most ready way to rob God of his glory. "Herein is love," says the Holy Ghost, "not that we loved God, but that he loved us" first (1 John 4:10–11). Now, you would invert this order, and say, "Herein is love, not that God loved me, but that I love him first." This is to take the glory of God from him: that, whereas he loves us without a cause that is in ourselves, and we have all cause in the world to love him, you would have the contrary, namely, that something should be in you for which God should love you, even your love to him; and that you should love God, before you know anything lovely in him—namely, whether he love you or not. This is a course of flesh's finding out that will never bring glory to God, nor peace to your own soul. Lay down, then, your *reasonings*; take up the love of the Father upon a *pure act of believing*, and that will open your soul to let it out unto the Lord in the communion of love.

To make yet some further improvement of this truth so opened and exhorted unto as before—it will discover unto us the *eminency and privilege of the saints of God*. Whatsoever low thoughts the sons of men may have of them, it will appear that they have meat to eat that the world knows not of. They have close communion and fellowship with the Father. They deal with him in the *interchange of love*. Men are generally esteemed according to the company they keep. It is an honor to stand in the presence of princes, though but as servants. What honor, then, have all the saints, to stand with boldness in the presence of the Father, and there to enjoy his bosom love! What a blessing did the queen of Sheba pronounce on the servants of Solomon, who stood before him and heard his wisdom [1 Kings 10:8]! How much more blessed, then, are they who stand continually before the God of Solomon, hearing his wisdom, enjoying his love! While others have their fellowship with Satan and their own lusts, making provision for them, and receiving perishing refreshments from them ("whose end is destruction, whose god is their belly, and whose glory is in their shame, who mind earthly things" [Phil. 3:19]), they have this sweet communion with the Father.

Moreover, what *a safe and sweet retreat* is here for the saints, in all the scorns, reproaches, scandals, misrepresentations which they undergo in the world. When a child is abused abroad in the streets by strangers, he runs with speed to the bosom of his father;[18] there he makes his complaint and is comforted. In all the hard censures and tongue-persecutions which the saints meet with in the streets of the world,[19] they may run with their moanings unto their Father and be comforted. "As one whom his mother comforts, so will I comfort you," says the Lord (Isa. 66:13). So that the soul may say, "If I have hatred in the world, I will go where I am sure of love. Though all others are hard to me, yet my Father is tender and full of compassion: I will go to him, and satisfy myself in him. Here I am accounted vile, frowned on, and rejected; but I have honor and love with him, whose kindness is better than life itself. There I shall have all things in the fountain, which others have but in the drops. There is in my Father's love every thing desirable: there is the sweetness of all mercies in the abstract itself, and that fully and durably."

Evidently, then, *the saints are the most mistaken men* in the world. If they say, "Come and have fellowship with us" (1 John 1:3), are not men

---

18. Isa. 26:20.

19. *Empaigmōn . . . peiran elabon* [received trial of mockings and beatings], Heb. 11:36. *Oneidismois . . . theatrizomenoi* [publicly exposed to insults and persecutions], Heb. 10:33.

ready to say, "Why, what are you? A sorry company of seditious, factious persons.[20] Be it known unto you, that we despise your fellowship. When we intend to leave fellowship with all honest men, and men of worth, then will we come to you." But, alas! how are men mistaken! Truly their fellowship is with the Father: let men think of it as they please, they have close, spiritual, heavenly refreshing in the mutual communication of love with the Father himself. How they are generally misconceived, the apostle declares, "As deceivers, and yet true; as unknown, and yet well known; as dying, and, behold, we live; as chastened, and not killed; as sorrowful, yet always rejoicing; as poor, yet making many rich; as having nothing, and yet possessing all things" (2 Cor. 6:8–10). And as it is thus in general, so in no one thing more than this, that they are looked on as poor, low, despicable persons, when indeed they are the only great and noble personages in the world. Consider the company they keep: it is with the Father—who so glorious? The merchandise they trade in, it is love—what so precious? Doubtless they are the excellent on the earth (Ps. 16:3).

Further; this will *discover a main difference between the saints and empty professors.*[21] As to the performance of duties, and so the enjoyment of outward privileges, fruitless professors often walk hand in hand with them; but now come to their secret retirements,[22] and what a difference is there! There the saints hold communion with God: hypocrites, for the most part, with the world and their own lusts—with them they converse and communicate; they hearken what they will say to them, and make provision for them, when the saints are sweetly wrapped up in the bosom of their Father's love. It is oftentimes even almost impossible that believers should, in outward appearance, go beyond them who have very rotten hearts: but this meat they have, which others know not of; this refreshment in the banqueting house, wherein others have no share—in the multitude of their thoughts, the comforts of God their Father refresh their souls.

Now, then (to draw toward a close of this discourse), if these things be so, "what manner of men ought we to be, in all manner of holy conversation?"[23] Even "our God is a consuming fire" [Heb. 12:29]. What communion is there between light and darkness [2 Cor. 6:14]? Shall sin and lust dwell in those thoughts which receive in and carry out love from

---

20. Acts 17:6; 28:22.
21. ones who make a religious confession
22. privacy and seclusion, usually leisure.
23. way of life

and unto the Father? Holiness becomes[24] his presence forever. An unclean spirit cannot draw nigh unto him—an unholy heart can make no abode with him. A lewd person will not desire to hold fellowship with a sober man; and will a man of vain and foolish imaginations hold communion and dwell with the most holy God? There is not any consideration of this love but is a powerful motive unto holiness, and leads thereunto. Ephraim says, "What have I to do any more with idols?"[Hos. 14:8] when in God he finds salvation. Communion with the Father is wholly inconsistent with loose walking. "If we say that we have fellowship with him, and walk in darkness, we lie, and do not the truth" (1 John 1:6). "He that says, 'I know him' [I have communion with him], and keeps not his commandments, is a liar, and the truth is not in him" (1 John 2:4). The most specious and glorious pretence made to an acquaintance with the Father, without holiness and obedience to his commandments, serves only to prove the pretenders to be liars. The love of the world and of the Father dwell not together.

And if this be so (to shut up all), how many that go under the name of Christians, come short of the truth of it! How unacquainted are the generality of professors with the mystery of this communion and the fruits of it! Do not many very evidently hold communion with their lusts and with the world, and yet would be thought to have a portion and inheritance among them that are sanctified? They have neither new name nor white stone [Rev. 2:17], and yet would be called the people of the Most High. May it not be said of many of them, rather, that God is not in all their thoughts [Ps. 10:4], than that they have communion with him? The Lord open the eyes of men, that they may see and know that walking with God is a matter not of form, but power! And so far of peculiar communion with the Father, in the instance of love which we have insisted on. "He is also faithful who has called us to the fellowship of his Son Jesus Christ our Lord" [1 Cor. 1:9]—of which in the next place.

---

24. suits, is fitting for.

PART 2

Of Communion with Each Person Distinctly—

Of Communion with the Son Jesus Christ

Chapter 1

Of that distinct communion which we have with the person of the Father we have treated in the foregoing chapters; we now proceed to the consideration of that which we have with his Son, Jesus Christ our Lord. Now the fellowship we have with the second person is with him as *Mediator*—in that office whereunto, by dispensation, he submitted himself for our sakes; being "made of a woman, made under the law, to redeem them that were under the law, that we might receive the adoption of sons" (Gal. 4:4–5). And herein I shall do these two things: (1) Declare that we have such fellowship with the Son of God. (2) Show wherein that fellowship or communion does consist.

We Have Fellowship with the Son of God

For the first, I shall only produce some few places of Scripture to *confirm* it, that it is so: "God is faithful, by whom you were called unto the fellowship of his Son Jesus Christ our Lord" (1 Cor. 1:9). This is that whereunto all the saints are called, and wherein, by the faithfulness of God, they shall be preserved, even fellowship with Jesus Christ our Lord. We are called of God the Father, as the Father, in pursuit of his love, to communion with the Son, as our Lord.

"Behold, I stand at the door, and knock: if any man hear my voice, and open the door, I will come in to him, and will sup with him, and he with me" (Rev. 3:20; cf. John 14:23). Certainly this is fellowship, or I know not what is. Christ will sup with believers: he refreshes himself with his own graces in them, by his Spirit bestowed on them. The Lord Christ is exceedingly delighted in tasting of the sweet fruits of the Spirit in the saints. Hence is that prayer of the spouse that she may have something for his entertainment when he comes to her: "Awake, O north wind; and come, you south; blow upon my garden, that the spices thereof may flow out. Let my Beloved come into his garden, and eat his pleasant fruits" (Song 4:15).[1] The souls of the saints are the garden of Jesus Christ, the good ground (Heb. 6:7)—a garden for delight; he rejoices in them; "his delights are with the sons of men" (Prov. 8:31); and he "rejoices over them" (Zeph. 3:17)—and a garden for fruit, yea, pleasant fruit; so he describes it: "A garden enclosed is my sister, my spouse; a spring shut up, a fountain sealed. Your plants are an orchard of pomegranates, with pleasant fruits; camphire, with spikenard, spikenard and saffron; calamus and cinnamon, with all trees of frankincense; myrrh and aloes, with all chief spices" (Song 4:12–14).[2] Whatever is sweet and delicious for taste, whatever savory and odoriferous,[3] whatever is useful and medicinal, is in this garden. There is all manner of spiritual refreshments, of all kinds whatever, in the souls of the saints, for the Lord Jesus. On this account is the spouse so earnest in the prayer mentioned for an increase of these things, that her Beloved may sup with her, as he has promised. "Awake, O north wind," etc.—"O that the breathings and workings of the Spirit of all grace might stir up all his gifts and graces in me, that the Lord Jesus, the beloved of my soul, may have meet[4] and acceptable entertainment from me." God complains of want of fruit in his vineyard (Isa. 5:2; Hos. 10:1). Want of good food for Christ's entertainment is that [which] the spouse feared and labors to prevent. A barren heart is not fit to receive him. And the delight he takes in the fruit of the Spirit is unspeakable. This he expresses at large: "I am come," says he; "I have eaten, I am refreshed" (Song 5:1). He calls it *p^eri m^egadim*, "The fruit of his sweetnesses"; or most pleasant to him. Moreover, as Christ sups with his saints, so he has promised they shall sup with him, to complete that fellowship they have with him. Christ provides for their entertainment in a most eminent manner. There are beasts killed, and wine is mingled,

---

1. Note that Owen (along with most interpreters in the seventeenth century) interpreted the Song of Solomon (or Canticles) christologically. As Owen says later in this chapter, "this whole book is taken up in the description of *the communion that is between the Lord Christ and his saints.*" For more on this, see Kelly Kapic's introduction, pp. 34–37.

2. The terms in this passage refer to various fragrant ointments, plants, and spices.

3. fragrant

4. fitting, appropriate.

and a table furnished (Prov. 9:2). He calls the spiritual dainties[5] that he has for them a "feast," a "wedding,"[6] "a feast of fat things, wine on the lees,"[7] etc. The fatted calf is killed for their entertainment. Such is the communion, and such is the mutual entertainment of Christ and his saints in that communion.

Song of Solomon 2:1–7, "I am the rose of Sharon, and the lily of the valleys. As the lily among thorns, so is my love among the daughters. As the apple tree among the trees of the wood, so is my Beloved among the sons. I sat down under his shadow with great delight, and his fruit was sweet to my taste," etc.

In the two first verses you have the description that Christ gives, first of himself, then of his church. Of himself; that is, what he is to his spouse: "I am the rose of Sharon, and the lily of the valleys" (v. 1). The Lord Christ is, in the Scripture, compared to all things of eminency in the whole creation.[8] He is in the heavens the *sun*, and the bright morning star; as the *lion* among the beasts, the lion of the tribe of Judah. Among the flowers of the field, here he is the *rose* and the *lily*. The two eminencies of flowers, sweetness of savor and beauty of color, are divided between these. The rose for sweetness and the lily for beauty ("Solomon in all his glory was not arrayed like one of these" [Matt. 6:29]) have the preeminence. Further, he is "the rose of Sharon," a fruitful plain, where the choicest herds were fed (1 Chron. 27:29); so eminent, that it is promised to the church that there shall be given unto her the excellency of Sharon (Isa. 35:2).[9] This fruitful place, doubtless, brought forth the most precious roses. Christ, in the savor of his love, and in his righteousness (which is as the garment wherein Jacob received his blessing, giving forth a smell as the smell of a pleasant field [Gen. 27:27]), is as this excellent rose, to draw and allure the hearts of his saints unto him. As God smelled a sweet savor from the blood of his atonement (Eph. 5:2); so from the graces wherewith for them he is anointed, his saints receive a refreshing, cherishing savor (Song 1:3). A sweet savor expresses that which is acceptable and delightful (Gen. 8:21). He is also "the lily of the valleys"; that of all flowers is the most eminent in beauty (Matt. 6:29). Most desirable is he,

---

5. that which is sweet, delicious.

6. Isa. 25:6; Matt. 22:8; Rev. 19:7.

7. wine that has been laid down for a significant period of time so that it ages properly

8. Mal. 4:2; Rev. 12:1; Luke 1:78 (*anatolē ex hupsous* ["the dawn from heaven"]); Num. 24:17; 2 Pet. 1:19; Rev. 22:16; Gen. 49:9; Mic. 5:8; Rev. 5:5.

9. Isa. 33:9; 65:10.

for the comeliness[10] and perfection of his person; incomparably fairer than the children of men: of which afterward. He, then, being thus unto them (abundantly satiating all their spiritual senses) their refreshment, their ornament,[11] their delight, their glory; in the next verse he tells us what they are to him: "As the lily among thorns, so is my beloved among the daughters" [Song 2:2]. That Christ and his church are likened unto and termed the same thing (as here the lily) is, as from their union by the indwelling of the same Spirit, so from that conformity and likeness that is between them (Rom. 8:29), and whereunto the saints are appointed. Now she is a lily, very beautiful unto Christ; "as the lily among thorns": (1) By the way of *eminency*; as the lily excels the thorns, so do the saints all others whatever, in the eye of Christ. Let comparison be made, so will it be found to be. (2) By the way of *trial*; the residue of the world being "pricking briers and grieving thorns to the house of Israel" (Ezek. 28:24). "The best of them is as a brier, the most upright is sharper than a thorn hedge" (Mic. 7:4). And thus are they among the daughters—even the most eminent collections of the most improved professors, that are no more but so. There cannot be in any greater comparison, a greater exaltation of the excellency of any thing. So, then, is Christ to them indeed (Song 2:1); so are they in his esteem, and indeed (v. 2). How he is in their esteem and indeed, we have (v. 3).

"As the apple tree among the trees of the wood, so is my Beloved among the sons. I sat down under his shadow with great delight, and his fruit was sweet to my taste." To carry on this intercourse, the spouse begins to speak her thoughts of, and to show her delight in, the Lord Christ; and as he compares her to the lily among the thorns, so she him to the *apple tree* among the trees of the wood. And she adds this reason of it, even because he has the two eminent things of trees, which the residue of them have not: (1) *fruit* for food; (2) *shade* for refreshment. Of the one she eats, under the other she rests; both with great delight. All other sons, either angels, the sons of God by creation (Job 1:6; 38:7), or the sons of Adam—the best of his offspring, the leaders of those companies which (v. 2) are called daughters, or sons of the old creation, the top branches of all its desirable things—are to a hungry, weary soul (such alone seek for shade and fruit) but as the fruitless, leafless trees of the forest, which will yield them neither food nor refreshment. "In Christ," says she, "there is fruit, fruit sweet to the taste; yea, 'his flesh is meat indeed, and his

10. attractiveness
11. adornment

blood is drink indeed'" (John 6:55). "Moreover, he has brought forth that everlasting righteousness which will abundantly satisfy any hungry soul, after it has gone to many a barren tree for food, and has found none. Besides, he abounds in precious and pleasant graces, whereof I may eat (Song 5:1); yea, he calls me to do so, and that abundantly." These are the fruits that Christ bears. They speak of a tree that brings forth all things needful for life, in food and raiment.[12] Christ is that tree of life, which has brought forth all things that are needful unto life eternal. In him is that righteousness which we hunger after (Matt. 5:6)—in him is that water of life, which whosoever drinks of will thirst no more (John 4:14). Oh, how sweet are the fruits of Christ's mediation to the faith of his saints! He that can find no relief in mercy, pardon, grace, acceptance with God, holiness, sanctification, etc., is an utter stranger to these things (wine on the lees[13]) that are prepared for believers. Also, he has shades for refreshment and shelter—shelter from wrath without, and refreshment because of weariness from within. The first use of the shade[14] is to keep us from the *heat* of the sun, as did Jonah's gourd. When the heat of wrath is ready to scorch the soul, Christ, interposing, bears it all. Under the shadow of his wings we sit down constantly, quietly, safely, putting our trust in him; and all this with great delight. Yea, who can express the joy of a soul safe[ly] shadowed from wrath under the covert[15] of the righteousness of the Lord Jesus! There is also refreshment in a shade from *weariness*. He is "as the shadow of a great rock in a weary land" (Isa. 32:2). From the power of *corruptions*, trouble of temptations, distress of persecutions, there is in him quiet, rest, and repose (Matt. 11:27–28).

Having thus mutually described each other, and so made it manifest that they cannot but be delighted in fellowship and communion, in the next verses that communion of theirs is at large set forth and described. I shall briefly observe four things therein: (1) *sweetness*; (2) *delight*; (3) *safety*; (4) *comfort*.

Sweetness

"He brought me to the banqueting house," or "house of wine" [Song 2:4]. It is all set forth under expressions of the greatest sweetness and

---

12. garments, clothing.
13. Isa. 25:6; Prov. 9:2.
14. Jonah 4:6; Isa. 25:4; 32:2; 2 Cor. 5:21; Gal. 3:13; Mal. 4:2.
15. shelter

most delicious refreshment—flagons,[16] apples, wine, etc. "*He* entertains me," says the spouse, "as some great personage." Great personages, at great entertainments, are had into the banqueting house—the house of wine and dainties. These are the preparations of grace and mercy—love, kindness, supplies revealed in the gospel, declared in the assemblies of the saints, exhibited by the Spirit. This "love is better than wine" (Song 1:2); it is "not meat and drink, but righteousness, and peace, and joy in the Holy Ghost."[17] Gospel dainties are sweet refreshments; whether these houses of wine be the *Scriptures*, the *gospel*, or the *ordinances* dispensed in the assemblies of the saints, or any eminent and signal manifestations of special love (as banqueting is not every day's work, nor used at ordinary entertainments), it is all one. Wine that cheers the heart of man, that makes him forget his misery (Prov. 31:6–7), that gives him a cheerful look and countenance (Gen. 49:12), is that which is promised. The grace exhibited by Christ in his ordinances is refreshing, strengthening, comforting, and full of sweetness to the souls of the saints. Woe be to such full souls as loathe these honeycombs! But thus Christ makes all his assemblies to be banqueting houses; and there he gives his saints entertainment.

Delight

The spouse is quite ravished with the sweetness of this entertainment, finding love and care and kindness bestowed by Christ in the assemblies of the saints. Hence she cries out, "Stay[18] me with flagons, comfort me with apples; for I am sick of love" (Song 2:5). Upon the discovery of the excellency and sweetness of Christ in the banqueting house, the soul is instantly overpowered and cries out to be made partaker of the fullness of it. She is "*sick of love*"—not (as some suppose) fainting for want of a sense of love, under the apprehension of wrath, but made sick and faint, even overcome, with the mighty actings of that divine affection, after she had once tasted of the sweetness of Christ in the banqueting house. Her desire deferred makes her heart sick [Prov. 13:12]; therefore she cries, "Stay me," etc.—"I have seen a glimpse of the 'King in his beauty'—tasted of the fruit of his righteousness; my soul melts in longing after him. Oh! support and sustain my spirit with his presence in his ordinances—those 'flagons and apples of his banqueting house'—or I

---

16. a large, spouted vessel for holding and pouring liquids, usually wine
17. Rom. 14:17; John 7:37; Prov. 27:7.
18. sustain

shall quite sink and faint! Oh, what have you done, blessed Jesus! I have seen you, and my soul is become as the chariots of Ammi-nadib [Song 6:12]. Let me have something from you to support me, or I die." When a person is fainting on any occasion, these two things are to be done: *strength* is to be used to support him, that he sink not to the ground; and *comfortable things* are to be applied, to refresh his spirits. These two the soul, overpowered and fainting with the force of its own love (raised by a sense of Christ's), prays for. It would have strengthening grace to support it in that condition, that it may be able to attend its duty; and consolations of the Holy Ghost, to content, revive, and satiate it, until it come to a full enjoyment of Christ. And thus sweetly and with delight is this communion carried on.

Safety

"His banner over me was love" (Song 2:4). The banner is an emblem of safety and protection—a sign of the presence of a host. Persons belonging to an army do encamp under their banner in security. So did the children of Israel in the wilderness; every tribe kept their camps under their own standard. It is also a token of success and victory (Ps. 20:5). Christ has a banner for his saints; and that is love. All their protection is from his love; and they shall have all the protection his love can give them. This safeguards them from hell, death—all their enemies. Whatever presses on them, it must pass through the banner of the love of the Lord Jesus. They have, then, great spiritual safety; which is another ornament or excellency of their communion with him.

Supportment and Consolation

"His left hand is under my head, and his right hand does embrace me" (Song 2:6). Christ here has the posture of a most tender friend toward any one in sickness and sadness. The soul faints with love—spiritual longings after the enjoyment of his presence; and Christ comes in with his embraces. He nourishes and cherishes his church (Eph. 5:29; Isa. 63:9). Now "the hand under the head" is supportment, sustaining grace, in pressures and difficulties; and "the hand that does embrace," the hand upon the heart, is joy and consolation—in both, Christ rejoicing, as the "bridegroom rejoices over the bride" (Isa. 62:5). Now, thus to lie in the arms of Christ's love, under a perpetual influence of supportment and refreshment, is certainly to hold communion with him. And hereupon verse 7, the spouse is most earnest for the continuance of his fellowship, charging all so to demean themselves, that her Beloved be not disquieted, or provoked to depart.

In brief, this whole book is taken up in the description of *the communion that is between the Lord Christ and his saints*; and therefore, it is very needless to take from thence any more particular instances thereof.

I shall only add that of Proverbs 9:1–5, "Wisdom has built her house, she has hewn out her seven pillars; she has killed her beasts; she has mingled her wine; she has also furnished her table. She has sent forth her maidens: she cries upon the highest places of the city, 'Whosoever is simple, let him turn in hither: as for him that wants understanding,' she says to him, 'Come, eat of my bread, and drink of the wine which I have mingled.'" The Lord Christ, the eternal Wisdom of the Father, and who of God is made unto us wisdom, erects a *spiritual house*, wherein he makes provision for the entertainment of those guests whom he so freely invites. His church is the house which he has built on a perfect number of pillars, that it might have a stable foundation: his slain beasts and mingled wine, wherewith his table is furnished, are those *spiritual fat things* of the gospel, which he has prepared for those that come in upon his invitation. Surely, to eat of this bread and drink of this wine, which he has so graciously prepared, is to hold fellowship with him; for in what ways or things are there nearer communion than in such?

I might further evince[19] this truth, by a consideration of *all the relations* wherein Christ and his saints do stand; which necessarily require that there be a communion between them, if we do suppose they are faithful in those relations: but this is commonly treated on, and something will be spoken to it in one signal instance afterward.

---

19. prove, evidence, make manifest.

Chapter 2

Wherein Our Fellowship with the Son Consists

Having manifested that the saints hold peculiar fellowship with the Lord Jesus, it next follows that we show wherein it is that they have this peculiar communion with him.

Now, this is in *grace*. This is everywhere ascribed to him by the way of eminency. "He dwelt among us, full of grace and truth" (John 1:14); grace in the truth and substance of it.[1] All that went before was but typical and in representation; in the truth and substance it comes only by Christ. "Grace and truth came by Jesus Christ" (v. 17); "and of his fullness have all we received, and grace for grace" (v. 16)—that is, we have communion with him in grace; we receive from him all manner of grace whatever; and therein have we fellowship with him.

So likewise in that *apostolic benediction*, wherein the communication of spiritual blessings from the several persons unto the saints is so exactly distinguished; it is grace that is ascribed to our Lord Jesus Christ, "The *grace* of the Lord Jesus Christ, and the love of God, and the communion of the Holy Ghost, be with you all" (2 Cor. 13:14).

Yea, Paul is so delighted with this, that he makes it his motto and the token whereby he would have his epistles known, "The salutation of Paul with mine own hand, which is the token in every epistle: so I write. The *grace* of our Lord Jesus Christ be with you all" (2 Thess. 3:17–18). Yea, he makes these two, "*Grace be with you*" and "The *Lord Jesus be with you*," to be equivalent expressions; for whereas he affirmed the one

---

1. Acts 15:11; Rom. 16:24; 1 Cor. 16:23; 2 Cor. 13:14; Gal. 6:18; Eph. 6:24.

to be the token in all his epistles, yet sometimes he uses the one only, sometimes the other of these, and sometimes puts them both together. This, then, is that which we are peculiarly to eye in the Lord Jesus, to receive it from him, even grace, gospel-grace, revealed in or exhibited by the gospel. He is the head-stone in the building of the temple of God, to whom "*Grace, grace,*" is to be cried (Zech. 4:7).

Grace is a word of various acceptations. In its most eminent significations it may be referred unto one of these three heads:

First, grace of *personal presence* and comeliness. So we say, "A graceful and comely person," either from himself or his ornaments.[2] This in Christ (upon the matter) is the subject of near one-half of the book of Canticles; it is also mentioned, "You are fairer than the children of men; grace is poured into your lips" (Ps. 45:2). And unto this first head, in respect of Christ, do I refer also that acceptation of grace which, in respect of us, I fix in the third place. Those inconceivable gifts and fruits of the Spirit which were bestowed on him, and brought forth in him, concur to his personal excellency; as will afterward appear.

Second, grace of *free favor and acceptance.*[3] "By this grace we are saved"; that is, the free favor and gracious acceptation of God in Christ. In this sense is it used in that frequent expression, "If I have found grace in your sight"; that is, if I be freely and favorably accepted before you. So he "gives grace" (that is, favor) "unto the humble" (James 4:6; Gen. 39:21; 41:37; Acts 7:10; 1 Sam. 2:26; 2 Kings 25:27, etc.).

Third, the *fruits of the Spirit,* sanctifying and renewing our natures, enabling unto good, and preventing from evil, are so termed. Thus the Lord tells Paul, "his grace was sufficient for him"; that is, the assistance against temptation which he afforded him (Col. 3:16; 2 Cor. 8:6–7; Heb. 12:28).

These two latter, as relating unto Christ in respect of us who receive them, I call *purchased grace*, being indeed purchased by him for us; and our communion with him therein is termed a "fellowship in his sufferings, and the power of his resurrection" (Phil. 3:10).

The Personal Grace of Christ

Let us begin with the first, which I call *personal grace*; and concerning that, do these two things: (1) Show *what it is* and wherein it consists; I

---

2. Prov. 1:9, 3:22, 34; Song 3:6–11, 5:9–16, etc.

3. Ezra 9:8; Acts 4:33; Luke 2:40; Esther 2:17; Ps. 84:11; Eph. 2:6; Acts 15:40; 18:27; Rom. 1:7; 4:4, 16; 5:2, 20; 11:5–6; 2 Thess. 2:16; Titus 3:7; Rev. 1:4, etc.

mean the personal grace of Christ; and (2) Declare how the saints *hold immediate communion with him therein.*

THE NATURE OF PERSONAL GRACE

To the handling of the first, I shall only premise this observation: It is Christ as mediator of whom we speak; and therefore, by the "grace of his person," I understand not—

The glorious excellencies of his Deity considered in itself, abstracting from the office which for us, as God and man, he undertook.

Nor the outward appearance of his human nature, neither when he conversed here on earth, bearing our infirmities (whereof, by reason of the charge that was laid upon him, the prophet gives quite another character [Isa. 52:14]), concerning which some of the ancients were very poetical in their expressions; nor yet as now exalted in glory—a vain imagination whereof makes many bear a false, a corrupted respect unto Christ, even upon carnal apprehensions of the mighty exaltation of the human nature; which is but "to know Christ after the flesh" (2 Cor. 5:16), a mischief much improved by the abomination of foolish imagery. But this is that which I intend—the graces of the person of Christ as he is vested with the office of mediation, this spiritual eminency, comeliness, and beauty, as appointed and anointed by the Father unto the great work of bringing home all his elect unto his bosom.

Now, in this respect the Scripture describes him as exceedingly excellent, comely, and desirable—far above comparison with the *chief*, choicest created good, or any endearment imaginable. "You are fairer than the children of men: grace is poured into your lips" (Ps. 45:2). He is, beyond comparison, more beautiful and gracious than any here below,[4] *yaph^e yaphîta*; the word is doubled, to increase its significance, and to exalt its subject beyond all comparison. *Shwphrk mlk' mshych' 'dyph mbny nsh'* says the Chaldee paraphrast:[5] "Your fairness, O king Messiah, is more excellent than the sons of men." *Pulcher admodum præ filiis hominum* ["You are exceedingly beautiful more than the sons of men"]—exceeding desirable. Inward beauty and glory is here expressed

---

4. Isa. 11:1; Jer. 23:5; 33:15; Zech. 3:8; 6:12.

5. I.e., author of a targum (expanded translation) written in Aramaic. Owen uses the term "Chaldee" to refer to biblical Aramaic, since he was working under the influence of an older (incorrect) theory that biblical Aramaic was essentially the language of the Neo-Babylonian (i.e., "Chaldean") Empire. Paraphrast means "paraphraser."

by that of outward shape, form, and appearance;[6] because that was so much esteemed in those who were to rule or govern. [In] Isaiah 4:2, the prophet, terming of him "the branch of the Lord" and "the fruit of the earth," affirms that he shall be "beautiful and glorious, excellent and comely," "for in him dwells all the fullness of the Godhead bodily" (Col. 2:9).

[In] Song 5:9, the spouse is inquired of as to this very thing, even concerning the personal excellencies of the Lord Christ, her beloved: "What is your Beloved" (say the daughters of Jerusalem) "more than another beloved, O you fairest among women? What is your Beloved more than another beloved?" and she returns this answer, "My Beloved is white and ruddy, the chiefest among ten thousand" (v. 10), and so proceeds to a particular description of him by his excellencies to the end of the chapter, and there concludes that "he is altogether lovely" (v. 16); whereof at large afterward. Particularly, he is here affirmed to be "white and ruddy"; a due mixture of which colors composes the most beautiful complexion.

First, he is *white* in the glory of his *Deity*, and *ruddy* in the preciousness of his *humanity*. "His teeth are white with milk, and his eyes are red with wine" (Gen. 49:12). Whiteness (if I may so say) is the complexion of glory. In that appearance of the Most High, the "Ancient of days," it is said, "His garment was white as snow, and the hair of his head like the pure wool" (Dan. 7:9); and of Christ in his transfiguration, when he had on him a mighty luster of the Deity, "His face did shine as the sun, and his raiment was white as the light" (Matt. 17:2);

---

6. *Hōs hēdu kalos hotan echei noun sōphrona, prōton men eidos axion turannidos.* ["How sweet is beauty when its brain has sense / first may his species be worthy of a kingdom." Porphyry, *Porphyrii Isagoge et in Aristotelis Categorias Commentarium: Sive Quinque Voces,* 4.1, line 1, ed. Adolfus Busse (Berlin: Typis et Impensis Georgii Reimer, 1887), 4; *Porphyry: Introduction,* trans. Jonathan Barnes (Oxford: Clarendon Press, 2003), 5. Cf. Menander, "The Maxims of Menander," line 555, *The Fragments of Attic Comedy,* vol. 3b, 3 vols. in 4, ed. and trans. John Maxwell Edmonds (Leiden: E. J. Brill, 1961), 949; Euripides, *Aileus Aiolos,* frag. 15, line 2, *Tragicorum Graecorum Fragmenta* ed. Augustus Nauck and Bruno Snell (Georg Olms Verlagsbuchhandlung Hildesheim, 1964), 367.] *Commendari se verecundiâ oris adeo sentiebat, ut apud senatum sic quondam jactaverit; usque adhuc certe animum meum probastis et vultum.* ["He was so conscious that the modesty of his expression was in his favor, that he once made this boast in the senate: 'So far, at any rate, you have approved my heart and my countenance.'" Suetonius, *Suetonius II,* Loeb Classical Library, trans. J. C. Rolfe (Cambridge, MA: Harvard University Press, 1959), 379.] *Formæ elegantia in Rege laudatur, non quod per se decor oris magni æstimari debeat, sed quia in ipso vultu sæpe reluceat generosa indoles.* ["Personal excellence is ascribed to the king, not that the beauty of the countenance, which of itself is not reckoned among the number of the virtues, ought to be very highly valued; but because a noble disposition of mind often shines forth in the very countenance of a man." John Calvin, *Commentary on the Book of Psalms,* trans. James Anderson (Grand Rapids, MI: Baker, 2003), 2:175.]

which, in the phrase of another evangelist, is "White as snow, so as no fuller on earth can white them" (Mark 9:3). It was a divine, heavenly, surpassing glory that was upon him (Rev. 1:14). Hence the angels and glorified saints, that always behold him and are fully translated into the image of the same glory, are still said to be in white robes.[7] His whiteness is his Deity, and the glory thereof. And on this account the Chaldee paraphrast ascribes this whole passage unto God. "They say," says he, "to the house of Israel, 'Who is the God whom you will serve?' etc. Then began the congregation of Israel to declare the praises of the Ruler of the world, and said, 'I will serve that God who is clothed in a garment white as snow, the splendor of the glory of whose countenance is as fire.'" He is also ruddy in the beauty of his humanity. Man was called Adam, from the red earth whereof he was made. The word here used[8] points him out as the second Adam, partaker of flesh and blood, because the children also partook of the same (Heb. 2:14). The beauty and comeliness of the Lord Jesus in the union of both these in one person, shall afterward be declared.

Secondly, he is *white* in the beauty of his *innocency* and holiness, and *ruddy* in the *blood* of his oblation.[9] Whiteness is the badge of innocence and holiness. It is said of the Nazarites, for their typical holiness, "They were purer than snow, they were whiter than milk" (Lam. 4:7). And the prophet shows us that scarlet, red, and crimson are the colors of sin and guilt; whiteness of innocency[10] (Isa. 1:18). Our Beloved was "a Lamb without blemish and without spot" (1 Pet. 1:19). "He did no sin, neither was guile found in his mouth" (1 Pet. 2:22). He was "holy, harmless, undefiled, separate from sinners" (Heb. 7:26); as afterward will appear. And yet he who was so white in his innocence, was made ruddy in his own blood; and that two ways: *Naturally*, in the pouring out of his blood, his precious blood, in that agony of his soul when thick drops of blood trickled to the ground (Luke 22:44); as also when the whips and thorns, nails and spears, poured it out abundantly: "There came forth blood and water" (John 19:34). He was ruddy by being drenched all

---

7. Rev. 3:4–5; 6:11; 7:9, 13; 19:14.

8. *dodi tsakh w᷃'adom*, Song 5:10.

9. offering, sacrifice.

10. *Alii candidum exponunt esse puris et probis, rubrum et cruentum reprobis ad eos puniendos ut Isaia, cap. lxiii. dicitur,* מַדּוּעַ אָדֹם לִלְבוּשֶׁךָ *Cur rubent vestimenta tua? quod nostri minus recte de Christi passione exponunt.* ["Others explain that white is for pure and upright things, and the bloody red for base things for those who will be punished as it is said in Isaiah chapter 63, *maddu'a 'adom lil᷃busheka*. "Why are your garments red?" Our [writers] explain this less correctly concerning Christ's passion." Jean Mercier.]

over in his own blood. And *morally*, by the imputation of sin, whose color is red and crimson. "God made him to be sin for us, who knew no sin" (2 Cor. 5:21). He who was white, became ruddy for our sakes, pouring out his blood an oblation for sin. This also renders him graceful: by his whiteness he fulfilled the law; by his redness he satisfied justice. "This is our Beloved, O you daughters of Jerusalem."

Thirdly, his endearing excellency in the *administration of his kingdom* is hereby also expressed (Rev. 6:2). He is white in love and mercy unto his own; red with justice and revenge toward his enemies (Isa. 63:3; Rev. 19:13).

There are three things in general wherein this *personal excellency* and grace of the Lord Christ does consist: (1) His *fitness* to save, from the *grace of union*, and the proper necessary effects thereof. (2) His *fullness* to save, from the *grace of communion*; or the free consequences of the grace of union. (3) His *excellency* to endear, from his *complete suitableness* to all the wants of the souls of men:

First, *his fitness to save*—his being *hikanos*, a fit Savior, suited to the work; and this, I say, is from his *grace of union*. The uniting of the natures of God and man in one person made him fit to be a Savior to the uttermost. He lays his hand upon God, by partaking of his nature (Zech. 13:7); and he lays his hand upon us, by being partaker of our nature (Heb. 2:14, 16): and so becomes a days-man,[11] or umpire, between both. By this means he fills up all the distance that was made by sin between God and us; and we who were far off are made nigh in him. Upon this account it was that he had room enough in his breast to receive, and power enough in his spirit to bear, all the wrath that was prepared for us. Sin was infinite only in respect of the *object*; and punishment was infinite in respect of the *subject*. This arises from his union.

Union is the conjunction of the two natures of God and man in one person (John 1:14; Isa. 9:6; Rom. 1:3; 9:5). The necessary consequences whereof are—

The *subsistence*[12] of the human nature in the person of the Son of God, having no subsistence of its own (Luke 1:35; 1 Tim. 3:16).

Koinōnia idiōmatōn—that *communication of attributes* in the person, whereby the properties of either nature are promiscuously[13] spoken

---

11. arbiter, mediator (days as in "day set for trial"); cf. Job 9:33, KJV.
12. mode or quality of existence
13. indiscriminately

of the person of Christ, under whatever name, of God or man, he be spoken of (Acts 20:28, 3:21).

The *execution* of his office of mediation in his single person, in respect of both natures: wherein is considerable, *Ho energōn*—the agent, Christ himself, God and man. He is the *principium quo, energētikon*—the principle that gives life and efficacy to the whole work; and then, secondly, the *principium quod*—that which operates, which is both natures distinctly considered. Thirdly, the *energeia*, or *drastikē tēs phuseōs kinēsis*—the effectual working itself of each nature. And, lastly, the *energēma*, or *apotelesma*—the effect produced, which arises from all, and relates to them all: so resolving the excellency I speak of into his personal union.

Second, *his fullness to save*, from the grace of communion or the effects of his union, which are free; and consequences of it, which is all the furniture[14] that he received from the Father by the unction of the Spirit, for the work of our salvation: "He is able also to save them to the uttermost that come unto God by him" (Heb. 7:25); having all fullness unto this end communicated unto him: "for it pleased the Father that in him should all fullness dwell" (Col. 1:19); and he received not "the Spirit by measure" (John 3:34). And from this fullness he makes out a suitable supply unto all that are his; "grace for grace" (John 1:16). Had it been given to him by measure, we had exhausted it.

Third, *his excellency to endear*, from his *complete suitableness* to all the wants of the souls of men. There is no man whatever, that has any want in reference unto the things of God, but Christ will be unto him that which he wants: I speak of those who are given him of his Father. Is he *dead*? Christ is *life* (Col. 3:4). Is he *weak*? Christ is the *power* of God and the *wisdom* of God (1 Cor. 1:24, 30). Has he the *sense of guilt* upon him? Christ is complete *righteousness*—"The LORD our Righteousness" (Jer. 23:6). Many poor creatures are sensible of their wants, but know not where their remedy lies. Indeed, whether it be life or light, power or joy, all is wrapped up in him.

This, then, for the present, may suffice in general to be spoken of the personal grace of the Lord Christ: He has *a fitness to save*, having pity and ability, tenderness and power, to carry on that work to the uttermost; and *a fullness to save*, of redemption and sanctification, of righteousness and the Spirit; and *a suitableness to the wants of all our souls*: whereby he becomes exceedingly desirable, yea, altogether lovely; as afterward will appear in particular. And as to this, in the first place,

---

14. endowments, qualities, capacities.

the saints have distinct fellowship with the Lord Christ; the manner whereof shall be declared in the ensuing chapter.

Only, from this entrance that has been made into the description of him with whom the saints have communion, some motives might be taken to stir us up whereunto; as also considerations to lay open the nakedness and insufficiency of all other ways and things unto which men engage their thoughts and desires, something may be now proposed. The daughters of Jerusalem—ordinary, common professors—having heard the spouse describing her Beloved (Song 5:10–16, etc.), instantly are stirred up to seek him together with her: "Whither is your Beloved turned aside? that we may seek him with you" (6:1). What Paul says of them that crucified him, may be spoken of all that reject him, or refuse communion with him: "Had they known him, they would not have crucified the Lord of glory" [1 Cor. 2:8]—Did men know him, were they acquainted in any measure with him, they would not so reject the Lord of glory. [He] himself calls them "simple ones," "fools," and "scorners"—that despise his gracious invitation (Prov. 1:22). There are none who despise Christ, but only they that know him not; whose eyes the god of this world has blinded, that they should not behold his glory [2 Cor. 4:4]. The souls of men do naturally seek something to rest and repose themselves upon—something to satiate and delight themselves with, with which they [may] hold communion; and there are two ways whereby men proceed in the pursuit of what they so aim at. Some set before them some certain end—perhaps pleasure, profit, or, in religion itself, acceptance with God; others seek after some end, but without any certainty, pleasing themselves now with one path, now with another, with various thoughts and ways, like them (Isa. 57:10)—because something comes in by the life of the hand, they give not over though weary. In whatsoever condition you may be (either in greediness pursuing some certain end, be it secular or religious; or wandering away in your own imaginations, wearying yourselves in the largeness of your ways), compare a little what you aim at, or what you do, with what you have already heard of Jesus Christ: if anything you design be like to him, if anything you desire be equal to him, let him be rejected as one that has neither form nor comeliness in him; but if, indeed, all your ways be but vanity and vexation[15] of spirit, in comparison of him, why do you spend your "money for that which is not bread, and your labor for that which satisfies not?" [Isa. 55:2].

---

15. annoyance

Use 1. You that are yet in the *flower of your days*, full of health and strength, and, with all the vigor of your spirits, do pursue some one thing, some another, consider, I pray, what are all your beloveds to this Beloved? What have you gotten by them? Let us see the peace, quietness, assurance of everlasting blessedness that they have given you. Their paths are crooked paths—whoever goes in them shall not know peace. Behold here a fit object for your choicest affections—one in whom you may find rest to your souls—one in whom there is nothing [that] will grieve and trouble you to eternity. Behold, he stands at the door of your souls, and knocks [Rev. 3:20]: Oh, reject him not, lest you seek him and find him not! Pray[16] study him a little; you love him not, because you know him not. Why does one of you spend his time in idleness and folly, and wasting of precious time, perhaps debauchedly? Why does another associate and assemble himself with them that scoff at religion and the things of God? Merely because you know not our dear Lord Jesus? Oh, when he shall reveal himself to you, and tell you he is Jesus whom you have slighted and refused, how will it break your hearts and make you mourn like a dove [Isa. 38:14; 59:11] that you have neglected him! and if you never come to know him, it had been better you had never been. While it is called today, then, harden not your hearts [Heb. 3:13].

Use 2. You that are, perhaps, seeking earnestly after a *righteousness, and are religious persons*, consider a little with yourselves—has Christ his due place in your hearts? Is he your all? Does he dwell in your thoughts? Do you know him in his excellency and desirableness? Do you indeed account all things "loss and dung" for his exceeding excellency [Phil. 3:8]? Or rather, do you prefer almost any thing in the world before it? But more of these things afterward.

---

16. i.e., I ask that you.

Chapter 3

The next thing that comes under consideration is the *way* whereby we hold communion with the Lord Christ, in respect of that personal grace whereof we have spoken. Now, this the Scripture manifests to be by the way of a *conjugal*[1] *relation*. He is married unto us, and we unto him; which spiritual relation is attended with suitable conjugal affections. And this gives us fellowship with him as to his personal excellencies.

This the spouse expresses: "My Beloved is mine, and I am his" (Song 2:16); "He is mine, I possess him, I have interest in him, as my head and my husband; and I am his, possessed of him, owned by him, given up unto him: and that as to my Beloved in a conjugal relation."

So Isaiah 54:5, "Your Maker is your husband; the LORD of hosts is his name; and your Redeemer the Holy One of Israel; the God of the whole earth shall he be called." This is yielded as the reason why the church shall not be ashamed nor confounded in the midst of her troubles and trials—she is married to her Maker, and her Redeemer is her husband. And setting out the mutual glory of Christ and his church in their walking together, he says it is "as a bridegroom decks himself with ornaments, and as a bride adorns herself with jewels" (Isa. 61:10). Such is their condition, because such is their relation; which he also further expresses, "As the bridegroom rejoices over the bride, so shall your God rejoice over you" (Isa. 62:5). As it is with such persons in the

---

1. marital

day of their espousals,[2] in the day of the gladness of their hearts [Song 3:11], so is it with Christ and his saints in this relation. He is a husband to them, providing that it may be with them according to the state and condition whereinto he has taken them.

To this purpose we have his faithful engagement: "I will," says he, "betroth[3] you unto me forever; yea, I will betroth you unto me in righteousness, and in judgment, and in lovingkindness, and in mercies. I will even betroth you unto me in faithfulness" (Hos. 2:19–20). And it is the main design of the ministry of the gospel, to prevail with men to give up themselves unto the Lord Christ, as he reveals his kindness in this engagement. Hence Paul tells the Corinthians that he had "espoused them unto one husband, that he might present them as a chaste virgin unto Christ" (2 Cor. 11:2). This he had prevailed upon them for, by the preaching of the gospel, that they should give up themselves as a virgin, unto him who had betrothed them to himself as a husband.

And this is a *relation* wherein the Lord Jesus is exceedingly delighted, and invites others to behold him in this his glory: "Go forth," says he, "O you daughters of Jerusalem, and behold king Solomon with the crown wherewith his mother crowned him in the day of his espousals, and in the day of the gladness of his heart" (Song 3:11). He calls forth the daughters of Jerusalem (all sorts of professors) to consider him in the condition of betrothing and espousing his church unto himself. Moreover, he tells them that they shall find on him two things eminently upon this account: (1) *Honor.* It is the day of his coronation, and his spouse is the crown wherewith he is crowned. For as Christ is a diadem of beauty and a crown of glory unto Zion (Isa. 28:5); so Zion also is a diadem and a crown unto him (Isa. 62:3). Christ makes this relation with his saints to be his glory and his honor. (2) *Delight.* The day of his espousals, of taking poor sinful souls into his bosom, is the day of the gladness of his heart. John was but the friend of the Bridegroom that stood and heard his voice when he was taking his bride unto himself, and he rejoiced greatly (John 3:29): how much more, then, must be the joy and gladness of the Bridegroom himself! even that which is expressed, "he rejoices with joy, he joys with singing" (Zeph. 3:17).

It is the gladness of the heart of Christ, the joy of his soul, to take poor sinners into this relation with himself. He rejoiced in the thoughts of it from eternity (Prov. 8:31); and always expresses the greatest willingness

---

2. wedding, wedding feast.
3. commit to marriage

to undergo the hard task required thereunto (Ps. 40:7–8; Heb. 10:7); yea, he was pained as a woman in travail, until he had accomplished it (Luke 12:50). Because he loved his church, he gave himself for it (Eph. 5:25), despising the shame and enduring the cross (Heb. 12:2), that he might enjoy his bride—that he might be for her, and she for him, and not for another (Hos. 3:3). This is joy, when he is thus crowned by his mother. It is believers that are mother and brother of this Solomon (Matt. 12:49–50). They crown him in the day of his espousals, giving themselves to him, and becoming his glory (2 Cor. 8:23).

Thus he sets out his whole communion with his church under this allusion, and that most frequently. The time of his taking the church unto himself is the day of his marriage; and the church is his bride, his wife (Rev. 19:7–8). The entertainment he makes for his saints is a wedding supper (Matt. 22:3). The graces of his church are the ornaments of his queen (Ps. 45:9–14); and the fellowship he has with his saints is as that which those who are mutually beloved in a conjugal relation do hold (Song 1). Hence Paul, in describing these two, makes sudden and insensible[4] transitions from one to the other [in] Ephesians 5:22–32, concluding the whole with an application unto Christ and the church.

It is now to be inquired, in the next place, how it is that we hold communion with the person of Christ in respect of conjugal relations and affections, and wherein this does consist. Now, herein there are some things that are common unto Christ and the saints, and some things that are peculiar to each of them, as the nature of this relation does require. The whole may be reduced unto these two heads: (1) *a mutual resignation of themselves one to the other*; (2) *mutual, consequential, conjugal affections.*[5]

There is a *mutual resignation*, or making over of their persons one to another. This is the first act of communion, as to the personal grace of Christ. Christ makes himself over to the soul, to be his, as to all the love, care, and tenderness of a husband; and the soul gives up itself wholly unto the Lord Christ, to be his, as to all loving, tender obedience. And herein is the main of Christ's and the saints' espousals. This, in the prophet, is set out under a parable of himself and a harlot: "You shall abide for me," says he unto her, "you shall not be for another, and I will be for you" (Hos. 3:3)—"Poor harlot," says the Lord Christ, "I have bought you unto myself with the price of mine own blood; and

---

4. imperceptible; barely able to be perceived.
5. Owen does not return to this second point until the beginning of chap. 4.

now, this is that which we will consent unto—*I will be for you, and you shall be for me*, and not for another."

Christ gives himself to the soul, with all his excellencies, righteousness, preciousness, graces, and eminencies, to be its Savior, head, and husband, forever to dwell with it in this holy relation. He looks upon the souls of his saints, likes them well, counts them fair and beautiful, because he has made them so. "Behold, you are fair, my companion; behold, you are fair; you have doves' eyes" (Song 1:15). Let others think what they please, Christ redoubles it, that the souls of his saints are very beautiful, even perfect, through his comeliness, which he puts upon them, "Behold, you are fair, you are fair" ([Song 1:15; cf.] Ezek. 16:14):[6] particularly, that their spiritual light is very excellent and glorious; like the eyes of a dove, tender, discerning, clear, and shining. Therefore he adds that pathetical[7] wish of the enjoyment of this his spouse, "O my dove," says he, "that are in the clefts of the rock, in the secret places of the stairs, let me see your countenance, let me hear your voice; for sweet is your voice, and your countenance is comely" (Song 2:14); "Do not hide yourself, as one that flies to the clefts of the rocks; be not dejected, as one that hides herself behind the stairs, and is afraid to come forth to the company that inquires for her. Let not your spirit be cast down at the weakness of your supplications, let me yet hear your sighs and groans, your breathing and partings to me; they are very sweet, very delightful: and your spiritual countenance, your appearance in heavenly things, is comely and delightful unto me." Neither does he leave her thus, but presses her hard to a closer [union] with him in this conjugal bond: "Come with me from Lebanon, my spouse, with me from Lebanon: look from the top of Amana, from the top of Shenir and Herman, from the lions' dens, from the mountains of the leopards" (Song 4:8); "You are in a wandering condition (as the Israelites of old), among lions and leopards, sins and troubles; come from thence unto me, and I will give you refreshment" (Matt. 11:28). Upon this invitation, the spouse boldly concludes that the desire of Christ is toward her (Song 7:10); that he does indeed love her and aim at taking her into this fellowship with himself. So, in carrying on this union, Christ freely bestows himself upon the soul. Precious and excellent as he is, he becomes ours. He makes himself to be so; and with him, all his graces. Hence says the

---

6. *Repetit non citra pathos, en tu pulchra es.* ["He repeats not without passion, behold you are beautiful." Joannis Merceri (Jean Mercier), *Commentarii Iobus et Solomonis, Proverbia, Ecclesiastem, Canticum Canticorum* (Luduni Batavorum [Leyden]: Ex Offiina Francisci Hackii, 1651), 612.]

7. affecting, moving.

spouse, "'My Beloved is mine'; in all that he is, he is mine." Because he is righteousness (Isa. 45:24–25), he is "The LORD our Righteousness" (Jer. 23:6). Because he is the wisdom of God and the power of God, he is "made unto us wisdom," etc. (1 Cor. 1:30). Thus, "the branch of the LORD is beautiful and glorious, and the fruit of the earth is excellent and comely for them that are escaped of Israel" (Isa. 4:2). This is the first thing on the part of Christ—*the free donation* and bestowing of himself upon us to be our Christ, our Beloved, as to all the ends and purposes of love, mercy, grace, and glory; whereunto in his mediation he is designed, in a marriage covenant never to be broken. This is the sum of what is intended: The Lord Jesus Christ, fitted and prepared, by the accomplishment and furniture of his person as mediator, and the large purchase of grace and glory which he has made, to be a husband to his saints, his church, tenders himself in the promises of the gospel to them in all his desirableness; convinces them of his goodwill toward them, and his all-sufficiency for a supply of their wants; and upon their consent to accept of him—which is all he requires or expects at their hands—he engages himself in a marriage covenant to be theirs forever.

On the part of the saints, it is their free, willing consent to receive, embrace, and submit unto the Lord Jesus, as their husband, Lord, and Savior—to abide with him, subject their souls unto him, and to be ruled by him forever.

Now, this in the soul is either *initial*, or the solemn consent at the first entrance of union; or *consequential*, in renewed acts of consent all our days. I speak of it especially in this latter sense, wherein it is proper unto communion; not in the former, wherein it primarily intends union.

There are two things that complete this *self-resignation* of the soul:

First, the *liking of Christ*, for his *excellency*, grace, and suitableness, far above all other beloveds whatever, preferring him in the judgment and mind above them all. In the place above mentioned (Song 5:9), the spouse being earnestly pressed, by professors at large, to give in her thoughts concerning the excellency of her Beloved in comparison of other endearments, answers expressly that he is "the chief of ten thousand, yea" [Song 5:10], "altogether lovely" (Song 5:16)—infinitely beyond comparison with the choicest created good or endearment imaginable. The soul takes a view of all that is in this world, "the lust of the flesh, the lust of the eyes, and the pride of life," and sees it all to be vanity—that "the world passes away, and the lust thereof" (1 John 2:16–17). These beloveds are [in] no way to be compared unto him. It views also legal righteousness, blamelessness before men, uprightness of conversation, duties upon conviction, and concludes of all as Paul does, "Doubtless, I count all these things loss for the excellency of the knowledge of Christ Jesus my Lord" (Phil. 3:8). So, also, does the church reject all appearing assistances whatever (Hos. 14:3)—as goodly as Asshur, as promising as idols—that God alone may be preferred. And this is the soul's entrance into conjugal communion with Jesus Christ as to personal grace—the constant preferring him above all pretenders to its affections, counting all loss and dung in comparison of him. Beloved peace, beloved natural relations, beloved wisdom and learning, beloved righteousness, beloved duties [are] all loss, compared with Christ.

Second, the *accepting of Christ* by the *will*, as its only husband, Lord, and Savior. This is called "receiving" of Christ (John 1:12); and is not intended only for that solemn act whereby at first entrance we close with him, but also for the constant frame of the soul in abiding with him and owning of him as such. When the soul consents to take Christ on his own terms, to save him in his own way,[8] and says, "Lord, I would have had you and salvation in my way, that it might have been partly of mine endeavors, and as it were by the works of the law; I am now willing to receive you and to be saved in your way—merely by grace: and though I would have walked according to my own mind, yet now I wholly give up myself to be ruled by your Spirit: for in you have I righteousness and strength (Isa. 45:24), in you am I justified and do glory"; then does it carry on communion with Christ as to the grace of his person. This it is to receive the Lord Jesus in his comeliness and eminency. Let believers exercise their hearts abundantly unto this thing. This is choice communion with the Son Jesus Christ. Let us receive him in all his excellencies, as he bestows himself upon us—be frequent in thoughts of faith, comparing him with other beloveds, sin, world, legal righteousness; and preferring him before them, counting them all loss and dung in comparison of him. And let our souls be persuaded of his sincerity and willingness in giving himself, in all that he is, as mediator unto us, to be ours; and let our hearts give up themselves unto him. Let us tell him that we will be for him, and not for another: let him know it from us; he delights to hear it, yea, he says, "Sweet is our voice, and our countenance is comely" [Song 2:14]—and we shall not fail in the issue of sweet refreshment with him.

---

8. Rom. 9:31–32; 10:3–4.

Digression 1

To strengthen our hearts in the resignation mentioned of ourselves unto the Lord Christ as our husband, as also to make way for the stirring of us up to those consequential conjugal affections of which mention shall afterward be made, I shall turn aside to a more full description of some of the personal excellencies of the Lord Christ, whereby the hearts of his saints are indeed endeared unto him.

In "The LORD our Righteousness," then, may these ensuing things be considered; which are exceeding suitable to prevail upon our hearts to give up themselves to be wholly his.

The Excellency of Christ's Deity

He is exceeding excellent and desirable in his *Deity*, and the glory thereof.[1] He is "*Jehovah our Righteousness*" (Jer. 23:6). In the rejoicing of Zion at his coming to her, this is the bottom: "Behold your God!" (Isa. 40:9). "We have seen his glory," says the apostle. What glory is that? "The glory of the only-begotten Son of God" (John 1:14). The choicest saints have been afraid and amazed at the beauty of an angel; and the stoutest sinners have trembled at the glory of one of those creatures in

---

1. Num. 21:5; 1 Cor. 10:9; Ps. 68:18; Eph. 4:8, 10; Ps. 97:7; Heb. 1:6; Ps. 102:25; Isa. 7:14; Luke 2:34; Rom. 9:5; 1 Pet. 2:6; Isa. 40:3; 44:6; 45:22; 48:12; Rom. 14:10; Rev. 1:11; Mal. 3:1; Ps. 2:12; Isa. 35:4; 52:5–6; 45:14–15; Zech. 2:8, 12; 3:1; 12:10; Matt. 16:16; Luke 1:16–17; John 5:18–19; 10:30; 1:1, 3, 10, 14; 6:62; 8:23, 58; Col. 1:16; Heb. 1:2, 10–12; John 3:13, 31; 16:28; Mic. 5:2; Prov. 8:23; John 17:5; Jer. 23:6; 1 John 5:20; Rev. 1:18, 4:8; Acts 20:28; 1 John 3:16; Phil. 2:6–8; 1 Tim. 3:16; Heb. 2:16; 1 John 4:3; Heb. 10:5; John 20:28; John 10:29–31; Matt. 16:16; Rom. 8:32; John 3:16, 18; Col. 1:15; John 17:10; Isa. 9:6; Col. 2:9; 1 Cor. 8:6; 2:8; Ps. 68:17.

a low appearance, representing but the back parts of their glory, who yet themselves, in their highest advancement, do cover their faces at the presence of our Beloved, as conscious to themselves of their utter disability to bear the rays of his glory (Isa. 6:2; John 12:39–41). He is "*the fellow of the* LORD *of hosts*" (Zech. 13:7). And though he once appeared in the form of a servant, yet then "he thought it not robbery to be equal with God" (Phil. 2:6). In the glory of this majesty he dwells in light inaccessible [1 Tim. 6:16]. We "cannot by searching find out the Almighty unto perfection: it is as high as heaven; what can we do? Deeper than hell; what can we know? The measure thereof is longer than the earth, and broader than the sea" (Job 11: 7–9). We may all say one to another of this, "Surely we are more brutish than any man, and have not the understanding of a man. We neither learned wisdom, nor have the knowledge of the holy. Who has ascended up into heaven, or descended? Who has gathered the wind in his fists? Who has bound the waters in a garment? Who has established all the ends of the earth? What is his name, and what is his Son's name, if you can tell?" (Prov. 30:2–4).

If any one should ask, now, with them in the Song of Solomon, what is in the Lord Jesus, our beloved, more than in other beloveds, that should make him so desirable and amiable and worthy of acceptation? What is he more than others? I ask, What is a *king* more than a *beggar*? Much [in] every way. Alas! this is nothing; they were born alike, must die alike, and after that is the judgment. What is an *angel* more than a *worm*? A worm is a creature, and an angel is no more; he has made the one to creep in the earth—made also the other to dwell in heaven. There is still a proportion between these, they agree in something; but what are all the nothings of the world to the God infinitely blessed for-evermore? Shall the dust of the balance, or the drop of the bucket be laid in the scale against him [Isa. 40:12, 15]? This is he of whom the sinners in Zion are afraid, and cry, "Who among us shall dwell with the devouring fire, who among us shall dwell with everlasting burnings?" [Isa. 33:14]. I might now give you a glimpse of his excellency in many of those properties and attributes by which he discovers himself to the faith of poor sinners; but as he that goes into a garden where there are innumerable flowers in great variety, gathers not all he sees, but crops here and there one and another, I shall endeavor to open a door and give an inlet[2] into the infinite excellency of the graces of the Lord Jesus,

_____

2. entrance

as he is "God blessed forevermore" [Rom. 9:5]—presenting the reader
with one or two instances, leaving him to gather for his own use what
further he pleases. Hence, then, observe—

The *endless, bottomless, boundless grace* and compassion that is in
him who is thus our husband, as he is the God of Zion. It is not the
grace of a *creature*, nor all the grace that can possibly at once dwell in
a created nature, that will serve our turn. We are too indigent[3] to be
suited with such a supply. There was a fullness of grace in the human
nature of Christ—he received not "the Spirit by measure" (John 3:34);
a fullness like that of light in the sun, or of water in the sea (I speak not
in respect of communication, but sufficiency); a fullness incomparably
above the measure of angels: yet it was not properly an infinite fullness—it was a created, and therefore a limited, fullness. If it could be
conceived as separated from the Deity, surely so many thirsty, guilty
souls, as every day drink deep and large draughts of grace and mercy
from him, would (if I may so speak) sink him to the very bottom; nay,
it could afford no supply at all, but only in a moral way. But when
the conduit of his humanity is inseparably united to the infinite, inex-
haustible fountain of the Deity, who can look into the depths thereof?
If, now, there be grace enough for sinners in an all-sufficient God, it
is in Christ; and, indeed, in any other there cannot be enough. The
Lord gives this reason for the peace and confidence of sinners, "You
shall not be ashamed, neither be you confounded; for you shall not
be put to shame" (Isa. 54:4). But how shall this be? So much sin, and
not ashamed! So much guilt, and not confounded! "Your Maker,"
says he, "is your husband; the LORD of hosts is his name; and your
Redeemer the Holy One of Israel; the God of the whole earth shall he
be called" [Isa. 54:5]. This is the bottom of all peace, confidence, and
consolation—the grace and mercy of our Maker, of the God of the
whole earth. So are kindness and power tempered[4] in him; he makes
us, and mars us—he is our God and our Goël,[5] our Redeemer. "Look
unto me," says he, "and be you saved; for I am God, and none else"
(Isa. 45:22), "Surely, shall one say, In the LORD have I righteousness"
(Isa. 45:24).

And on this ground it is that if all the world should (if I may so say)
set themselves to drink free grace, mercy, and pardon, drawing water

---

3. lacking, impoverished, deficient.
4. balanced
5. from the Hebrew participle of the verb *gaal* ("to redeem").

continually from the wells of salvation;[6] if they should set themselves to draw from one single promise, an angel standing by and crying, "Drink, O my friends, yea, drink abundantly, take so much grace and pardon as shall be abundantly sufficient for the world of sin which is in every one of you"—they would not be able to sink the grace of the promise one hair's breadth. There is enough for millions of worlds, if they were; because it flows into it from an infinite, bottomless fountain. "Fear not, O worm Jacob, I am God, and not man" [Isa. 41:14] is the bottom of sinners' consolation. This is that "head of gold" mentioned (Song 5:11), that most precious fountain of grace and mercy. This infiniteness of grace, in respect of its spring and fountain, will answer all objections that might hinder our souls from drawing nigh to communion with him, and from a free embracing of him. Will not this suit us in all our distresses? What is our finite guilt before it? Show me the sinner that can spread his iniquities to the dimensions (if I may so say) of this grace. Here is mercy enough for the greatest, the oldest, the most stubborn transgressor—"Why will you die, O house of Israel?" [Ezek. 18:31]. Take heed of them who would rob you of the Deity of Christ. If there were no more grace for me than what can be treasured up in a mere man, I should rejoice [if] my portion might be under rocks and mountains.

Consider, hence, his *eternal, free, unchangeable love.* Were the love of Christ unto us but[7] the love of a mere man, though never so excellent, innocent, and glorious, it must have a *beginning*, it must have an *ending*, and perhaps be *fruitless.* The love of Christ in his human nature toward his [people] is exceeding, intense, tender, precious, compassionate, abundantly heightened by a sense of our miseries, feeling of our wants, experience of our temptations; all flowing from that rich stock of grace, pity, and compassion, which, on purpose for our good and supply, was bestowed on him: but yet this love, as such, cannot be infinite nor eternal, nor from itself absolutely unchangeable. Were it no more, though not to be paralleled nor fathomed, yet our Savior could not say of it, as he does, "As the Father has loved me, so have I loved you" (John 15:9). His love could not be compared with and equaled unto the divine love of the Father, in those properties of eternity, fruitfulness, and unchangeableness, which are the chief anchors of the soul, rolling itself on the bosom of Christ. But now—

---

6. Song 5:1; Isa. 55:1; Rev. 22:17; John 7:37–38.

7. i.e., nothing more than.

Christ's Love Is Eternal

It is *eternal*: "Come you near unto me, hear you this; I have not," says he, "spoken in secret from the beginning; from the time that it was, there am I: and now the Lord GOD, and his Spirit, has sent me" (Isa. 48:16). He himself is "yesterday, today, and forever" (Heb. 13:8); and so is his love, being his who is "Alpha and Omega, the first and the last, the beginning and the ending, which is, which was, and which is to come" (Rev. 1:11).[8]

Christ's Love Is Unchangeable

Unchangeable. Our love is *like ourselves*; as we are, so are all our affections: so is the love of Christ *like himself.* We love one one day, and hate him the next. He changes, and we change also: this day he is our right hand, our right eye; the next day, "Cut him off, pluck him out" (Gal. 4:14–15). Jesus Christ is still the same; and so is his love. "In the beginning he laid the foundation of the earth; and the heavens are the works of his hands; they shall perish, but he remains: they all shall wax[9] old as does a garment; and as a vesture[10] shall he fold them up, and they shall be changed: but he is the same, and his years fail not" (Heb. 1:10–12). He is the LORD, and he changes not; and therefore we are not consumed. Whom he loves, he loves unto the end.[11] His love is such as never had beginning, and never shall have ending.

Christ's Love Is Fruitful

It is also *fruitful*—fruitful in all gracious issues and effects. A man may love another as his own soul, yet perhaps that love of his cannot help him. He may thereby pity him in prison, but not relieve him; bemoan him in misery, but not help him; suffer with him in trouble, but not ease him. We cannot love grace into a child, nor mercy into a friend; we cannot love them into heaven, though it may be the great desire of our soul. It was love that made Abraham cry, "O that Ishmael might live before you!" [Gen. 17:18], but it might not be. But now the love of Christ, being the love of God, is *effectual and fruitful* in producing all the good things which he wills unto his beloved. He loves life, grace,

---

8. Due to textual criticism, this verse has different wording in modern translations.

9. grow, become.

10. garment, covering, robe.

11. Mal. 3:6; John 13:1.

and holiness into us; he loves us also into covenant, loves us into heaven. Love in him is properly to will good to anyone: whatever good Christ by his love wills to any, that willing is *operative* of that good.

These three qualifications of the love of Christ make it exceedingly eminent, and him exceeding desirable. How many millions of sins, in every one of the elect, every one whereof were enough to condemn them all, has this love overcome! What mountains of unbelief does it remove! Look upon the conversation of any one saint, consider the frame of his heart, see the many stains and spots, the defilements and infirmities, wherewith his life is contaminated, and tell me whether the love that bears with all this be not to be admired. And is it not the same toward thousands every day? What streams of grace, purging, pardoning, quickening, assisting, do flow from it every day! This is our Beloved, O you daughters of Jerusalem [Song 5:16].

The Excellency of Christ's Humanity

He is desirable and worthy [of] our acceptation, as considered in his *humanity*; even therein also, in reference to us, he is exceedingly desirable. I shall only, in this, note unto you two things: (1) its *freedom from sin*; (2) its *fullness of grace*—in both which regards the Scripture sets him out as exceedingly lovely and amiable.

Christ Was Free from Sin

He was *free from sin*—the Lamb of God, without spot, and without blemish (1 Pet. 1:19); the male of the flock, to be offered unto God, the curse falling on all other oblations, and them that offer them (Mal. 1:14). The purity of the snow is not to be compared with the whiteness of this lily, of this rose of Sharon (Song 2:1), even from the womb: "For such a high priest became us, who is holy, harmless, undefiled, separate from sinners" (Heb. 7:26). Sanctified persons, whose stains are in any measure washed away, are exceeding fair in the eye of Christ himself. "You are all fair," says he, "my love, you have no spot in you."[12] How fair, then, is he who never had the least spot or stain!

It is true, Adam at his creation had this spotless purity (Eccles. 7:29); so had the angels: but they came immediately from the hand of God, without concurrence of any *secondary* cause. Jesus Christ is a plant

---

12. Song 1:15–16; 4:1, 7, 10.

and root out of a dry ground (Isa. 53:2), a blossom from the stem of Jesse, a bud from the loins of sinful man—born of a sinner, after there had been no innocent flesh in the world for four thousand years, every one upon the roll of his genealogy being infected therewith. To have a flower of wonderful rarity to grow in *paradise*, a garden of God's own planting, not sullied[13] in the least, is not so strange; but, as the psalmist speaks [Ps. 107:35–37?] (in another kind), to hear of it in a *wood*, to find it in a *forest*, to have a spotless bud brought forth in the *wilderness* of corrupted nature, is a thing which angels may desire to look into. Nay, more, this whole nature was not only defiled, but also accursed; not only unclean, but also guilty—guilty of Adam's transgression, in whom we have all sinned. That the human nature of Christ should be derived from hence free from guilt, free from pollution, this is to be adored.

OBJECTION AND ANSWER

But you will say, "How can this be? Who can bring a clean thing from an unclean? How could Christ take our nature, and not the defilements of it, and the guilt of it? If Levi paid tithes in the loins of Abraham (Heb. 7:9–10), how is it that Christ did not sin in the loins of Adam?"

There are two things in *original sin*:

First, *guilt of the first sin*, which is imputed to us. We all sinned in him. *Eph ho pantes hemarton* (Rom. 5:12), whether we render it relatively ("in whom") or illatively[14] ("being all have sinned"), all is one: that one sin is the sin of us all—"*omnes eramus unus ille homo.*"[15] We were all in covenant with him; he was not only a natural head, but also a federal head unto us. As Christ is to believers (Rom. 5:17; 1 Cor. 15:22), so was he to us all; and his transgression of that covenant is reckoned to us.

Second, there is the *derivation* of a polluted, corrupted nature from him: "Who can bring a clean thing out of an unclean?" "That which is born of the flesh is flesh" and nothing else; whose wisdom and mind is corrupted also: a polluted fountain will have polluted streams.[16] The *first person* corrupted *nature*, and that *nature* corrupts *all persons* following. Now, from both these was Christ most free:

---

13. polluted, soiled.

14. inferentially

15. "We all were that one man." Augustine, *The City of God*, NPNF[1] 2:251; PL 41, col. 386.

16. Job 14:4; Rom. 8:7, *phronēma tēs sarkos* ["the fleshly mind"]; John 3:16; Col. 2:18, *noos tēs sarkos* ["the fleshly mind"].

He was *never federally in Adam*, and so not liable to the imputation of his sin on that account. It is true that sin was imputed to him when he was made sin (2 Cor. 5:21); thereby he took away the sin of the world (John 1:29): but it was imputed to him in the covenant of the Mediator, through his voluntary susception,[17] and not in the covenant of Adam, by a legal imputation. Had it been reckoned to him as a descendant from Adam, he had not been[18] a fit high priest to have offered sacrifices for us, as not being "separate from sinners" (Heb. 7:26). Had Adam stood in his innocence, Christ had not been[19] incarnate to have been a mediator for sinners; and therefore the counsel of his incarnation (Gen. 3:15), morally, took not place until after the fall.[20] Though he was in Adam in a natural sense from his first creation, in respect of the purpose of God (Luke 3:23, 38), yet he was not in him in a law sense until after the fall: so that, as to his own person, he had no more to do with the first sin of Adam, than with any personal sin of [any] one whose punishment he voluntarily took upon him; as we are not liable to the guilt of those progenitors[21] who followed Adam, though naturally we were no less in them than in him. Therefore did he, all the days of his flesh, serve God in a covenant of works; and was therein accepted with him, having done nothing that should disannul[22] the virtue of that covenant as to him. This does not, then, in the least take off from his perfection.

For the *pollution of our nature*, it was prevented in him from the instant of conception: "The Holy Ghost shall come upon you, and the power of the Highest shall overshadow you: therefore also that holy thing that shall be born of you shall be called the Son of God" (Luke 1:35). He was "made of a woman" (Gal. 4:4); but that portion whereof he was made was sanctified by the Holy Ghost, that what was born thereof should be a holy thing. Not only the conjunction and union of soul and body, whereby a man becomes partaker of his whole nature, and therein of the pollution of sin, being a son of Adam, was prevented by the sanctification of the Holy Ghost, but it also accompanied the *very separation of his bodily substance* in the womb unto that sacred

---

17. reception

18. i.e., would not have been.

19. i.e., would not have been.

20. "The counsel of his incarnation" refers to the righteous agreement of the triune counsel (Father, Son, and Holy Spirit) that, in light of humanity's fall into sin the Son should become incarnate (i.e., become the God-man, by assuming a human nature in addition to his divine nature).

21. ancestors

22. annul, cancel, make void.

purpose whereunto it was set apart: so that upon all accounts he is "holy, harmless, undefiled" [Heb. 7:26]. Add now hereunto, that he "did no sin, neither was guile found in his mouth" (1 Pet. 2:22); that he "fulfilled all righteousness" (Matt. 3:15); his Father being always "well pleased" with him (v. 17), on the account of his perfect obedience; yea, even in that sense wherein he charges his angels with folly, and those inhabitants of heaven are not clean in his sight; and his excellency and desirableness in this regard will lie before us. Such was he, such is he; and yet for our sakes was he contented not only to be esteemed by the vilest of men to be a transgressor, but to undergo from God the punishment due to the vilest sinners. Of which afterward.

Christ Was Full of Grace

The *fullness of grace* in Christ's *human nature* sets forth the amiableness and desirableness thereof. Should I make it my business to consider his perfections, as to this part of his excellency—what he had from the womb (Luke 1:35), what received growth and improvement as to exercise in the days of his flesh (Luke 2:52), with the complement of them all in glory—the whole would tend to the purpose in hand. I am but taking a view of these things *in transitu*.[23] These two things lie in open sight to all at the first consideration: all grace was in him, for the *kinds* thereof; and all *degrees* of grace, for its perfections; and both of them make up that fullness that was in him. It is created grace that I intend; and therefore I speak of the kinds of it: it is grace inherent in a created nature, not infinite; and therefore I speak of the degrees of it.

For the *fountain* of grace, the Holy Ghost, he received not him "by measure" (John 3:34); and for the communications of the Spirit, "it pleased the Father that in him should all fullness dwell" (Col. 1:19)—"that in all things he might have the preeminence" [Col. 1:18]. But these things are commonly spoken unto.

This is the *Beloved* of our souls, "holy, harmless, undefiled"; "full of grace and truth"[24]—

- full, to a sufficiency for every end of grace
- full, for practice, to be an example to men and angels as to obedience

---

23. Lat. in passing.
24. John 1:14, 16; 1 Cor. 11:1; Eph. 5:2; 1 Pet. 2:21; Matt. 3:17; Heb. 2:18; 7:25.

- full, to a certainty of uninterrupted communion with God
- full, to a readiness of giving supply to others
- full, to suit him to all the occasions and necessities of the souls of men
- full, to a glory not unbecoming a subsistence in the person of the Son of God
- full, to a perfect victory, in trials, over all temptations
- full, to an exact correspondence to the whole law, every righteous and holy law of God
- full to the utmost capacity of a limited, created, finite nature
- full, to the greatest beauty and glory of a living temple of God
- full, to the full pleasure and delight of the soul of his Father
- full, to an everlasting monument of the glory of God, in giving such inconceivable excellencies to the Son of man.

And this is the second thing considerable for the endearing of our souls to our Beloved.

Christ Is All This in One Person

Consider that he is *all this in one person.* We have not been treating of *two*, a God and a man; but of one who *is* God and man.[25] That Word that was with God in the beginning, and was God (John 1:1) is also made flesh (v. 14)—not by a conversion of itself into flesh; not by appearing in the outward shape and likeness of flesh; but by assuming

---

25. *Qui, propter homines liberandos ab æternâ morte, homo factus est, et ita ad susceptionem humilitatis nostræ, sine suæ majestatis diminutione inclinans, ut manens quod erat, assumensque quod non erat; veram servi formam, ei formæ, in qua Deo patri est æqualis, adunaret, ut nec inferiorem absumeret glorificatio, nec superiorem minueret assumptio; salvâ enim proprietate utriusque substantiæ, et in unam coëunte personam, suscipitur a majestate humilitas, a virtute infirmitas, a mortalitate æternitas, et ad rependendum nostræ conditionis debitum, natura inviolabilis naturæ est unita passibili,* etc. ["With the purpose of delivering man from eternal death, became man: so bending Himself to take on Him our humility without decrease in His own majesty, that remaining what He was and assuming what He was not, He might unite the true form of a slave to that form in which He is equal to God the Father, and join both natures together by such a compact that the lower should not be swallowed up in its exaltation nor the higher impaired by its new associate. Without detriment therefore to the properties of either substance which then came together in one person, majesty took on humility, strength weakness, eternity mortality: and for the paying off of the debt, belonging to our condition, inviolable nature was united with passible nature. . . ." Leo the Great, *Serm*, I, *De Nat.*, "On the Feast of the Nativity" in *Sermons of Leo the Great: Sermon XXI*, NPNF[2] 12:129; PL 54, cols. 191C–192A.]

that holy thing that was born of the virgin (Luke 1:35), into personal union with himself. So "the mighty God" (Isa. 9:6) is a "child given" to us; that holy thing that was born of the virgin is called "the Son of God" (Luke 1:35). That which made the man Christ Jesus to be *a man* was the union of soul and body; that which made him *that man*, and without which he was not *the man*, was the subsistence of *both* united in the person of the Son of God. As to the proof hereof, I have spoken of it elsewhere at large;[26] I now propose it only in general, to show the amiableness of Christ on this account. Here lies, hence arises, the grace, peace, life, and security of the church—of all believers; as by some few considerations may be clearly evinced:

Christ Was Fit to Suffer and to Bear Our Punishment

Hence was he *fit* to suffer and able to bear whatever was due unto us,[27] in that very action wherein the "Son of man gave his life a ransom for many" (Matt. 20:28). "God redeemed his church with his own blood" (Acts 20:28); and therein was the "love of God seen, that he gave his life for us" (1 John 3:16). On this account was there *room* enough in his breast to receive the points of all the *swords* that were sharpened by the law against us (Zech. 13:7); and *strength* enough in his shoulders to bear the *burden* of that curse that was due to us (Ps. 89:19). Thence was he so *willing* to undertake the work of our redemption, "Lo, I come to do your will, O God" (Heb. 10:7–8)—because he knew his ability to go through with it. Had he not been *man*, he could not have suffered; had he not been *God*, his suffering could not have availed either himself or us—he had not[28] satisfied; the suffering of a mere man could not bear any proportion to that which in any respect was infinite. Had the great and righteous God gathered together all the sins that had been committed by his elect from the foundation of the world, and searched the bosoms of all that were to come to the end of the world, and taken them all, from the sin of their nature to the least deviation from the

---

26. John Owen, *Vindiciae Evangelicae* [*Mystery of the Gospel Vindicated* (1655), *Works* 12].

27. *Deus versus, et homo verus in unitatem Domini temperatur, ut, quod nostris remediis congruebat, unus atque idem Dei hominumque mediator et mori possit ex uno, et resurgere possit ex altero.* ["And true God and true man were combined to form one Lord, so that, as suited the needs of our case, one and the same Mediator between God and men, the Man Christ Jesus, could both die with the one and rise again with the other." Leo the Great, "On the Feast of the Nativity," in *Sermons of Leo the Great: Sermon XXI*, NPNF[2] 12:129; PL 54, col. 192A.]

28. i.e., he could not have.

rectitude[29] of his most holy law, and the highest provocation of their regenerate and unregenerate condition, and laid them on a mere holy, innocent, creature—Oh how would they have overwhelmed him, and buried him forever out of the presence of God's love! Therefore does the apostle premise that glorious description of him to the purging of our sin: "He has spoken unto us by his Son, whom he has appointed heir of all things, by whom also he made the worlds; who being the brightness of his glory, and the express image of his person, and upholding all things by the word of his power," has "purged our sins" (Heb. 1:2–3). It was he that purged our sins, who was the Son and heir of all things, by whom the world was made—the brightness of his Father's glory, and express image of his person; he did it, he alone was able to do it. "God was manifested in the flesh" (1 Tim. 3:16) for this work. The sword awaked against him that was the fellow of the Lord of hosts (Zech. 13:7); and by the wounds of that great shepherd are the sheep healed (1 Pet. 2:24–25).

Christ Became a Fountain of Grace to All Who Believe

Hence does he become an *endless*, bottomless fountain of grace to all them that believe. The fullness that it pleased the Father to commit to Christ, to be the great *treasury* and storehouse of the church, did not, does not, lie in the human nature, considered in itself; but in the person of the mediator, God and man. Consider wherein his communication of grace does consist, and this will be evident. The foundation of all is laid in his satisfaction, merit, and purchase; these are the morally procuring cause of all the grace we receive from Christ. Hence all grace becomes to be his (John 16:14–15); all the things of the new covenant, the promises of God, all the mercy, love, grace, glory promised, became, I say, to be his. Not as though they were all actually invested, or did reside and were in the human nature, and were from thence *really* communicated to us by a participation of a portion of what did so inhere: but they are *morally* his, by a compact, to be bestowed by him as he thinks good, as he is mediator, God and man;[30] that is, the only begotten Son made flesh, "from whose fullness we receive, and grace for grace" (John 1:16). The real communication of grace is by Christ sending the Holy Ghost to regenerate us, and to create all the habitual grace, with the daily supplies thereof, in our hearts, that we are made partakers of. Now the

---

29. uprightness
30. Isa. 53:11–12; John 1:16; Col. 1:19–20.

Holy Ghost is thus sent by Christ as mediator, God and man, as is at large declared (John 14–16); of which more afterward. This, then, is that which I intend by this fullness of grace that is in Christ, from whence we have both our beginning and all our supplies; which makes him, as he is the Alpha and Omega of his church (Rev. 1:11[31]), the beginner and finisher of our faith (Heb. 12:2), excellent and desirable to our souls. Upon the payment of the great price of his blood, and full acquitment[32] on the satisfaction he made, all grace whatsoever (of which at large afterward) becomes, in a moral sense, his, at his disposal; and he bestows it on, or works it in, the hearts of his by the Holy Ghost, according as, in his infinite wisdom, he sees it needful. How glorious is he to the soul on this consideration! That is most excellent to us which suits us in a wanting condition—that which gives bread to the hungry, water to the thirsty, mercy to the perishing. All our reliefs are thus in our Beloved. Here is the *life* of our souls, the *joy* of our hearts, our *relief* against sin and *deliverance* from the wrath to come.

Christ Was a Fit Mediator

Thus is he *fitted* for a mediator, a days-man, an umpire between God and us—being one with him, and one with us, and one in himself in this oneness, in the unity of one person. His ability and universal fitness for his office of mediator are hence usually demonstrated. And herein is he "Christ, the power of God, and the wisdom of God" (1 Cor. 1:24). Herein shines out the infinitely glorious wisdom of God; which we may better admire than express. What soul that has any acquaintance with these things falls not down with reverence and astonishment? How glorious is he that is the Beloved of our souls! What can be wanting that should encourage us to take up our rest and peace in his bosom? Unless all ways of relief and refreshment be so obstructed by unbelief, that no consideration can reach the heart to yield it the least assistance, it is impossible but that from hence the soul may gather that which will endear it unto him with whom we have to do. Let us dwell on the thoughts of it. This is the *hidden mystery*; great without controversy; admirable to eternity. What poor, low, perishing things do we spend our contemplations on! Were we to have no advantage by this astonishing dispensation, yet its excellency, glory, beauty, depths, deserve the flower of our inquiries, the vigor of our spirits, the substance of our time; but

---

31. Due to textual criticism, this verse has a different wording in modern translations.
32. aquittal, discharge, release.

when, with, our life, our peace, our joy, our inheritance, our eternity, our all, lies herein, shall not the thoughts of it always dwell in our hearts, always refresh and delight our souls?

Christ Was Exalted and Invested with All Authority

He is excellent and glorious in this—in that he is *exalted and invested with all authority*. When Jacob heard of the exaltation of his son Joseph in Egypt, and saw the chariots that he had sent for him, his spirit fainted and recovered again, through abundance of joy and other overflowing affections (Gen. 45:26–27). Is our Beloved lost, who for our sakes was upon the earth poor and persecuted, reviled, killed? No! He was dead, but he is alive, and, lo, he lives forever and ever, and has the keys of hell and of death (Rev. 1:18). Our Beloved is made a lord and ruler (Acts 2:36). He is made a king; God sets him his king on his holy hill of Zion (Ps. 2:6);[33] and he is crowned with honor and dignity, after he had been "made a little lower than the angels for the suffering of death" (Heb. 2:7–9). And what is he made king of? "All things are put in subjection under his feet" (v. 8). And what power over them has our Beloved? "All power in heaven and earth" (Matt. 28:18). As for men, he has power given him "over all flesh" (John 17:2). And in what glory does he exercise this power? He gives eternal life to his elect; ruling them in the power of God (Mic. 5:4), until he bring them to himself: and for his enemies, his arrows are sharp in their hearts (Ps. 45:5); he dips his vesture in their blood (Isa. 63:3 [cf. Rev. 19:13]). Oh, how glorious is he in his authority over his enemies! In this world he terrifies, frightens, awes, convinces, bruises their hearts and consciences—fills them with fear, terror, disquietment,[34] until they yield him feigned obedience; and sometimes with outward judgments bruises, breaks, turns the wheel upon them—stains all his vesture with their blood—fills the earth with their carcasses (Ps. 110:6), and at last will gather them all together—beast, false prophet, nations, etc.—and cast them into that lake that burns with fire and brimstone (Rev. 19:20).

He is gloriously exalted above *angels* in this his authority, good and bad, "far above all principality, and power, and might, and dominion, and every name that is named, not only in this world, but also in that

---

33. Gen. 49:10; Num. 24:17, 19; Ps. 2:1–9; 89:19–25; 110:1–3; Isa. 11:1, 4; 32:1–2; 53:12; 63:1–3; Jer. 23:5–6; Dan. 7:13–14; Luke 2:11; 19:38; John 5:22–23; Acts 2:34–36, 5:31; Phil. 2:9–11; Eph. 1:20–22; Rev. 5:12–14; 19:16.

34. disturbance, uneasiness, anxiety, unrest.

which is to come" (Eph. 1:20–22). They are all under his feet—at his command and absolute disposal. He is at the right hand of God, in the highest exaltation possible, and in full possession of a kingdom over the whole creation; having received a "*name* above every name," etc. (Phil. 2:9). Thus is he

- glorious in his *throne*, which is at "the right hand of the Majesty on high" (Heb. 1:3)
- glorious in his *commission*, which is "all power in heaven and earth" (Matt. 28:18)
- glorious in his *name*, a name above every name—"Lord of lords, and King of kings" (Rev. 19:16)
- glorious in his *scepter*—"a scepter of righteousness is the scepter of his kingdom" (Ps. 45:6)
- glorious in his *attendants*—"his chariots are twenty thousand, even thousands of angels" (Ps. 68:17), among them he rides on the heavens, and sends out the voice of his strength, attended with ten thousand times ten thousand of his holy ones (Dan. 7:10)
- glorious in his *subjects*—all creatures in heaven and in earth, nothing is left that is not put in subjection to him (Eph. 1:22)
- glorious in his *way of rule*, and the administration of his kingdom—full of sweetness, efficacy, power, serenity, holiness, righteousness, and grace, in and toward his elect—of terror, vengeance, and certain destruction toward the rebellious angels and men
- glorious in the *issue of his kingdom*, when every knee shall bow before him, and all shall stand before his judgment-seat (Phil. 2:10–11).

And what a little portion of his glory is it that we have pointed to! This is the beloved of the church—its head, its husband; this is he with whom we have communion: but of the whole exaltation of Jesus Christ I am elsewhere to treat at large.

Having insisted on these generals, for the further carrying on the motives to communion with Christ, in the relation mentioned, taken from his excellencies and perfections, I shall reflect on the description given of him by the spouse in the Canticles, to this very end and purpose:

My Beloved is white and ruddy, the chiefest among ten thousand. His head is as the most fine gold, his locks are bushy, and black as a raven.

His eyes are as the eyes of doves by the rivers of waters, washed with milk,
and fitly set. His cheeks are as a bed of spices, as sweet flowers: his lips
like lilies, dropping sweet-smelling myrrh. His hands are as gold rings, set
with the beryl: his belly is as bright ivory overlaid with sapphires. His legs
are as pillars of marble, set upon sockets of fine gold: his countenance is
as Lebanon, excellent as the cedars. His mouth is most sweet: yea, he is
altogether lovely. This is my Beloved, and this is my friend, O daughters
of Jerusalem. (Song 5:10–16)

The general description given of him (v. 10) has been before considered;
the ensuing particulars are instances to make good the assertion that he
is "the chiefest among ten thousand."

The spouse begins with his *head* and *face* (vv. 11–13). In his head,
she speaks first in general, unto the *substance* of it—it is "fine gold";
and then in particular, as *to its ornaments*—"his locks are bushy, and
black as a raven."

"His Head Is as the Most Fine Gold"

"*His head is as the most fine gold*," or, "His head gold, solid gold";
so some—"made of pure gold"; so others—*chrusion kephalē*, say the
LXX [Septuagint[35]], retaining part of both the Hebrew words, *ketem
pazs—"massa auri."*[36]

Two things are eminent in gold—splendor or glory, and duration.
This is that which the spouse speaks of the head of Christ. His head is
his government, authority, and kingdom. Hence it is said, "A crown of
pure gold was on his head" (Ps. 21:3); and his head is here said to be
gold, because of the crown of gold that adorns it—as the monarchy in

---

35. Greek translation of the Old Testament.

36. William Goold, the eighteenth-century editor of Owen's *Works*, writes: "So the words are
quoted in all editions of this treatise. Fully to develop the meaning of the allusion, it seems necessary
that the whole of the Septuagint rendering should be quoted: *Kephalē autou chrusion kephaz.* It is
the last word in which part of both the Hebrew words is said to be retained. There is some difficulty
in fixing the import of *paz*. Gesenius, William refers us to Ps. 19:10, in proof that it means fine,
as distinguished from common gold; from *pazaz*, a root not used in Hebrew, but signifying, in the
cognate dialect of Arabic, to separate, to purify metals. Some connect the term with Uphaz, a district
from which gold was procured (Jer. 10:9). Schultens, Albert derives the word from *kazaz*, to leap,
to spring up into notice, in allusion to the amount of gold discovered on the surface of the earth,
through the previous disintegration of the rock in which it was disseminated, and when a shower
has washed it from the soil by which it was covered. There is coincidence between the etymology
of the word suggested by the Dutch critic, and the fact that the largest quantities of gold and gold
ore have been discovered, not by excavation, but by the washing of detritus in regions of primary
and transitory strata where the eruption of igneous rocks has occurred: 'As for the earth, . . . it has
dust of gold' (Job 28:5–6)."

Daniel that was most eminent for glory and duration is termed a "head of gold" (Dan. 2:38). And these two things are eminent in the kingdom and authority of Christ:

It is a *glorious* kingdom; he is full of glory and majesty, and in his majesty he rides "prosperously" (Ps. 45:3–4). "His glory is great in the salvation of God: honor and majesty are laid upon him: he is made blessed forever and ever" (Ps. 21:5–6). I might insist on particulars, and show that there is not any thing that may render a kingdom or government glorious, but it is in this of Christ in all its excellencies. It is a *heavenly*, a *spiritual*, a *universal*, and *unshaken* kingdom; all which render it glorious. But of this, [it was discussed] somewhat before.

It is *durable*, yea, eternal—solid gold. "His throne is forever and ever" (Ps. 45:6); "of the increase of his government there shall be no end, upon the throne of David, and upon his kingdom, to order it, and to establish it with judgment and with justice from henceforth even forever" (Isa. 9:7). "His kingdom is an everlasting kingdom" (Dan. 7:27)—"a kingdom that shall never be destroyed" (Dan. 2:44); for he must reign until all his enemies be subdued. This is that head of gold—the splendor and eternity of his government.

And if you take the head in a natural sense, either the glory of his Deity is here attended to, or the fullness and excellency of his wisdom, which the head is the seat of. The allegory is not to be straitened, while we keep to the analogy of faith.[37]

The Ornaments of His Head

For the *ornaments* of his head; his locks, they are said to be "bushy," or curled, "black as a raven." His curled locks are black—"as a raven" is added by way of illustration of the blackness, not with any allusion to the nature of the raven. Take the head spoken of in a *political* sense: his locks of hair—said to be *curled*, as seeming to be *entangled*, but really falling in perfect order and beauty, as bushy locks—are his thoughts, and counsels, and ways, in the administration of his kingdom. They are *black* or *dark*, because of their *depth* and unsearchableness—as God is said to dwell in thick darkness; and *curled* or *bushy*, because of their exact *interweavings*, from his infinite wisdom. His thoughts are many as the hairs of the head, seeming to be perplexed and entangled, but

---

37. Analogy of faith (*analogia fidei*) is the general sense of the meaning of Scripture, whereby clear and crucial Scripture passages are used to interpret unclear or ambiguous passages. For Owen's view on the analogy of faith, see *Works* 4:199, 216; 21:315–16.

really set in a comely order, as curled bushy hair; deep and unsearchable, and dreadful to his enemies, and full of beauty and comeliness to
his beloved. Such are, I say, the thoughts of his heart, the counsels of
his wisdom, in reference to the administrations of his kingdom: dark,
perplexed, involved, to a carnal eye; in themselves, and to his saints,
deep, manifold, ordered in all things, comely, desirable.

In a *natural* sense, black and curled locks denote comeliness, and
vigor of youth. The strength and power of Christ, in the execution of
his counsels, in all his ways, appears glorious and lovely.

The next thing described in him is his *eyes*. "His eyes are as the eyes
of doves by the rivers of waters, washed with milk, and fitly set" (Song
5:12). The reason of this allusion is obvious: doves are tender birds, not
birds of prey; and of all others they have the most bright, shining, and
piercing eye; their delight also in streams of water is known. Their being
washed in milk—or clear, white, crystal water—adds to their beauty.
And they are here said to be "fitly set"; that is, in due proportion for
beauty and luster—as a precious stone in the foil or fullness of a ring,
as the word signifies.

Eyes being for *sight*, discerning, knowledge, and acquaintance with
the things that are to be seen; the knowledge, the understanding, the
discerning Spirit of Christ Jesus, are here intended. In the allusion used
four things are ascribed to them: (1) tenderness; (2) purity; (3) discerning; and, (4) glory:

The tenderness and compassion of Christ toward his church is here
intended. He looks on it with the eyes of gall-less doves; with tenderness
and careful compassion; without anger, fury, or thoughts of revenge.
So is the eye interpreted, "The eyes of the LORD your God are upon
that land." Why so? "It is a land that the LORD your God cares for"
(Deut. 11:12)—cares for it in mercy. So are the eyes of Christ on us, as
the eyes of one that in tenderness cares for us; that lays out his wisdom,
knowledge, and understanding, in all tender love, in our behalf. He is
the stone, that foundation-stone of the church, whereon "are seven
eyes" (Zech. 3:9); wherein is a perfection of wisdom, knowledge, care,
and kindness, for its guidance.

Purity—as washed doves' eyes for purity. This may be taken either
subjectively, for the excellency and immixed cleanness and purity of
his sight and knowledge in himself; or objectively, for his delighting to
behold purity in others. "He is of purer eyes than to behold iniquity"
(Hab. 1:13). "He has no pleasure in wickedness; the foolish shall not
stand in his sight" (Ps. 5:4–5). If the righteous soul of Lot was vexed

with seeing the filthy deeds of wicked men (2 Pet. 2:8), who yet had eyes of flesh in which there was a mixture of impurity, how much more do the pure eyes of our dear Lord Jesus abominate all the filthiness of sinners! But herein lies the excellency of his love to us, that he takes care to take away our filth and stains, that he may delight in us; and seeing we are so defiled, that it could no otherwise be done, he will do it by his own blood, "Even as Christ also loved the church, and gave himself for it, that he might sanctify and cleanse it, with the washing of water by the word, that he might present it to himself a glorious church, not having spot, or wrinkle, or any such thing; but that it should be holy, and without blemish" (Eph. 5:25–27). The end of this undertaking is that the church might be thus gloriously presented unto himself, because he is of purer eyes than to behold it with joy and delight in any other condition. He leaves not his spouse until he says of her, "You are all fair, my love; there is no spot in you" (Song 4:7). Partly, he takes away our spots and stains by the "renewing of the Holy Ghost" (Titus 3:5), and wholly adorns us with his own righteousness: and that because of the purity of his own eyes, which "cannot behold iniquity" [Hab. 1:13]—that he might present us to himself holy.

Discerning. He sees as doves, quickly, clearly, thoroughly—to the bottom of that which he looks upon. Hence, in another place it is said that his "eyes are as a flame of fire" (Rev. 1:14). And why so? That the churches might know that he is he which "searches the reins and hearts" (Rev. 2:23). He has discerning eyes, nothing is hid from him; all things are open and naked before him with whom we have to do. It is said of him, while he was in this world, that "Jesus knew all men, and needed not that any should testify of man; for he knew what was in man" (John 2:24–25). His piercing eyes look through all the thick coverings of hypocrites, and the show of pretences that is on them. He sees the inside of all; and what men are there, that they are to him. He sees not as we see, but ponders *the hidden man* of the heart [1 Pet. 3:4]. No humble, broken, contrite soul, shall lose one sigh or groan after him, and communion with him; no pant of love or desire is hid from him—he sees in secret; no glorious performance of the most glorious hypocrite will avail with him—his eyes look through all, and the filth of their hearts lies naked before him.

Beauty and glory are here intended also. Every thing of Christ is beautiful, for he is "altogether lovely" (Song 5:16), but most glorious [is he] in his sight and wisdom: he is the wisdom of God's eternal wisdom itself; his understanding is infinite. What spots and stains are in all our knowledge! When it is made perfect, yet it will still be finite and limited. His is without spot of darkness, without foil of limitedness. Thus, then, is he beautiful and glorious: his "head is of gold, his eyes are doves' eyes, washed in milk, and fitly set" [Song 5:11–12].

The next thing insisted on is his *cheeks*. "His cheeks are as a bed of spices; as sweet flowers," or "towers of perfumes" (Song 5:13) [marginal reading], or well-grown flowers. There are three things evidently pointed at in these words: (1) a *sweet savor*, as from spices, and flowers, and towers of perfume; (2) *beauty and order*, as spices set in rows or beds, as the words import;[38] (3) *eminency* in that word, as sweet or well-grown, great flowers.

These things are in the cheeks of Christ. The Chaldee paraphrast, who applies this whole song to God's dealings with the people of the Jews, makes these cheeks of the church's husband to be the two tables of stone, with the various lines drawn in them; but that allusion is strained, as are most of the conjectures of that scholiast.[39]

The cheeks of a man are the seat of *comeliness* and manlike courage. The comeliness of Christ, as has in part been declared, is from his fullness of grace in himself for us. His manly courage respects the administration of his rule and government, from his fullness of authority; as was before declared. This comeliness and courage the spouse, describing Christ as a beautiful, desirable personage, to show that spiritually he is so, calls his cheeks; so to make up his parts, and proportion. And to them does she ascribe—

A sweet *savor*, order, and eminency. A sweet savor; as God is said to smell a sweet savor from the grace and obedience of his servants (Gen. 8:21, the LORD smelled a savor of rest from the sacrifice of Noah), so do the saints smell a sweet savor from his grace laid up in Christ (Song 1:3). It is that which they rest in, which they delight in, which they are refreshed with. As the smell of aromatical spices and flowers pleases the natural sense, refreshes the spirits, and delights the person; so do the graces of Christ to his saints. They please their spiritual sense, they refresh their drooping spirits, and give delight to their souls. If he be nigh them, they smell his raiment, as Isaac the raiment of Jacob. They say, "It is as the smell of a field which the LORD has blessed" (Gen. 27:27); and their souls are refreshed with it.

---

38. signify
39. scholar who writes explanatory notes

Order and *beauty* are as spices set in a garden bed. So are the graces of Christ. When spices are set in order, anyone may know what is for his use, and take and gather it accordingly. Their answering, also, one to another makes them beautiful. So are the graces of Christ; in the gospel they are distinctly and in order set forth, that sinners by faith may view them, and take from him according to their necessity. They are ordered for the use of saints in the promises of the gospel. There is light in him, and life in him, and power in him, and all consolation in him—a constellation of graces, shining with glory and beauty. Believers take a view of them all, see their glory and excellency, but fix especially on that which, in the condition wherein they are, is most useful to them. One takes light and joy; another, life and power. By faith and prayer do they gather these things in this bed of spices. Not any that comes to him goes away unrefreshed. What may they not take, what may they not gather? What is it that the poor soul wants? Behold, it is here provided, set out in order in the promises of the gospel; which are as the beds wherein these spices are set for our use: and on the account hereof is the covenant said to be "ordered in all things" (2 Sam. 23:5).

Eminency. His cheeks are "a tower of perfumes" held up, made conspicuous, visible, eminent. So it is with the graces of Christ, when held out and lifted up in the preaching of the gospel. They are a tower of perfumes—a sweet savor to God and man.

The next clause of that verse is, "His lips are like lilies, dropping sweet-smelling myrrh." Two perfections in things natural are here alluded unto: First, the glory of *color* in the lilies, and the sweetness of *savor* in the myrrh. The glory and beauty of the lilies in those countries was such as that our Savior tells us that "Solomon, in all his glory, was not arrayed like one of them" (Matt. 6:29); and the savor of myrrh such as, when the Scripture would set forth any thing to be an excellent savor, it compares it thereunto (Ps. 45:8); and thereof was the sweet and holy ointment chiefly made (Ex. 30:23–25): mention is also made frequently of it in other places, to the same purpose. It is said of Christ that "grace was poured into his lips" (Ps. 45:2); whence men wondered or were amazed—*tois logois tēs charitos* [Luke 4:22]—"at the words of grace" that proceeded out of his mouth. So that by the lips of Christ, and their dropping sweet-smelling myrrh, the word of Christ, its savor, excellency, and usefulness is intended. Herein is he excellent and glorious indeed, surpassing the excellencies of those natural things which yet are most precious in their kind—even in the glory, beauty, and usefulness of his word. Hence they that preach his word to the saving of the souls of men are said to be a "sweet savor unto God" (2 Cor. 2:15); and the savor of the knowledge of God is said to be manifested by them (v. 14). I might insist on the several properties of myrrh, whereto the word of Christ is here compared—its bitterness in taste, its efficacy to preserve from putrefaction, its usefulness in perfumes and unctions[40]—and press the allegory in setting out the excellencies of the word in allusions to them; but I only insist on generals. This is that which the Holy Ghost here intends: the word of Christ is sweet, savory, precious unto believers; and they see him to be excellent, desirable, beautiful in the precepts, promises, exhortations, and the most bitter threats thereof.

The spouse adds, "His hands are as gold rings set with the beryl" [Song 5:14]. The word "beryl," in the original, is "*Tarshish*," which the Septuagint has retained, not restraining it to any peculiar precious stone; the onyx, say some; the chrysolite, say others—any precious stone shining with a sea-green color, for the word signifies the sea also. Gold rings set with precious, glittering stones, are both valuable and desirable, for profit and ornament: so are the hands of Christ; that is, all his works—the effects, by the cause. All his works are glorious; they are all fruits of wisdom, love, and bounty. "And his belly is as bright ivory, overlaid with sapphires" [Song 5:14]. The smoothness and brightness of ivory, the preciousness and heavenly color of the sapphires, are here called in, to give some luster to the excellency of Christ. To these is his belly, or rather his bowels (which takes in the heart also), compared. It is the inward bowels, and not the outward bulk that is signified. Now, to show that by "bowels" in the Scripture, ascribed either to God or man, affections are intended, is needless. The tender love, unspeakable affections and kindness, of Christ to his church and people is thus set out. What a beautiful sight is it to the eye, to see pure polished ivory set up and down with heaps of precious sapphires! How much more glorious are the tender affections, mercies, and compassion of the Lord Jesus unto believers!

The *strength* of his kingdom, the *faithfulness* and *stability* of his promises—the height and glory of his person in his dominion—the sweetness and excellency of communion with him, is set forth in these words: "His legs are as pillars of marble set upon sockets of fine gold; his countenance is as Lebanon, excellent as the cedars: his mouth is most sweet" (Song 5:15).

---

40. ointments

When the spouse has gone thus far in the description of him, she concludes all in this general assertion: "He is wholly desirable—altogether to be desired or beloved" (v. 16). As if she should have said: "I have thus reckoned up some of the perfections of the creatures (things of most value, price, usefulness, beauty, glory, here below), and compared some of the excellencies of my Beloved unto them. In this way of allegory I can carry things no higher; I find nothing better or more desirable to shadow out and to present his loveliness and desirableness: but, alas! all this comes short of his perfections, beauty, and comeliness; 'he is *all wholly* to be desired, to be beloved'"—

- Lovely in his *person*—in the glorious all-sufficiency of his Deity, gracious purity and holiness of his humanity, authority and majesty, love and power.

- Lovely in his *birth* and incarnation; when he was rich, for our sakes becoming poor—taking part of flesh and blood, because we partook of the same; being made of a woman, that for us he might be made under the law, even for our sakes.

- Lovely in the whole *course* of his life, and the more than angelical holiness and obedience which, in the depth of poverty and persecution, he exercised therein—doing good, receiving evil; blessing, and being cursed, reviled, reproached, all his days.

- Lovely in his *death*; yea, therein most lovely to sinners—never more glorious and desirable than when he came broken, dead, from the cross. Then had he carried all our sins into a land of forgetfulness; then had he made peace and reconciliation for us; then had he procured[41] life and immortality for us.

- Lovely in his whole *employment*, in his great undertaking—in his *life, death, resurrection, ascension*; being a mediator between God and us, to recover the glory of God's justice, and to save our souls—to bring us to an enjoyment of God, who were set at such an infinite distance from him by sin.

- Lovely in the glory and majesty wherewith he is *crowned*. Now he is set down at the right hand of the Majesty on high; where, though he be terrible to his enemies, yet he is full of mercy, love, and compassion, toward his beloved ones.

---

41. gained, obtained.

- Lovely in all those *supplies of grace and consolations*, in all the dispensations of his Holy Spirit, whereof his saints are made partakers.
- Lovely in all the *tender care, power, and wisdom*, which he exercises in the protection, safe-guarding, and delivery of his church and people, in the midst of all the oppositions and persecutions whereunto they are exposed.
- Lovely in all his *ordinances*, and the whole of that spiritually glorious worship which he has appointed to his people, whereby they draw nigh and have communion with him and his Father.
- Lovely and glorious in the *vengeance* he takes, and will finally execute, upon the stubborn enemies of himself and his people.
- Lovely in the *pardon* he has purchased and does dispense—in the reconciliation he has established, in the grace he communicates, in the consolations he does administer, in the peace and joy he gives his saints, in his assured preservation of them unto glory.

What shall I say? There is no end of his excellencies and desirableness—"He is altogether lovely. This is our beloved, and this is our friend, O daughters of Jerusalem."

Digression 2

Wisdom and Knowledge in Christ

A second consideration of the excellencies of Christ, serving to *endear* the hearts of them who stand with him in the relation insisted on, arises from that which, in the mistaken apprehension of it is the great darling of men, and in its true notion the great aim of the saints; which is *wisdom and knowledge*. Let it be evinced that all true and solid knowledge is laid up in, and is only to be attained from and by, the Lord Jesus Christ; and the hearts of men, if they are but true to themselves and their most predominate principles, must needs be engaged to him. This is the great design of all men, taken off from professed slavery to the world and the pursuit of sensual, licentious courses—that they may be *wise*: and what ways the generality of men engage in for the compassing[1] of that end shall be afterward considered. To the glory and honor of our dear Lord Jesus Christ, and the establishment of our hearts in communion with him, the design of this digression is to evince that all wisdom is laid up in him, and that from him alone it is to be obtained.

[In] 1 Corinthians 1:24 the Holy Ghost tells us that "Christ is the power of God, and the wisdom of God"—not the *essential* Wisdom of God, as he is the eternal Son of the Father (upon which account he is called "Wisdom" in Prov. 8:12–13), but as he is *crucified* (1 Cor. 1:23). As he is crucified, so he is the wisdom of God; that is, all that wisdom which God lays forth for the discovery and manifestation of himself,

---

1. attaining, achieving.

and for the saving of sinners, which makes foolish all the wisdom of the world—that is all in Christ crucified; held out in him, by him, and to be obtained only from him. And thereby in him do we see the glory of God (2 Cor. 3:18). For he is not only said to be "the wisdom of God," but also to be "made unto us wisdom" (1 Cor. 1:30). He is made, not by creation, but ordination and appointment, wisdom unto us; not only by teaching us wisdom (by a metonymy of the effect for the cause[2]), as he is the great prophet of his church, but also because by the knowing of him we become acquainted with the wisdom of God—which is our wisdom; which is a metonymy of the adjunct.[3] This, however verily promised, is thus only to be had. The sum of what is contended for is asserted in [these] terms: "In him are hid all the treasures of wisdom and knowledge" (Col. 2:3).

There are two things that might seem to have some color in claiming a title and interest in this business: (1) *civil* wisdom and prudence, for the management of affairs; (2) *ability* of learning and literature—but God rejects both these, as of no use at all to the end and intent of true wisdom indeed. There is in the world that which is called "understanding," but it comes to nothing. There is that which is called "wisdom," but it is turned into folly, "God brings to nothing the understanding of the prudent, and makes foolish this wisdom of the world" (1 Cor. 1:19–20). And if there be neither wisdom nor knowledge (as doubtless there is not) without the knowledge of God (Jer. 8:9), it is all shut up in the Lord Jesus Christ: "No man has seen God at any time; the only begotten Son, which is in the bosom of the Father, he has revealed him" (John 1:18). He is not seen at another time, nor known upon any other account, but only the revelation of the Son. He has manifested him from his own bosom; and therefore it is said that he is "the true Light, which lights every man that comes into the world" (John 1:9)—the true Light, which has it in himself: and none has any but from him; and all have it who come unto him. He who does not so, is in darkness.

The sum of all true wisdom and knowledge may be reduced to these three heads: (1) The *knowledge of God*, his nature and his properties. (2) The *knowledge of ourselves* in reference to the will of God concerning us. (3) Skill to walk in *communion* with God:

---

2. i.e., the effect is named but the cause is meant.
3. i.e., an addition is named but the subject is meant.

True Wisdom and Knowledge Consist in Knowing the Works of God

The knowledge of the works of God, and the chief end of all, does necessarily attend these. (1) In these three is summed up all true wisdom and knowledge; and, (2) not any of them is to any purpose to be obtained, or is manifested, but only in and by the Lord Christ.

THE ATTRIBUTES OF GOD

God, by the work of the creation, by the creation itself, did reveal himself in many of his properties unto his creatures capable of his knowledge—his power, his goodness, his wisdom, his all-sufficiency are thereby known. This the apostle asserts in Romans 1:19–21. He calls it *to gnōston tou theou* (v. 19)—that is, his eternal power and Godhead (v. 20); and a knowing of God (v. 21): and all this by the creation.[4] But yet there are some properties of God which all the works of creation cannot in any measure reveal or make known—as his *patience, longsuffering,* and *forbearance.* For all things being made good (Gen. 1:31), there could be no place for the exercise of any of these properties, or manifestation of them. The whole fabric of heaven and earth considered in itself, as at first created, will not discover any such thing as patience and forbearance in God;[5] which yet are eminent properties of his nature, as himself proclaims and declares (Ex. 34:6–7).

Wherefore the Lord goes further; and by the works of his *providence,* in preserving and ruling the world which he made, discovers and reveals

---

4. *Epei oun to genomenon ho kosmos estin ho xumpas, ho touton theōrōn tacha an akousai par autou, ōs eme pepoiēken ho theos.* ["Since, then, what has come into being is the whole universe, if you contemplate this, you might hear it say, 'a god made me.'" Plotinus, *Plotinus: Enneads III.1–9,* Loeb Classical Library, trans. A. H. Armstrong (Cambridge, MA: Harvard University Press, 1967), 53.]

5. *Quamvis speciali cura atque indulgentia Dei, populum Israeliticum constat electum, omnesque alias nationes suas vias ingredi, hoc est, secundum propriam permissæ sunt vivere voluntatem, non ita tamen se æterna Creatoris bonitas ab illis hominibus avertit, ut eus ad cognoscendum atque metuendum nullis significationibus admoneret.* ["It is true that God's special care and mercy chose the people of Israel as His own, while other nations were left to walk in their own ways, that is, to live according to their own choosing. Yet the eternal goodness of their Creator did not turn away from them so as not to admonish them with some tokens of His own, of their duty to know and fear Him." Prosper of Aquitaine, *De Vocatione Gentium* 2, 4, *The Call of All Nations,* vol. 14 of Ancient Christian Writers, trans. and ann. P. DeLetter (New York; Ramsey, NJ: Paulist Press, 1978), 95.] *Cœlum et terra, et omnia quæ in eis sunt, ecce undique mihi dicunt ut te amem, nec cessant dicere omnibus, ut sint inexcusabiles.* ["And also the heaven, and earth, and all that is therein, behold, on every side they say that I should love Thee; nor do they cease to speak unto all, 'so that they are without excuse.'" Augustine, *The Confessions of Saint Augustine,* NPNF[1] 1:144; PL 32, col. 0782.]

these properties also. For whereas by cursing the earth, and filling all the elements oftentimes with signs of his anger and indignation, he has, as the apostle tells us, "revealed from heaven his wrath against all ungodliness and unrighteousness of men" (Rom. 1:18); yet not proceeding immediately to destroy all things, he has manifested his patience and forbearance to all. This Paul tells us: "He suffered[6] all nations to walk in their own ways; yet he left not himself without witness, in that he did good, and gave rain from heaven and fruitful seasons, filling their hearts with food and gladness" (Acts 14:16–17). A large account of his goodness and wisdom herein the psalmist gives us throughout Psalm 104. By these ways he bare witness to his own goodness and patience; and so it is said, "He endures with much longsuffering," etc. (Rom. 9:22). But now, here all the world is at a stand; by all this they have but an obscure glimpse of God, and see not so much as his back parts. Moses saw not that, until he was put into the rock (Ex. 33:22); and that rock was Christ (1 Cor. 10:4). There are some of the most eminent and glorious properties of God (I mean, in the manifestation whereof he will be most glorious; otherwise his properties are not to be compared) that there is not the least glimpse to be attained of out of the Lord Christ, but only by and in him; and some that comparatively we have no light of but in him; and of all the rest no *true* light but by him:

Of the first sort, whereof not the least guess and imagination can enter into the heart of man but only by Christ, are *love* and *pardoning mercy*:

Love; I mean *love unto sinners*. Without this, man is of all creatures most miserable; and there is not the least glimpse of it that can possibly be discovered but in Christ. The Holy Ghost says, "God is love" (1 John 4:8, 16); that is, not only of a loving and tender nature, but one that will exercise himself in a dispensation of his love, eternal love, toward us—one that has purposes of love for us from of old, and will fulfill them all toward us in due season. But how is this demonstrated? How may we attain an acquaintance with it? He tells us, "In this was manifested the love of God, because that God sent his only begotten Son into the world, that we might live through him" (1 John 4:9). This is the only discovery that God has made of any such property in his nature, or of any thought of exercising it toward sinners—in that he has sent Jesus Christ into the world, that we might live by him. Where now is the wise, where is the scribe, where is the disputer of this world, with all

---

6. allowed, permitted, tolerated.

their wisdom [1 Cor. 1:20]? Their voice must be that of the hypocrites in Zion (Isa. 33:14–15). That wisdom which cannot teach me that God is love, shall ever pass for folly. Let men go to the sun, moon, and stars, to showers of rain and fruitful seasons, and answer truly what by them they learn hereof. Let them not think themselves wiser or better than those that went before them, who, to a man, got nothing by them, but being left inexcusable.

Pardoning mercy, or grace. Without this, even his love would be fruitless. What discovery may be made of this by a sinful man, may be seen in the father of us all; who, when he had sinned, had no reserve for mercy, but hid himself (Gen. 3:8). He did it *l'ruakh hayyom*, when the wind did but a little blow at the presence of God; and he did it foolishly, thinking to "hide himself among trees!" (Ps. 139:7–8). "The law was given by Moses, but grace and truth came by Jesus Christ" (John 1:17)—grace in the truth and substance. Pardoning mercy, that comes by Christ alone; that pardoning mercy which is manifested in the gospel, and wherein God will be glorified to all eternity (Eph. 1:6). I mean not that general mercy, that velleity[7] of acceptance which some put their hopes in:[8] that *pathos* (which to ascribe unto God is the greatest dishonor that can be done him) shines not with one ray out of Christ; it is wholly treasured up in him and revealed by him. Pardoning mercy is God's free, gracious acceptance of a sinner upon satisfaction made to his justice in the blood of Jesus; nor is any discovery of it, but as relating to the satisfaction of justice, consistent with the glory of God. It is a mercy of inconceivable condescension in forgiveness, tempered with exact justice and severity.[9] God is said "to set forth Christ to be a propitiation through faith in his blood, to declare his righteousness in the remission of sins" (Rom. 3:25); his righteousness is also manifested in the business of forgiveness of sins: and therefore it is everywhere said to be wholly in Christ (Eph. 1:7). So that this gospel grace and pardoning mercy is alone purchased by him, and revealed in him. And this was the main end of all typical

---

7. inclination, mere desire, wish.

8. *Hestō dē eleos, lupē tis epi phainomenō kakō phthartikō kai lupērō tou anaxiou tugchanein.* ["Let pity then be a kind of pain excited by the sight of evil, deadly or painful, which befalls one who does not deserve it." Aristotle, *The "Art" of Rhetoric*, Loeb Classical Library, trans. John Henry Freese (Cambridge, MA: Harvard University Press, 1967), 225.] *Quid autem misericordia, nisi alienæ miseriæ quædam in nostro corde compassio; quâ alicui, si possumus, subvenire compellimur?* ["And what is compassion but a fellow-feeling for another's misery, which prompts us to help him if we can?" Augustine, *The City of God*, NPNF[1] 2:169; PL 41, col. 0261.]

9. *katakauchatai eleos kriseōs* ("mercy rejoices against judgment"), James 2:13.

institutions—to manifest that remission and forgiveness is wholly wrapped up in the Lord Christ, and that out of him there is not the least conjecture to be made of it, nor the least morsel to be tasted. Had not God set forth the Lord Christ, all the angels in heaven and men on earth could not have apprehended that there had been any such thing in the nature of God as this grace of pardoning mercy [1 Pet. 1:12]. The apostle asserts the full manifestation as well as the exercise of this mercy to be in Christ only: "After that the kindness and love of God our Savior toward man appeared" (Titus 3:4–5)—namely, in the sending of Christ, and the declaration of him in the gospel. Then was this pardoning mercy and salvation not by works discovered.

And these are of those properties of God whereby he will be known, whereof there is not the least glimpse to be obtained but by and in Christ; and whoever knows him not by these, knows him not at all. They know an idol, and not the only true God. He that has not the Son, the same has not the Father (1 John 2:23); and not to have God as a Father, is not to have him at all; and he is known as a Father only as he is love, and full of pardoning mercy in Christ. How this is to be had the Holy Ghost tells us: "The Son of God is come and has given us an understanding, that we may know him that is true" (1 John 5:20). By him alone we have our understanding to know him that is true. Now, these properties of God Christ reveals in his doctrine, in the revelation he makes of God and his will, as the great prophet of the church (John 17:6). And on this account the knowledge of them is exposed to all, with an evidence unspeakably surmounting that which is given by the creation to his eternal power and Godhead. But the life of this knowledge lies in an acquaintance with his person, wherein the express image and beams of this glory of his Father do shine forth (Heb. 1:3); of which before.

There are other properties of God which, though also otherwise discovered, yet are so clearly, eminently, and savingly only in Jesus Christ: (1) his *vindictive justice* in punishing sin; (2) his *patience, forbearance,* and *longsuffering* toward sinners; (3) his *wisdom,* in managing things for his own glory; (4) his *all-sufficiency,* in himself and unto others. All these, though they may receive some lower and inferior manifestations out of Christ, yet they clearly shine only in him; so as that it may be our wisdom to be acquainted with them.

His *vindictive justice.* God has, indeed, [in] many ways manifested his indignation and anger against sin; so that men cannot but know that it is "the judgment of God, that they which commit such things are worthy of death" (Rom. 1:32). He has in the law threatened to kindle a fire in his anger that shall burn to the very heart of hell. And even in many providential dispensations, "his wrath is revealed from heaven against all the ungodliness of men" (Rom. 1:18). So that men must say that he is a God of *judgment*. And he that shall but consider that the angels for sin were cast from heaven, shut up under chains of everlasting darkness unto the judgment of the great day (the rumor whereof seems to have been spread among the Gentiles, whence the poet makes his Jupiter threaten the inferior rebellious deities with that punishment[10]); and how Sodom and Gomorrah were condemned with an overthrow, and burned into ashes, that they might be "examples unto those that should after live ungodly" (2 Pet. 2:6); cannot but discover much of God's vindictive justice and his anger against sin. But far more clear does this shine into us in the Lord Christ:

First, in him God has manifested the *naturalness* of this righteousness unto him, in that it was impossible that it should be diverted from sinners without the interposing of a propitiation. Those who lay the necessity of satisfaction merely upon the account of a free act and determination of the will of God, leave, to my apprehension, no just and indispensable foundation for the death of Christ, but lay it upon a supposition of that which might have been otherwise.[11] But plainly, God, in that he spared not his only Son, but made his soul an offering for sin, and would admit of no atonement but in his blood, has abundantly manifested that it is of necessity to him (his holiness and righteousness requiring it) to render indignation, wrath, tribulation, and anguish unto sin.[12] And the knowledge of this *naturalness* of vindictive justice, with the *necessity* of its execution on supposition of sin, is the only true and useful knowledge of it. To look upon it as that which God may exercise or forbear, makes his justice not a property of his nature, but a free act of his *will*; and a *will to punish* where one may do otherwise without injustice, is rather ill-will than justice.

---

10. *Ē min helōn rhipsō ex Tartaron ēeroenta / Tēle mal hēchi bathiston hupo chthonos esti berethron / Entha sidēreiai te pulai kai chalkeos oudos / Tosson enerth Aideō, hoson ouranos est apo gaiēs.* ["I shall take him and hurl him into the murky Tartarus, far, far away, where is the deepest gulf beneath the earth, the gates whereof are of iron and the threshhold of bronze, as far beneath Hades as heaven is above the earth." Homer, *The Illiad I*, Loeb Classical Library, trans. A. T. Murray (Cambridge, MA: Harvard University Press, 1954), 339.]

11. John Owen, *Vid. Diatrib. De Just. Divin.* ["A Dissertation on Divine Justice: or, the Claims of Vindicatory Justice Vindicated" (1653), *Works*, 10:481–624.]

12. Rom. 8:32; Isa. 53:10; Heb. 10:7–9; Rom. 1:32; 2 Thess. 1:5–6; Ps. 5:5–6; Hab. 1:13; Ps. 119:137.

Second, in the *penalty* inflicted on Christ for sin, this justice is far more gloriously manifested than otherwise. To see, indeed, a world, made good and beautiful, wrapped up in wrath and curses, clothed with thorns and briers; to see the whole beautiful creation made subject to vanity, given up to the bondage of corruption; to hear it groan in pain under that burden; to consider legions of angels, most glorious and immortal creatures, cast down into hell, bound with chains of darkness, and reserved for a more dreadful judgment for one sin; to view the ocean of the blood of souls spilt to eternity on this account[13]—will give some insight into this thing. But what is all this to that view of it which may be had by a spiritual eye in the Lord Christ? All these things are worms, and of no value in comparison of him. To see him who is the wisdom of God, and the power of God (1 Cor. 1:30), always beloved of the Father (Matt. 3:17); to see him, I say, fear, and tremble, and bow, and sweat, and pray, and die; to see him lifted up upon the cross, the earth trembling under him, as if unable to bear his weight; and the heavens darkened over him, as if shut against his cry; and himself hanging between both, as if refused by both; and all this because our sins did meet upon him[14]—this of all things does most abundantly manifest the severity of God's vindictive justice. Here, or nowhere, is it to be learned.

His *patience*, *forbearance*, and *longsuffering* toward sinners. There are many glimpses of the patience of God shining out in the works of his providence; but all exceedingly beneath that discovery of it which we have in Christ, especially in these three things:

First, the *manner* of its discovery. This, indeed, is evident to all, that God does not ordinarily *immediately punish* men upon their offences. It may be learned from his constant way in governing the world: notwithstanding all provocations, yet he does good to men; causing his sun to shine upon them, sending them rain and fruitful seasons, filling their hearts with food and gladness.[15] Hence it was easy for them to conclude that there was in him abundance of goodness and forbearance. But all this is yet in much darkness, being the exurgency[16] of men's reasonings from their observations; yea, the management of it [God's patience] has been such as that it has proved a snare almost universally unto them

---

13. Gen. 3:17–19, 8:21; Rom. 8:21–22; 2 Pet. 2:4–6; 3:6; Jude 6–7.

14. Matt. 26:37–38; Mark 14:33; Luke 22:43–44; Heb. 5:7; Matt. 27:51; Mark 15:33–34; Isa. 53:6.

15. Matt. 5:45; Acts 14:17–18.

16. urgent force

toward whom it has been exercised (Eccl. 8:11), as well as a temptation to them who have looked on (Job 21:7; Ps. 73:2–4, etc.; Jer. 12:1; Hab. 1:13). The discovery of it in Christ is utterly of another nature. In him the very nature of God is discovered to be love and kindness; and that he will exercise the same to sinners, he has promised, sworn, and solemnly engaged himself by covenant. And that we may not hesitate about the aim which he has herein, there is a stable bottom and foundation of acting suitably to those gracious properties of his nature held forth—namely, the reconciliation and atonement that is made in the blood of Christ. Whatever discovery were made of the patience and lenity of God unto us, yet if it were not withal revealed that the other properties of God, as his justice and revenge for sin, had their actings also assigned to them to the full, there could be little consolation gathered from the former. And therefore, though God may teach men his goodness and forbearance, by sending them rain and fruitful seasons, yet withal at the same time, upon all occasions, "revealing his wrath from heaven against the ungodliness of men" (Rom. 1:18), it is impossible that they should do anything but miserably fluctuate and tremble at the event of these dispensations; and yet this is the best that men can have out of Christ, the utmost they can attain unto. With the present possession of good things administered in this patience, men might, and did for a season, take up their thoughts and satiate themselves; but yet they were not in the least delivered from the bondage they were in by reason of death, and the darkness attending it.[17] The law reveals no patience or forbearance in God; it speaks, as to the issue of transgressions, nothing but sword and fire, had not God interposed by an act of sovereignty. But now, as was said, with that revelation of forbearance which we have in Christ, there is also a discovery of the satisfaction of his justice and wrath against sin; so that we need not fear any actings from them to interfere with the works of his patience, which are so sweet unto us. Hence God is said to be "in Christ, reconciling the world to himself" (2 Cor. 5:19); manifesting himself in him as one that has now no more to do for the manifestation of all his attributes—that is, for the glorifying of himself—but only to forbear, reconcile, and pardon sin in him.

---

17. *Animula vagula, blandula* / *Hospes comesque corporis* / *Quæ nunc abibis in loca* / *Pallida, rigida, nudula?* / *Nec ut soles dabis jocos.* ["Deer fleeting sweeting, little soul / My body's comrade and its guest, / What region now must be thy goal, / Poor little wan, numb, naked soul, / Unable, as of old, to jest?" "Hadrian's Dying Farewell to His Soul," in *Minor Latin Poets*, vol. 2, Loeb Classical Library, trans. J. Wight Duff and Arnold M. Duff (Cambridge, MA: Harvard University Press, 1998), 445.]

Second, in the *nature* of it. What is there in that forbearance which out of Christ is revealed? Merely a not immediate punishing upon the offense, and, withal, giving and continuing temporal mercies;[18] such things as men are prone to abuse, and may perish with their bosoms full of them to eternity. That which lies hid in Christ, and is revealed from him, is full of love, sweetness, tenderness, kindness, grace. It is the Lord's waiting to be gracious to sinners; waiting for an advantage to show love and kindness, for the most eminent endearing of a soul unto himself: "Therefore will the LORD wait, that he may be gracious unto you; and therefore will he be exalted, that he may have mercy upon you" (Isa. 30:18). Neither is there any revelation of God that the soul finds more sweetness in than this. When it [i.e., one's soul] is experimentally convinced that God from time to time has passed by many, innumerable iniquities, he is astonished to think that God should do so; and admires that he did not take the advantage of his provocations to cast him out of his presence. He finds that, with infinite wisdom, in all longsuffering, he has managed all his dispensations toward him to recover him from the power of the devil, to rebuke and chasten his spirit for sin, to endear him unto himself—there is, I say, nothing of greater sweetness to the soul than this: and therefore the apostle says that all is "through the forbearance of God" (Rom. 3:25). God makes way for complete forgiveness of sins through this his forbearance; which the other does not.

Third, they differ in their *ends and aims*. What is the aim and design of God in the dispensation of that forbearance which is manifested and may be discovered out of Christ? The apostle tells us, "What if God, willing to show his wrath, and to make his power known, endured with much longsuffering the vessels of wrath fitted for destruction?" (Rom. 9:22). It was but to leave them inexcusable, that his power and wrath against sin might be manifested in their destruction. And therefore he calls it "a suffering of them to walk in their own ways" (Acts 14:16); which elsewhere he holds out as a most dreadful judgment—to wit, in respect of that issue whereto it will certainly come; as "I gave them up unto their own hearts' lusts, and they walked in their own counsels" (Ps. 81:12): which is as dreadful a condition as a creature is capable of falling into in this world.[19] He calls it a "winking at the sins of their

---

18. Rom. 2:4–5; 9:22.

19. *Eos, quibus indulgere videtur, quibus parcere, molles venturis malis (Deus) format.* ["Those, however, whom he seems to favour, whom he seems to spare, he is really keeping soft against ills to come." Seneca, *Seneca: Moral Essays I*, Loeb Classical Library, trans. John W. Basore (Cambridge, MA: Harvard University Press, 1958), 29.] *Pro dii immortales! Cur interdum in hominum sceleribus*

ignorance"; as it were, taking no care nor thought of them in their dark condition, as it appears by the antithesis, "But now he commands all men everywhere to repent" (Acts 17:30). He did not take so much notice of them then as to command them to repent, by any clear revelation of his mind and will. And therefore the exhortation of the apostle—"Despise you the riches of his goodness and forbearance and long suffering, not knowing that the goodness of God leads you to repentance?" (Rom. 2:4)—is spoken to the Jews, who had advantages to learn the natural tendency of that goodness and forbearance which God exercises in Christ; which, indeed, leads to repentance: or else he does in general intimate that, in very reason, men ought to make another use of those things than usually they do, and which he charges them with, "But after our hardness and impenitent heart" (Rom. 2:5), etc. At best, then, the patience of God unto men out of Christ, by reason of their own incorrigible stubbornness, proves but like the waters of the river Phasis, that are sweet at the top and bitter in the bottom;[20] they swim for a while in the sweet and good things of this life (Luke 16:25); wherewith being filled, they sink to the depth of all bitterness.

But now, evidently and directly, the end of that patience and forbearance of God which is exercised in Christ, and discovered in him to us, is the saving and bringing into God those toward whom he is pleased to exercise them. And therefore Peter tells you that he is "longsuffering toward us, not willing that any should perish, but that all should come to repentance" (2 Pet. 3:9)—that is, all us toward whom he exercises forbearance; for that is the end of it, that his will concerning our repentance and salvation may be accomplished. And the nature of it, with its end, is well expressed: "This is as the waters of Noah unto me: for as I have sworn that the waters of Noah should no more go over the earth, so have I sworn that I would not be wroth"[21] (Isa. 54:9), etc. It is God's taking a course, in his infinite wisdom and goodness, that we shall not be destroyed notwithstanding our sins; and therefore, these two things

---

maximis, aut connivetis, aut praesentis fraudis poenas in diem reservatis! ["Why, immortal Gods, when men commit the greatest crimes do ye sometimes overlook them or reserve to some future day punishment for a crime of the present?" Cicero, *Pro Caelio*, 24, *Cicero XII: Pro Caelio, De provinciis consularibus, and Pro Balbo*, Loeb Classical Library, trans. R. Gardner (Cambridge, MA: Harvard University Press, 1999), 479.]

20. *Kata men tou epirrheontos bapsanta, gluku to hudōr animēsasthai ei de eis bathos tis kathēken tēn kalpin, halmuron.* ["If one should dip just beneath the surface, it is possible to draw out fresh water, but then, by sinking the cup deeper, to draw out salty water." Arrian of Nicomedia, *Arrian: Periplus Ponti Euxini*, ed. and trans. Aiden Little (London: Bristol Classical Press, 2003), 61.]

21. wrathful

are laid together in God, as coming together from him, "The God of patience and consolation" (Rom. 15:5): his patience is a matter of the greatest consolation. And this is another property of God, which, though it may break forth in some rays, to some ends and purposes, in other things, yet the treasures of it are hid in Christ; and none is acquainted with it, unto any spiritual advantage, that learns it not in him.

His *wisdom*, his infinite wisdom, in managing things for his own glory, and the good of them toward whom he has thoughts of love. The Lord, indeed, has laid out and manifested infinite wisdom in his works of creation, providence, and governing of his world:[22] in wisdom has he made all his creatures. "How manifold are his works! In wisdom has he made them all; the earth is full of his riches" (Ps. 104:24). So in his providence, his supportment and guidance of all things, in order to one another, and his own glory, unto the ends appointed for them; for all these things "come forth from the LORD of hosts, who is wonderful in counsel, and excellent in working" (Isa. 28:29). His law also is forever to be admired, for the excellency of the wisdom therein (Deut. 4:7–8). But yet there is that which Paul is astonished at, and wherein God will forever be exalted, which he calls "the depth of the riches of the wisdom and knowledge of God" (Rom. 11:33)—that is only hid in and revealed by Christ. Hence, as he is said to be "the wisdom of God" (1 Cor. 1:20, 30) and to be "made unto us wisdom" (1 Cor. 1:30); so the design of God, which is carried along in him and revealed in the gospel, is called "the wisdom of God" and a "mystery; even the hidden wisdom which God ordained before the world was; which none of the princes of this world knew" (1 Cor. 2:7–8). [In] Ephesians 3:10 it is called "the manifold wisdom of God"; and to discover the depth and riches of this wisdom, he tells us in that verse that it is such, that principalities and powers, that very angels themselves, could not in the least measure get any acquaintance with it, until God, by gathering of a church of sinners, did actually discover it. Hence Peter informs us that they who are so well acquainted with all the works of God, do yet bow down and desire with earnestness to look into these things (the things of the wisdom of

---

22. *Si amabilis est sapientia cum cognitione rerum conditarum, quam amabilis est sapientia, quæ condidit omnia ex nihilo!* ["If wisdom with the knowledge of created things is lovely, how lovely is the wisdom, which created all things from nothing!" This quote is not found in Owen's citation, Augustine, *Meditations* (PL 40, cols. 897–942), a work once attributed to Augustine; cf. *Meditations of Saint Augustine*, trans. Matthew J. O'Connell and ed. John E. Rottelle (Villanova, PA: Augustinian Press, 1995). Rather, it is found in another work that has also been attributed to Augustine: *De spiritu et anima liber unus*, PL 40, col. 828.]

God in the gospel) (1 Pet. 1:12). It asks a man much wisdom to make a curious work, fabric, and building; but if one shall come and deface it, to raise up the same building to more beauty and glory than ever, this is excellence of wisdom indeed. God in the beginning made all things good, glorious, and beautiful. When all things had an innocence and beauty, the clear impress of his wisdom and goodness upon them (Gen. 1:31), they were very glorious; especially man, who was made for his special glory. Now, all this beauty was defaced by sin, and the whole creation rolled up in darkness, wrath, curses, confusion, and the great praise of God buried in the heaps of it.[23] Man, especially, was utterly lost, and came short of the glory of God, for which he was created (Rom. 3:23). Here, now, does the depth of the riches of the wisdom and knowledge of God open itself. A design in Christ shines out from his bosom, that was lodged there from eternity, to recover things to such an estate as shall be exceedingly to the advantage of his glory, infinitely above what at first appeared, and for the putting of sinners into inconceivably a better condition than they were in before the entrance of sin. He appears now glorious; he is known to be a God pardoning iniquity and sin,[24] and *advances the riches of his grace*: which was his design (Eph. 1:6). He has infinitely vindicated his justice also, in the face of men, angels, and devils, in setting forth his Son for a propitiation (Rom. 3:24–25). It is also to our advantage; we are more fully established in his favor, and are carried on toward a more exceeding weight of glory than formerly was revealed (2 Cor. 4:17). Hence was that ejaculation of one of the ancients, "O *felix culpa, quæ talem meruit redemptorem!*"[25] Thus Paul tells us, "Great is the mystery of godliness" (1 Tim. 3:16), and that "without controversy." We receive "grace for grace" (John 1:16)—for that grace lost in Adam, better grace in Christ. Confessedly, this is a depth of wisdom indeed. And of the love of Christ to his church, and his union with it, to carry on this business, "This is a great mystery," says the apostle (Eph. 5:32); great wisdom lies herein.

So, then, this also is hid in Christ—the great and unspeakable riches of the wisdom of God, in *pardoning* sin, *saving* sinners, satisfying *justice*, fulfilling the *law*, repairing his own *honor*, and providing for us a

---

23. Gen. 3:17–18; Rom. 1:18.

24. Exod. 33:18–19; 34:6–7.

25. Lat. "O happy fault, that merited such and so great a Redeemer!" Owen also uses this same expression in his sermon "A Vision of Unchangeable, Free Mercy," in *Works*, 8:35. This translation is Owen's own, found in that sermon. Originally this expression comes from the Exultent Hymn, apparently used in the Roman liturgy between the fifth and seventh centuries.

more exceeding weight of glory; and all this out of such a condition as wherein it was impossible that it should enter into the hearts of angels or men how ever the glory of God should be repaired, and one sinning creature delivered from everlasting ruin. Hence it is said, that at the last day God "shall be glorified in his saints, and admired in all them that believe" (2 Thess. 1:10). It shall be an admirable thing, and God shall be forever glorious in it, even in the bringing of believers to himself. To save sinners through believing, shall be found to be a far more admirable work than to create the world of nothing.

His *all-sufficiency* is the last of this sort that I shall name.

God's all-sufficiency in himself is his absolute and universal perfection, whereby nothing is wanting *in* him, nothing *to* him: No accession can be made to his fullness, no decrease or wasting can happen thereunto. There is also in him an all-sufficiency for others; which is his power to impart and communicate his goodness and himself so to them as to satisfy and fill them, in their utmost capacity, with whatever is good and desirable to them. For the first of these—his all-sufficiency for the communication of his *goodness*, that is, in the outward effect of it—God abundantly manifested in the creation, in that he made all things good, all things perfect; that is, to whom nothing was wanting in their own kind—he put a stamp of his own goodness upon them all. But now for the latter—his giving *himself* as an all-sufficient God, to be *enjoyed* by the creatures, to hold out all that is in him *for the satiating and making them blessed*—that is alone discovered by and in Christ. In him he is a Father, a God in covenant, wherein he has promised to lay out himself for them; in him has he promised to give himself into their everlasting fruition, as their exceeding great reward.

And so I have insisted on the second sort of properties in God, whereof, though we have some obscure glimpse in other things, yet the clear knowledge of them, and acquaintance with them, is only to be had in the Lord Christ.

That which remains is briefly to declare that not any of the properties of God whatever can be known, savingly and to consolation, but only in him; and so, consequently, all the wisdom of the knowledge of God is hid in him alone, and from him to be obtained.

SAVING KNOWLEDGE OF AND COMFORT FROM GOD'S ATTRIBUTES ARE FOUND ONLY IN CHRIST

There is no *saving knowledge of any property of God*, nor such as brings *consolation*, but what alone is to be had in Christ Jesus, being laid up in him, and manifested by him. Some eye the justice of God, and know that this is his righteousness, "that they which do such things" (as sin) "are worthy of death" (Rom. 1:32). But this is to no other end but to make them cry, "Who amongst us shall dwell with the devouring fire?" (Isa. 33:14). Others fix upon his patience, goodness, mercy, forbearance; but it does not at all lead them to repentance; but "they despise the riches of his goodness, and after their hardness and impenitent hearts treasure up unto themselves wrath against the day of wrath" (Rom. 2:4–5). Others, by the very works of creation and providence, come to know "his eternal power and Godhead; but they glorify him not as God, nor are thankful, but become vain in their imagination, and their foolish hearts are darkened" (Rom. 1:21). Whatever discovery men have of truth out of Christ, they "hold it captive under unrighteousness" (v. 18). Hence Jude tells us that "in what they know naturally, as brute beasts, in those things they corrupt themselves" (v. 10).

That we may have a saving knowledge of the properties of God, attended with consolation, these three things are required: (1) that God has *manifested* the glory of them all in a way of doing good unto us. (2) that he will yet *exercise* and lay them out to the utmost in our behalf. (3) that, being so *manifested and exercised*, they are fit and powerful to bring us to the everlasting fruition of himself; which is our blessedness. Now, all these three lie hid in Christ; and the least glimpse of them out of him is not to be attained.

This is to be received, that God has actually *manifested* the glory of all his attributes in a way of doing us good. What will it avail our souls, what comfort will it bring unto us, what endearment will it put upon our hearts unto God, to know that he is infinitely righteous, just, and holy, unchangeably true and faithful, if we know not how he may preserve the glory of his justice and faithfulness in his comminations[26] and threatenings, but only in our ruin and destruction? If we can from thence only say it is a righteous thing with him to recompense tribulation unto us for our iniquities? What fruit of this consideration had Adam in the garden (Genesis 3)? What sweetness, what encouragement, is there in knowing that he is *patient* and *full of forbearance*, if the glory of these is to be exalted in enduring the vessels of wrath fitted for destruction? Nay, what will it avail us to hear him proclaim himself "The LORD, the LORD God, merciful and gracious, abundant in goodness and truth," yet, withal, that he will "by no means clear the guilty" (Ex. 34:6–7)—so shutting

---

26. denunciations, threats.

up the exercise of all his other properties toward us, upon the account of our iniquity? Doubtless, not at all. Under this naked consideration of the properties of God, justice will make men fly and hide (Genesis 3; Isa. 2:21; 33:15–16)—patience [will] render them obdurate[27] (Eccl. 8:11). Holiness utterly deters them from all thoughts of approach unto him (Josh. 24:19). What relief have we from thoughts of his immensity and omnipresence, if we have cause only to contrive how to fly from him (Ps. 139:11–12), if we have no pledge of his gracious presence with us? This is that which brings salvation, when we shall see that God has glorified all his properties in a way of doing us good. Now, this he has done in Jesus Christ. In him has he made his justice glorious, in making all our iniquities to meet upon him, causing him to bear them all, as the scape-goat in the wilderness; not sparing him, but giving him up to death for us all[28]—so exalting his justice and indignation against sin in a way of freeing us from the condemnation of it (Rom. 3:25; 8:33–34). In him has he made his truth glorious, and his faithfulness, in the exact accomplishment of all his absolute threatenings and promises. That fountain-threat and commination whence all others flow: "In the day you eat thereof you shall die the death" (Gen. 2:17); seconded with a curse (Deut. 27:26): "Cursed is everyone that continues not," etc. (Gal. 3:10)—is in him accomplished, fulfilled, and the truth of God in them laid in a way to our good. He, by the grace of God, tasted death for us (Heb. 2:9); and so delivered us who were subject to death (Heb. 2:15); and he has fulfilled the curse, by being made a curse for us (Gal. 3:13). So that in his very threatenings his truth is made glorious in a way to our good. And for his promises, "They are all yea, and in him Amen, unto the glory of God by us" (2 Cor. 1:20). And for his mercy, goodness, and the riches of his grace, how eminently are they made glorious in Christ, and advanced for our good! God has set him forth to declare his righteousness for the forgiveness of sin; he has made way in him forever to exalt the glory of his pardoning mercy toward sinners. To manifest this is the great design of the gospel, as Paul admirably sets it out (Eph. 1:5–8). There must our souls come to an acquaintance with them, or forever live in darkness.

Now, this is a *saving knowledge*, and full of consolation, when we can see all the properties of God made glorious and exalted in a way of doing us good. And this wisdom is hid only in Jesus Christ. Hence, when he desired his Father to glorify his *name* (John 12:24)—to make

---

27. hardened, unyielding, obstinate.
28. Isa. 53:5–6; Lev. 16:21; Rom. 8:32.

in him his name (that is, his nature, his properties, his will) all glorious in that work of redemption he had in hand—he was instantly answered from heaven, "I have both glorified it and will glorify it again" [John 12:28]. He will give it its utmost glory in him.

That God will yet *exercise* and lay out those properties of his to the utmost in our behalf. Though he has made them all glorious in a way that may tend to our good, yet it does not absolutely follow that he will *use* them for our good; for do we not see innumerable persons perishing everlastingly, notwithstanding the manifestation of himself which God has made in Christ. Wherefore further, God has committed all his properties into the hand of Christ, if I may so say, to be managed in our behalf and for our good. He is "the power of God, and the wisdom of God" (1 Cor. 1:24); he is "the LORD our Righteousness" (Jer. 23:6) and is "made unto us of God wisdom, and righteousness, sanctification, and redemption" (1 Cor. 1:30). Christ having glorified his Father in all his attributes, he has now the exercise of them committed to him, that he might be the captain of salvation [Heb. 2:10] to them that do believe; so that if, in the righteousness, the goodness, the love, the mercy, the all-sufficiency of God, there be any thing that will do us good, the Lord Jesus is fully interested with the dispensing of it in our behalf. Hence God is said to be "in him, reconciling the world unto himself" (2 Cor. 5:18). Whatever is in him, he lays it out for the reconciliation of the world, in and by the Lord Christ; and he becomes "the LORD our Righteousness" (Isa. 45:24–25). And this is the second thing required.

There remains only, then, that these attributes of God, so manifested and exercised, are *powerful and able* to bring us to the everlasting fruition of him. To evince this, the Lord wraps up the whole covenant of grace in *one* promise, signifying no less: "I will be your God." In the covenant, God becomes our God, and we are his people; and thereby all his attributes are ours also. And lest that we should doubt—when once our eyes are opened to see in any measure the inconceivable difficulty that is in this thing, what unimaginable obstacles on all hands there lie against us—that all is not enough to deliver and save us, God has, I say, wrapped it up in this expression, Genesis 17:1: "I am," says he, "God Almighty" (all-sufficient)[29]—"I am wholly able to perform all my undertakings, and to be your exceeding great reward. I can

---

29. *Shaddai, Aquila interpretatur alkimon, quod nos robustum et ad omnia perpetranda sufficientem possumus dicere.* ["Shaddai, Aquila translated as "strong," because we can say that he is firm and equipped to do all things." Jerome, *Epistles* cxxxvi; PL 22, col. 429.]

remove all difficulties, answer all objections, pardon all sins, conquer all opposition: I am God all-sufficient." Now, you know in whom this covenant and all the promises thereof are ratified, and in whose blood it is confirmed—to wit, in the Lord Christ alone; in him only is God an all-sufficient God to any, and an exceeding great reward. And hence Christ himself is said to "save to the uttermost them that come to God by him" (Heb. 7[:25]). And these three things, I say, are required to be known, that we may have a saving acquaintance, and such as is attended with consolation, with any of the properties of God; and all these being hid only in Christ, from him alone it is to be obtained.

This, then, is the first part of our first demonstration—that all true and sound wisdom and knowledge is laid up in the Lord Christ, and from him alone to be obtained; because our wisdom, consisting, in a main part of it, in the knowledge of God, his nature, and his properties, this lies wholly hid in Christ, nor can possibly be obtained but by him.

True Wisdom and Knowledge Consist in the Knowledge of Ourselves

For the *knowledge of ourselves*, which is the second part of our wisdom,[30] this consists in these three things, which our Savior sends his Spirit to convince the world of—even "sin, righteousness, and judgment" (John 16:8). To know ourselves in reference unto these three is a main part of true and sound wisdom; for they all respect the supernatural and immortal end whereunto we are appointed; and there is none of these that we can attain unto but only in Christ.

KNOWING OURSELVES IN REFERENCE TO SIN

In respect of *sin*. There is a sense and knowledge of sin left in the *consciences* of all men by nature. To tell them what is good and evil in many things, to approve and disapprove of what they do, in reference to a *judgment* to come, they need not go further than themselves (Rom. 2:14–15). But this is obscure, and relates mostly to greater sins, and is in sum that which the apostle gives us, "They know the judgment of God, that they which do such things are worthy of death" (Rom. 1:32). This he places among the common presumptions and notions that are

---

30. *Hē sophia esti tōn timiōtatōn.* [This is an abridgement of Aristotle's larger sentence that reads, "That *Wisdom* is both Scientific Knowledge and Intuitive Intelligence as regards the things *of the most exalted* nature." *Aristotle: The Nicomachean Ethics*, trans. H. Rackham (Cambridge, MA: Harvard University Press, 1962), 344–45 (bk. 6 ch. 7.5)].

received by mankind—namely, that it is "righteous with God, that they who do such things are worthy of death" (Rom. 1:32).[31] And if that be true, which is commonly received, that no nation is so barbarous or rude, but it retains *some sense of a Deity*; then this also is true, that there is no nation but has *a sense of sin*, and the displeasure of God for it. For this is the very first notion of God in the world, that he is the rewarder of good and evil.[32] Hence were all the sacrifices, purgings,

---

31. *To dikaiōma tou theou epignontes hoti hoi ta toiauta prassontes axioi thanatou eisin* [Rom. 1:32]. *Perfecto demum scelere, magnitudo ejus intellecta est.* ["But only with the comtemplation of the crime was its magnitude realized by the Caesar." Tacitus, *The Annals of Tacitus*, in *Tacitus IV: The Annals, Books XIII–XVI*, Loeb Classical Library, trans. John Jackson (Cambridge, MA: Harvard University Press, 1937), 123.] *To chrēma pascheis? tis s apollusin nosos; / He sunesis, hoti sunoida dein eirgasmenos.* ["Menelaus: 'What aileth thee? What sickness ruineth thee?' Orestes: 'Conscience!—to know I have wrought a fearful deed.'" *Orestes*, from *Euripides II: Electra, Orestes, Iphigeneia in Taurica, Andromache, Cyclops*, Loeb Classical Library, trans. Arthur S. Way (Cambridge, MA: Harvard University Press, 1958), 157.]

32. *Primus est deorum cultus, Deos credere: deinde reddere illis majestatem suam, reddere bonitatem, sine qua nulla majestas est. Scire illos esse qui præsident mundo: qui universa vi sua temperant: qui humani generis tutelam gerunt.* ["The first way to worship the gods is to believe in the gods; the next to acknowledge their majesty, to acknowledge their goodness without which there is no majesty. Also, to know that they are supreme commanders in the universe, controlling all things by their power and acting as guardians of the human race." Seneca, "Epistle 95," from *Seneca: Ad Lucilium epistulae morales in Three Volumes*, vol. 3, Loeb Classical Library, trans. Richard Gummere (Cambridge, MA: Harvard University Press, 1953), 89.] *Neque honor ullus deberi potest Deo, si nihil præstat colenti; nec ullus metus, si non irascitur non colenti.* ["And no honour can be due to God, if He affords nothing to His worshipers; and no fear, if He is not angry with him who does not worship Him." Lactantius, *A Treatise on the Anger of God: Addressed to Donatus*, ANF 7:262; PL 36, col. 0755.] *Raro antecedentem scelestum / Deseruit pede pœna claudo.* ["Rarely does Retribution fail to catch up with the criminal despite her limping gate." Horace, *Odes*, in *Odes and Epodes*, Loeb Classical Library, trans. and ed. Niall Rudd (Cambridge, MA: Harvard University Press, 2004), 147.] *Quo fugis Encelade? quascunque accesseris oras, / Sub Jove semper eris.* [Whither are you feeling, Enceladus? Whatever shores you reach, you will always be under Jupiter. Attributed to Virgil, as cited by John Gill, *Complete Body of Doctrinal and Practical Divinity*, 2 vols. (Grand Rapids, MI: Baker, 1978), 1:63.] *Hos tu / Evasisse putes, quos diri conscia facti / Mens habet attonitos, et surdo verbere cædit!* ["But why should you suppose that a man escapes punishment whose mind is ever kept in terror by the consciousness of an evil deed which lashes him with unheard blows." Juvenal, *Satire XIII*, from *Juvenal and Persius*, Loeb Classical Library, trans. G. G. Ramsey (Cambridge, MA: Harvard University Press, 1965), 261.] *Oiei su tous thanontas ō Nikostrate, / Truphēs hapasēs metalabontas en biō, / Pepheugenai, to theion ōs lelēthotas; / Estin Dikēs ophthalmos, hos ta panth hora. / Kai gar kath hadēn duo tribous nomizomen, / Mian dikaiōn, heteran d asebōn, ein hodon. / K ei tous duo kalupsei hē gē, Phasio chronō / Harpaz, apelthōn, klept, aposterei, kuka. / Mēden planēthēs, estai kan hadou krisis. / Hēnper poiēsei theos ho pantōn despotēs, / ou tounoma phoberon oud an onomasami egō.* ["Think'st thou, Nicostratus, the dead, who here / Enjoyed whate'er of good life offers man, / Escape the notice of Divinity, / As if they might forgotten be of Him? / Nay, there's an eye of Justice watching all; / For if the good and bad find the same end, / Then go thou, rob, steal, plunder, at thy will, / Do all the evil that to thee seems good. / Yet be not thou deceived; for underneath / There is a throne and place of judgment set, / Which God the Lord of all shall occupy; Whose name is terrible, nor shall I dare . . . , etc. / Philemon, as quoted by Justin Martyr in *Justin on the Sole Government of God*, ANF 1:290–91; PG 6, col. 320A-B. Cf. a similar quote

expiations, which were so generally spread over the face of the earth. But this was and is but very dark, in respect of that knowledge of sin with its appurtenances,[33] which is to be obtained.

A further knowledge of sin, upon all accounts whatever, is given by the law; that law which was "added because of transgressions" (Gal. 3:19; cf. Rom. 7:13). This revives *doctrinally* all that sense of good and evil which was at first implanted in man; and it is a glass, whereinto whosoever is able *spiritually* to look, may see sin in all its ugliness and deformity. The truth is, look upon the *law* in its purity, holiness, compass, and perfection; its *manner of delivery,*[34] with dread, terror, thunder, earthquakes, fire; the *sanction of it,* in death, curse, wrath; and it makes a wonderful discovery of sin, upon every account: its pollution, guilt, and exceeding sinfulness are seen by it. But yet all this does not suffice to give a man a true and thorough conviction of sin. Not but that the glass is clear, but of ourselves we have not eyes to look into it; the rule is straight, but we cannot apply it: and therefore Christ sends his Spirit to convince the world of sin (John 16:8); who, though, as to some ends and purposes, he makes use of the law, yet the work of *conviction,* which alone is a useful knowledge of sin, is his peculiar work. And so the discovery of sin may also be said to be by Christ—to be part of the wisdom that is hid in him [Col. 2:3]. But yet there is a twofold regard besides this, of his sending his Spirit to convince us, wherein this wisdom appears to be hid in him: First, because there are some near *concernments* of sin, which are more clearly held out in the Lord Christ's being made sin for us, than any other way. Secondly, in that there is no knowledge to be had of sin, so as to give it a *spiritual and saving improvement,* but only in him.

For the first, there are four things in sin that clearly shine out in the cross of Christ: (1) the *desert*[35] of it; (2) man's *impotency* by reason of it; (3) the *death* of it; (4) a *new end put to it.*

The *desert* of sin does clearly shine in the cross of Christ upon a twofold account: (1) of the *person* suffering for it; (2) of the *penalty* he underwent.

Of the person suffering for it. This the Scripture oftentimes very emphatically sets forth, and lays great weight upon: "God so loved the

---

attributed to the comic poet Diphilus in Clement of Alexander, *The Miscellanies, or Stromata,* ANF 2:472; PG 9, col. 532A.]

33. apparatus, instruments.

34. Ex. 19:18–20; Deut. 4:11; Heb. 12:18–21.

35. that which it deserves, punishment.

world, that he gave his only begotten Son" (John 3:16). It was his only
Son that God sent into the world to suffer for sin. "He spared not his
own Son, but delivered him up for us all" (Rom. 8:32). To see a slave
beaten and corrected, it argues a fault committed; but yet perhaps the
demerit of it was not very great. The correction of a son argues a great
provocation; that of an only son, the greatest imaginable. Never was sin
seen to be more abominably sinful and full of provocation than when
the burden of it was upon the shoulders of the Son of God. God having made his Son, the Son of his love, his only begotten, full of grace
and truth, sin for us (2 Cor. 5:21), to manifest his indignation against
it, and how utterly impossible it is that he should let the least sin go
unpunished, he lays hand on him (Zech. 13:7) and spares him not. If sin
be imputed to the dear Son of his bosom (Isa. 53:6), as upon his own
voluntary assumption of it it was—for he said to his Father, "Lo, I come
to do your will" (Heb. 10:7), and all our iniquities did meet on him—he
will not spare him anything of the due desert of it. Is it not most clear
from hence, even from the blood of the cross of Christ, that such is the
demerit of sin, that it is altogether impossible that God should pass by
any, the least, unpunished? If he would have done it for any, he would
have done it in reference to his only Son; but he spared him not.

Moreover, God is not at all delighted with, nor desirous of, the blood,
the tears, the cries, the inexpressible torments and sufferings, of the Son
of his love (for he delights not in the anguish of any—"he does not afflict
willingly, nor grieve the children of men" [Lam. 3:33], much less the
Son of his bosom); only he required that his law be fulfilled, his justice
satisfied, his wrath atoned for sin; and nothing less than all this would
bring it about. If the debt of sin might have been compounded for at a
cheaper rate, it had never been held up at the price of the blood of Christ.
Here, then, soul, take a view of the desert of sin; behold it far more
evident than in all the threatenings and curses of the law. "I thought,
indeed," may you say from thence, "that sin, being found on such a
poor worm as I am, was worthy of death; but that it should have this
effect if charged on the Son of God—*that* I never once imagined."

Consider also, further, what he suffered. For though he was so excellent a one, yet perhaps it was but a light affliction and trial that he
underwent, especially considering the strength he had to bear it. Why,
whatever it were, it made this "fellow of the LORD of hosts" (Zech.
13:7), this "lion of the tribe of Judah" (Rev. 5:5), this "mighty one"

(Ps. 89:19), "the wisdom and power of God,"[36] to tremble, sweat, cry, pray, wrestle, and that with strong supplications.[37] Some of the popish[38] devotionists tell us that one drop, the least, of the blood of Christ, was abundantly enough to redeem all the world; but they err, not knowing the desert of sin, nor the severity of the justice of God. If one drop less than was shed, one pang less than was laid on, would have done it, those other drops had not been shed, nor those other pangs laid on. God did not cruciate[39] the dearly-beloved of his soul for nought. But there is more than all this:

It pleased God to bruise him, to put him to grief, to make his soul an offering for sin, and to pour out his life unto death (Isa. 53:5–6). He hid himself from him—was far from the voice of his cry, until he cried out, "My God, my God, why have you forsaken me?" (Ps. 22:1). He made him sin (2 Cor. 5:21) and a curse for us (Gal. 3:13); executed on him the sentence of the law; brought him into an agony, wherein he sweat thick drops of blood, was grievously troubled, and his soul was heavy unto death. He that was the power of God, and the wisdom of God, went stooping under the burden, until the whole frame of nature seemed astonished at it. Now this, as I said before that it discovered the indignation of God against sin, so it clearly holds out the desert of it. Would you, then, see the true demerit of sin?—take the measure of it from the mediation of Christ, especially his cross. It brought him who was the Son of God, equal unto God, God blessed forever, into the form of a servant (Phil. 2:7), who had not where to lay his head. It pursued him all his life with afflictions and persecutions; and lastly brought him under the rod of God; there [it] bruised him and brake[40] him—slew the Lord of life (1 Cor. 2:7) [cf. Acts 3:15]. Hence is deep humiliation for it, upon the account of him whom we have pierced (Zech. 12:10). And this is the first spiritual view of sin we have in Christ.

The wisdom of understanding our *impotency*, by reason of sin, is wrapped up in him. By our impotency, I understand two things: (1) Our *disability* to make any *atonement* with God for sin. (2) Our *disability to answer* his mind and will, in all or any of the *obedience* that he requires, by reason of sin.

---

36. Prov. 8:22; 1 Cor. 1:24.
37. Matt. 26:37–38; Mark 14:33–34; Luke 22:44; Heb. 5:7.
38. a negative label for Roman Catholicism, relating to belief in papal supremacy.
39. torment, torture.
40. past participle of *broke*

For the first, that alone is discovered in Christ. Many inquiries have the sons of men made after an atonement—many ways have they entered into to accomplish it. After this they inquire, "Will any manner of sacrifices, though appointed of God, as burnt-offerings, and calves of a year old; though very costly, thousands of rams, and ten thousand rivers of oil; though dreadful and tremendous, offering violence to nature, as to give my children to the fire" (Mic. 6:6–7)—will any of these things make an atonement? David does positively, indeed, determine this business, "None of them" (of the best or richest of men) "can by any means redeem his brother, nor give to God a ransom for him; for the redemption of their soul is precious, and it ceases forever" (Ps. 49:7–8). It cannot be done—no atonement can be made; yet men would still be doing, still attempting: hence did they heap up sacrifices,[41] some costly, some bloody and inhuman. The Jews, to this day, think that God was atoned for sin by the sacrifices of bulls and goats, and the like. And the Socinians[42] acknowledge no atonement, but what consists in men's repentance and new obedience. In the cross of Christ are the mouths of all stopped as to this thing. For—

First, God has there discovered that *no sacrifices for sin*, though of his own *appointment*, could ever make them *perfect* that offered them (Heb. 10:11). Those sacrifices could never take away sin (Ps. 40:6–7)—those services could never make them perfect that performed them, as to the conscience (Heb. 9:9); as the apostle proves (Heb. 10:1). And thence the Lord rejects all sacrifices and offerings whatever, as to any such end and purpose (vv. 6–8), Christ, in their stead,[43] saying, "Lo, I come"; and by him we are "justified from all things, from which we could not be justified by the law" (Acts 13:39). God, I say, in Christ, has condemned all sacrifices, as wholly insufficient in the least to make an atonement for sin. And how great a thing it was to instruct the sons of men in this wisdom, the event has manifested.

Second, he has also written *vanity* on all other endeavors whatever that have been undertaken for that purpose. By setting forth his only Son "to be a propitiation" (Rom. 3:24–26), he leaves no doubt upon the spirits of men that in themselves they could make no atonement; for "if righteousness were by the law, then were Christ dead in vain"

---

41. John Owen, *Diatrib. De Just. Divin.* ["A Dissertation on Divine Justice: or, the Claims of Vindicatory Justice Vindicated" (1653), *Works* 10:512–24.]

42. A frequent target of Owen's polemics, the Socinians were a heterodox sect led by Laelius Socinus (d. 1562 in Zürich) and his nephew Faustus Socinus (d. 1604).

43. place

[Gal. 2:21]. To what purpose should he be made a propitiation, were not we ourselves weak and without strength to any such purpose? So the apostle argues, when we had no power, then did he by death make an atonement (Rom. 5:6, 8–9).

This, wisdom then, is also hid in Christ. Men may see by other helps, perhaps, far enough to fill them with dread and astonishment (as those in Isa. 33:14); but such a sight and view of it as may lead a soul to any comfortable settlement about it—that only is discovered in this treasury of heaven, the Lord Jesus.

Our disability to answer the mind and will of God, in all or any of the *obedience* that he requires, is in him only to be discovered. This, indeed, is a thing that many will not be acquainted with to this day. To teach a man that he cannot do what he ought to do, and for which he condemns himself if he do it not, is no easy task. Man rises up with all his power to plead against a conviction of impotency. Not to mention the proud conceits and expressions of the philosophers,[44] how many that would be called Christians do yet creep, by several degrees, in the persuasion of a power of fulfilling the law! And from whence, indeed, should men have this knowledge that we have not? *Nature* will not teach it[45]—that is proud and conceited; and it is one part of its pride, weakness, and corruption, not to know it at all. The *law* will not teach it: for though that will show us what *we have done amiss*, yet it will not discover to us that *we could not do better*; yea, by requiring exact obedience of us, it takes for granted that such power is in us for that purpose: it takes no notice that we have *lost* it; nor does it concern it so to do. This, then, also lies hid in the Lord Jesus. "The law of the Spirit of life in Christ Jesus has made me free from the law of sin and death. For what the law could not do, in that it was weak through the flesh, God sending his own Son in the likeness of sinful flesh, and for sin, condemned sin in the flesh; that the righteousness of the law might be fulfilled in us" (Rom. 8:2–4). The law can bring forth no righteousness, no obedience; it is weak to any such purpose, by reason of the flesh, and that corruption that is come on us. These two things are done in Christ, and by him: First, *sin is condemned* as to its guilt, and we set free from that; the righteousness of the law by his obedience is fulfilled

---

44. *Quia unusquisque sibi virtutem acquirit; nemo sapientum de ea gratias Deo egit.* ["Because everyone obtains virtue for himself; none of the philosophers gave thanks to God for it." Cicero.]

45. *Natura sic apparet vitiata, ut hoc majoris vitii sit non videre.* ["It is apparent that nature is so corrupted, that it does not see its own rather large taint." Cf. Augustine, *On Nature and Grace*, NPNF[1] 5:140; PL 44, col. 274.]

in us, who could never do it ourselves. And, secondly, that *obedience* which is required of us, *his Spirit works* it in us. So that that perfection of obedience which we have in him is imputed to us; and the sincerity that we have in obedience is from his Spirit bestowed on us. And this is the most excellent glass, wherein we see our impotency; for what need we his perfect obedience to be made ours, but that we have not, can not attain any? What need we his Spirit of life to quicken us, but that we are dead in trespasses and sins?

The *death* of sin—sin dying in us now, in some measure, while we are alive. This is a third concernment of sin which it is our wisdom to be acquainted with; and it is hid only in Christ. There is a twofold dying of sin: as to the *exercise* of it in our mortal members; and as to the *root*, principle, and power of it in our souls. The first, indeed, may be learned in part out of Christ. Christ-less men may have sin dying in them, as to the outward exercise of it. Men's bodies may be disabled for the service of their lusts, or the practice of them may not consist with their interest. Sin is never *more alive* than when it is thus dying.[46] But there is a dying of it as to the root, the principle of it—the daily decaying of the strength, power, and life of it; and this is to be had alone in Christ. Sin is a thing that of itself is not apt to die or to decay, but to get ground, and strength, and life, in the subject wherein it is, to eternity; prevent all its actual eruptions, yet its original *enmity* against God will still grow. In believers it is still dying and decaying, until it be utterly abolished. The opening of this treasury you have: "Know you not, that so many of us as were baptized into Jesus Christ were baptized into his death?" Therefore we are buried with him by baptism into death, that like as Christ was raised from the dead by the glory of the Father, even so we also should walk in newness of life. For if we have been planted together in the likeness of his death, we shall be also in the likeness of his resurrection; knowing this, that our old man is crucified with him, that the body of sin might be destroyed, that henceforth we should not serve sin" (Rom. 6:3–6). This is the design of the apostle in the beginning of that chapter, not only to manifest whence is the principle and rise of our mortification and the death of sin, even from the death and blood of Christ; but also the manner of sin's continuance and dying in us, from the manner of Christ's dying for sin. He was crucified for us, and thereby sin was crucified in us; he died for us, and the body of sin is destroyed, that we should not serve sin; and as

---

46. Cf. John Owen, "On the Mortification of Sin," in *Overcoming Sin and Temptation*, ed. Kelly M. Kapic and Justin Taylor (Wheaton, IL: Crossway, 2006), 37–139. Also *Works*, 6:1–86.

he was raised from the dead, that death should not have dominion over him, so also are we raised from sin, that it should not have dominion over us. This wisdom is hid in Christ only. Moses at his dying day had all his strength and vigor; so have sin and the law to all out of Jesus: at their dying day, sin is [in] no way decayed. Now, next to the receiving of the righteousness prepared for us, to know this is the chief part of our wisdom. To be truly acquainted with the *principle* of the dying of sin, to feel virtue and power flowing from the cross of Christ to that purpose, to find sin crucified in us, as Christ was crucified for us—this is wisdom indeed, that is in him alone.

There is a *glorious end* whereunto sin is appointed and ordained, and discovered in Christ, that others are unacquainted with. Sin in its own nature tends merely to the dishonor of God, the debasement of his majesty, and the ruin of the creature in whom it is; hell itself is but the filling of wretched creatures with the fruit of their own devices.[47] The comminations and threats of God in the law do manifest one other end of it, even the demonstration of the vindictive justice of God, in measuring out unto it a meet recompense of reward (2 Thess. 1:6). But here the law stays (and with it all other light) and discovers no other use or end of it at all. In the Lord Jesus there is the *manifestation* of another and more glorious end; to wit, the praise of God's *glorious grace* (Eph. 1:6) in the pardon and forgiveness of it—God having taken order in Christ that that thing which tended merely to his dishonor should be managed to his infinite glory, and that which of all things he desires to exalt (Heb. 8:6–13)—even that he may be known and believed to be a "God pardoning iniquity, transgression and sin" [Mic. 7:18]. To return, then, to this part of our demonstration:

In the knowledge of ourselves, in reference to our eternal condition, does much of our wisdom consist. There is not anything wherein, in this depraved condition of nature, we are more concerned than sin; without a knowledge of that, we know not ourselves. "Fools make a mock of sin" [Prov. 14:9]. A true saving knowledge of sin is to be had only in the Lord Christ: in him may we see the desert of our iniquities, and their pollution, which could not be borne or expiated but by his blood; neither is there any wholesome view of these but in Christ. In him and his cross is discovered our universal impotency, either of *atoning God's justice* or *living up to his will*. The death of sin is procured by, and discovered in, the death of Christ; as also the manifestation of the riches of God's

---

47. Prov. 1:31; Jer. 17:10.

grace in the pardoning thereof. A real and experimental acquaintance, as to ourselves, with all which, is our wisdom; and it is that which is of more value than all the wisdom of the world.

KNOWING OURSELVES IN REFERENCE TO RIGHTEOUSNESS

Righteousness is a second thing whereof the Spirit of Christ convinces the world, and the main thing that it is our wisdom to be acquainted with. This all men are persuaded of, that God is a most righteous God (that is a natural notion of God which Abraham insisted on: "Shall not the Judge of all the earth do right?" Gen. 18:25). They "know that this is the judgment of God, that they who commit such things are worthy of death" (Rom. 1:32); that "it is a righteous thing with him to recompense tribulation unto offenders" (2 Thess. 1:6). He is "a God of purer eyes than to behold evil" (Hab. 1:13); and therefore, "the ungodly cannot stand in judgment" (Ps. 1:5). Hence the great inquiry of every one (who lies in any measure under the power of it), convinced of immortality and the judgment to come, is concerning the righteousness wherewith to appear in the presence of this righteous God. This more or less they are solicitous about all their days; and so, as the apostle speaks, "through the fear of death they are all their lifetime subject to bondage" (Heb. 2:15)—they are perplexed with fears about the issue of their righteousness, lest it should end in death and destruction.

Unto men set upon this inquiry, that which first and naturally presents itself, for their direction and assistance, assuredly promising them a righteousness that will abide the trial of God, provided they will follow its direction, is *the law*. The law has many fair pleas to prevail with a soul to close with it for a righteousness before God. It was given out from God himself for that end and purpose; it contains the whole obedience that God requires of any of the sons of men; it has the promise of life annexed[48] to it: "Do this, and live" [Luke 10:28]; "The doers of the law are justified" [Rom. 2:13]; and, "If you will enter into life, keep the commandments" [Matt. 19:17]—yea, it is most certain that it must be wholly fulfilled, if we ever think to stand with boldness before God. This being some part of the plea of the law, there is no man that seeks after righteousness but does, one time or another, attend to it and attempt its direction. Many do it every day, who yet will not own that so they do. This, then, they set themselves about—laboring to correct their lives,

48. joined, added, united, attached.

amend their ways, perform the duties required, and so follow after a righteousness according to the prescript of the law. And in this course do many men continue long with much perplexity—sometimes hoping, oftener fearing; sometimes ready to *give quite over*; sometimes *vowing to continue* (their consciences being no way satisfied, nor righteousness in any measure attained) all their days. After they have wearied themselves perhaps for a long season, in the largeness of their ways, they come at length, with fear, trembling, and disappointment, to that conclusion of the apostle: "By the works of the law no flesh is justified" [Gal. 2:16]; and with dread cry that if God mark what is done amiss, there is no standing before him. That they have this issue, the apostle witnesses, "Israel, who followed after the law of righteousness, has not attained to the law of righteousness.[49] Wherefore? Because they sought it not by faith, but as it were by the works of the law" (Rom. 9:31–32). It was not solely for want of endeavor in themselves that they were disappointed, for they earnestly followed after the law of righteousness; but from the nature of the thing itself—it would not bear it. Righteousness was not to be obtained that way; "For," says the apostle, "if they which are of the law be heirs, faith is made void, and the promise made of none effect; because the law works wrath" (Rom. 4:14–15). The law itself is now such as that it cannot give life: "If there had been a law given which would have given life, verily righteousness should have been by the law" (Gal. 3:21). And he gives the reason in the next verse why it could not give life; because "the Scripture concludes all under sin" [Gal. 3:22]; that is, it is very true, and the Scripture affirms it, that all men are sinners, and the law speaks not one word to sinners but death and destruction: therefore the apostle tells us plainly that God himself found fault[50] with this way of attaining righteousness (Heb. 8:7–8). He complains of it; that is, he declares it insufficient for that end and purpose.

Now, there are two considerations that discover unto men the vanity and hopelessness of seeking righteousness in this path:

First, that they have *already sinned*: "For all have sinned,[51] and come short of the glory of God" (Rom. 3:23). This they are sufficiently sensible of, that although they could for the time to come fulfill the whole law, yet there is a score, a reckoning, upon them already, that they know

---

49. *diōkōn nomon dikaiosunēs eis nomon dikaiosunēs ouk ephthase* ("pursuing the law of righteousness, they did not attain the law of righteousness" [Rom. 9:31]). Note: the second use of *dikaiosunēs* is not in the original text of Scripture.

50. *memphomenos* (lit. "finding fault" [Heb. 8:7]).

51. *pantes hemarton* ("all have sinned" [Rom. 3:23; 5:12]).

not how to answer for. Do they consult their guide, the law itself,[52] how they may be eased of the account that is past? It has not one word of direction or consolation; but bids them prepare to *die*. The sentence is gone forth, and there is no escaping.

Second, that if all *former debts* should be blotted out, yet they are no way able for the *future* to fulfill the law; they can as well move the earth with a finger, as answer the perfection thereof: and therefore, as I said, on this twofold account, they conclude that this labor is lost. "By the works of the law shall no flesh be justified" (Gal. 3:11–12).

Wherefore, secondly: being thus disappointed by *the severity and inexorableness* of the law, men generally betake themselves to some other way, that may *satisfy* them as to those considerations which took them off from their former hopes; and this, for the most part, is by fixing themselves upon some ways of atonement to satisfy God, and helping out the rest with hopes of mercy. Not to insist on the ways of atonement and expiation which the Gentiles had pitched on; nor on the many ways and inventions—by works satisfactory of their own, supererogations[53] of others, indulgences, and purgatory in the close—that the papists[54] have found out for this end and purpose; it is, I say, proper to all convinced persons, as above, to seek for a righteousness, partly by an endeavor to satisfy for what is past, and partly by hoping after general mercy. This the apostle calls a seeking for it "as it were by the works of the law"[55] (Rom. 9:32); not directly, "but as it were" by the works of the law, making up one thing with another. And he tells us what issue they have in this business: "Being ignorant of God's righteousness, and going about to establish their own righteousness, they have not submitted themselves unto the righteousness of God" (Rom. 10:3). They were by it enemies to the righteousness of God. The ground of this going about to establish their own righteousness was that they were ignorant of the righteousness of God. Had they known the righteousness of God, and what exact conformity to his will he requires, they had never[56] undertaken such a fruitless business as to have compassed it "as it were by the works of

---

52. Deut. 27:26; Gal. 3:10.

53. According to the Roman Catholic doctrine of *opera supererogationis*, supererogatory acts—that is, actions that go beyond the call of duty and the requirements for salvation—produced a superabundance of merit that was deposited in a spiritual treasury of the church and could be used by ordinary sinners for the remittance of their sins.

54. a negative label for Roman Catholics, due to their belief in papal supremacy. From the Latin *papa* ("pope").

55. *hōs ex ergōn nomou* ("as it were by works of the law" [Rom. 9:32]).

56. i.e., would never have.

the law." Yet this many will stick on a long time. Something they do, something they hope for; some old faults they will buy off with new obedience. And this pacifies their consciences for a season; but when the Spirit comes to convince them of righteousness [John 16:8], neither will this hold. Wherefore—

The matter comes at length to this issue—they look upon themselves under this twofold qualification:

As *sinners*, obnoxious[57] to the law of God and the curse thereof; so that unless that be satisfied, that nothing from thence shall ever be laid to their charge, it is altogether in vain once to seek after an appearance in the presence of God.

As *creatures* made to a supernatural and eternal end; and therefore bound to answer the whole mind and will of God in the obedience required at their hands. Now, it being before discovered to them that both these are beyond the compass of their own endeavors, and the assistance which they have formerly rested on, if their eternal condition be of any concern to them, their wisdom is to find out a righteousness that may answer both these to the utmost.

Now, both these are to be had only in the Lord Christ, who is our righteousness. This wisdom, and all the treasures of it, are hid in him.

He expiates former iniquities, he satisfies for sin, and procures remission of it. "Being justified freely by his grace, through the redemption that is in Christ Jesus: whom God has set forth to be a propitiation through faith in his blood, to declare his righteousness for the remission of sins that are past, through the forbearance of God" (Rom. 3:24–25). "All we like sheep," etc. (Isa. 53:6). "Through his blood we have redemption, the forgiveness of sins" (Eph. 1:7) "God spared not his own Son, but delivered," etc. (Rom. 8:32). This, even this alone, is our righteousness; as to that first part of it which consists in the removal of the whole guilt of sin, whereby we are come short of the glory of God. On this account it is that we are assured that none shall ever lay anything to our charge, or condemn us (Rom. 8:33–34)—there being "no condemnation to them that are in Christ Jesus" (v. 1). We are purged by the sacrifice of Christ, so as to have "no more conscience of sin" (Heb. 10:2); that is, troubles in conscience about it. This wisdom is hid only in the Lord Jesus; in him alone is there an atonement discovered: and give me the wisdom which shall cut all scores concerning sin, and let the world take what remains. But—

---

57. liable, subject to, exposed, made susceptible to harm.

There is yet something more *required*; it is not enough that we are not *guilty*, we must also be *actually righteous*—not only all sin is to be answered for, but all righteousness is to be fulfilled. By taking away the guilt of sin, we are as persons innocent; but something more is required to make us to be considered as persons obedient. I know nothing to teach me that an innocent person shall go to heaven, be rewarded, if he be no more but so. Adam was innocent at his first creation, but he was to "do this," to "keep the commandments," before he entered into "life": he had no title to life by innocence. This, then, moreover, is required, that the whole law be fulfilled, and all the obedience performed that God requires at our hands. This is the soul's second inquiry; and it finds a resolution only in the Lord Christ: "For if, when we were enemies, we were reconciled to God by the death of his Son, much more, being reconciled, we shall be saved by his life" (Rom. 5:10). His death reconciled us; then are we saved by his life. The actual obedience which he yielded to the whole law of God is that righteousness whereby we are saved; if so be we are found in him, not having on our own righteousness which is of the law, but the righteousness which is of God by faith (Phil. 3:9). This I shall have occasion to handle more at large hereafter.

To return, then: It is not, I suppose, any difficult task to persuade men, convinced of immortality and judgment to come, that the main of their wisdom lies in this, even to find out such a righteousness as will accompany them forever, and abide the severe trial of God himself. Now, all the wisdom of the world is but folly, as to the discovery of this thing. The utmost that man's wisdom can do is but to find out most wretched, burdensome, and vexatious ways of perishing eternally. All the treasures of this wisdom are hid in Christ; he "of God is made unto us wisdom and righteousness" (1 Cor. 1:30).

Knowing Ourselves in Reference to Judgment

Come we to the last thing, which I shall but touch upon; and that is *judgment*. The true wisdom of this also is hid in the Lord Christ; I mean, in particular, that judgment that is for to come: so at present I take the word in that place [John 16:8]. Of what concernment this is to us to know, I shall not speak—it is that whose influence upon the sons of men is the principle of their discriminating themselves from the beasts that perish.[58] Neither shall I insist on the obscure intimations of it[59] which are given by the present proceedings of Providence in governing the world; nor that greater light of it which shines in the threats and promises of the law. The wisdom of it is in two regards hid in the Lord Jesus: (1) as to the *truth* of it; (2) as to the *manner* of it:

For the *truth* of it; and so in and by him it is confirmed, and that two ways: (1) by his *death*; (2) by his *resurrection*:

By his death. God, in the death of Christ, punishing and condemning sin in the flesh of his own Son, in the sight of men, angels, and devils, has given an abundant assurance of a righteous and universal judgment to come; wherefore, or upon what account imaginable, could he be induced to lay such a load on him, but that he will certainly reckon one day with the sons of men for all their works, ways, and walkings before him. *The death of Christ is a most solemn exemplar of the last judgment.* Those who own him to be the Son of God will not deny a judgment to come.

By his resurrection. Pistin paraschōn pasin (Acts 17:31)—he has given faith and assurance of this thing to all, by raising Christ from the dead, having appointed him to be the judge of all; in whom and by whom he will judge the world in righteousness. And then—

And, lastly, for the *manner* of it: that it shall be by him who has loved us, and given himself for us—who is himself the righteousness that he requires of our hands; and on the other side, by him who has been, in his *person, grace, ways, worship, servants,* reviled, despised, contemned[60] by the men of the world—which holds out unspeakable consolation on

---

58. *Bene et compositè C. Cæsar . . . de vita et morte disseruit, falsa, credo, existimans, ea quæ de infernis memorantur; diverso itinere malos a bonis loca tetra, inculta, fœda atque formidolosa habere.* ["In fine and finished phrases did Gaius Caesar . . . speak of life and death, regarding as false, I presume, the tales which are told of the Lower World, where they say that the wicked take a different path from the good, and they dwell in the regions that are gloomy, desolate, unsightly, and full of fears." Marcus Porcius Cato, as quoted in *The War with Catiline*, from Sallust, Loeb Classical Library, trans. J. C. Rolfe (Cambridge, MA: Harvard University Press, 1965), 103.] *All esti kai tō onti to amkbioskesthai, kai ek tōn tethneōtōn tous zōntas gignesthai, kai tas tōn tethneōtōn psuchas einai kai tais men agathais ameinon einai tais de kakais kakion.* ["And it is a fact that the living are generated from the dead and that the souls of the dead exist (and that the good fare better and the bad worse)." Plato, *Phaedo*, Loeb Classical Library, trans. Arnold North Fowler (Cambridge, MA: Harvard University Press, 1971), 252–53.]

59. "*Devenêre locos lætos, et amœna vireta / Fortunatorum nemorum, sedesque beatas,*" etc. Virgil, *Aeneid,* vi. 638. ["They came to a land of joy, the green pleasaunces and happy seats of the Blissful Groves." Virgil, *Virgil I: Eclogues, Georgics, Aeneid I–VI,* Loeb Classical Library, trans. H. R. Fairclough (Cambridge, MA: Harvard University Press, 1960), 551.]

60. to despise with contempt, scorn, disdain.

the one hand, and terror on the other: so that the wisdom of this also is hid in Christ.

And this is the second part of our first demonstration. Thus the knowledge of ourselves, in reference to our supernatural end, is no small portion of our wisdom. The things of the greatest concernment hereunto are sin, righteousness, and judgment; the wisdom of all which is alone hid in the Lord Jesus: which was to be proved.

True Wisdom and Knowledge Consist in the Skill of Walking with God

The third part of our wisdom is to walk with God. Now, that one may walk with another, six things are required: (1) agreement; (2) acquaintance; (3) a way; (4) strength; (5) boldness; (6) an aiming at the same end. All these, with the wisdom of them, are hid in the Lord Jesus.

WALKING WITH ANOTHER REQUIRES AGREEMENT

Agreement. The prophet tells us that two cannot walk together unless they be agreed (Amos 3:3). Until agreement be made, there is no communion, no walking together. God and man by nature (or while man is in the state of nature) are at the greatest enmity. He declares nothing to us but wrath (Rom. 1:18); whence we are said to be children of it; that is, born obnoxious to it (Eph. 2:3): and while we remain in that condition, "the wrath of God abides on us" (John 3:36). All the discovery that God makes of himself unto us is, that he is inexpressibly provoked; and therefore preparing wrath against the day of wrath, and the revelation of his righteous judgment. The day of his and sinners' meeting is called "the day of wrath" (Rom. 2:5–6). Neither do we come short in our enmity against him; yea, we first began it, and we continue longest in it. To express this enmity, the apostle tells us, that our very minds, the best part of us, are "enmity against God" (Rom. 8:7–8); and that we neither are, nor will, nor can be, subject to him; our enmity manifesting itself by universal rebellion against him: whatever we do that seems otherwise, is but hypocrisy or flattery; yea, it is a part of this enmity to lessen it. In this state the wisdom of walking with God must needs be most remote from the soul. He is "light, and in him is no darkness at all";[61] we are darkness, and in us there is no light at all. He is life, a "living God"; we are dead, dead sinners—dead

---

61. Gk. *skotia en autō ouk estin oudemia*, 1 John 1:5; Eph. 5:8; 2:1; Ex. 15:11; 1 John 4:8; Titus 3:3.

in trespasses and sin. He is "holiness," and glorious in it; we wholly defiled—an abominable thing. He is "love"; we full of hatred—hating and being hated. Surely this is no foundation for agreement, or, upon that, of walking together: nothing can be more remote than this frame from such a condition. The foundation, then, of this, I say, is laid in Christ, hid in Christ. "He," says the apostle, "is our peace; he has made peace" for us (Eph. 2:14–15). He slew the enmity in his own body on the cross (v. 16).

He takes out of the way the *cause of the enmity* that was between God and us—sin and the curse of the law. He makes an end of sin, and that by making atonement for iniquity (Dan. 9:24); and he blots out the handwriting of ordinances (Col. 2:14), redeeming us from the curse, by "being made a curse for us" (Gal. 3:13).

He destroys him who would *continue the enmity* and make the breach[62] wider, "Through death he destroyed him that had the power of death, that is, the devil" (Heb. 2:14); and [he] "spoiled principalities and powers" (Col. 2:15).

He made "*reconciliation* for the sins of the people" (Heb. 2:17); he made by his blood an atonement with God, to turn away that wrath which was due to us, so making peace. Hereupon God is said to be "in Christ, reconciling the world unto himself" (2 Cor. 5:19)—being reconciled himself (v. 18), he lays down the enmity on his part, and proceeds to what remains—to slay the enmity on our part, that we also may be reconciled. And this also—

He does; for "by our Lord Jesus Christ we do receive the atonement" (Rom. 5:11), accept of the peace made and tendered, laying down our enmity to God; and so confirming an agreement betwixt us in his blood. So that "through him we have an access unto the Father" (Eph. 2:18). Now, the whole wisdom of this agreement, without which there is no walking with God, is hid in Christ; out of him God on his part is a consuming fire—we are as stubble fully dry, yet setting ourselves in battle array against that fire: if we are brought together we are consumed. All our approachings to him out of Christ are but to our detriment; in his blood alone have we this agreement. And let not any of us once suppose that we have taken any step in the paths of God with him, that any one duty is accepted, that all is not lost as to eternity, if we have not done it upon the account hereof.

---

62. gap

WALKING WITH ANOTHER REQUIRES ACQUAINTANCE

There is required *acquaintance*, also, to walking together. Two may *meet together* in the same way, and have no quarrel between them, no enmity; but if they are mere strangers one to another, they *pass by* without the least communion together. It does not suffice that the enmity between God and us be taken away; we must also have acquaintance given us with him. Our not knowing of him is a great cause and a great part of our enmity. Our understandings are "darkened," and we are "alienated from the life of God," etc. (Eph. 4:18). This also, then, must be added, if we ever come to walk with God, which is our wisdom. And this also is hid in the Lord Christ, and comes forth from him. It is true there are sundry other means, as his word and his works, that God has given the sons of men, to make a discovery of himself unto them, and to give them some acquaintance with him, that, as the apostle speaks, "they should seek the Lord, if haply[63] they might find him" (Acts 17:27); but yet, as that knowledge of God which we have by his works is but very weak and imperfect, so that which we have by the word, the letter of it, by reason of our blindness, is not saving to us if we have no other help; for though that be light as the sun in the firmament, yet if we have no eyes in our heads, what can it avail us?—no saving acquaintance with him, that may direct us to walk with him, can be obtained. This also is hid in the Lord Jesus, and comes forth from him, "He has given us an understanding, that we should know him that is true" (1 John 5:20)—all other light whatever without his giving us an understanding, will not do it. He is the true Light, which lights everyone that is enlightened (John 1:9). He opens our understandings that we may understand the Scriptures (Luke 24:45)—none has known God at any time, "but he has revealed him" (John 1:18). God dwells in that "light which no man can approach unto" (1 Tim. 6:16). None has ever had any such acquaintance with him as to be said to have seen him, but by the revelation of Jesus Christ. Hence he tells the Pharisees that, notwithstanding all their great knowledge which they pretended, indeed they had "neither heard the voice of God at any time, nor seen his shape" (John 5:37). They had no manner of spiritual acquaintance with God, but he was unto them as a man whom they had never heard nor seen. There is no acquaintance with God as love, and full of kindness, patience, grace, and pardoning mercy (on which knowledge of him alone we can walk with him), but only in Christ; but of this fully before. This, then, also is hid in him.

---

63. perhaps, perchance.

Walking with Another Requires a Way

There must, moreover, be a way wherein we must walk with God. God did at the beginning assign us a path to walk in with him, even the path of innocence and exact holiness, in a covenant of works. This path, by sin, is so filled with thorns and briers, so stopped up by curses and wrath, that no flesh living can take one step in that path; a *new way* for us to walk in must be found out, if ever we think to hold communion with God. And this also lies upon the former account. It is hid in Christ. All the world cannot, but *by and in him*, discover a path that a man may walk one step with God in. And therefore the Holy Ghost tells us that Christ has consecrated, dedicated, and set apart for that purpose "a new and living way" into the holiest of all (Heb. 10:20); a *new* one, for the first, old one was useless; a *living* one, for the other is dead: therefore, says he, "Let us draw near" (v. 22); having a way to walk in, let us draw near. And this way that he has prepared is no other but himself. In answer to them who would go to the Father, and hold communion with him, he tells them, "I am the way; and no man comes to the Father but by me" (John 14:6). He is *the medium of all communication* between God and us. In him we meet; in him we walk. All influences of love, kindness, mercy, from God to us, are through him; all our returns of love, delight, faith, obedience unto God, are all through him—he being that "one way" God so often promises his people: and it is a glorious way (Isa. 35:8)—a high way, a way of holiness, a way that none can err in that once enter it; which is further set out (Isa. 42:16). All other ways, all paths but this, go down to the chambers of death; they all lead to walk contrary to God.

Walking with Another Requires Strength

But suppose all this—that agreement be made, acquaintance given, and a way provided; yet if we have no *strength* to walk in that way, what will all this avail us? This also, then, must be added; of ourselves we are of no strength (Rom. 5:6)—poor weaklings, not able to go a step in the ways of God. When we are set in the way, either we throw ourselves down, or temptations cast us down, and we make no progress: and the Lord Jesus tells us plainly that "without him we can do nothing" (John 15:5); not anything at all that shall have the least acceptation with God. Neither can all the creatures in heaven and earth yield us the least assistance. Men's contending to do it in their own power, comes to nothing. This part of this, wisdom also is hid in Christ. All strength to walk with God is from him. "I can do all things through Christ, which strengthens me," says St. Paul (Phil. 4:13), who denies that of ourselves we have any sufficiency (2 Cor. 3:5). We that can do nothing in ourselves, we are such weaklings, can do all things in Jesus Christ, as giants; and therefore in him we are, against all oppositions in our way, "more than conquerors" (Rom. 8:37); and that because "from his fullness we receive grace for grace" (John 1:16). From him have we the Spirit of life and power, whereby he bears, as on eagles' wings, swiftly, safely, in the paths of walking with God. Any step that is taken in any way, by strength that is not immediately from Christ, is one step toward hell. He first takes us by the arm and teaches us to go, until he leads us on to perfection. He has milk and strong meat to feed us; he strengthens us with all might, and is with us in our running the race that is set before us. But yet—

WALKING WITH ANOTHER REQUIRES BOLDNESS

Whence should we take this *confidence* as to walk with God; even our God, who is "a consuming fire"? (Heb. 12:29). Was there not such a dread upon his people of old, that it was taken for granted among them that if they saw God at any time, it was not to be endured—they must *die*? Can any, but with extreme horror, think of that dreadful appearance that he made unto them of old upon Mount Sinai; until Moses himself, who was their mediator, said, "I exceedingly fear and quake"? (Heb. 12:21), and all the people said, "Let not God speak with us, lest we die"? (Ex. 20:19). Nay, though men have apprehensions of the goodness and kindness of God, yet upon any discovery, of his glory, how do they tremble, and are filled with dread and astonishment! Has it not been so with the "choicest of his saints"? (Hab. 3:16; Isa. 6:5; Job 42:5-6). Whence, then, should we take to ourselves this boldness, to walk with God? This the apostle will inform us in Hebrews 10:19; it is "by the blood of Jesus": so Ephesians 3:12, "In him we have boldness, and access with confidence"—not standing afar off, like the people at the giving of the law, but drawing nigh to God with boldness; and that upon this account: The dread and terror of God entered by sin; Adam had not the least thought of hiding himself until he had sinned. The *guilt* of sin being on the conscience, and this being *a common notion* left in the hearts of all, that God is a most righteous revenger thereof; this fills men with dread and horror at an apprehension of his presence, fearing that he is come to call their sins to remembrance. Now, the Lord Jesus, by the sacrifice and the atonement that he has made, has taken away this conscience of sin; that is, a dread of revenge from God upon the account of the guilt thereof. He has removed the slaying sword of the law, and on that account gives us great boldness with God; discovering him unto us now, no longer as a revenging Judge, but as a tender, merciful, and reconciled Father. Moreover, whereas there is on us by nature a spirit of bondage, filling us with innumerable tormenting fears, he takes it away, and gives us "the Spirit of adoption, whereby we cry Abba, Father," and behave ourselves with confidence and gracious boldness, as children: for "where the Spirit of the Lord is, there is liberty" (2 Cor. 3:17); that is, a freedom from all that dread and terror which the administration of the law brought with it. Now, as there is no sin that God will more severely revenge than any boldness that man takes with him out of Christ; so there is no grace more acceptable to him than that boldness which he is pleased to afford us in the blood of Jesus. There is, then—

WALKING WITH ANOTHER REQUIRES THE SAME DESIGN AND END

But one thing more to add; and that is, that two cannot walk together unless they have the *same design* in hand, and aim at the same *end*. This also, in a word, is given us in the Lord Jesus. The end of God is the advancement of his own glory; none can aim at this end, but only in the Lord Jesus. The sum of all is that the whole wisdom of our walking with God is hid in Christ, and from him only to be obtained; as has been manifest by an enumeration of particulars.

And so have I brought my first demonstration of what I intended unto a close, and manifested that all true wisdom and knowledge is laid up in, and laid out by, the Lord Jesus; and this by an induction of the chief particular heads of those things wherein confessedly our wisdom does consist. I have but one more to add, and therein I shall be brief.

Wisdom and Knowledge apart from Christ

Secondly, then, I say this truth will be further manifested by the consideration of the *insufficiency* and vanity of anything else that may lay claim or pretend to a title to wisdom.

There be two things in the world that do pass under this account: (1) The one is *learning* or *literature*; skill and knowledge of arts, sciences, tongues, with the knowledge of the things that are past. (2) *Prudence and skill* for the management of ourselves in reference to others, in civil affairs, for public good; which is much the fairest flower within the border of nature's garden. Now, concerning both these, I shall briefly evince: First, that they are utterly *insufficient* for the compassing and obtaining of those *particular ends* whereunto they are designed. Second, that both of them *in conjunction*, with their utmost improvement, cannot reach the true general end of wisdom. Both which considerations will set the crown, in the issue, upon the head of Jesus Christ.

Neither Learning nor Prudence Individually Can Achieve Their Particular Ends

LEARNING CANNOT ACHIEVE ITS PARTICULAR END

We begin with the first of these, and that as to the first particular. *Learning* itself, if it were all in one man, is not able to compass the particular end whereto it is designed; which writes "vanity and vexation" upon the forehead thereof.

The *particular end of literature* (though not observed by many, men's eyes being fixed on false ends, which compel them in their progress *"aberrare a scopo"*[64]) is none other but to remove some part of that curse which is come upon us by sin. Learning is the product of the soul's struggling with the curse for sin. Adam, at his first creation, was completely furnished with all that *knowledge* (excepting only things not then in being, neither in themselves nor in any natural causes, as that which we now call *tongues*, and those things that are the subject of *story*), as far as it lies in a needful tendency to the utmost end of man, which we now press after. There was no straitness, much less darkness, upon his understanding, that should make him sweat for a way to improve, and make out those general conceptions of things which he had. For his knowledge of nature, it is manifest, from his imposition of suitable names on all the creatures (the particular reasons of the most of which to us are lost); wherein, from the approbation given of his nomination of things in the Scripture, and the significance of what yet remains evident, it is most apparent it was done upon a clear acquaintance with their natures. Hence Plato could observe that he was most wise that first imposed names on things; yea, had more than human wisdom.[65] Were

---

64. Lat. "to wander from its aim."

65. *Oimai men egō ton alēthestaton logon peri toutōn einai, ō Sōkrates, meizō tina dunamin einai ē anthrōpeian, tēn themenēn ta prōta onomata tois pragmasin.* ["I think the truest theory of the matter, Socrates, is that the power which first gave names to things is more than human." Plato,

the wisest man living, yea, a general collection of all the wise men in the world, to make an experiment of their skill and learning, in giving names to all living creatures, suitable to their natures and expressive of their qualities, they would quickly perceive the loss they have incurred. Adam was made *perfect*, for the whole end of ruling the creatures and living to God, for which he was made; which, without the knowledge of the nature of the one and the will of the other, he could not be. All this being lost by sin, a multiplication of tongues also being brought in, as a curse for an after rebellion (Gen. 11:3), the whole design of learning is but to *disentangle the soul from this issue of sin*. Ignorance, darkness, and blindness, is come upon the understanding; acquaintance with the works of God, spiritual and natural, is lost; strangeness of communication is given, by multiplication of tongues; tumultuating[66] of passions and affections, with innumerable darkening prejudices, are also come upon us. To remove and take this away—to disentangle the mind in its reasonings, to recover an acquaintance with the works of God, to subduct[67] the soul from under the effects of the curse of division of tongues—is the aim and tendency of literature. This is the *"aliquid quo tendit"*;[68] and he that has any other aim in it, *"Passim sequitur corvum testâque lutoque."*[69] Now, not to insist upon that vanity and vexation of spirit, with the innumerable evils wherewith this enterprise is attended, this is that I only say, it is in itself no way sufficient for the attainment of its end, which writes vanity upon its forehead with characters not to be obliterated. To this purpose I desire to observe these two things:

That the *knowledge* aimed at to be recovered was given unto man in order to his *walking* with God, unto that *supernatural end* whereunto he was appointed. For after he was furnished with all his endowments, the law of life and death was given to him, that he might know wherefore he received them. Therefore, knowledge in him was spiritualized and sanctified: even that knowledge which he had by nature, in respect of its principle and end, was *spiritual*.

Plato VI: Cratylus, Parmenides, Greater Hippias, Lesser Hippias, Loeb Classical Library, trans. H. N. Fowler (Cambridge, MA: Harvard University Press, 1953), 183.]

66. agitation, disturbing, stirring up.

67. remove from use, influence.

68. "the something to which it aims."

69. "Have you any goal in life? Is there any target at which you aim? Or are you just taking random shots at ravens with potsherds and clods?" Persius, *Juvenal and Persius*, Loeb Classical Library, trans. G. G. Ramsey (Cambridge, MA: Harvard University Press, 1965), 351.

That the *loss* of it is part of that *curse* which was inflicted on us for sin. Whatever we come short in of the state of the first man in innocence, whether in loss of good or addition of evil, it is all of the curse for sin. Besides, that blindness, ignorance, darkness, deadness, which is everywhere ascribed to us in the state of nature, does fully comprise that also whereof we speak.

On these two considerations it is most apparent that learning can no way of itself attain the end it aims at. For—

That light which by it is discovered (which, the Lord knows, is very little, *weak*, *obscure*, *imperfect*, *uncertain*, *conjectural*, for a great part only enabling men to quarrel with and oppose one another, to the reproach of reason, yet I say, that which is attained by it) is not in the least measure by it *spiritualized*, or brought into that order of living to God, and with God, wherein at first it lay. This is wholly beyond its reach. As to this end, the apostle assures us that the utmost issue that men come to is darkness and folly (Rom. 1:21–22). Who knows not the profound inquiries, the subtile disputations, the acute reasonings, the admirable discoveries of Socrates, Plato, and Aristotle, and others? What, as to the purpose in hand, did they attain by all their studies and endeavors? *Emōranthēsan*, says the apostle—"They became fools." He that, by general consent, bears the *crown* of reputation for wisdom from them all, with whom to have lived was counted an inestimable happiness,[70] died like a fool, sacrificing a cock to Æsculapius.[71] And another [apostle assures us] that Jesus Christ alone is "the true Light" that lights us (John 1:9). And there is not any that has any true light, but what is immediately from him. After all the learning of men, if they have nothing else, they are still natural men, and perceive not the things of God. Their light is still but darkness; and how great is that darkness [cf. Matt. 6:23]! It is the Lord Jesus alone who is anointed to open the eyes of the blind. Men cannot spiritualize a notion, nor lay it in any order to the glorifying of God. After all their endeavors, they are still blind and dark, yea, darkness itself, knowing nothing as they

---

70. *Ei de tis tōn aretēs ephiemenōn ōphelimōterō tini Sōkratous sunegeneto, ekeinon egō ton andra axiomakaristotaton nomizō.* ["And if among those who make virtue their aim any one has ever been brought into contact with a person more helpful than Socrates, I count that man worthy to be called most blessed." Xenophon, *Xenophon: Anabasis IV-VII Symposium and Apology*, Loeb Classical Library, ed. O. J. Todd and Carleton L. Brownson (Cambridge, MA.: Harvard University Press, 1961), 509.]

71. Just before his death, Socrates commanded Crito to sacrifice a cock to Æsculapius, or Asclepius, the Greek demigod of medicine and healing. See Plato, *Phaedo*, 118a.

should. I know how the men of these attainments are apt to say, "Are we blind also?" with great contempt of others; but God has blasted all their pride:[72] "Where," says he, "is the wise? where is the scribe?" etc. (1 Cor. 1:20). I shall not add what Paul has further cautioned us, to the seeming condemning of philosophy as being fitted to make spoil of souls; nor what Tertullian with some other of the ancients have spoken of it,[73] being very confident that it was the *abuse*, and not the true *use* and advantage of it, that they opposed. But—

The *darkness and ignorance* that it strives to remove, being come upon us as a curse, it is not in the least measure, as it is a curse, able to remove it or take it away. He that has attained to the greatest height of literature, yet if he has nothing else—if he have not Christ—is as much under the curse of blindness, ignorance, stupidity, dullness, as

---

72. *O Sapientia superba irridens Christum crucifixum!* ["Oh, proud wisdom! thou laughest to scorn the crucified Christ." Augustine, *Lectures or Tractatus on the Gospel According to John*, NPNF¹ 7:15; PL 35, col. 1390.]

73. *Hæreses a philosophiâ subornantur. Inde Æones, et formæ nescio quæ, trinitas hominis apud Valentinum, Platonicus fuerat; inde Marcionis Deus melior de tranquillitate, a Stoicis venerat. Et ut anima interire dicatur, ab Epicureis observatur, et ut carnis restitutio negetur, de unâ omnium philosophorum scholâ sumitur: . . . Quid ergo Athenis et Hierosolymis? quid Academiæ et Ecclesiæ? quid hæreticis et Christianis? Nostra institutio de porticu Salomonis est. Nobis curiositate opus non est post Jesum Christum; nec inquisitione post evangelium. Cum credimus, nihil desideramus ultra credere. Hoc enim priùs credimus, non esse quod ultra credere debeamus.* ["Heresies are instigated by philosophy. From this source came the Aeons, and I know not what forms and the trinity of man in the system of Valentinus, who was of Plato's school. From the same source came Marcion's better god, with tranquility; he came of the Stoics. Then, again, the opinion that the soul dies is held by the Epicureans; while the denial of the restoration of the body is taken from the aggregate school of all the philosophers. . . . What indeed has Athens to do with Jerusalem? What is there between the Academy and the Church? what between heretics and Christians? Our instruction comes from 'the porch of Solomon.' We need no curiosity after Christ Jesus, no inquisition after the gospel! With our faith, we desire no further belief. For this is our first faith, that there is nothing which we ought to believe besides." Cf. Tertullian, *On the Prescription Against Heresies*, ANF 3:246; PL 2, cols. 19A–19B, 20B–21A.] *Epeidēper hikanōs ek tōn proeirēmenōn ta tōn philosophōn humōn ele legktai pragmata pasēs agnoias kai apatēs phanenta plērē.* Cf. "Since, therefore, it has been sufficiently proved that the opinions of your philosophers are obviously full of all ignorama and deceit." Justin Martyr, *Hortatory Address to the Greeks*, chap. 11, ANF, 1:278. *Mounon emoi philon eske logōn kleos, hous sunageiran / Antoliē te, dusis te, kai Hellados euchos Athenai, / Tois epi poll emogēsa polun chronon, alla kai autou, / Prēneas en dapedō Christou proparoithen ethēka, / Eixantas megaloio theou logō hos rha kaluptei Panta phrenos Broteēs strepton polueidea muthon.* [Cf. "The frame that goes with letters was the only thing that absorbed me. East and West combined to procure me that, and Athens, the glory of Greece. I labored much for a long time in the craft of letters; but even these two I laid prostrate before the feet of Christ in subjection to the Word of the great God. It overshadows all the twisted, variegated products of the human mind." Gregory of Nazianzus, *Carmen de vita sua, Concerning His Own Affairs*, in *St. Gregory of Nazianzus: Three Poems*, trans. Denise Molaise Meehan (Washington DC: Catholic University Press of America, 1987), 28; PG 37, col. 977.]

the poorest, silliest soul in the world. The curse is only removed in him who was made a curse for us. Everything that is penal is taken away only by him on whom all our sins did meet in a way of punishment; yea, upon this account. The *more abilities* the mind is furnished with, the more it *closes with the curse*, and strengthens itself to act its enmity against God. All that it receives does but help it to set up high thoughts and imaginations against the Lord Christ. So that this knowledge comes short of what in particular it is designed unto; and therefore cannot be that solid wisdom we are inquiring after.

There be sundry other things whereby it were easy to blur the countenance of this wisdom; and, from its intricacy, difficulty, uncertainty, unsatisfactoriness—betraying its followers into that which they most profess to avoid, blindness and folly—to write upon it "vanity and vexation of spirit." I hope I shall not need to add any thing to clear myself for not giving a due esteem and respect unto literature, my intendment[74] being only to cast it down at the feet of Jesus Christ, and to set the crown upon his head.

Prudence Cannot Achieve Its Particular End

Neither can the second part of the choicest wisdom out of Christ attain the peculiar end whereunto it is appointed; and that is *prudence in the management of civil affairs*—than which no perishing thing is more glorious—nothing more useful for the common good of human kind. Now, the immediate end of this prudence is to keep *the rational world* in bounds and order, to draw circles about the sons of men, and to keep them from passing their allotted bounds and limits, to the mutual disturbance and destruction of each other. All manner of trouble and disturbance arises from irregularity: one man breaking in upon the rights, usages, interests, relations of another, sets this world at variance.[75] The sum and aim of all wisdom below is to cause all things to move in their proper sphere, whereby it would be impossible there should be any more interfering than is in the celestial orbs, notwithstanding all their diverse and various motions: to keep all to their own allotments, within the compass of the lines that are fallen unto them, is the special end of this wisdom.

---

74. intention
75. dissent, discord.

Now, it will be a very easy task to demonstrate that all civil prudence whatever[76] (besides the vexation of its attainment, and loss being attained) is no way able to compass this end. The present condition of affairs throughout the world, as also that of former ages, will abundantly testify it; but I shall further discover the vanity of it for this end in some few observations. And the

First is that, through the *righteous judgment* of God lopping off the top flowers of the pride of men, it frequently comes to pass that those who are furnished with the greatest abilities of this kind do lay them out to a direct contrary end unto that which is their natural tendency and aim. From whom, for the most part, are all the commotions in the world—the breaking up of bounds, setting the whole frame of nature on fire? Is it not from such men as these? Were not men so wise, the world, perhaps, would be more quiet, when the end of wisdom is to keep it in quietness. This seems to be a curse that God has spread upon the wisdom of the world, in the most in whom it is, that it shall be employed in *direct opposition* to its proper end.

That God has made this a *constant path* toward the advancement of his own glory, even to leaven the wisdom and the counsels of the wisest of the sons of men with folly and madness, that they shall, in the depth of their policy, advise things for the compassing of the ends they do propose[77] as unsuitable as anything that could proceed out of the mouth of a child or a fool, and as directly tending to their own disappointment and ruin as anything that could be invented against them. "He destroys the wisdom of the wise, and brings to nothing the understanding of the prudent" (1 Cor. 1:19). This he largely describes [in] Isaiah 19:11–14. Drunkenness and staggering is the issue of all their wisdom; and that upon this account—the Lord gives them the spirit of giddiness[78] (so also Job 5:12–14). They meet with darkness

---

76. *Hō gēras hōs epachthes anthrōpoisin ei, kai pantachē luperon, ou kath hen monon, en hō gar ouden dunameth oud ischuomen, su tēnikauth hēmas didaskeis eu phronein.* ["Old Age, was ever a trouble such as you, / not here and there a pang, but through and through? / You teach us to be wise and prudent men / When we've lost health and strength, and not till then." Although Owen attributed this quote to Nicostratus, this quote has actually been attributed to Pherecrates, an Old Attic Comedy poet who lived about a century before Nicostratus. See *The Fragments of Attic Comedy*, 3 vols. in 4, ed. and trans. John Maxwell Edmonds (Leiden, E. J. Brill, 1957) 1:283; PCG, ed. Ralph Kassel and C. Austin, 7:219.]

77. *Isthuc est sapere, non quod ante pedes modò est, / Videre; sed etiam illa quæ futura sunt, / Prospicere.* ["That's real wisdom . . . not merely to see what lies under your feet but to foresee the future." Terence, *The Brothers*, in *Terence II: Phormio, Mother-in-law, Brothers*, Loeb Classical Library, trans. and ed. John Barsby (Cambridge, MA: Harvard University Press, 2001), 297.]

78. incapable of serious thought or attention, akin to intoxication.

in the daytime,[79] when all things seem clear about them, and a man would wonder how men should miss their way, then will God make it darkness to such as these (so Ps. 33:10). Hence God, as it were, sets them at work and undertakes their disappointment, "Go about your counsels," says the Lord, "and I will take order that it shall come to nought" (Isa 8:9–10). And Psalm 2:3–4, when men are deep at their plots and contrivances, God is said to have them in derision, to laugh them to scorn, seeing the poor worms industriously working out their own ruin. Never was this made more clear than in the days wherein we live. Scarcely have any wise men been brought to destruction, but it has evidently been through their own *folly*; neither has the wisest counsel of most been one jot better than madness.

That this wisdom, which should tend to *universal quietness*, has almost constantly given universal disquietness unto themselves in whom it has been most eminent. "In much wisdom is much grief" (Eccles. 1:18). And in the issue, some of them have made away with themselves, as Ahithophel [2 Sam. 17:1–23]; and the most of them have been violently dispatched by others. There is, indeed, no end of the folly of this wisdom.[80] The great men of the world carry away the reputation of it—really it is found in few of them. They are, for the most part, common events, whereunto they contribute not the least mite, which are ascribed to their care, vigilance, and foresight. Mean men, that have learned to adore what is above them, reverence the meetings and conferences of those who are in greatness and esteem. Their weakness and folly is little known. Where this wisdom has been most eminent, it has dwelt so close upon the borders of atheism, been attended with such falseness and injustice, that it has made its possessors wicked and infamous.

I shall not need to give any more instances to manifest the insufficiency of this wisdom for the attaining of its own peculiar and immediate end. This is the vanity of anything whatever—that it comes short of the mark it is directed unto. It is far, then, from being true and solid wisdom, seeing on the forehead thereof you may read "Disappointment."

---

79. Isa. 29:14; 47:10; Jer. 49:7; Obad. 8.

80. *Prudens futuri temporis exitum / Caliginosa nocte premit Deus: / Ridetque, si mortalis ultra / Fas trepidat.* ["God in his providence hides future events in murky darkness, and laughs if a mere mortal frets about what is beyond his control." Horace, *Odes and Epodes*, Loeb Classical Library, trans. and ed. Niall Rudd (Cambridge, MA: Harvard University Press, 2004), 213.]

And this is the first reason why true wisdom cannot consist in either of these—because they come short even of the particular and immediate ends they aim at. But—

Learning and Prudence Together Cannot Achieve the General End of Wisdom

Secondly, *both these in conjunction*, with their utmost improvement, are not able to reach the true general end of wisdom. This assertion also falls under an easy demonstration, and it were a facile[81] thing to discover their disability and unsuitableness for the true end of wisdom; but it is so professedly done by him who had the largest portion of both of any of the sons of men (Solomon in his Preacher), that I shall not any further insist upon it.

To draw, then, unto a close: if true and *solid wisdom* is not in the least to be found amongst these, if the *pearl* be not hid in this field, if these two are but vanity and disappointment, it cannot but be to no purpose to seek for it in anything else below, these being amongst them incomparably the most excellent; and therefore, with one accord, let us set the crown of this wisdom on the head of the Lord Jesus.

Let the reader, then, in a few words, take a view of the *tendency* of this whole digression. To draw our hearts to the more cheerful entertainment of and delight in the Lord Jesus, is the aim thereof. If all wisdom be laid up in him, and by an interest in him only to be attained—if all things beside him and without him that lay claim thereto are folly and vanity—let them that would be wise learn where to repose their souls.

---

81. effortless

Chapter 4

Communion between Christ and the Soul

The communion begun, as before declared, between Christ and the soul,[1] is in the next place carried on by suitable *consequential affections*—affections suiting such a relation. Christ having given himself to the soul, loves the soul; and the soul having given itself unto Christ, loves him also. Christ loves his own, yea, "loves them to the end" (John 13:1); and the saints they love Christ, they "love the Lord Jesus Christ in sincerity" (Eph. 6:24).

Now the love of Christ, wherewith he follows his saints, consists in these four things: (1) delight; (2) valuation; (3) pity, or compassion; (4) bounty. The love, also, of the saints unto Christ may be referred to these four heads: delight; valuation; chastity; duty.

Two of these are of the *same kind*, and two *distinct*; as is required in this relation, wherein all things stand not on equal terms.

The first thing on the part of Christ is *delight*. Delight is the flowing of love and joy—the rest and complacence of the mind in a suitable, desirable good enjoyed.[2] Now, Christ delights exceedingly in his saints: "As the bridegroom rejoices over the bride, so shall your God rejoice over you" (Isa. 62:5). Hence he calls the day of his espousals, the day

---

1. Owen here resumes the theme of chap. 3, which he began by exploring the way we have communion with Christ in relation to personal grace. The first point was that Christ and believers have a mutual resignation to each other. He now moves on to the second point, namely, that the communion between Christ and the soul is carried on by suitable consequential affections.

2. *Hēdonē mallon en ēremia estin, ē en kinēsei.* ["There is essentially a truer pleasure in rest than in motion." Aristotle, *The Nicomachean Ethics,* Loeb Classical Library, trans. H. Rackham (Cambridge, MA: Harvard University Press, 1945), 449.] *Teleioi de tēn energeian hē hēdonē.* ["But the pleasure perfects the activity." Aristotle, *The Nicomachean Ethics*, Loeb Classical Library, trans. H. Rackham (Cambridge, MA: Harvard University Press, 1945), Book X, chap. iv.

of the "gladness of his heart" (Song 3:11). It is known that usually this
is the most *unmixed* delight that the sons of men are in their pilgrimage made partakers of. The delight of the bridegroom in the day of his
espousals is the height of what an expression of delight can be carried
unto. This is in Christ answerable to the relation he takes us into. His
heart is glad in us, without sorrow. And every day while we live is his
wedding day. It is said of him, "The LORD your God in the midst of
you" (that is, dwelling amongst us, taking our nature, John 1:14) "is
mighty; he will save, he will rejoice over you with joy; he will rest in
his love, he will joy over you with singing" (Zeph. 3:17); which is a full
description of delight, in all the parts of it—joy and exultation, rest and
complacence. "I rejoiced," says he, "in the habitable parts of the earth,
and my delights were with the sons of men" (Prov. 8:31). The thoughts
of communion with the saints were the joy of his heart from eternity.
On the compact and agreement that was between his Father and him,
that he should divide a portion with the strong, and save a remnant for
his inheritance, his soul rejoiced in the thoughts of that pleasure and
delight which he would take in them, when he should actually take
them into communion with himself. Therefore in the preceding verse it
is said he was by him as *'amon*, say we, "As one brought up with him,"
alumnus (the LXX renders it *harmozousa* and the Latin, with most other
translations, [renders it] *cuncta componens*, or *disponens*). The word,
taken *actively*, signifies him whom another takes into his care to breed
up, and disposes of things for his advantage. So did Christ take us then
into his care, and rejoiced in the thoughts of the execution of his trust.
Concerning them he says, "Here will I dwell, and here will I make my
habitation forever" [cf. 2 Chron. 6:2]. For them has he chosen for his
temple and his dwelling place, because he delights in them. This makes
him take them so nigh himself in every relation. As he is God, they are
his temple; as he is a king, they are his subjects (he is the king of saints);
as he is a head, they are his body (he is the head of the church); as he
is a firstborn, he makes them his brethren ("he is not ashamed to call
them brethren" [Heb. 2:11]).

   I shall choose out one particular from among many as an instance
for the proof of this thing; and that is this: Christ *reveals his secrets*,
his mind, unto his saints, and enables them to reveal the secrets of
their hearts to him—an evident demonstration of great delight. It was
Samson's carnal delight in Delilah that prevailed with him to reveal unto
her those things which were of greatest concernment unto him; he will
not hide his mind from her, though it cost him his life [Judges 16]. It is

only a bosom *friend* into whom we will *unbosom* ourselves. Neither is there, possibly, a greater evidence of delight in close communion than this, that one will reveal his heart unto him whom he takes into society, and not entertain him with things common and vulgarly known. And therefore have I chose this instance, from amongst a thousand that might be given, of this delight of Christ in his saints.

He, then, communicates his mind unto his saints, and unto *them only*—his mind, the counsel of his love, the thoughts of his heart, the purposes of his bosom, for our eternal good—his mind, the ways of his grace, the workings of his Spirit, the rule of his scepter, and the obedience of his gospel. All *spiritual* revelation is by Christ. He is "the true Light, that lights every man that comes into the world" (John 1:9). He is the "Day-spring," the "Day-star," and the "Sun,"[3] so that it is impossible any light should be but by him. From him it is that "the secret of the LORD is with them that fear him, and he shows them his covenant" (Ps. 25:14); as he expresses it at large: "You are my friends, if you do whatsoever I command you.[4] Henceforth I call you not servants; for the servant knows not what his lord does: but I have called you friends; for all things[5] that I have heard of my Father I have made known unto you" (John 15:14–15). He makes them as his friends, and uses them as friends—as bosom friends, in whom he is delighted. He makes known all his mind unto them; every thing that his Father has committed to him as Mediator to be revealed (Acts 20:24). And the apostle declares how this is done: "'God has revealed these things unto us by his Spirit;' for we have received him, 'that we might know the things that are freely given us of God'" (1 Cor. 2:10–11). He sends us his Spirits as he promised, to make known his mind unto his saints and to lead them into all truth. And thence the apostle concludes, "We have known the mind of Christ" (1 Cor. 2:16), "for he uses us as friends, and declares it unto us" (John 1:18). There is not anything in the heart of Christ, wherein

---

3. Mal. 4:2; Luke 1:78; 2 Pet. 1:19.

4. *Voluntatem Dei nosse quisquam desiderat? fiat amicus Deo, quia si voluntatem hominis nosse vellet, cujus amicus non esset, omnes ejus impudentiam et stultitiam deriderent.* ["And if anyone desires to know God's will, let him first become a friend with God, because anyone wishing to know a human person's will without being his friend, would find everybody mocking his shameless folly." Augustine, *On Genesis: A Refutation of the Manichees*, in *On Genesis*, The Works of Saint Augustine: A Translation for the 21st Century, trans. Edmund Hill (Hyde Park, NY: New City Press, 2002), 42; PL 34, col. 175.]

5. *Vox panta ex subjecta materia, restrictionem ad doctrinam salutis requirit.* ["Every voice that is subject to matter requires restraint for the doctrine of salvation." Paulus Tarnovius, *Pauli Tarnovii in S. Johannis Evangelium commentarius* (Rostochii: Hallervordius, 1629).]

these his friends are concerned, that he does not reveal to them. All his *love*, his *goodwill*, the *secrets* of his covenant, the *paths* of obedience, the *mystery* of faith, is told them.

And all this is spoken in opposition to *unbelievers*, with whom he has no *communion*. These know nothing of the mind of Christ as they ought: "The natural man receives not the things that are of God" (1 Cor. 2:14). There is a wide difference between understanding *the doctrine of the Scripture* as in the letter, and a true knowing the mind of Christ. This we have by special unction from Christ (1 John 2:27), "We have an unction from the Holy One, and we know all things" (1 John 2:20).

Now, the things which in this communion Christ reveals to them that *he delights in*, may be referred to these two heads: (1) Himself. (2) His kingdom.

Himself. "He that loves me shall be loved of my Father; and I will love him, and will manifest myself unto him" (John 14:21)—"manifest myself in all my graces, desirableness, and loveliness; he shall know me as I am, and such I will be unto him—a Savior, a Redeemer, the chief of ten thousand." He shall be acquainted with the true worth and value of the pearl of price; let others look upon him as having neither form nor comeliness, as no way desirable, he will manifest himself and his excellencies unto them in whom he is delighted, that they shall see him altogether lovely. He will veil himself to all the world; but the saints with open face shall behold his beauty and his glory, and so be translated into the image of the same glory, as by the Spirit of the Lord (2 Cor. 3:18).

His kingdom. They shall be acquainted with the *government of his Spirit* in their hearts; as also with his rule and the administration of authority in his word and among his churches.

Thus, in the first place, does he manifest his *delight* in his saints—he communicates his *secrets* unto them. He gives them to know his person, his excellencies, his grace, his love, his kingdom, his will, the riches of his goodness, and the bowels of his mercy, more and more, when the world shall neither see nor know any such thing.

Second, he enables his saints to *communicate* their mind, to reveal their souls, unto him, that so they may walk together as intimate friends. Christ knows *the minds of all*. He knows what is in man, and needs not that any man testify of him (John 2:25). He searches the hearts and tries the reins of all (Rev. 2:23). But all know not how to communicate their mind to Christ. It will not avail a man at all that Christ knows his mind; for so he does of every one, whether he will or no—but that a man can make his heart known unto Christ, this is consolation. Hence the prayers of the saints are incense, odors (Rev. 8:3); and those of others are howling, cutting off a dog's neck, offering of swine's blood[6]—an abomination unto the Lord. Now, three things are required to enable a man to communicate his heart unto the Lord Jesus:

Assistance for the work; for of ourselves we cannot do it. And this the saints have by the Spirit of Jesus: "Likewise the Spirit also helps our infirmities: for we know not what we should pray for as we ought; but the Spirit itself makes intercession for us with groanings which cannot be uttered. And he that searches the hearts knows what is the mind of the Spirit, because he makes intercession for the saints according to the will of God" (Rom. 8:26–27). All endeavors, all attempts for communion with God, without the supplies of the Spirit of supplications, without his effectual working in the heart, is of no value, nor to any purpose. And this *opening* of our hearts and bosoms to the Lord Jesus is that wherein he is exceedingly delighted. Hence is that affectionate call of his unto us, to be treating with him on this account: "O my dove, that are in the secret places of the stairs, let me see your countenance, let me hear your voice; for sweet is your voice, and your countenance is comely" (Song 2:14). When the soul on any account is driven to hide itself—in any neglected condition, in the most unlikely place of abode—then does he call for this communication of itself by prayer to him; for which he gives the assistance of the Spirit mentioned.

A way whereby to approach unto God with our desires. This, also, we have by him provided for us: "Thomas says unto Jesus, Lord, we know not whither you go; and how can we know the way? Jesus says unto him, I am the way[7] [and the truth and the life]; no man comes unto the Father, but by me" (John 14:5–6). That way which we had of going unto God at our *creation* is quite shut up by *sin*. The sword of the law, which has fire put into it by sin, turns every way, to stop all passages unto communion with God. Jesus Christ has "consecrated a new and living way"[8] (for the saints) "through the veil, that is to say, his flesh" (Heb. 10:20). He has consecrated and set it apart for believers, and for them alone. Others pretend to go to God with their prayers, but they come

---

6. Hos. 7:14; Isa. 66:3; Prov. 28:9.

7. *Vera via vitæ*. ["The true way of life." Theodore Beza.]

8. *Via nullius ante trita solo. Prosphaton kai zōsan, recens interfectam; tamen viventem*. ["The road never before traveled on earth; new and living, just put to death, yet alive." Cf. *Lucretius: De Rerum Natura*, Loeb Classical Library, trans. W. H. D. Rouse (Cambridge, MA: Harvard University Press, 1975), 77; Heb. 10:20; Tertullian, *The Five Books Against Marcion*, ANF 3:309; PL 2, col. 0303B.]

not nigh him. How can they possibly come to the end who go not in the way? Christ only is the way to the throne of grace; none comes to God but by him. "By him we have an access in one Spirit unto the Father" (Eph. 2:18). These two things, then, the saints have for the opening of their hearts at the throne of grace—*assistance* and a *way*. The assistance of the Spirit, without which they are nothing; and the way of Christ's mediation, without which God is not to be approached unto.

Boldness to go unto God. The voice of sinners in themselves, if once acquainted with the terror of the Lord, is: "Who among us shall dwell with the devouring fire? Who among us shall dwell with everlasting burnings?" (Isa. 33:14). And no marvel; shame and trembling before God are the proper issues of sin (Gen. 3:8–9). God will revenge that carnal, atheistic boldness which sinners out of Christ do use toward him. But we have now "boldness to enter into the holiest by the blood of Jesus, by a new and living way, which he has consecrated for us, through the veil, that is to say, his flesh: and having a high priest over the house of God, we may draw near with a true heart, in full assurance of faith" (Heb. 10:20). The truth is, such is the glory and terror of the Lord, such the infinite perfection of his holiness, that, on clear sight of it, it will make the soul conclude that of itself it cannot serve him[9]; nor will it be to any advantage, but add to the fierceness of his destruction, once to draw nigh to him. It is in Christ alone, and on the account alone of his oblation and intercession, that we have any boldness to approach unto him. And these three advantages have the saints of communicating their minds unto the Lord Christ, which he has provided for them, because he delights in them.

To touch a little by the way, because this is of great importance, I will instance in one of these, as I might in every one, that you may see the difference between a spiritual revealing of our minds unto Christ in this acceptable manner, and that praying upon conviction which others practice; and this shall be from the first—namely, the assistance we have by the Spirit.

The Spirit of Christ reveals to us *our own wants*, that we may reveal them unto him: "We know not what we should pray for as we ought" (Rom. 8:26);[10] no teachings under those of the Spirit of God are able to make our souls acquainted with their own wants—its burdens, its temptations. For a soul to know its wants, its infirmities, is a heavenly

---

9. Josh. 24:19; Ex. 20:19; Deut. 5:25, 18:16; Isa. 33:14; Mic. 6:6–7.
10. Isa. 38:14.

discovery. He that has this assistance, his prayer is more than half made before he begins to pray.[11] His conscience is affected with what he has to do; his mind and spirit contend within him, there especially where he finds himself most straitened. He brings his burden on his shoulders, and unloads himself on the Lord Christ. He finds (not by a perplexing conviction, but a holy sense and weariness of sin) where he is dead, where dull and cold, wherein unbelieving, wherein tempted above all his strength, where the light of God's countenance is wanting. And all these the soul has a sense of by the Spirit—an inexpressible sense and experience. Without this, prayer is not prayer; men's voices may be heard, but they speak not in their hearts.[12] Sense of want is the spring of desire—natural, of natural; spiritual, of spiritual. Without this sense given by the Holy Ghost, there is neither desire nor prayer.

The *expressions*, or the words of such persons, come exceeding *short of the laboring of their hearts*; and therefore, in and after their supplications, "the Spirit makes intercession with sighs and groans that cannot be uttered" [Rom. 8:26].[13] Some men's words go exceedingly beyond their hearts. Did their spirits come up to their expressions, it were well. He that has this assistance can provide no clothing that is large and broad enough to set forth the desires of his heart; and therefore, in the close of his best and most fervent supplications, such a person finds a double dissatisfaction in them: (1) That they are not *a righteousness* to be rested on (Isa. 64:6); that if God should mark what is in them amiss, they could not abide the trial (Ps. 130:3). (2) That his heart in them is not *poured out*, nor delivered in any proportion to the holy desires and laborings that were conceived therein; though he may in Christ have great refreshment by them. The more they [saints] speak, the more they find they have left unspoken.

The intercession of the saints thus assisted is *according to the mind of God*; that is, they are guided by the Spirit to make requests for those things unto God which it is his will they should desire—which he knows to be good for them, useful and suitable to them, in the condition wherein they are. There are many ways whereby we may know when we make our supplications according to the will of God. I shall instance[14] only in one; that is, when we do it according to the promise: when our prayers

---

11. *Huperentugchanein, est advocatorum qui clientibus desideria dictant.* ["To intercede is characteristic of advocates who repeatedly state their desires to their clients."]

12. 1 Sam. 1:13.

13. Isa. 38:14; Ex. 14:15.

14. i.e., provide an example.

are regulated by the promise, we make them according to the will of God. So David [says], "Remember the word upon which you have caused me to hope" (Ps. 119:49). He prays, and regulates his desire by the word of promise wherein he had trusted. But yet, men may ask that which is in the promise, and yet not have their prayers regulated by the promise. They may pray for what is in the promise, but not as it is in the promise. So James says some "ask and receive not, because they ask amiss, that they may spend it on their lusts" (James 4:3). Though the things which God would have us ask be requested, yet if not according as he would have us do it, we ask amiss.

Two things are required, that we may pray for the things in the promise, as they are in the promise:

First, that we look upon them as *promised*, and promised in Christ; that is, that all the reason we have whence we hope for attaining the things we ask for, is from the mediation and purchase of Christ, in whom all the promises are yea and amen [2 Cor. 1:20]. This it is to ask the Father in Christ's name—God as a father, the fountain; and Christ as the procurer of them.

Second, that we ask for them for the *end* of the promise, not to spend on our lusts. When we ask pardon for sin, with secret reserves in our hearts to continue in sin, we ask the choicest mercy of the covenant, to spend it on our lusts.[15] The end of the promise the apostle tells us, "Having these promises, let us cleanse ourselves from all pollution of the flesh and spirit, perfecting holiness in the fear of God" (2 Cor. 7:1). When we ask what is in the promise, as it is in the promise, to this end of the promise, our supplications are according to the will of God. And this is the first conjugal affection that Christ exercises toward believers—*he delights in them*; which that he does is evident, as upon other considerations innumerable, so from the instance given.

In return hereunto, for the carrying on of the communion between them, *the saints' delight in Christ*; he is their joy, their crown, their rejoicing, their life, food, health, strength, desire, righteousness, salvation, blessedness: without him they have nothing; in him they shall find all things. "God forbid that I should glory, save in the cross of our Lord Jesus Christ" (Gal. 6:14). He has, from the foundation of the world, been the hope, expectation, desire, and delight of all believers. The promise of him was all (and it was enough) that God gave Adam in his inexpressible distress, to relieve and comfort him (Gen. 3:15). Eve

---

15. Ps. 78:35–37.

perhaps supposed that the promised seed had been born in her firstborn, when she said, "I have gotten a man from the LORD" (so most properly, '*et* denoting the fourth case[16]); and this was the matter of her joy (Gen. 4:1). Lamech having Noah given to him as a type of Christ and salvation by him, cries out, "This same shall comfort us concerning our work and toil of our hands, because of the ground which the LORD has cursed" (Gen. 5:29); he rejoices in him who was to take away the curse, by being made a curse for us. When Abraham was in the height of his glory, returning from the conquest of the kings of the east, that came against the confederate kings of the vale of Sodom, God appears to him with a glorious promise, "Fear not, Abram: I am your shield, and your exceeding great reward" (Gen. 15:1) What now could his soul more desire? Alas! he cries (as Reuben afterward, upon the loss of Joseph), "The child is not, and whither shall I go?" [Gen. 37:30]. "Lord GOD, what wilt you give me, seeing I go childless?" (Gen. 15:2). "You have promised that in my seed shall all the earth be blessed; if I have not that seed, ah! what good will all other things do me?" Thence it is said that he "rejoiced to see the day of Christ; he saw it, and was glad" (John 8:56); the thoughts of the coming of Christ, which he looked on at the distance of two thousand years, was the joy and delight of his heart. Jacob, blessing his sons, lifted up his spirit when he comes to Judah, in whom he considered the Shiloh to come (Gen. 49:8–9); and a little after, wearied with the foresight and consideration of the distresses of his posterity, this he diverts to for his relief, as that great delight of his soul: "I have waited for your Salvation, O God" [Gen. 49:18]—for him who was to be the salvation of his people. But it would be endless to instance in particulars. Old Simon sums up the whole: Christ is God's salvation, and Israel's glory (Luke 2:30–31); and whatever was called the glory of old, it was either himself or a type of him. The glory of man is their delight. Hence, he is called "The Desire of all nations" (Hag. 2:7). Him whom their soul loves and delights in, [they] desire and long after. So is the saints' delight in him made a description of him, by way of eminence: "The Lord whom you seek shall suddenly come to his temple, even the messenger of the covenant whom you delight in" (Mal. 3:1). "He whom you seek, whom you delight in" is the description of Christ. He is their delight and desirable one, the person of their desire. To fix on something in particular:

---

16. Owen believes that the preposition "from" should be dropped so that '*et* is in apposition to Yahweh (i.e., "I have gotten a man, [namely,] Yahweh").

In that pattern of communion with Jesus Christ which we have in the Canticles, this is abundantly insisted on. The spouse tells us that she sits down under his shadow with great delight (Song 2:3). And this delight to be vigorous and active, she manifests several ways; wherein we should labor to find our hearts in like manner toward him:

First, by her exceeding *great care to keep his company* and society, when once she had obtained it: "I charge you, O you daughters of Jerusalem, by the roes, and by the hinds of the field, that you stir not up, nor awake my love till he please" (Song 2:7). Having obtained sweet communion with Christ, described in the verses foregoing (of which before), here she expresses her delight in it and desire of the continuance of it; and therefore, following on the allusion formerly insisted on, she speaks as one would do to her companion, [as one] that had rest with one she loved: "I charge you, by all that is dear to you—by the things you most delight in, which among the creatures are most lovely, all the pleasant and desirable things that you can think of—that you disturb him not." The sum of her aim and desire is, that nothing may fall out, nothing of sin or provocation happen, that may occasion Christ to depart from her, or to remove from that dispensation wherein he seemed to take that rest in her: "O stir him not up until he please!" that is, never.[17] *Ha'ahabah*—love itself in the abstract, to express a *pathos*, or earnest affection; for so that word is often used. When once the soul of a believer has obtained sweet and real communion with Christ, it looks about him, watches all temptations, all ways whereby sin might approach, to disturb him in his enjoyment of his dear Lord and Savior, his rest and desire. How does it charge itself not to omit anything, nor to do anything that may interrupt the communion obtained! And because the common *entrance* of temptations, which tend to the *disturbance* of that rest and complacency which Christ takes in the soul, is from delightful diversions from actual communion with him; therefore is desire strong and active that the companions of such a soul, those with whom it does converse, would not, by their proposals or allurements, divert it into any such frame as Christ cannot delight nor rest in. A believer that has gotten Christ in his arms is like one that has found great spoils, or

---

17. *Æternitatem temporis juxta sensum mysticum in se includit, ut alias in Scriptura; quia nunquam a tali somno, id est, conjunctione cum sponso, excitari velit.* [[The passage] mentions an eternity of time according to the mystical sense, as elsewhere in Scripture; since she wishes never to be roused from such sleep, that is from union with her spouse. Joannis Mercerii (Jean Mercier), *Commentarii Iobus et Solomonis, Proverbia, Ecclesiastem, Canticum Canticorum* (Luduni Batavorum [Leyden]: Ex Offiina Francisci Hackii, 1651), 615.]

a pearl of price. He looks about him every way, and fears everything that may deprive him of it. Riches make men watchful; and the actual sensible possession of him, in whom are all the riches and treasure of God, will make men look about them for the keeping of him. The line of *choicest communion* is a line of the greatest *spiritual solicitousness*: *carelessness* in the enjoyment of Christ pretended is a manifest evidence of a *false* heart.

Second, the spouse manifests her delight in him by the utmost impatience of his absence, with desires still of nearer communion with him.[18] "Set me as a seal upon your heart, as a seal upon your arm: for love is strong as death; jealousy is cruel as the grave: the coals thereof are coals of fire, which has a most vehement flame" (Song 8:6). The allusion is doubtless from the high priest of the Jews, in his spiritual representation of the church before God. He had a breastplate which he is said to wear on his heart (Ex. 28:29), wherein the names of the children of Israel were engraven, after the manner of seals or signets, and he bare them for a memorial before the Lord. He had the like also upon his shoulders, or on his arms (Ex. 28:11–12); both representing the priesthood of Christ, who bears the names of all his before his Father in the "holy of holies" (Heb. 9:24). Now the seal on the heart is near, inward, tender love and care, which gives an impression and image on the heart of the thing so loved. "Set me," says the spouse, "as a seal upon your heart" [Song 8:6]; "Let me be constantly fixed in your most tender and affectionate love; let me always have a place in your heart; let me have an engraving, a mighty impression of love, upon your heart, that shall never be obliterated." The soul is never satisfied with thoughts of Christ's love to it. "O that it were more, that it were more! that I were as a 'seal on his heart!'" is its language. The soul knows, indeed, on serious thoughts, that the love of Christ is inconceivable and cannot be increased; but it would fain[19] work up itself to an apprehension of it: and therefore she adds here, "Set me as a seal upon your arm." The heart is the *fountain*, but close and hidden; the arm is *manifestation and power*. "Let," says the spouse, "your love be manifested to me in your tender and powerful persuasion of me." Two things are evident in this request: the continual mindfulness of Christ of the soul, as having its condition still in his eye, engraven on his arm (Isa. 49:15–16), with the exalting of his power for the preservation of it, suitable to the love

---

18. Hag. 2:23; Jer. 22:24.
19. eager, well-disposed, be delighted to.

of his heart unto it; and the manifestation of the hidden love and care of the heart of Christ unto the soul, being made visible on his arm, or evident by the fruit of it. This is that which she would be assured of; and without a sense whereof there is no rest to be obtained.

The reason she gives of this earnestness in her supplications is that which principally evinces her delight in him: "Love is strong as death, jealousy is cruel as the grave," or "hard as hell" [Song 8:6]. This is the intention of what is so loftily set out by so many metaphors in this and the following verse: "I am not able to bear the workings of my love to you, unless I may always have society and fellowship with you. There is no satisfying of my love without it. It is as the grave, that still says Give, give (Prov. 30:15). Death is not satisfied without its prey; if it have not *all*, it has *nothing*: let what will happen, if death has not its whole desire, it has nothing at all. Nor can it be withstood in its appointed season; no ransom will be taken. So is my love; if I have you not wholly, I have nothing. Nor can all the world bribe it to a diversion; it will be no more turned aside than death in its time. Also, I am not able to bear my jealous thoughts: I fear you do not love me, that you have forsaken me; because I know I deserve not to be beloved. These thoughts are hard as hell; they give no rest to my soul: if I find not myself on your heart and arm, I am as one that lies down in *a bed of coals*." This also argues a holy greediness of delight.

Third, she further manifests this by her solicitousness, trouble, and *perplexity* in his loss and withdrawings. Men bewail[20] the loss of that whose whole enjoyment they delight in; we easily bear the absence of that whose presence is not delightful. This state of the spouse is discovered: "By night[21] on my bed I sought him whom my soul loves:[22] I sought him, but I found him not. I will rise now, and go about the city in the streets, and in the broad ways I will seek him whom my soul loves: I sought him, but I found him not. The watchmen that go about the city found me: to whom I said, Saw you him whom my soul loves?" (Song 3:1–3). It is night now with the soul—a time of darkness and trouble, or affliction.

---

20. wail, cry out, lament.

21. Isa. 50:10.

22. *Eleganter periphrasi utitur loco nominis proprii, ut vim amoris sui exprimat. . . . Ista repetitio assensum indicat et studium quo eum quærebat, et mœrorem quo angebatur, quod occurrere non posset.* ["Elegantly she uses circumlocution in the place of the personal name, so that she may express the force of her love. . . . Such repetition indicates the favor and zeal with which she was seeking him, and the grief with which she was vexed, because she could not meet him." Joannis Merceri (Jean Mercier), *Commentarii Iobus et Solomonis, Proverbia, Ecclesiastem, Canticum Canticorum*, 618–19.]

Whenever Christ is absent, it is night with a believer. He is the *sun;*[23] if he go down upon them, if his beams be eclipsed, if in his light they see no light, it is all darkness with them. Here, whether the coming of the night of any trouble on her made her discover Christ's absence, or the absence of Christ made it night with her, is not expressed. I rather think the latter; because, setting that aside, all things seem to be well with her. The absence of Christ will indeed make it night, dark as darkness itself, in the midst of all other glowing consolations. But is the spouse contented with this dispensation? She is upon her bed—that is, of ease (the bed, indeed, sometimes signifies tribulation [Rev. 2:22]; but in this book, everywhere, rest and contentment: here is not the least intimation of any tribulation but what is in the want of Christ); but in the greatest peace and opportunity of ease and rest, a believer finds none in the absence of Christ: though he be on his bed, having nothing to disquiet him, he rests not, if Christ, his rest, be not there. She "sought him." Seeking of Christ by night, on the bed (that is, alone, in immediate inquest,[24] and in the dark), has two parts: searching of our own souls for the cause of his *absence*; secondly, searching the promises for his *presence*.

The soul finding not Christ present in his *wonted*[25] manner, *warming, cherishing, reviving it* with love, nigh to it, supping with it, always filling its thoughts with himself, dropping myrrh and sweet tastes of love into it; but, on the contrary, that other thoughts crowd in and perplex the heart, and Christ is not nigh when inquired after; it presently inquires into the cause of all this,[26] calls itself to an account what it has *done*, how it has *behaved itself*, that it is not with it as at other times—that Christ has withdrawn himself, and is not nigh to it in the wonted manner. Here it accomplishes a diligent search; it considers the love, tenderness, and kindness of the Lord Jesus, what delight he takes in abiding with his saints, so that his departure is not without cause and provocation. "How," says it, "have I demeaned myself, that I have lost my Beloved? Where have I been wandering after other lovers?" And when the miscarriage is found out, it abounds in revenge and indignation.

Having driven this to some *issue*, the soul applies itself to the promises of the covenant, wherein Christ is most graciously exhibited unto it; considers one, ponders another, to find a taste of him—it considers diligently if it can see the delightful countenance and favor of Christ in

---

23. Mal. 4:2.
24. inquiry, investigation.
25. accustomed
26. 2 Cor. 13:5.

them or no. But now, if (as it often falls out) the soul finds nothing but the *carcass*, but the bare *letter*, in the promise—if it come to it as to the grave of Christ, of which it may be said (not in itself, but in respect of the seeking soul), "He is risen, he is not here"—this amazes the soul, and it knows not what to do. As a man that has a jewel of great price, having no occasion to use it, lays it aside, as he supposes, in a safe place; in an agony and extremity of want going to seek for his jewel, he finds it not in the place he expected, and is filled with amazement, and knows not what to do—so is it with this pearl of the gospel. After a man has sold all that he has for it, and enjoyed it for a season, then to have it missing at a time of need, it must needs perplex him. So was it with the spouse here. "I sought him," says she, "but I found him not" [Song 3:1]; a thing which not seldom befalls us in our communion with Christ.

But what does she now do? Does she give over and search no more? Nay; but says she, "'I will arise' [Song 3:2]; I will not so give over. I must have Christ, or die. I will now arise" (or, "let me arise") "and go about this business."

She resolves to put herself upon *another course*, a more *vigorous inquest*: "I will arise and make use of other means besides those of private prayer, meditation, self-searching, and inquiring into the promises," which she had insisted on before. It carries—

Resolution, and a zealous, violent casting off that frame wherein she had lost her love. "'I will arise';[27] I will not rest in this frame: I am undone if I do." So, sometimes God calls his church to arise and shake itself out of the dust. Abide not in that condition.

Diligence. "I will now take another course; I will leave no way unattempted, no means untried, whereby I may possibly recover communion with my Beloved."

This is the condition of a soul that finds not the wonted presence of Christ in its private and more retired inquiries—dull in prayer, wandering in meditations, rare in thoughts of him—"I will not bear this frame: whatever way God has appointed, I will, in his strength, vigorously pursue, until this frame be altered and I find my Beloved."

Then the way she puts herself upon *is to go about the city*. Not to insist upon particulars, nor to strain the parts of the allegory too far, the city here intended is the city of God, the *church*; and the passing through the broad and narrow streets is the diligent inquiry that the spouse makes in all the paths and ordinances given unto it. This, then,

---

27. Isa. 52:2; 60:1.

is the next thing the soul addresses itself unto in the want of Christ: when it finds him not in any private endeavors, it makes vigorous application to the ordinances of public worship; in prayer, in preaching, in administration of the seals, does it look after Christ. Indeed, the great inquiry the souls of believers make, in every ordinance, is after Christ. So much as they find of him, so much sweetness and refreshment have they, and no more. Especially when under any desertion, they rise up to this inquiry: they listen to every word, to every prayer, to find if any thing of Christ, any light from him, any life, any love, appears to them. "Oh, that Christ would at length meet me in this or that sermon, and recover my poor heart to some sight of his love—to some taste at kindness!" The solicitousness of a believer in his inquest after Christ, when he finds not his presence, either for grace or consolation, as in former days, is indeed inexpressible. Much of the frame of such a heart is couched in the redoubling of the expression, "I sought him, I sought him"; setting out an inconceivable passion and suitably industrious desire. Thus, being disappointed at home, the spouse proceeds.

But yet see the *event* of this also: "She sought him, but found him not." It does sometimes so fall out, all will not do: "They shall seek him, and not find him"; they shall not come nigh him. Let them that enjoy anything of the presence of Christ take heed what they do; if they provoke him to depart, if they lose him, it may cost them many a bitter inquiry before they find him again. When a soul prays and meditates, searches the promises in private; when it with earnestness and diligence attends all ordinances in public, and all to get one glimpse of the face of Jesus Christ, and all in vain, it is a sad condition.

What now follows in this estate? "The watchmen found me," etc. (Song 3:3). That these watchmen of the city of God are the watchmen and officers of the church is confessed. And it is of sad consideration that the Holy Ghost does sometimes in this book take notice of them on no good account. Plainly, chapter 5:7, they turn persecutors. It was Luther's saying, "*Nunquam periclitatur religio nisi inter reverendissimos.*"[28] Here they are of a more gentle temper,[29] and seeing the poor disconsolate soul, they seem to take notice of her condition.

It is the duty, indeed, of faithful watchmen, *to take notice of poor, troubled, deserted souls*—not to keep at a distance, but to be willing to assist. And a truly pressed soul on the account of Christ's absence

---

28. "Religion is never in danger except among the most revered."
29. character, constitution, quality.

cannot cover its love, but must be inquiring after him: "Saw you him whom my soul loves?" [Song 3:3]. "This is my condition: I have had sweet enjoyment of my blessed Jesus—he is now withdrawn from me. Can you help me? Can you guide me to my consolation? What acquaintance have you with him? When saw you him? How did he manifest himself to you, and wherein?" All these laborings in his absence sufficiently discover the soul's delight in the presence of Christ. Go one step further, to the discovery that it made of him once again, and it will yet be more evident. "It was but a little that I passed from them, but I found him whom my soul loves: I held him, and would not let him go, until I had brought him into my mother's house, and into the chamber of her that conceived me. I charge you, O you daughters of Jerusalem" (Song 3:4–5), etc.

First, she tells you how she *came* to him: "She found him"—what ways and by what means is not expressed. It often so falls out in our communion with Christ, when private and public means fail, and the soul has nothing left but *waiting silently* and walking humbly, Christ appears; that his so doing may be evidently of grace. Let us not at any time give over in this condition. When all ways are past, the summer and harvest are gone without relief—when neither bed nor watchmen can assist—let us wait a little, and we shall see the Salvation of God. Christ honors his immediate absolute actings sometimes, though ordinarily he crowns his ordinances. Christ often manifests himself immediately, and out of ordinances, to them that wait for him in them—that he will do so to them that despise them, I know not. Though he will meet men unexpectedly in his way, yet he will not meet them at all out of it. Let us wait as he has appointed; let him appear as he pleases. How she deals with him when found is *next* declared: "She held him, and would not let him go," etc. [Song 3:4]. They are all expressions of the greatest joy and delight imaginable. The sum is: having at length come once more to an enjoyment of sweet communion with Christ, the soul lays fast hold on him by faith (*kratein*, "to hold fast," is an act of faith), refuses to part with him any more, in vehemency of love—tries to keep him in ordinances in the house of its mother, the church of God; and so uses all means for the confirming of the mutual love between Christ and her: all the expressions, all the allusions used, evidencing delight to the utmost capacity of the soul. Should I pursue all the instances and testimonies that are given hereunto, in that one book of the Song of Solomon, I must enter upon an exposition of the greatest part of it; which is not my present business. Let the hearts of the saints that are acquainted with these things be allowed to make the close. What is it they long for, they rejoice in? What is it that satisfies them to the utmost, and gives sweet complacency to their spirits in every condition? What is it whose *loss* they fear, whose *absence* they cannot bear? Is it not this their Beloved, and he alone?

This, also, they further manifest *by their delight in every thing that peculiarly belongs to Christ*, as his, in this world. This is an evidence of delight, when, for his sake whom we delight in, we also delight in everything that belongs to him. Christ's great interest in this world lies in his people and his ordinances—his household and their provision. Now in both these do the saints exceedingly delight, for his sake. Take an instance in both kinds in one man, namely, David, "In the saints and the excellent" (or the noble) "of the earth is all my delight; my delight in them" (Ps. 16:3). Christ says of his church that she is "*Hephzi-bah*," "My delight in her" (Isa. 62[:4]). Here says David of the same, "*Hephzi-bam*—"My delight in them." As Christ delights in his saints, so do they in one another, on his account. "Here," says David, "is all my delight." Whatever contentment he took in any other persons, it was nothing in comparison of the delight he took in them. Hence, mention is made of "laying down our lives for the brethren," or any common cause wherein the interest of the community of the brethren does lie.

Secondly, for the ordinances, consider the same person. Psalms 42, 84, and 48 are such plentiful testimonies throughout, as we need no further inquiring; nor shall I go forth to a new discourse on this particular.

And this is the first mutual consequential act of conjugal affection, in this communion between Christ and believers: *he delights in them, and they delight in him.* He delights in their prosperity, has pleasure in it; they delight in his honor and glory, and in his presence with them. For his sake they delight in his servants (though by the world contemned) as the most excellent in the world; and in his ordinances, as the wisdom of God—which are foolishness to the world.

Chapter 5

Christ values his saints, values believers (which is the second branch of that conjugal affection he bears toward them), having taken them into the relation whereof we speak. I shall not need to insist long on the demonstration hereof; heaven and earth are full of evidences of it. Some few considerations will give life to the assertion. Consider them, then, (1) *absolutely*; (2) *in respect of others*; and you will see what a valuation he puts upon them:

All that ever he did or does, all that ever he underwent or suffered as mediator, was for their sakes. Now, these things were so great and grievous, that had he not esteemed them above all that can be expressed, he had never engaged to their performance and undergoing. Take a few instances:

For their sakes was he "made *flesh*" (John 1:14); "manifested in the flesh" (1 Tim. 3:16). "Forasmuch then as the children are partakers of flesh and blood, he also himself likewise took part of the same" (Heb. 2:14). And the height of this valuation of them the apostle aggravates.[1] "Verily he took not on him the nature of angels, but he took on him the seed of Abraham" (v. 16); he had no such esteem of angels. Whether you take *epilambamesthai* (properly to "take," or to "take hold of") as our translators, and so supply the word "nature," and refer the whole unto Christ's incarnation, who therein took our nature on him, and not the nature of angels; or for *analambanesthai*, to "help" (he did not help nor succor[2] fallen angels, but he did help and succor the seed of

---

1. adds to the weight of (in the sense of the Latin *aggravare*, "to make heavier").
2. assist, relieve.

Abraham[3]), and so consider it as the fruit of Christ's incarnation—it is all one, as to our present business: his preferring the seed of Abraham before angels, his valuing them above the other, is plainly expressed. And observe that he came to help the seed of Abraham—that is, *believers*.[4] His esteem and valuation is of them only.

For their sakes he was so made flesh, as that there was an *emptying*, an *exinanition*[5] of himself [Phil. 2:8], and an eclipsing of his glory, and a becoming poor for them, "you know the grace of our Lord Jesus Christ, that, though he was rich, yet for our sakes he became poor" (2 Cor. 8:9). Being rich in eternal glory with his Father (John 17:5), he became poor for believers. The same person that was rich was also poor. That the riches here meant can be none but those of the Deity is evident by its opposition to the poverty which as man he undertook. This is also more fully expressed: "Who being in the form of God, counted it no robbery to be equal to God, but he emptied himself, taking the form of a servant, and being made in the fashion of a man, and found in form as a man," etc. (Phil. 2:6–7). That the "form of God" is here the essence of the Deity, sundry things inevitably evince; as—

That he was therein *equal* to God,[6] that is, his Father. Now, nothing but God is equal to God. Not Christ as he is mediator, in his greatest glory (John 14:28)—nothing but that which is infinite, is equal to that which is infinite.

The *form of God* is opposed to the *form of a servant*; and that form of a servant is called the "fashion of a man" (Phil. 2:8)—that fashion wherein he was found when he gave himself to death, wherein as a man he poured out his blood and died. *Morphēn doulou labōn* (he "took the form of a servant") is expounded in the next words, *en homoiōmati anthrōpōn genomenos*—an expression used to set out his incarnation (Rom. 8:3). God sent him *en homoiōmati sarkos amartias* in taking true flesh, he was "in the likeness of sinful flesh." Now, in thus doing, it is said *eauton ekenōse*—"he humbled, emptied himself, made himself of no reputation." In the very taking of flesh, there was a condescension, a debasing of the person of the Son of God; it could not be without it. If God humbled himself to "behold the things that are in heaven, and in the earth" (Ps. 113:6), then certainly it was an inconceivable condescension

---

3. See John Owen, *Vindiciae Evangelicae* [*Mystery of the Gospel Vindicated* (1655), *Works*, 12:205–36].

4. Rom. 4:17; Gal. 3:7.

5. abasement, humiliation.

6. See Owen, *Vindiciae Evangelicae*, 205–36.

and abasement, not only to *behold*, but *take upon him* (into personal union) our nature with himself. And though nothing could possibly be taken off from the essential glory of the Deity, yet that person appearing in the fashion of a man, and form of a servant, the glory of it, as to the manifestation, was eclipsed; and he appeared quite another thing than what indeed he was, and had been from eternity (Isa. 53:2). Hence he prays that his Father would "glorify him with the glory he had with him before the world was" (John 17:5), as to the manifestation of it. And so, though the divine nature was not abased, the person was.

For their sakes he so humbled and emptied himself, in taking flesh, as to become therein a *servant*—in the eyes of the world of no esteem nor account; and a true and real servant unto the Father.[7] For their sakes he humbled himself and became obedient. All that he did and suffered in his life comes under this consideration; all which may be referred to these three heads: (1) *Fulfilling all righteousness* (Matt. 3:15). (2) *Enduring all manner of persecutions* and hardships. (3) *Doing all manner of good to men.* He took on him, for their sakes, a life and course pointed to (Heb. 5:7–8)—a life of prayers, tears, fears, obedience, suffering; and all this with cheerfulness and delight, calling his employment his "meat and drink," and still professing that the law of this obedience was in his heart (Heb. 10:7–8)—that he was content to do this will of God. He that will sorely revenge the least opposition that is or shall be made to him by others, was content to undergo any thing, all things, for believers.

He stays not here, but (for the consummation of all that went before) for their sakes he becomes *obedient to death*, the death of the cross. So he professes to his Father: "For their sakes I sanctify myself" (John 17:19)—"I dedicate myself as an offering, as a sacrifice, to be killed and slain." This was his aim in all the former, that he might die; he was born, and lived, that he might die (Heb. 2:14–15). He valued them above his life. And if we might stay to consider a little what was in this death that he underwent for them, we should perceive what a price indeed he put upon them. *The curse of the law* was in it (Gal. 3:13); the *wrath of God* was in it (2 Cor. 5:21); the *loss of God's presence* was in it (Ps. 22:1). It was a fearful cup that he tasted of, and drank of, that they might never taste of it (Matt. 26:39). A man would not for ten thousand worlds be willing to undergo that which Christ underwent for us in that one thing of desertion from God, were it attended with no more distress but what

---

7. Isa. 42:1, 19; John 14:31.

a mere creature might possibly emerge from under. And what thoughts we should have of this himself tells us, "Greater love has no man than this, that a man lay down his life for his friends" (John 15:13). It is impossible there should be any greater demonstration or evidence of love than this. What can any one do more? And yet he tells us in another place that it has another aggravation and heightening: "God commends his love toward us, in that, while we were yet sinners, Christ died for us" (Rom. 5:8). When he did this for us we were sinners, and enemies, whom he might justly have destroyed. What more can be done?—to die for us when we were sinners! Such a death, in such a manner, with such attendancies of wrath and curse—a death accompanied with the worst that God had ever threatened to sinners—argues as high a valuation of us as the heart of Christ himself was capable of.

For one to part with his glory, his riches, his ease, his life, his love from God—to undergo loss, shame, wrath, curse, death, for another—is an evidence of a dear valuation; and that it was all on this account, we are informed (Heb. 12:2). Certainly Christ had a dear esteem of them, that, rather than they should perish—that they should not be his, and be made partakers of his glory—he would part with all he had for their sakes (Eph. 5:25–26).

There would be no end should I go through all the instances of Christ's valuation of believers, in all their deliverances, afflictions, in all conditions of *sinning and suffering*—what he has done, what he does in his intercession, what he delivers them from, what he procures for them; all telling out this one thing—they are the apple of his eye, his jewel, his diadem, his crown.

In comparison of others. All the *world* is nothing to him in comparison of them. They are his *garden*; the rest of the world, a *wilderness*. "A garden enclosed is my sister, my spouse; a spring shut up, a fountain sealed" (Song 4:12). They are his *inheritance*; the rest, his enemies, of no regard with him. So Isaiah 43:3–4, "I am the LORD your God, the Holy One of Israel, your Savior: I gave Egypt for your ransom, Ethiopia and Seba for you. Since you were precious[8] in my sight, you have been honorable, and I have loved you: therefore will I give men for you, and people for your life." The reason of this dealing of Christ with his church, in parting with all others for them, is because he loves her. She

---

8. *Amorem istum non esse vulgarem ostendit, dum nos pretiosos esse dicit.* [Cf. "He means that this love is not of an ordinary kind when he says that we are 'precious.'" John Calvin, *Commentary on the Book of the Prophet Isaiah*, 4 vols., trans. Rev. William Pringle, in *Calvin's Commentaries* (1850; reprint, Grand Rapids, MI: Baker, 1989), 3:323.]

is precious and honorable in his sight; thence he puts this great esteem upon her. Indeed, he disposes of all nations and their interests according as is for the good of believers. In all the siftings of the nations, the eye of God is upon the house of Israel; not a grain of them shall perish (Amos 9:9). Look to heaven; *angels* are appointed to minister for them (Heb. 1:14). Look into the world; the *nations* in general are either blessed for their sakes,[9] or destroyed on their account[10]—preserved to try them, or rejected for their cruelty toward them; and will receive from Christ their final doom according to their deportment[11] toward these despised ones.[12] On this account are the pillars of the earth borne up, and patience is exercised toward the perishing world. In a word, there is not the meanest,[13] the weakest, the poorest believer on the earth, but Christ prizes him more than all the world besides. Were our hearts filled much with thoughts hereof, it would tend much to our consolation.

To answer this, *believers also value Jesus Christ*; they have an esteem of him above all the world, and all things in the world. You have been in part acquainted with this before, in the account that was given of their delight in him, and inquiry after him. They say of him in their hearts continually, as David, "Whom have I in heaven but you? And none upon earth I desire beside you" (Ps. 73:25). Neither heaven nor earth will yield them an object any way comparable to him, that they can delight in.

They value him above all other things and persons. "*Mallem,*" said one, "*ruere cum Christo, quam regnare cum Cæsare. Pulchra terra, pulchrum coelum, sed pulcherrimus dominus Jesus*"[14]—Christ and a dungeon, Christ and a cross, is infinitely sweeter than a crown, a scepter without him, to their souls. So was it with Moses, "He esteemed the reproach of Christ greater riches than the treasures in Egypt" (Heb. 11:26). The reproach of Christ is the worst consequent that the wickedness of the world or the malice of Satan can bring upon the followers of him. The treasures of Egypt were in those days the greatest in the world; Moses despised the very best of the world, for the worst of the cross of Christ. Indeed, [Christ] himself has told believers, that if they

---

9. Gen. 12:3; Mic. 5:7–8.

10. Isa. 34:8; 61:2; 63:4.

11. conduct, behavior, demeanor.

12. Matt. 25:41–46.

13. lowly, debased.

14. Martin Luther: "Indeed, I would rather fall with Christ, than reign with Caesar. The earth is beautiful, heaven is beautiful, but the Lord Jesus is most beautiful."

love anything better than him, father or mother, they are not worthy of him [Matt. 10:37]. A despising of all things for Christ is the very first lesson of the gospel. "Give away all, take up the cross and follow me" [Matt. 16:24] was the way whereby he tried his disciples of old; and if there be not the same mind and heart in us, we are none of his.

They value him above their lives. "My life is not dear, that I may perfect my course with joy, and the ministry I have received of the Lord Jesus" (Acts 20:24)—"Let life and all go, so that I may serve him; and, when all is done, enjoy him, and be made like to him." It is known what is reported of Ignatius when he was led to martyrdom: "Let what will," said he, "come upon me, only so I may obtain Jesus Christ."[15] Hence they of old rejoiced when whipped, scourged, put to shame, for his sake (Acts 5:41; Heb. 11). All is welcome that comes from him, or for him. The lives they have to live, the death they have to die, is little, is light, upon the thoughts of him who is the stay of their lives and the end of their death. Were it not for the refreshment which daily they receive by thoughts of him, they could not live—their lives would be a burden to them; and the thoughts of enjoyment of him made them cry with Paul, "Oh that we were dissolved!" [cf. 2 Cor. 5:1]. The stories of the martyrs of old and of late, the sufferers in giving witness to him under the dragon and under the false prophet, the neglect of life in women and children on his account, contempt of torments, while his name sweetened all, have rendered this truth clear to men and angels.

They value him above all spiritual excellencies, and all other righteousness whatever, "Those things which were advantage to me, I esteemed loss for the excellency of the knowledge of Christ Jesus my Lord; for whose sake I have lost all things, and do esteem them common, that I may gain Christ, and be found in him" (Phil. 3:7–8). Having recounted the excellencies which he had, and the privileges which he enjoyed, in his Judaism—which were all of a spiritual nature, and a participation wherein made the rest of his countrymen despise all the world, and look upon themselves as the only acceptable persons with God, resting on them for righteousness—the apostle tells us what is his esteem of

---

15. *Nun archomai einai mathētēs, ouden toutōn tōn horōmenōn epithumō, hina ton Iēsoun Christon heurō. Pur, stauros, thēria, sugklasis osteōn, kai tōn melōn diaspasmos, kai pantos tou sōmatos suntribē, kai basanoi tou diabolou eis eme elthōsin, hina Iesou Christou apolausō.* ["Now do I begin to be a disciple, and desire none of the things visible that I may find Jesus Christ. Let fire and cross and attacks of wild beasts, let wrenching of bones, cutting apart of limbs, crushing of the whole body, tortures of the devil—let all these come upon me if only I may attain unto the joy which is in Christ." Jerome, *Lives of Illustrious Men,* NPNF[2] 3:367; PL 32, col. 636A.]

them, in comparison of the Lord Jesus. They are "loss and dung" [Phil. 3:8]—things that for his sake he had really suffered the loss of; that is, whereas he had for many years been a zealot of the law, seeking after a righteousness as it were by the works of it (Rom. 9:32), instantly[16] serving God day and night to obtain the promise (Acts 26:7), living in all good conscience from his youth (Acts 23), all the while very zealous for God and his institutions—now [he] willingly casts away all these things, looks upon them as loss and dung, and could not only be contented to be without them, but, as for that end for which he sought after them, he abhorred them all. When men have been strongly convinced of their duty, and have labored many years to keep a good conscience (Acts 23:1)—have prayed, and heard, and done good, and denied themselves, and been zealous for God (Rom. 10:2–3), and labored with all their might to please him (Acts 26:7), and so at length to come to enjoy him; they had rather part with all the world, life and all, than with this they have wrought.[17] You know how unwilling we are to part with anything we have labored and beaten our heads about? How much more when the things are so excellent, as our duty to God, blamelessness of conversation, hope of heaven, and the like, which we have beaten our hearts about. But now, when once Christ appears to the soul, when he is known in his excellency, all these things, as without him, have their paint washed off, their beauty fades, their desirableness vanishes, and the soul is not only contented to part with them all, but puts them away as a defiled thing and cries, "In the Lord Jesus only is my righteousness and glory" (cf. Isa. 45:24). Proverbs 3:13–15, among innumerable testimonies, may be admitted to give witness hereunto: "Happy is the man that finds wisdom, and the man that gets understanding. For the merchandise of it is better than the merchandise of silver, and the gain thereof than fine gold. She is more precious than rubies: and all the things that you can desire are not to be compared unto her." It is of Jesus Christ, the Wisdom of God, the eternal Wisdom of the Father, that the Holy Ghost speaks; as is evident from the description which is given hereof (Proverbs 8). He and his ways are better than silver and gold, rubies, and all desirable things; as in the gospel he likens himself to the "pearl in the field," which when the merchant man finds, he sells all that he has, to purchase (Matt. 13:45–46).[18] All goes for Christ—all righteousness without him,

---

16. insistently

17. John 9:40; Rom. 9:30–31.

18. *Principium culmenque omnium rerum pretii, margaritæ tenent.* ["The first place therefore and the topmost rank among all things of price is held by pearls." Pliny the Elder, *Pliny: Natural*

all ways of religion, all goes for that one pearl. The glory of his Deity, the excellency of his person, his all-conquering desirableness, ineffable love, wonderful undertaking, unspeakable condescensions, effectual mediation, complete righteousness, lie in their eyes, ravish their hearts, fill their affections, and possess their souls. And this is the second mutual conjugal affection between Christ and believers; all which, on the part of Christ, may be referred unto two heads:

First, all that he parted with, all that he did, all that he suffered, all that he does as mediator; he parted with, did, suffered, does on the account *of his love to and esteem of believers.*[19] He parted with the greatest glory, he underwent the greatest misery, he does the greatest works that ever were, because he loves his spouse—because he values believers. What can more, what can further be spoken? How little is the depth of that which is spoken fathomed! How unable are we to look into the mysterious recesses of it! He so loves, so values his saints, as that, having from eternity undertaken to bring them to God, he rejoices his soul in the thoughts of it; and pursues his design through heaven and hell, life and death, by suffering and doing, in mercy and with power; and ceases not until he bring it to perfection. For—

Second, he does so value them, as that he will not *lose* any of them to *eternity*, though all the world should combine to take them out of his hand. When in the days of his flesh he foresaw what opposition, what danger, what rocks they should meet with, he cried out, "Holy Father, keep them" (John 17:11)—"Let not one of them be lost"; and tells us plainly that no man shall take his sheep out of his hand (John 10:28). And because he was then in the form of a servant, and it might be supposed that he might not be able to hold them, he tells them true, as to his present condition of carrying on the work of mediation, his "Father was greater than he" (John 14:28); and therefore to him he committed them, and none should take them out of his Father's hand (John 10:29). And whereas the world, afflictions, and persecutions, which are without, may be conquered, and yet no security given but that sin from within, by the assistance of Satan, may prevail against them to their ruin; as he has provided against Satan, in his promise that the gates of hell shall not prevail against them, so he has taken care that sin itself shall not destroy them. Herein, indeed, is the depth of his love to be contemplated, that

History, in *Pliny: Natural History III, Libri VII–XI*, Loeb Classical Library, trans. H. Rackham (Cambridge, MA: Harvard University Press, 1967), 235.]

19. Gal. 2:20; John 13:34; Rev. 1:5–6; Eph. 5:25–26; Heb. 10:9–10.

whereas his holy soul hates every sin (it is a burden, an abomination, a new wound to him), and his poor spouse is sinful (believers are full of sins, failings, and infirmities), he hides all, covers all, bears with all, rather than he will lose them; by his power preserving them from such sins as a remedy is not provided for in the covenant of grace. Oh, the world of sinful follies that our dear Lord Jesus bears with on this account! Are not our own souls astonished with the thoughts of it? Infinite patience, infinite forbearance, infinite love, infinite grace, infinite mercy, are all set on work for this end, to answer this his valuation of us.

On our part it may also be referred to two heads:

First, that, upon the discovery of him to our souls, they rejoice to *part* with all things wherein they have delighted or reposed their confidence, *for him and his sake*, that they may enjoy him.[20] Sin and lust, pleasure and profit, righteousness and duty, in their several conditions, all shall go, so they may have Christ.

Second, that they are willing to part with all things rather than with him, when they do enjoy him (Matt. 10:37). To think of parting with peace, health, liberty, relations, wives, children; it is offensive, heavy, and grievous to the best of the saints: but their souls cannot bear the thoughts of parting with Jesus Christ; such a thought is cruel as the grave. The worst thoughts that, in any fear, in desertions (Song 8:6), they have of hell, is that they shall not enjoy Jesus Christ.[21] So they may enjoy him here, hereafter be like him, be ever with him, stand in his presence; they can part with all things freely, cheerfully, be they never so beautiful, in reference to this life or that which is to come.

The third conjugal affection on the part of Christ is *pity and compassion*. As a man "nourishes and cherishes his own flesh,[22] so does the Lord his church" (Eph. 5:29). Christ has a fellow feeling with his saints in all their troubles, as a man has with his own flesh. This act of the conjugal love of Christ relates to the many trials and pressures of afflictions that his saints meet with here below. He does not deal with

---

20. Matt. 13:45–46; Phil. 3:8.

21. *Kai touto moi tōn en hadou kolaseōn baruteron an eiē.* ["And I think that this might be fiercer than the punishments in hell." Basil.]

22. *Fateor insitam esse nobis corporis nostri caritatem.* ["I confess that we all have an inborn affection for our body." Lucius Annaeus Seneca, Epistle XIV, in *Moral Epistles*, 3 vols., trans. Richard M. Gummere, The Loeb Classical Library (Cambridge, MA: Harvard University Press, 1917–1925), 1:85.] *Generi animantium omni est a natura tributum ut se, vitam, corpusque tueatur.* ["First of all, Nature has endowed every species of living creature with the instinct of self-preservation." Cicero, *Cicero: De Officiis*, trans. Walter Miller (New York: G. P. Putman's Sons, 1956), 13.]

believers as the Samaritans with the Jews, that fawned on them in their prosperity, but despised them in their trouble; he is as a tender father (Ps. 103:13), who, though perhaps he love all his children alike, yet he will take most pains with, and give most of his presence unto, one that is sick and weak, though therein and thereby he may be made most froward,[23] and, as it should seem, hardest to be borne with. And (which is more than the pity of any father can extend to) he himself suffers with them and takes share in all their troubles.

Now all the sufferings of the saints in this world, wherein their head and husband exercises pity, tenderness, care, and compassion toward them, are of two sorts, or may be referred to two heads: (1) temptations; (2) afflictions.

Temptations (under which head I comprise sin also, whereto they tend); as in, from, and by their own infirmities; as also from their adversaries without. The frame of the heart of Christ, and his deportment toward them in this condition, you have, "We have not a high priest which cannot be touched with the feeling of our infirmities" (Heb. 4:15). We have not such a one as cannot. The two negations do vehemently affirm that we have such a high priest as can be, or is, touched. The word "touched" comes exceedingly short of expressing the original word; it is *sumpathēsai*—to "suffer together."[24] "We have," says the apostle, "such a high priest as can, and consequently does, suffer with us—endure our infirmities." And in what respect he suffers with us in regard of our infirmities, or has a fellow-feeling with us in them, he declares in the next words, "He was tempted like as we are" (v. 15). It is as to our infirmities, our temptations, spiritual weakness;[25] therein,

---

23. stubbornly contrary, obstinate.

24. *Hoc quidem certum est, hoc vocabulo, summum illum consensum membrorum et capitis (id est, ecclesiæ et Christi) significari, de quo toties Paulus disserit. Deinde ut cum de Deo loquitur, ita, etiam de Christo glorioso disserens Scriptura, ad nostrum captum se demittit. Gloriosum autem ad dextram patris Christum sedere credimus; ubi dicitur nostris malis affici, quod sibi factum ducat quicquid nobis fit injuriæ, ideo clamans e cœlis, Saul cur me presequeris? Altiores speculationes scrutari, nec utile nec tutum existimo.* ["Indeed it is certain that, by this word, that supreme agreement between the members and the head (that is, between the church and Christ) is signified, about which Paul is generally discussing. Next, that when he speaks about God, thus, and discussing the Scriptures about the glorious Christ, he brings himself down to our comprehension. However we believe that the glorious Christ sits at the right hand of the Father; where he is said to be affected by our calamities, because he would regard as having been done to himself whatever may be injurious to us, for that reason shouting from heaven, 'Saul why do you persecute me?' I think that loftier speculations examine what is neither profitable nor safe." Theodore Beza, *Jesu Christi Domini Nostri Novum Testamentum, sive Novum Foedus* (Cantabrigiae: Ex Officina Rogeri Danielis, 1642), 665.]

25. Rom. 8:26; 1 Cor. 11:32; 2 Cor. 11:30; 12:9, 10; Gal. 4:13.

in particular, has he a compassionate sympathy and fellow-feeling with us. Whatever be our infirmities, so far as they are our temptations, he does suffer with us under them, and compassionates us. Hence at the last day he says, "I was a hungered," etc. (Matt. 25:35). There are two ways of expressing a fellow-feeling and suffering with another: (1) *Per benevolam condolentiam*—a "friendly grieving." (2) *Per gratiosam opitulationem*—a "gracious supply": both are eminent in Christ:

He *grieves and labors* with us.[26] "The angel of the LORD answered and said, O LORD of hosts, how long will you not have mercy on Jerusalem?" (Zech. 1:12). He speaks as one intimately affected with the state and condition of poor Jerusalem; and therefore he has bid all the world take notice that what is done to them is done to him (Zech. 2:8–9); yea, to "the apple of his eye."[27]

In the second he abounds. "He shall feed his flock like a shepherd, he shall gather the lambs with his arm, and carry them in his bosom, and gently lead them that are with young" (Isa. 40:11). Yea, we have both here together—*tender compassionateness and assistance.* The whole frame wherein he is here described[28] is a frame of the greatest tenderness, compassion, condescension that can be imagined.[29] His people are set forth under many infirmities; some are lambs, some great with young, some very tender, some burdened with temptations—nothing in any of them all strong or comely. To them all Christ is a shepherd that feeds his own sheep and drives them out to pleasant pasture;[30] where, if he sees a poor weak lamb, does not thrust him on, but takes him into his

---

26. Acts 9:4; Isa. 63:9.

27. Deut. 32:10; Ps. 17:8.

28. *En ipse capellas / Protinus æger ago; hanc etiam vix Tityre duco,* etc. ["See, heartsick, I myself am driving my goats along, and here, Tityrus, is one I scarce can lead." Virgil, *Virgil I: Eclogues, Georgics, Aeneid I–VI,* Loeb Classical Library, trans. H. R. Fairclough (Cambridge, MA: Harvard University Press, 1960), 2.]

29. *Quod frequentur in Scriptura, pastoris nomen Deus usurpat, personamque induit, non vulgare est teneri in nos amoris signum. Nam quum humilis et abjecta sit loquendi forma, singulariter erga nos affectus sit oportet, qui se nostrâ causa ita demittere non gravatur: mirum itaque nisi tam blanda et familiaris invitatio ad eum nos alliciat.* ["God, in the Scripture, frequently takes to himself the name, and puts on the character of a shepherd, and this is no mean token of his tender love toward us. As this is a lowly and homely manner of speaking, He who does not disdain to stoop so low for our sake, must bear a singularly strong affection toward us. It is therefore wonderful, that when he invites us to himself with such gentleness and familiarity, we are not drawn or allured to him, that we may rest in safety and peace under his guardianship." John Calvin, *Commentary upon the Book of Psalms,* vol. 1 of *Calvin's Commentaries Volume IV,* trans. James Anderson (Grand Rapids, MI: Baker, 2003), 391–92.]

30. Heb. 13:20; 1 Pet. 2:25; 5:4; Ps. 23:1; Zech. 13:7; Isa. 40:11; Ezek. 34:23; John 10:11, 14, 16.

bosom, where he both eases and refreshes him: he leads him gently and tenderly. As did Jacob [lead] them that were burdened with young (Gen. 33:13), so does our dear Lord Jesus with his flock, in the several ways and paths wherein he leads them. When he sees a poor soul—weak, tender, halting, ready to sink and perish—he takes him into his arms, by some gracious promise administered to him, carries him, bears him up when he is not able to go one step forward. Hence is his great quarrel with those shepherds, "Woe be to you shepherds! The diseased have you not strengthened, neither have you healed that which was sick, neither have you bound up that which was broken, neither have you brought again that which was driven away, neither have you sought that which was lost" (Ezek. 34:4). This is that which our careful, tender husband would have done.

So mention being made of his compassionateness and fellow-suffering with us (Heb. 4:15), it is added, v. 16, that he administers *charin eis eukairon boētheian*—seasonable grace, grace for help in a time of need. This is an evidence of compassion, when, like the Samaritan, we afford[31] seasonable help. To lament our troubles or miseries, without affording help, is to no purpose. Now, this Christ does; he gives *eukairon boētheian*—seasonable help. Help being a thing that regards want, is always excellent; but its coming in season puts a crown upon it. A pardon to a malefactor,[32] when he is ready to be executed, is sweet and welcome. Such is the assistance given by Christ. All his saints may take this as a sure rule, both in their temptations and afflictions: when they can want them, they shall not want relief; and when they can bear no longer, they shall be relieved (1 Cor. 10:13).

So it is said *emphatically* of him: "In that he himself has suffered being tempted, he is able to succor them that are tempted" (Heb. 2:18). It is true, there is something in all our temptations more than was in the temptation of Christ. There is something in ourselves to take part with every temptation; and there is enough in ourselves to tempt us, though nothing else should appear against us (James 1:14–15). With Christ it was not so (John 14:30). But this is so far from taking off his compassion toward us, that, on all accounts whatever, it does increase it; for if he will give us succor because we are tempted, the sorer our temptations are, the more ready will he be to succor us. Take some instances

---

31. supply
32. criminal

of Christ's giving *eukairon boētheian*—"seasonable help" in and under temptations unto sin. Now this he does several ways:

By keeping the soul which is liable to temptation and exposed to it, *in a strong habitual bent* against that sin that he is obnoxious to the assaults of. So it was in the case of Joseph: Christ knew that Joseph's great trial, and that whereon if he had been conquered he had been undone, would lie upon the hand of his mistress tempting him to lewdness; whereupon he kept his heart in a steady frame against that sin, as his answer without the least deliberation argues (Gen. 39:9). In other things, wherein he was not so deeply concerned, Joseph's heart was not so fortified by habitual grace; as it appears by his swearing by the life of Pharaoh (Gen. 42:15). This is one way whereby Christ gives suitable help to his, in tenderness and compassion. The saints, in the course of their lives, by the company, society, business, they are cast upon, are liable and exposed to temptations great and violent, some in one kind, some in another. Herein is Christ exceedingly kind and tender to them, in fortifying their hearts with abundance of grace as to that sin unto temptations whereunto they are most exposed; when perhaps in other things they are very weak and are often surprised.

Christ sometimes, by some strong *impulse* of actual grace, recovers the soul *from the very borders of sin*. So it was in the case of David (1 Sam. 24:4–6). "He was almost gone," as he speaks himself; "his feet had well-nigh slipped." The temptation was at the door of prevalence, when a mighty impulse of grace recovers him. To show his saints what they are, their own weakness and infirmity, he sometimes suffers them to go to the very edge and brow of the hill, and then causes them to hear a word behind them saying, "This is the right way, walk in it"—and that with power and efficacy; and so recovers them to himself.

By taking away the *temptation itself*, when it grows so strong and violent that the poor soul knows not what to do. This is called "delivering the godly out of temptation" (2 Pet. 2:9), as a man is plucked out of the snare, and the snare left behind to hold another. This have I known to be the case of many, in sundry perplexing temptations. When they have been quite weary, have tried all means of help and assistance, and have not been able to come to a comfortable issue, on a sudden, unexpectedly, the Lord Christ, in his tenderness and compassion, rebukes Satan, that they hear not one word more of him as to their temptation. Christ comes in in the storm, and says, "Peace, be still."

By giving in *fresh supplies of grace*, according as temptations do grow or increase. So was it in the case of Paul: "My grace is sufficient for you" (2 Cor. 12:9). The temptation, whatever it were, grew high; Paul was earnest for its removal; and receives only this answer, of the sufficiency of the grace of God for his supportment, notwithstanding all the growth and increase of the temptation.

By giving them *wisdom* to make a *right, holy, and spiritual improvement* of all temptations. James bids us "count it all joy when we fall into divers temptations" (James 1:2): which could not be done were there not a holy and spiritual use to be made of them; which also himself manifests in the words following. There are manifold uses of temptations, which experienced Christians, with assistance suitable from Christ, may make of them. This is not the least, that by them we are brought to know ourselves. So Hezekiah was left to be tried, to know what was in him. By temptation, some bosom, hidden corruption is oftentimes discovered, that the soul knew not of before. As it was with Hazael in respect of enormous crimes (2 Kings 8:13), so in lesser things with the saints. They would never have believed there had been such lusts and corruptions in them as they have discovered upon their temptations. Yea, diverse [people] having been tempted to one sin, have discovered another that they thought not of; as some, being tempted to pride, or worldliness, or looseness of conversation, have been startled by it, and led to a discovery of neglect of many duties and much communion with God, which before they thought not of. And this is from the tender care of Jesus Christ, giving them in suitable help; without which no man can possibly make use of or improve a temptation. And this is a suitable help indeed, whereby a temptation which otherwise, or to other persons, might be a deadly wound, proves the lancing of a festered sore, and the letting out of corruption that otherwise might have endangered the life itself. So, "If need be you are in heaviness through manifold temptations" (1 Pet. 1:6).

When the soul is at any time more or less overcome by temptations, Christ in his tenderness relieves it with mercy and pardon; so that his [soul] shall not sink utterly under their burden (1 John 2:1–2).

By one, more, or all of these ways, does the Lord Jesus manifest his [soul] conjugal tenderness and compassion toward the saints, in and under their temptations.

Christ is compassionate toward them in their afflictions: "In all their affliction he is afflicted" (Isa. 63:9); yea, it seems that all our afflictions (at least those of one sort—namely, which consist in persecutions) are his in the first place, [and] ours only by participation. We "fill up the measure of the afflictions of Christ" (Col. 1:24).[33] Two things evidently manifest this compassionateness in Christ:

His interceding with his Father for their relief (Zech. 1:12). Christ intercedes on our behalf, not only in respect of our *sins*, but also our *sufferings*; and when the work of our afflictions is accomplished, we shall have the relief he intercedes for (Heb. 7:25). The Father always hears him; and we have not a deliverance from trouble, a recovering of health, ease of pain, freedom from any evil that ever laid hold upon us, but it is given us on the intercession of Jesus Christ. Believers are unacquainted with their own condition, if they look upon their mercies as dispensed in a way of common providence. And this may, indeed, be a cause why we esteem them no more, are no more thankful for them, nor fruitful in the enjoyment of them: we see not how, by what means, nor on what account, they are dispensed to us. The generation of the people of God in the world are at this day alive, undevoured, merely on the account of the intercession of the Lord Jesus. His compassionateness has been the fountain of their deliverances. Hence oftentimes he rebukes their sufferings and afflictions, that they shall not act to the utmost upon them when they are under them. He is with them when they pass through fire and water (Isa. 43:2–3).

In that he does and will, in the winding up of the matter, so sorely *revenge the quarrel* of their sufferings upon their enemies. He avenges his elect that cry unto him; yea, he does it speedily. The controversy of Zion leads on the day of his vengeance (Isa. 34:8). He looks upon them sometimes in distress, and considers what is the state of the world in reference to them. Zechariah 1:11, "We have walked to and fro through the earth, and, behold, all the earth sits still, and is at rest," say his messengers to him, whom he sent to consider the world and its condition during the affliction of his people. This commonly is the condition of the world in such a season, "They are at rest and quiet, their hearts are abundantly satiated; they drink wine in bowls, and send gifts to one another."[34] Then Christ looks to see who will come in for their succor (Isa. 59:16–17); and finding none engaging himself for their relief, by

---

33. *Tōn pathēmatōn Christi duo sunt genera: proterēmata, quæ passus est in corpore suo, et husterēmata, quæ in sanctis.* ["There are two kinds of Christ's sufferings: the former, which he suffered in his own body, and the latter, which are among the saints." A possible source for the original quote may be from Jerome Zanchi, *D. Hieronymi Zanchi in Epistolam ad Colossenses*, col. 276 in *Operum theologicorum D. Hieronymi*, vol. 6 (Genevae: Excudebat Matthæus Berjon, 1605).]

34. Amos 6:3–6; Rev. 11:10.

the destruction of their adversaries, himself undertakes it. Now, this vengeance he accomplishes [in] two ways:

Temporally, upon *persons, kingdoms, nations, and countries* (a type whereof you have, Isa. 63:1–6); as he did it upon the old Roman world (Rev. 6:15–16). And this also he does two ways:

First, by *calling* out here and there an eminent *opposer*, and making him an example to all the world. So he dealt with Pharaoh: "For this cause have I raised you up" (Ex. 9:16). So he does to this day; he lays his hand upon eminent adversaries—fills one with fury, another with folly, blasts a third, and makes another wither, or destroys them utterly and terribly. As a provoked lion, he lies not down without his prey.

Second, in general, in the *vials of his wrath* which he will in these latter days pour out upon the antichristian world, and all that partake with them in their thoughts of vengeance and persecution. He will miserably destroy them, and make such work with them in the issue, that whosoever hears, both his ears shall tingle.

In eternal vengeance will he plead with the adversaries of his beloved (Matt. 25:41–46; 2 Thess. 1:6; Jude 15). It is hence evident that Christ abounds in pity and compassion toward his beloved. Instances might be multiplied, but these things are obvious, and occur to the thoughts of all.

In answer to this, I place in the saints chastity unto Christ, in every state and condition. That this might be the state of the church of Corinth, the apostle made it his endeavor. "I have espoused you to one husband, that I may present you as a chaste virgin to Christ. But I fear, lest by any means, as the serpent beguiled Eve through his subtlety, so your minds should be corrupted from the simplicity that is in Christ" (2 Cor. 11:2–3). And so is it said of the followers of the Lamb, on Mount Zion, "These are they which were not defiled with women, for they are virgins" (Rev. 14:4). What defilement that was they were free from, shall be afterward declared.

Now, there are three things wherein this chastity consists:

First, the not taking any thing *into their affections and esteem* for those ends and purposes for which they have received Jesus Christ. Here the Galatians failed in their conjugal affection to Christ; they preserved not themselves chaste to him. They had received Christ for life, and justification, and him only; but being after a while overcome with charms, or bewitched, they took into the same place with him the righteousness of the law (Gal. 3:1). How Paul deals with them hereupon is known. How sorely, how pathetically does he admonish them, how severely reprove them, how clearly convince them of their madness and folly! This, then, is the first chaste affection believers bear in their heart to Christ: having received him for their righteousness and salvation before God, for the fountain, spring, and well-head[35] of all their supplies, they will not now receive any other thing into his room and in his stead. As to instance, in one particular: We receive him for our acceptance with God (1 Cor. 1:30). All that here can stand in competition with him for our affections, must be our own endeavors for a righteousness to commend us to God (Rom. 10:4). Now, this must be either before we receive him, or after. [As] for all duties and endeavors, of whatsoever sort, for the pleasing of God before our receiving of Christ, you know what was the apostle's frame (Phil. 3:8–10). All endeavors, all advantages, all privileges he rejects with indignation, as loss—with abomination, as dung; and winds up all his aims and desires in Christ alone and his righteousness, for those ends and purposes. But the works we do after we have received Christ are of another consideration. Indeed, they are acceptable to God; it pleases him that we should walk in them. But as to that end for which we receive Christ, they are of no other account than the former (Eph. 2:8–10). Even the works we do after believing—those which we are created unto in Christ Jesus, those that God has ordained that believers "should walk in them"—as to justification and acceptance with God (here called salvation) are excluded. It will one day appear that Christ abhors the janglings of men about the place of their own works and obedience, in the business of their acceptation with God; nor will the saints find any peace in adulterous thoughts of that kind. The chastity we owe unto him requires another frame. The necessity, usefulness, and excellency of gospel obedience shall be afterward declared. It is marvelous to see how hard it is to keep some professors to any faithfulness with Christ in this thing—how many disputes have been managed,[36] how many distinctions invented, how many shifts and evasions studied, to keep up something, in some place or other, to some purpose or other, that they may dally with. Those that love him indeed are otherwise minded.

Herein, then, of all things, do the saints endeavor to keep their affections chaste and loyal to Jesus Christ. He is made unto them of God

---

35. source, spring, fountain.

36. *Perfice hoc precibus pretio ut hæream in parte aliqua tandem.* ["Contrive somehow by persuasion or bribery for me to retain some footing with Thais." Terence, *Eunuch,* in *Terence I: Women of Andros, the Self-Tormentor, Eunuch,* Loeb Classical Library, ed. and trans. John Barsby (Cambridge, MA: Harvard University Press, 2001), line 1055, 437.]

"righteousness"; and they will own nothing else to that purpose: yea, sometimes they know not whether they have any interest in him or no—he absents and withdraws himself; they still continue solitary, in a state of widowhood, refusing to be comforted, though many things offer themselves to that purpose, because he is not. When Christ is at any time absent from the soul, when it cannot see that it has any interest in him, many lovers offer themselves to it, many woo its affections, to get it to rest on this or that thing for relief and succor; but though it go mourning never so long, it will have nothing but Christ to lean upon. Whenever the soul is in the wilderness, in the saddest condition, there it will stay until Christ come for to take it up, until it can come forth leaning upon him (Song 8:5). The many instances of this that the book of Canticles affords us, we have in part spoken of before.

This does he who has communion with Christ: he watches diligently over his own heart, that nothing creep into its affections, to give it any peace or establishment before God, but Christ only. Whenever that question is to be answered, "Wherewith shall I come before the LORD, and appear before the high God?" he does not gather up, "This or that I will do"; or, "Here and there I will watch, and amend my ways"; but instantly he cries, "In the Lord Jesus have I righteousness; all my desire is, to be found in him, not having on my own righteousness."[37]

Second, in *cherishing that Spirit, that holy Comforter, which Christ sends to us*, to abide with us in his room and stead. He tells us that he sends him to that purpose (John 16:7). He gives him to us, *vicariam navare operam*,[38] says Tertullian—to abide with us forever, for all those ends and purposes which he has to fulfill toward us and upon us; he gives him to dwell in us, to keep us, and preserve us blameless for himself. His name is in him and with him: and it is upon this account that whatever is done to any of Christ's is done to him, because it is done to them in whom he is and dwells by his Spirit. Now, herein do the saints preserve their conjugal affections entire to Christ, that they labor by all means not to grieve his Holy Spirit, which he has sent in his stead to abide with them. This the apostle puts them in mind of, "Grieve not the Holy Spirit" (Eph. 4:30).

There be two main ends for which Christ sends his Spirit to believers: (1) for their *sanctification*; (2) for their *consolation*: to which two

---

37. Isa. 45:24; Phil. 3:9; Hab. 2:1–4.

38. Lat. "to perform the work on his behalf" [cf. Tertullian, "De Praescriptionibus Adverusus Haereticos (On Prescription Against Heretics)," ANF 3:249; PL 2, col. 26b].

all the particular acts of purging, teaching, anointing, and the rest that are ascribed to him, may be referred. So there be two ways whereby we may grieve him: (1) in respect of *sanctification*; (2) in respect of *consolation*.

In respect of *sanctification*. He is the Spirit of holiness—holy in himself, and the author of holiness in us: he works it in us (Titus 3:5), and he persuades us to it, by those motions of his which are not to be quenched (1 Thess. 5:19). Now this, in the first place, grieves the Spirit, when he is carrying on in us and for us a work so infinitely for our advantage, and without which we cannot see God, that we should run cross[39] to him, in ways of unholiness, pollution, and defilement. So the connection of the words in the place before mentioned manifests (Eph. 4:28–31); and thence does Paul bottom his powerful and most effectual persuasion unto holiness, even from the abode and indwelling of this Holy Spirit with us (1 Cor. 3:16–17). Indeed, what can grieve a loving and tender friend more than to oppose him and slight him when he is most intent about our good—and that a good of the greatest consequence to us. In this, then, believers make it their business to keep their hearts loyal and their affections chaste to Jesus Christ. They labor instantly not to grieve the Holy Spirit by loose and foolish, by careless and negligent walking, which he has sent to dwell and abide with them. Therefore shall no anger, wrath, malice, envy dwell in their hearts; because they are contrary to the holy, meek Spirit of Christ, which he has given to dwell with them. They attend to his motions, make use of his assistance, improve his gifts, and nothing lies more upon their spirits than that they may walk worthy of the presence of this holy substitute of the Lord Jesus Christ.

As to *consolation*. This is the second great end for which Christ gives and sends his Spirit to us; who from thence, by the way of eminency, is called "The Comforter." To this end he seals us, anoints us, establishes us, and gives us peace and joy. Of all which I shall afterward speak at large. Now, there be two ways whereby he may be grieved as to this end of his mission, and our chastity to Jesus Christ thereby violated:

By placing our comforts and joys in other things, and not being filled with joy in the Holy Ghost. When we make creatures or creature comforts—anything whatever but what we receive by the Spirit of Christ—to be our joy and our delight, we are false with Christ. So was it with Demas, who loved the present world (2 Tim. 4:10). When the

---

39. in contradiction, against.

ways of the Spirit of God are grievous and burdensome to us—when we say, "When will the Sabbath be past, that we may exact all our labors?"—when our delight and refreshment lies in earthly things—we are unsuitable to Christ. May not his Spirit say, "Why do I still abide with these poor souls? I provide them joys unspeakable and glorious; but they refuse them, for perishing things. I provide them spiritual, eternal, abiding consolations, and it is all rejected for a thing of nought." This Christ cannot bear; wherefore, believers are exceeding careful in this, not to place their joy and consolation in any thing but what is administered by the Spirit. Their daily work is to get their hearts crucified to the world and the things of it, and the world to their hearts; that they may not have living affections to dying things: they would fain look on the world as a crucified, dead thing, that has neither form nor beauty; and if at any times they have been entangled with creatures and inferior contentment, and have lost their better joys, they cry out to Christ, "O restore to us the joys of your Spirit!"

He is grieved when, through *darkness and unbelief*, we will not, do not, receive those consolations which he tenders[40] to us, and which he is abundantly willing that we should receive. But of this I shall have occasion to speak afterward, in handling our communion with the Holy Ghost.

[Christ is compassionate] in [*keeping*] *his institutions*, or matter and manner of his worship. Christ marrying his church to himself, taking it to that relation, still expresses the main of their chaste and choice affections to him to *lie in their keeping his institutions and his worship according to his appointment*. The breach of this he calls "adultery" everywhere, and "whoredom." He is a "jealous God"; and he gives himself that title only in respect of his institutions. And the whole apostasy of the Christian church unto false worship is called "fornication"; and the church that leads the others to false worship, the "mother of harlots" (Rev. 17:5). On this account, those believers who really attend to communion with Jesus Christ, do labor to keep their hearts chaste to him in his ordinances, institutions, and worship; and that [in] two ways:

First, *they will receive nothing, practice nothing, own nothing in his worship, but what is of his appointment*. They know that from the foundation of the world he never did allow, nor ever will, that in any thing the will of the creatures should be the measure of his honor or the principle of his worship, either as to matter or manner. It was a

---

40. offers

witty and true sense that one gave of the second commandment: *Non imago, non simulachrum prohibetur; sed non facies tibi;*[41] it is a making to ourselves, an inventing, a finding out, ways of worship, or means of honoring God, not by him appointed, that is so severely forbidden. Believers know what entertainment all will-worship finds with God: "Who has required these things at your hand?" [Isa. 1:12] and, "In vain do you worship me, teaching for doctrines the traditions of men" [Matt. 15:9]—is the best it meets with. I shall take leave to say what is upon my heart, and what (the Lord assisting) I shall willingly endeavor to make good against all the world—namely, that that principle, *that the church has power to institute and appoint any thing or ceremony belonging to the worship of God*, either as to matter or to manner, beyond the orderly observance of such circumstances as necessarily attend such ordinances as Christ himself has instituted, *lies at the bottom of all the horrible superstition and idolatry, of all the confusion, blood, persecution, and wars*, that have for so long a season spread themselves over the face of the Christian world; and that it is the design of a great part of the Revelation to make a discovery of this truth. And I doubt not but that the great controversy which God has had with this nation for so many years, and which he has pursued with so much anger and indignation, was upon this account: that, contrary to that glorious light of the gospel which shone among us, the wills and fancies of men, under the name of order, decency, and the authority of the church (a chimera[42] that none knew what it was, nor wherein the power of it did consist, nor in whom reside), were imposed on men in the ways and worship of God. Neither was all that pretence of glory, beauty, comeliness, and conformity, that then was pleaded, any thing more or less than what God does so describe in the church of Israel (Ezek. 16:25) and forwards. Hence was the Spirit of God in prayer derided; hence was the powerful preaching of the gospel despised; hence was the Sabbath decried; hence was holiness stigmatized and persecuted—to what end? That Jesus Christ might be deposed from the sole privilege and power of law-making in his church; that the true husband might be thrust aside, and adulterers of his spouse embraced; that taskmasters might be appointed in and over his house, which he never gave to his church (Eph. 4:11); that a ceremonious, pompous, outward show worship, drawn from Pagan, Judaical,[43] and

---

41. "Not an image, not an idol is forbidden; but a face not turned toward you."
42. vain, fanciful illusion.
43. Jewish

Antichristian observations, might be introduced—of all which there is not one word, tittle,[44] or iota,[45] in the whole book of God. This, then, they who hold communion with Christ are careful of: they will admit of nothing, practice nothing, in the worship of God, private or public, but what they have his warrant for; unless it comes in his name, with "Thus says the Lord Jesus," they will not hear "an angel from heaven." They know the apostles themselves were to teach the saints only what Christ commanded them (Matt. 28:20). You know how many in this very nation, in the days not long since past, yea, how many thousands, left their native soil and went into a vast and howling wilderness in the utmost parts of the world to keep their souls undefiled and chaste to their dear Lord Jesus, as to this of his worship and institutions.

Second, *they readily embrace, receive, and practice everything that the Lord Christ has appointed.* They inquire diligently into his mind and will, that they may know it. They go to him for directions, and beg of him to lead them in the way they have not known. The 119th Psalm may be a pattern for this. How does the good, holy soul breathe after instruction in the ways and ordinances, the statutes and judgments, of God! This, I say, they are tender[46] in: whatever is of Christ, they willingly submit unto, accept of, and give up themselves to the constant practice thereof; whatever comes on any other account they refuse.

Christ manifests and evidences his love to his saints in a *way of bounty*—in that rich, plentiful provision he makes for them. It has "pleased the Father that in him should all fullness dwell" (Col. 1:19); and that for this end, that "of his fullness we might all receive, and grace for grace" (John 1:16). I shall not insist upon the particulars of that provision which Christ makes for his saints, with all those influences of the Spirit of life and grace that daily they receive from him—that bread that he gives them to the full, the refreshment they have from him; I shall only observe this, that the Scripture affirms him to do all things for them in an abundant manner, or to do it richly, in a way of bounty. Whatever he gives us—his grace to assist us, his presence to comfort us—he does it abundantly. You have the general assertion of it: "Where sin abounded, grace did much more abound" (Rom. 5:20). If grace abound much more in comparison of sin, it is abundant grace indeed; as will easily be granted by any that shall consider how sin has

---

44. a small distinguishing mark, such as a diacritic, accent, or the dot over an *i* (cf. Matt. 5:18).
45. The ninth letter of the Greek alphabet, referring to a tiny portion.
46. careful

abounded, and does, in every soul. Hence he is said to be able, and we are bid to expect that he should do for us "exceeding abundantly above all that we ask or think" (Eph. 3:20). Is it pardoning mercy we receive of him? Why, he does "*abundantly* pardon" (Isa. 55:7); he will multiply or add to pardon—he will add pardon to pardon, that grace and mercy shall abound above all our sins and iniquities. Is it the Spirit he gives us? He sheds him upon us *richly* or "*abundantly*" (Titus 3:6); not only bidding us drink of the water of life freely, but also bestowing him in such a plentiful measure, that rivers of water shall flow from them that receive him (John 7:38–39)—that they shall never thirst any more when have drank of him. Is it grace that we receive of him? He gives that also in a way of bounty; we receive "*abundance of grace*" (Rom. 5:17); he "abounds toward us in all wisdom and prudence" (Eph. 1:8). Hence is that invitation (Song 5:1). If in any things, then, we are straitened, it is in ourselves; Christ deals bountifully with us. Indeed, the great sin of believers is that they make not use of Christ's bounty as they ought to do; that we do not every day take of him mercy in abundance. The oil never ceases till the vessels cease; supplies from Christ fail not but only when our faith fails in receiving them.

Then our return to Christ is in a way of duty. Unto this two things are required:

First, that we *follow after* and practice holiness in the power of it, as it is obedience unto Jesus Christ. Under this formality, as obedience to him, all gospel obedience is called, "whatsoever Christ commands us" (Matt. 28:20); and says he, "you are my friends, if you do whatsoever I command you" (John 15:14); and it is required of us that we live to him who died for us (2 Cor. 5:15)—live to him in all holy obedience—live to him as our Lord and King. Not that I suppose there are peculiar precepts and a peculiar law of Jesus Christ, in the observance whereof we are justified, as the Socinians fancy; for surely the gospel requires of us no more, but "to love the Lord our God with all our hearts, and all our souls" [Matt. 22:37]—which the law also required—but that the Lord Jesus having brought us into a condition of acceptance with God wherein our obedience is well-pleasing to him, and we being to honor him as we honor the Father, that we have a respect and peculiar regard to him in all our obedience. So Titus 2:14, he has purchased us unto himself. And thus believers do in their obedience; they eye Jesus Christ—

As the author of their faith and obedience, for whose sake it is "given to them to believe" (Phil. 1:29); and who by his Spirit works that obedience in them. So the apostle (Heb. 12:1–2); in the course of our obedience we still look to Jesus, "the author of our faith." Faith is here both the grace of faith, and the fruit of it in obedience.

As him in, for, and by whom we have acceptance with God in our obedience. They know all their duties are weak, imperfect, not able to abide the presence of God; and therefore they look to Christ as him who bears the iniquity of their holy things, who adds incense to their prayers, gathers out all the weeds of their duties, and makes them acceptable to God.

As one that has renewed the commands of God unto them, with mighty obligations unto obedience. So the apostle, "The love of Christ constrains us" (2 Cor. 5:14–15); of which afterward.

They consider him as God, equal with his Father, to whom all honor and obedience is due. So Revelation 5:13. But these things I have, not long since, opened in another treatise,[47] dealing about the worship of Christ as mediator. This, then, the saints do in all their obedience; they have a special regard to their dear Lord Jesus. He is, on all these accounts, and innumerable others, continually in their thoughts. His love to them, his life for them, his death for them—all his kindness and mercy constrains them to live to him.

Second, by laboring *to abound in fruits of holiness.* As he deals with us in a way of bounty, and deals out unto us abundantly, so he requires that we abound in all grateful, obediential[48] returns to him. So we are exhorted to "be always abounding in the work of the Lord" (1 Cor. 15:58). This is that I intend: the saints are not satisfied with that measure that at any time they have attained, but are still pressing, that they may be more dutiful, more fruitful to Christ.

And this is a little glimpse of some of that communion which we enjoy with Christ. It is but a little, from him who has the least experience of it of all the saints of God; who yet has found that in it which is better than ten thousand worlds; who desires to spend the residue of the few and evil days of his pilgrimage in pursuit hereof—in the contemplation of the excellencies, desirableness, love, and grace of our dear Lord Jesus, and in making returns of obedience according to his will: to whose soul, in the midst of the perplexities of this wretched world, and cursed rebellions of his own heart, this is the great relief, that "He that shall come will come, and will not tarry" [Heb. 10:37]. "The Spirit and the bride say, Come; and let him that reads say, Come. Even so, come, Lord Jesus" [Rev. 22:17].

---

47. Owen, *Vindiciae Evangelicae*, 433–43.
48. obedient

Chapter 6

Communion with Christ in Purchased Grace

Our process is now to communion with Christ in *purchased grace*, as it was before proposed[1]—"That we may know him, and the power of his resurrection, and the fellowship of his sufferings, and be made conformable to his death" (Phil. 3:10).

By purchased grace, I understand all that righteousness and grace which Christ has procured, or wrought out for us, or does by any means make us partakers of, or bestows on us for our benefit, by anything that he has done or suffered, or by anything he continues to do as mediator: First, *What this purchased grace is, and wherein it does consist*; secondly, *How we hold communion with Christ therein*; are the things that now come under consideration.[2]

What Is Purchased Grace?

The first may be considered [in] two ways: (1) in respect of the *rise and fountain* of it; (2) [in respect] of its *nature*, or wherein it consists.[3]

It has a threefold rise, spring, or causality in Christ: (1) the *obedience* of his life; (2) the *suffering* of his death; (3) his continued *intercession*. All the actions of Christ as mediator, leading to the communication of

---

1. Chap. 2 (of part 2) began the topic of our fellowship with Christ by first exploring the "personal grace of Christ." Here Owen picks this up again and begins the second head: the "purchased grace of Christ."
2. Owen will return to this second point in chap. 8 (of part 2).
3. Owen will return to this second point in chap. 7 (of part 2).

271

grace unto us, may be either referred to these heads, or to some things that are subservient to them or consequents of them.

For the nature of this grace wherein we have communion with Christ, flowing from these heads and fountains, it may be referred to these three: (1) Grace of *justification*, or acceptance with God; which makes a relative change in us, as to state and condition. (2) Grace of *sanctification*, or holiness before God; which makes a real change in us, as to principle and operation. (3) Grace of *privilege*; which is mixed, as we shall show, if I go forth to the handling thereof.

The Rise and Fountain of Purchased Grace

Now, that we have communion with Christ in this purchased grace, is evident on this single consideration—that there is almost nothing that Christ has done, which is a spring of that grace whereof we speak, but we are said to do it with him. We are "crucified" with him (Gal. 2:20); we are "dead" with him (2 Tim. 2:11; Col. 3:3); and "buried" with him (Rom. 6:4; Col. 2:12); we are "quickened together with him" (Col. 2:13); "risen" with him (Col. 3:1). "He has quickened us together with Christ, and has raised us up together, and made us sit together in heavenly places" (Eph. 2:5–6). In the actings of Christ, there is, by virtue of the compact between him as mediator and the Father, such an assured foundation laid of the communication of the fruits of those actings unto those in whose stead he performed them, that they are said, in the participation of those fruits, to have done the same things with him. The life and power of which truth we may have occasion hereafter to inquire into:

The Obedience of Christ's Life

The first fountain and spring of this grace, wherein we have our communion with Christ, is first to be considered; and that is the *obedience of his life*: concerning which it must be declared—(1) What it is that is *intended* thereby, and wherein it consists. (2) What *influence* it has into the grace whereof we speak.

To the handling of this I shall only premise this observation—namely, that in the order of *procurement*, the life of Christ (as was necessary) precedes his death; and therefore we shall handle it in the first place: but in the order of *application*, the benefits of his death are bestowed on us antecedently, in the nature of the things themselves, unto those of his life; as will appear, and that necessarily, from the state and condition wherein we are.

By the *obedience of the life of Christ*, I intend the universal conformity of the Lord Jesus Christ, as he was or is, in his being mediator, to the whole will of God; and his complete actual fulfilling of the whole of every law of God, or doing of all that God in them required. He might have been perfectly holy by obedience to the law of creation, the moral law, as the angels were; neither could any more, as a man walking with God, be required of him: but he submitted himself also to every law or ordinance that was introduced upon the occasion of sin, which, on his own account, he could not be subject to, it becoming him to "fulfill all righteousness"[4] (Matt. 3:15), as he spoke in reference to a newly-instituted ceremony.

That obedience is properly ascribed unto Jesus Christ as mediator, the Scripture is witness, both as to name and thing, "Though he were a Son, yet learned he obedience," etc. (Heb. 5:8); yea, he was obedient in his sufferings, and it was that which gave life to his death (Phil. 2:8). He was obedient to death: for therein "he did make his soul an offering for sin," or, "his soul made an offering for sin" (Isa. 53:10); as it is interpreted, "he poured out his soul to death," or, "his soul poured out itself unto death" (Isa. 53:12). And he not only sanctified himself to be an offering (John 17:19), but he also "offered up himself" (Heb. 9:14), an "offering of a sweet savor to God" (Eph. 5:2). Hence, as to the whole of his work, he is called the Father's "servant" (Isa. 42:1, 19), and he professes of himself that he "came into the world to do the will of God, the will of him that sent him" [John 6:38]; for which he manifests "his great readiness" (Heb. 10:7)—all which evince his obedience. But I suppose I need not insist on the proof of this, that Christ, in the work of mediation, and as mediator, was obedient, and did what he did willingly and cheerfully, in obedience to God.

---

4. *Vox hæc dikaiosunē hoc quidem loco latissimè sumitur, ita ut significet non modo to nomimon, sed et quicquid ullam æqui atque honesti habet rationem; nam lex Mosis de hoc baptismo nihil præscripserat.* ["This expression 'righteousness' is taken in this place most broadly, so that it may signify not only what pertains to the law but also whatever has any account of equity and virtue; for the law of Moses had ordered nothing concerning this baptism." Hugo Grotius, *Opera omnia theologica* (Basil: Apud E. & J.R. Thurnisios, Fratres, 1732), 2:24.] *Per dikaiosunē Christus hic non designat justitiam legalem, sed, ut ita loqui liceat, personalem; to prepon personæ, et to kathēkon muneri.* ["By 'righteousness' Christ does not designate legal righteousness here, but, that it may be permitted to speak thus, personal; 'what is fitting' for the person, and 'what is suitable' for the office." Antonius Walæus.] *Ebaptisthē de kai enēsteusen, ouk autos a porrhupseōs ē nēsteias chreian echōn, ē katharseōs, ho tē phusei katharos kai hagios.* ["But He was baptized, and then fasted, not having Himself any need of cleansing, or of fasting, or of purgation, who was by nature pure and holy." Clement, *Constitutions of the Holy Apostles*, ANF 7:460; PG 1, col. 1013A.]

Now, this obedience of Christ may be considered two ways: (1) as to the habitual root and fountain of it; (2) as to the actual parts or duties of it:

The *habitual righteousness of Christ* as mediator in his human nature was the absolute, complete, exact conformity of the soul of Christ to the will, mind, or law of God; or his perfect habitually inherent righteousness. This he had necessarily from the grace of union; from whence it is that that which was born of the virgin was a "holy thing" (Luke 1:35). It was, I say, necessary consequentially, that it should be so; though the effecting of it were by the free operations of the Spirit (Luke 2:52). He had an all-fullness of grace on all accounts. This the apostle describes: "Such a high priest became us, holy, harmless, undefiled, separate from sinners" (Heb. 7:26). Every way separate and distant from sin and sinners he was to be; whence he is called "the Lamb of God, without spot or blemish" (1 Pet. 1:19). This habitual holiness of Christ was inconceivably above that of the angels. He who "charges his angels with folly"[5] (Job 4:18); "who puts no trust in his saints; and in whose sight the heavens" (or their inhabitants) "are not clean" (Job 15:15); always embraces him in his bosom, and is always well pleased with him (Matt. 3:17). And the reason of this is because every other creature, though never so holy, has the Spirit of God by measure; but he was not given to Christ "by measure" (John 3:34); and that because it pleased him that in him "should all fullness dwell" (Col. 1:19). This habitual grace of Christ, though not absolutely infinite, yet, in respect of any other creature, it is as the water of the sea to the water of a pond or pool. All other creatures are depressed from perfection by this—that they subsist in a created, dependent being; and so have the fountain of what is communicated to them without them. But the human nature of Christ subsists in the person of the Son of God; and so has the bottom and fountain of its holiness in the strictest unity with itself.

The *actual obedience of Christ*, as was said, was his willing, cheerful, obediential performance of every thing, duty, or command that God, by

---

5. *Sensus est de angelis, qui si cum Deo conferantur, aut si eos secum Deus conferat, non habens rationem eorum quæ in illis posuit, et dotium ac donorum quæ in illos contulit, et quibus eos exornavit et illustravit, inveniat eos stolidos. Sanè quicquid habent angeli, a Deo habent.* ["The reference is to the angels, which if they should be compared with God, or if God should compare them with himself, not taking account of the things which he has put in them, both [having their reason which he placed in them, and] their endowments and gifts which he gave to them, and with which things he has furnished and adorned them, he would find them dull. Certainly whatever the angels have, they have from God."] Joannis Merceri (Jean Mercier), *Commentarii Iobus et Solomonis, Proverbia, Ecclesiastem, Canticum Canticorum* (Luduni Batavorum [Leyden]: Ex Offiina Francisci Hackii, 1651), 31.]

virtue of any law whereto we were subject and obnoxious, did require; and [his obedience], moreover, to the peculiar law of the mediator. Hereof, then, are two parts:

First, that whatever was *required* of us by virtue of any law—that he did and fulfilled. Whatever was required of us by the law of nature, in our state of innocence; whatever kind of duty was added by morally positive or ceremonial institutions; whatever is required of us in way of obedience to righteous judicial laws—he did it all. Hence he is said to be "made under the law" (Gal. 4:4); subject or obnoxious to it, to all the precepts or commands of it. So, Matthew 3:15, he said it became him to "fulfill all righteousness"[6]—*pasan dikaiosunēn*—all manner of righteousness whatever; that is, everything that God required, as is evident from the application of that general axiom to the baptism of John. I shall not need, for this, to go to particular instances, in the duties of the law of nature—to God and [to] his parents; of morally positive [duties], in the Sabbath, and other acts of worship; of the ceremonial law, in circumcision, and observation of all the rites of the Judaical church; of the judicial, in paying tribute to governors—it will suffice, I presume, that on the one hand he "did no sin, neither was guile found in his mouth"; and on the other, that he "fulfilled all righteousness": and thereupon the Father was always well pleased with him. This was that which he owned of himself, that he came to do the will of God; and he did it.

Second, there was a *peculiar law of the mediator*, which respected himself merely, and contained all those acts and duties of his which are not for our imitation. So that obedience which he showed in dying was peculiarly to this law:[7] "I have power to lay down my life: this commandment have I received of my Father" (John 10:18). As mediator, he received this peculiar command of his Father, that he should lay down his life, and take it again; and he was obedient thereunto. Hence we say, he who is mediator did some things merely as a man, subject to the law of God in general; so he prayed for his persecutors—those

---

6. *Fuit legis servituti subjectus, ut eam implendo nos ab ea redimeret, et ab ejus servitute.* ["He was made subject to the bondage of the law, in order that by fulfilling it he might deliver us from it, and from its bondage." Theodore Beza, *Jesu Christi Domini Nostri Novum Testamentum, sive Novum Foedus* (Cantabrigiae: Ex Officina Rogeri Danielis, 1642), 560.]

7. *Proprium objectum obedientiæ est præceptum, tacitum vel expressum, id est, voluntas superioris quocunque modo innotescat.* ["One's own object of obedience is the law, whether silent or expressed, that is, provided that the will of the superior in whatever place is made known." Aquinas, *Summa Theologiæ* II–II.2.5.3, 61 vols., trans. T.C. O'Brien (London: Blackfriars, 1964–1981), 31:83 (Latin text on page 82)]. Deut. 18:18; Acts 3:22; John 12:49; 14:31; 6:38; 5:30.

that put him to death (Luke 23:34)—some things as mediator; so he prayed for his elect only (John 17:9). There were not worse in the world, really and evidently, than many of them that crucified him; yet, as a man, subject to the law, he forgave them, and prayed for them. When he prayed as mediator, his Father always heard him and answered him (John 11:41); and in the other prayers he was accepted as one exactly performing his duty.

This, then, is the obedience of Christ; which was the first thing proposed to be considered. The next is—

That it has an influence into the grace of which we speak, wherein we hold communion with him—namely, our *free acceptation* with God; what that influence is, must also follow in its order.

For his *habitual righteousness*, I shall only propose it under these two considerations:

That upon this supposition, that it was *needful* that we should have a mediator that was God and man in one person, as it could not otherwise be, so it must needs be that he must be holy. For although there be but one primary necessary effect of the hypostatical union (which is the subsistence of the human nature in the person of the Son of God), yet that he that was so united to him should be a "holy thing," completely holy, was necessary also—of which before.

That the *relation* which this righteousness of Christ has to the grace we receive from him is only this—that thereby he was *ikanos*—fit to do all that he had to do for us. This is the intendment of the apostle (Heb. 7:26). Such a one "became us"; it was needful he should be such a one, that he might do what he had to do. And the reasons hereof are two:

Had he not been completely furnished with habitual grace, he could never have *actually* fulfilled the righteousness which was required at his hands. It was therein that he was able to do all that he did. So [he] himself lays down the presence of the Spirit with him as the bottom and foundation of his going forth to his work (Isa. 61:1).

He could not have been *a complete and perfect* sacrifice, nor have answered all the types and figures of him, that were complete and without blemish.[8] But now, Christ having this habitual righteousness,

---

8. *Præcipitur, Lev. xxii. 20, ne offeratur pecus in quo sit mum, id est corporis vitium: mum, efficitur mōmos 'culpa:' unde Christus dicutur amōmos, 'inculpatus'; opponitur autem mum, to tamim, hoc est 'integrum.' Ibid., ver. 19, et sic Exod. 12:5, præcipitur de agno paschali, ut sitomim id est 'integer,' omnis scilicet vitii expers. Idem præcipitur de agnis jugis sacrificii, Num. 28:3, quibus ipsa nimirum sanctitas Christi tanquam victimæ paræfigurata est.* ["It is commanded in Leviticus 22:20, that a sheep be not offered in which there is a *mum*, that is a blemish of the body: from *mum* it is

if he had never yielded any continued obedience to the law actively, but had suffered as soon after his incarnation as Adam sinned after his creation, he had been a fit sacrifice and offering; and therefore, doubtless, his following obedience has another use besides to fit him for an oblation, for which he was most fit without it.

For Christ's obedience to the *law of mediation*, wherein it is not coincident[9] with his passive obedience, as they speak (for I know that expression is improper); it was that which was requisite for the discharging of his office, and is not imputed unto us, as though we had done it, though the *apotelesmata*[10] and fruits of it are; but is of the nature of his intercession, whereby he provides the good things we stand in need of, at least subserviently to his oblation and intercession—of which more afterward.

About his *actual fulfilling* of the law, or doing all things that of us are required, there is some doubt and question; and about it there are three several opinions:

That this *active obedience* of Christ has no further influence into our justification and acceptance with God, but as it was *preparatory* to his blood-shedding and oblation; which is the sole cause of our justification, the whole righteousness which is imputed to us arising from thence.

That it may be considered two ways: (1) As it is *purely obedience*; and so it has no other state but that before mentioned. (2) As it was accomplished with suffering, and joined with it, as it was part of his humiliation, so it is *imputed* to us, or is part of that upon the account whereof we are justified.

That this obedience of Christ, being done *for* us, is reckoned graciously of God *unto* us; and upon the account thereof are we accepted as righteous before him. My intendment is not to handle this difference in the way of a controversy, but to give such an understanding of the whole as may speedily be reduced to the practice of godliness and consolation; and this I shall do in the ensuing observations:

---

rendered *mōmos*, 'blame': wherefore Christ is called *amōmos*, 'blameless': however *mum* is opposed to *to tamum*, that is, 'blameless.' In verse 19 of the same passage as well as in Exodus 12:5, it is commanded concerning the Passover lamb, that it be *tamim*, that is, 'blameless,' namely, free from every blemish. The same is commanded concerning the lambs of the double offering, in Numbers 28:3, in which certainly the same purity of Christ as the sin offering was, as it were, prefigured." Johannes Piscator, *Commentary on 1 Peter* (1 Pet. 1:19).]

9. matching point for point; in exact agreement.

10. fulfillment.

That the obedience that Christ yielded to the law in general is not only to the peculiar law of the mediator, though he yielded it *as mediator*. He was incarnate as mediator (Heb. 2:14; Gal. 4:4); and all he afterward did, it was as our mediator. For that cause "came he into the world" and did and suffered whatever he did or suffered in this world. So that of this expression, *as mediator*, there is a twofold sense: for it may be taken strictly, as relating solely to the law of the mediator, and so Christ may be said to do as mediator only what he did in obedience to that law; but in the sense now insisted on, whatever Christ did as a man subject to any law, he did it as mediator, because he did it as part of the duty incumbent on him who undertook so to be.

That whatever *Christ did as mediator*, he did it for them whose mediator he was, or in whose stead and for whose good he executed the office of a mediator before God. This the Holy Ghost witnesses: "What the law could not do, in that it was weak through the flesh, God sending his own Son in the likeness of sinful flesh, and for sin, condemned sin in the flesh, that the righteousness of the law might be fulfilled in us" (Rom. 8:3–4); because [of] that [which] we could not in that condition of weakness whereinto we are cast by sin—come to God, and be freed from condemnation by the law—God sent Christ as a mediator, to do and suffer whatever the law required at our hands for that end and purpose, that we might not be condemned, but accepted of God. It was all to this end—"That the righteousness of the law might be fulfilled in us"; that is, which the law required of us, consisting in duties of obedience. This Christ performed for us. This expression of the apostle, "God sending his own Son in the likeness of sinful flesh, and for sin, condemned sin in the flesh"—if you will add to it that of Galatians 4:4, that he was so sent forth as that he was *hupo nomon genomenos*, "made under the law" (that is, obnoxious to it, to yield all the obedience that it does require)—comprises the whole of what Christ did or suffered; and all this, the Holy Ghost tells us, was for us (Rom. 10:4).

That the end of this *active obedience* of Christ cannot be assigned to be, that he might be *fitted for his death and oblation*. For he answered all types, and was every way *ikanos* (fit to be made an offering for sin), by his union and habitual grace. So that if the obedience Christ performed be not reckoned to us, and done upon our account, there is no just cause to be assigned why he should live here in the world so long as he did, in perfect obedience to all the laws of God. Had he died before, there had been perfect innocence, and perfect holiness, by his habitual grace, and infinite virtue and worth from the dignity of his person; and surely he yielded not that long course of all manner of obedience, but for some great and special purpose in reference to our salvation.

That had not the obedience of Christ been for us (in what sense we shall see instantly), it might in his life have been required of him to yield obedience *to the law of nature*, the alone law which he could be liable to as a man; for an innocent man in a covenant of works, as he was, needs no other law, nor did God ever give any other law to any such person (the law of creation is all that an innocent creature is liable to, with what symbols of that law God is pleased to add). And yet to this law also was his subjection voluntary; and that not only consequentially, because he was born upon his own choice, not by any natural course, but also because as mediator, God and man, he was not by the institution of that law obliged unto it; being, as it were, exempted and lifted above that law by the hypostatical union: yet, when I say his subjection hereunto was voluntary, I do not intend that it was merely arbitrary and at choice whether he would yield obedience unto it or no[11]—but on supposition of his undertaking to be a mediator, it was necessary it should be so—but that he voluntarily and willingly submitted unto, and so became really subject to the commands of it. But now, moreover, Jesus Christ yielded perfect obedience to all those laws which came upon us by the occasion of sin, as the ceremonial law; yea, those very institutions that signified the washing away of sin, and repentance from sin, as the baptism of John, which he had no need of himself. This, therefore, must needs be for us.

That the obedience of Christ cannot be reckoned amongst his *sufferings*, but is clearly *distinct* from it, as to all formalities. Doing is one thing, suffering another; they are in diverse *predicaments*, and cannot be coincident.

See, then, briefly what we have obtained by those considerations; and then I shall intimate what is the stream issuing from this first spring or fountain of purchased grace, with what influence it has thereinto:

First, by the obedience of the life of Christ you see what is intended—*his willing submission unto, and perfect, complete fulfilling of, every law of God that any of the saints of God were obliged unto.* It is true, every act almost of Christ's obedience, from the blood of his circumcision to the blood of his cross, was attended with suffering, so that his whole

---

11. *Obedientia importat necessitatem respectu ejus quod præcipitur, et voluntatem respectu impletionis præcepti.* ["Obedience includes obligation in regard to that which is commanded, and the will in regard to the fulfillment of the command." Aquinas, *Summa Theologiae* 3, q. 47, 2, 2.]

life might, in that regard, be called a death; but yet, looking upon his willingness and obedience in it, it is distinguished from his sufferings peculiarly so called, and termed his *active righteousness*.[12] This is, then, I say, as was showed, that complete, absolutely perfect accomplishment of the whole law of God by Christ, our mediator; whereby he not only "did no sin, neither was there guile found in his mouth" [1 Pet. 2:22], but also most perfectly fulfilled all righteousness, as he affirmed it became him to do.

Secondly, that *this obedience was performed by Christ not for himself, but for us, and in our stead.* It is true, it must needs be, that while he had his conversation in the flesh he must be most perfectly and absolutely holy; but yet the prime intendment of his accomplishing of holiness—which consists in the complete obedience of his whole life to any law of God—that was no less for us than his suffering death. That this is so, the apostle tells us: "God sent forth his Son, made of a woman, made under the law, to redeem them that were under the law" (Gal. 4:4–5). This Scripture, formerly named, must be a little further insisted on. He was both made of a woman, and made under the law; that is, obedient to it for us. The end here, both of the incarnation and obedience of Christ to the law (for that must needs be understood here by the phrase *hupo nomon genomenos*—that is, disposed of in such a condition as that he must yield subjection and obedience to the law), was all to redeem us. In these two expressions, "made of a woman, made under the law," the apostle does not knit his incarnation and death together, with an exclusion of the obedience of his life. And he was so made under the law, as those were under the law whom he was to redeem. Now, we were under the law, not only as *obnoxious to its penalties*, but as *bound to all the duties of it.* That this is our being "under the law," the apostle informs us, "Tell me, you that desire to be under the law" (Gal. 4:21). It was not the penalty of the law they desired to be under, but to be under it in respect of obedience. Take away, then, the end, and you destroy the means. If Christ were not incarnate nor made under the law for himself, he did not yield obedience for himself;

---

12. *In vita passivam habuit actionem; in morte passionem activam sustinuit; dum salutem operatur in medio terræ.* ["In life he offered passive action; in death he underwent active passion; all the while he was working salvation in the midst of earth." While the translation is not yet published (and may slightly change in the editing process), the passage occurs in Bernard's "Sermon for Wednesday in Holy Week," in *Bernard of Clairvaux: Sermons for the Lenten and Easter Seasons*, Cistercian Fathers Series 52 (Kalamazoo, MI: Cistercian Publications, forthcoming); brackets in translation.]

it was all for us, *for our good*. Let us now look forward, and see what influence this has into our acceptation.

Thirdly, then, I say *this perfect, complete obedience of Christ to the law is reckoned unto us*. As there is a truth in that, "The day you eat you shall die" [Gen. 2:17]—death is the reward of sin, and so we cannot be freed from death but by the death of Christ (Heb. 2:14–15); so also is that no less true, "Do this, and live" [Luke 10:28]—that life is not to he obtained unless all be done that the law requires. That is still true, "If you wilt enter into life, keep the commandments" (Matt. 19:17). They must, then, be kept by us, or our surety. Neither is it of any value which by some is objected, that if Christ yielded perfect obedience to the law for us, then are we no more bound to yield obedience; for by his undergoing death, the penalty of the law, we are freed from it. I answer, How did Christ undergo death? Merely as it was penal. How, then, are we delivered from death? Merely as it is penal. Yet we must die still; yea, as the last conflict with the effects of sin, as a passage to our Father, we must die. Well, then, Christ yielded perfect obedience to the law; but how did he do it? Purely as it stood in that *conditional* [*arrangement*], "Do this, and live." He did it in the strength of the grace he had received; he did it as a means of life, to procure life by it, as the tenor of a covenant. Are we, then, freed from this obedience? Yes; but how far? From doing it in our own strength; from doing it for this end, that we may obtain life everlasting. It is vain that some say confidently that we must yet work for life; it is all one as to say we are yet under the old covenant, "*Hoc fac, et vives*":[13] we are not freed from obedience, as a way of walking with God, but we are, as a way of working to come to him: of which at large afterward.

"By the righteousness of one the free gift came upon all men unto justification of life: by the obedience of one shall many be made righteous," says the Holy Ghost (Rom. 5:18–19). By his obedience to the law are we made righteous; it is reckoned to us for righteousness. That the passive obedience of Christ is here only intended is false:

First, it is opposed to the *disobedience* of Adam, which was *active*. The *dikaiōma* is opposed *paraptōmati*—the righteousness to the fault. The fault was an active transgression of the law, and the obedience opposed to it must be an active accomplishment of it. Besides, obedience placed singly, in its own nature, denotes an action or actions conformable to the law; and therein came Christ, not to destroy but to fulfill

---

13. Vulgate: "Do this and you shall live" (Luke 10:28).

the law (Matt. 5:17)—that was the design of his coming, and so for us; he came to fulfill the law for us (Isa. 9:6), and [was] born to us (Luke 2:11). This also was in that will of the Father which, out of his infinite love, he came to accomplish. *Secondly*, it cannot clearly be evinced that there is any such thing, in propriety of speech, as *passive obedience*; *obeying is doing*, to which passion or suffering cannot belong: I know it is commonly called so, when men obey until they suffer; but properly it is not so.

So also, Philippians 3:9, "And be found in him, not having my own righteousness, which is of the law, but that which is through the faith of Christ, the righteousness which is of God by faith." The righteousness we receive is opposed to our own obedience to the law; opposed to it, not as something in another kind, but as something in the same kind excluding that from such an end which the other obtains. Now this is the obedience of Christ to the law—himself thereby being "made to us righteousness" (1 Cor. 1:30).

[In] Rom. 5:10 the issue of the death of Christ is placed upon reconciliation; that is, a slaying of the enmity and restoring us into that condition of peace and friendship wherein Adam was before his fall. But is there no more to be done? Notwithstanding that there was no wrath due to Adam, yet he was to obey, if he would enjoy eternal life. Something there is, moreover, to be done in respect of us, if, after the slaying of the enmity and reconciliation made, we shall enjoy life: "Being reconciled by his death," we are saved by that perfect obedience which in his life he yielded to the law of God. There is distinct mention made of reconciliation, through a non-imputation of sin (as Ps. 32:1; Luke 1:77; Rom. 3:25; 2 Cor. 5:19); and justification through an imputation of righteousness (Jer. 23:6; Rom. 4:5; 1 Cor. 1:30)—although these things are so far from being separated that they are reciprocally affirmed of one another: which, as it does not evince an identity, so it does an eminent conjunction. And this last we have by the life of Christ.

This is fully expressed in that typical representation of our justification before the Lord: Zech. 3:3–5. Two things are there expressed to belong to our free acceptation before God: *the taking away of the guilt of our sin*, our filthy robes; this is done by the death of Christ. Remission of sin is the proper fruit thereof; but there is more also required, even *a collation of righteousness*, and thereby a right to life eternal. This is here called "change of raiment"; so the Holy Ghost expresses it again, where he calls it plainly "the garments of salvation," and "the robe of righteousness"

(Isa. 61:10). Now this is only made ours by the obedience of Christ, as the other by his death.

Objection. "But if this be so, then are we as *righteous as Christ himself*, being righteous with his righteousness."

Answer. But first, here is a great difference—if it were no more than that this righteousness was *inherent in Christ*, and properly his own, it is only reckoned or *imputed* to us, or freely bestowed on us, and we are made righteous with that which is not ours. But, secondly, the truth is, that Christ was not righteous with that righteousness for *himself*, but for *us*; so that here can be no comparison: only this we may say, we are righteous with his righteousness which he wrought for us, and that completely.

And this, now, is the rise of the purchased grace whereof we speak, the obedience of Christ; and this is the influence of it into our acceptation with God. Whereas the guilt of sin, and our obnoxiousness to punishment on that account, is removed and taken away (as shall further be declared) by the death of Christ; and whereas, besides the taking away of sin, we have need of a complete righteousness, upon the account whereof we may be accepted with God; this obedience of Christ, through the free grace of God, is imputed unto us for that end and purpose.

This is all I shall for the present insist on to this purpose. That the passive righteousness of Christ only is imputed to us in the non-imputation of sin, and that on the condition of our faith and new obedience, so exalting them into the room of the righteousness of Christ, is a thing which, in communion with the Lord Jesus, I have as yet no acquaintance with. What may be said in the way of argument on the one side or other must be elsewhere considered.

THE DEATH AND OBLATION OF CHRIST

The second spring of our communion with Christ in purchased grace is his death and oblation. He lived for us, he died for us; he was ours in all he did, in all he suffered.[14] I shall be the more brief in handling of

---

14. *Tantane me tenuit vivendi, nate, voluptas, / Ut pro me hostili paterer succedere dextræ, / Quem genui? tuane hæc genitor per vulnera servor, / Morte tua vivens?* ["My son! And did such joy of life possess me, that in my stead I suffered thee to meet the foeman's sword—thee whom I begat? Am I, thy father, saved by these wounds of thine, and living by thy death?" *Virgil II: Aeneid VII–XII, the Minor Poems*, Loeb Classical Library, trans. H. R. Fairclough (Cambridge, MA: Harvard University Press, 1960), 229.]

this, because on another design I have elsewhere at large treated of all the concernments of it.[15]

Now, the death of Christ, as it is a spring of that purchased grace wherein we have communion with him, is in the Scripture proposed under a threefold consideration: (1) of a *price*; (2) of a *sacrifice*; (3) of a *penalty*.

In the first regard, its proper effect is *redemption*; in the second, *reconciliation* or atonement; in the third, *satisfaction*; which are the great ingredients of that purchased grace whereby, in the first place, we have communion with Christ.

It is a *price*. "We are bought with a price" (1 Cor. 6:20); being "not redeemed with silver and gold, and corruptible things, but with the precious blood of Christ" (1 Pet. 1:18–19): which therein answers those things in other contracts.[16] He came to "give his life a ransom for many" (Matt. 20:28)—a price of redemption (1 Tim. 2:6). The proper use and energy of this expression in the Scripture, I have elsewhere declared.[17]

Now, the proper effect and issue of the death of Christ as a price or ransom is, as I said, redemption. Now, redemption is the deliverance of anyone from bondage or captivity, and the miseries attending that condition, by the intervention or interposition[18] of a price or ransom, paid by the redeemer to him by whose authority the captive was detained:

First in general, it is a *deliverance*. Hence Christ is called "The Deliverer" (Rom. 11:26); giving himself to "deliver us" (Gal. 1:4). He is "Jesus, who delivers us from the wrath to come" (1 Thess. 1:10).

Second, it is the delivery of one from *bondage* or captivity. We are, without him, all prisoners and captives, "bound in prison" (Isa. 61:1); "sitting in darkness, in the prison house" (Isa. 42:7; 49:9); "prisoners in the pit wherein there is no water" (Zech. 9:11); "the captives of the mighty, and the prey of the terrible" (Isa. 49:25); under a "captivity that must be led captive" (Ps. 68:18): this puts us in "bondage" (Heb. 2:15).

---

15. John Owen, *Vindiciae Evangelicae*, chaps. 20–22 [*Mystery of the Gospel Vindicated* (1655), *Works* 12:419–33].

16. *Nil quidem emitur nisi interveniente pretio; sed hoc tamen additum magnam emphasin habet.* ["Indeed, nothing is bought except with a price agreed upon; but this addition, however, has great emphasis." Theodore Beza, *Jesu Christi Domini Nostri Novum Testamentum, sive Novum Foedus* (Cantabrigiae: Ex Officina Rogeri Danielis, 1642), 474.]

17. Cf. John Owen, *The Death of Death in the Death of Christ* (1647), *Works*, 10:258–61.

18. interjection, intervention.

Third, the person committing thus to prison and into bondage is *God himself*. To him we owe "our debts" (Matt. 6:12; 18:23–27); against him are our offenses (Ps. 51:4); he is the judge and lawgiver (James 4:12). To sin is to rebel against him. He shuts up men under disobedience (Rom. 11:32); and he shall cast both body and soul of the impenitent into hell-fire (Matt. 10:28). To his wrath are men obnoxious (John 3:36) and lie under it by the sentence of the law, which is their prison.

Fourth, the *miseries* that attend this condition are innumerable. Bondage to Satan, sin, and the world comprises the sum of them; from all which we are delivered by the death of Christ, as a price or ransom. "God has delivered us from the power of darkness, and has translated us into the kingdom of his dear Son; in whom we have redemption through his blood" (Col. 1:13–14). And he "redeems us from all iniquity" (Titus 2:14); "from our vain conversation" (1 Pet. 1:18–19); even from the guilt and power of our sin; purchasing us to himself "a peculiar people, zealous of good works" (Titus 2:14): so dying for the "redemption of transgressions" (Heb. 9:15); redeeming us also from the world (Gal. 4:5).

Fifth, and all this is by the *payment of the price mentioned into the hand of God*, by whose supreme authority we are detained captives, under the sentence of the law. The debt is due to the great householder (Matt. 18:23–24); and the penalty, his curse and wrath: from which by it we are delivered (Rev. 1:5).

This the Holy Ghost frequently insists on. "Being justified freely by his grace, through the redemption that is in Christ Jesus; whom God has set forth to be a propitiation through faith in his blood, to declare his righteousness for the remission of sins" (Rom. 3:24–25).[19] And this is the first consideration of the death of Christ, as it has an influence into the procurement of that grace wherein we hold communion with him.

It was a *sacrifice* also. He had a body prepared him (Heb. 10:5); wherein he was to accomplish what by the typical oblations and burnt-offerings of the law was prefigured. And that body he offered (Heb. 10:10)—that is, his whole human nature; for "his soul" also was made "an offering for sin" (Isa. 53:10): on which account he is said to offer himself (Eph. 5:2; Heb. 1:3; 9:26). He gave himself a sacrifice to God of a sweet-smelling savor; and this he did willingly,[20] as became him

---

19. 1 Cor. 6:20; 1 Pet. 1:18; Matt. 20:28; 1 Tim. 2:6; Eph. 1:7; Col. 1:13; Gal. 3:13.

20. *Observatum est a sacrificantibus, ut si hostia quæ ad aras duceretur, fuisset vehementer reluctata, ostendissetque se invitam altaribus admoveri, amoveretur, quia invito Deo eam offerri putabant; quæ vero stetisset oblata, hanc volenti numini dari existimabant.* ["It has always been

who was to be a sacrifice—the law of this obedience being written in his heart (Ps. 40:8); that is, he had a readiness, willingness, desire for its performance.

Now, the end of sacrifices, such as his was, bloody and for sin (Rom. 5:10; Heb. 2:17), was atonement and reconciliation. This is everywhere ascribed to them, that they were to make atonement; that is, in a way suitable to their nature. And this is the tendency of the death of Christ, as a sacrifice, atonement, and reconciliation with God. Sin had broken friendship between God and us (Isa. 63:10); whence his wrath was on us (John 3:36); and we are by nature obnoxious to it (Eph. 2:3). This is taken away by the death of Christ, as it was a sacrifice (Dan. 9:24). "When we were enemies, we were reconciled to God by the death of his Son" (Rom. 5:10). And thereby do we "receive the atonement" (v. 11); for "God was in Christ reconciling the world to himself, not imputing to them their sins and their iniquities" (2 Cor. 5:19–21; so also, Eph. 2:12–16, and in sundry other places). And this is the second consideration of the death of Christ; which I do but name, having at large insisted on these things elsewhere.

It was also a *punishment*—a punishment in our stead. "He was wounded for our transgressions, he was bruised for our iniquities: the chastisement of our peace was upon him" (Isa. 53:5). God made all our iniquities (that is, the punishment of them) "to meet upon him" (v. 6). "He bare the sins of many" (v. 12); "his own self bare our sins in his own body on the tree" (1 Pet. 2:24); and therein he "who knew no sin, was made sin for us" (2 Cor. 5:21). What it is in the Scripture to bear sin (see Deut. 19:15; 20:17; Num. 14:33; Ezek. 18:20). The nature, kind, matter, and manner of this punishment I have, as I said before, elsewhere discussed.

Now, bearing of punishment tends directly to the giving satisfaction to him who was offended, and on that account inflicted the punishment.

---

the practice at a sacrifice to remove any victim that struggled violently on being led to the altar and showed reluctance to approach it, on the ground that such an offering was deemed to be unwelcome to the god. If, however, the victim stood quietly at the altar, the offering was held to be acceptable to the deity." Macrobius, *The Saturnalia*, trans. Percival Vaughan Davies (New York: Columbia University Press, 1969), 206.] *Hoc quoque notandum, vitulos ad aras humeris hominum allatos non fere litare; sicut nec claudicante, nec aliena hostia placari deos; neque trahente se ab aris.* ["It should also be noted that calves are usually not acceptable if carried to the alters on a man's shoulders, and also that the gods are not propitiated if the victim is lame or is not of the appropriate sort, or if it drags itself away from the altar." Pliny the Elder, *Pliny: Natural History*, in *Pliny: Natural History III Libri VII–XI*, Loeb Classical Library, trans. H. Rackham (Cambridge, MA: Harvard University Press, 1967), 129.]

Justice can desire no more than a proportional punishment, due to the offense. And this, on his own voluntary taking of our persons, undertaking to be our mediator, was inflicted on our dear Lord Jesus. His substituting himself in our room being allowed of by the righteous Judge, satisfaction to him does thence properly ensue.

And this is the threefold consideration of the death of Christ, as it is a principal spring and fountain of that grace wherein we have communion with him; for, as will appear in our process, the single and most eminent part of purchased grace is nothing but the natural exurgency of the threefold effect of the death of Christ, intimated to flow from it on the account of the threefold consideration insisted on. This, then, is the second rise of purchased grace, which we are to eye, if we will hold communion with Christ in it—his death and blood-shedding, under this threefold notion of a price, an offering, and punishment. But—

The Intercession of Christ

This is not all: the Lord Christ goes further yet; he does not leave us so, but follows on the work to the utmost. "He died for our sins, and rose again for our justification" (Rom. 4:25). He rose again to carry on the complete work of purchased grace—that is, by his intercession; which is the third rise of it. In respect of this, he is said to be "able to save them to the uttermost that come unto God by him, seeing he ever lives to make intercession for them" (Heb. 7:25).

Now, the intercession of Christ, in respect of its influence into purchased grace, is considered two ways:

First, as a *continuance and carrying* on of his oblation, for the making out of all the fruits and effects thereof unto us. This is called his "appearing in the presence of God for us" (Heb. 9:24); that is, as the high priest, having offered the great offering for expiation of sin, carried in the blood thereof into the most holy place, where was the representation of the presence of God, so to perfect the atonement he made for himself and the people; so the Lord Christ, having offered himself as a sweet-smelling sacrifice to God, being sprinkled with his own blood, appears in the presence of God, as it were to mind[21] him of the engagement made to him, for the redemption of sinners by his blood, and the making out the good things to them which were procured thereby. And so this appearance of his has an

---

21. remind

influence into purchased grace, inasmuch as thereby he puts in his claim for it in our behalf.

Second, he procures *the Holy Spirit* for us, effectually to collate and bestow all this purchased grace upon us. That he would do this, and does it, for us, we have his engagement (John 14:16). This is purchased grace, in respect of its fountain and spring—of which I shall not speak further at present, seeing I must handle it at large in the matter of the communion we have with the Holy Ghost.

Chapter 7

The Nature of Purchased Grace

The fountain of that purchased grace wherein the saints have communion with Christ being discovered, in the next place the nature of this grace itself may be considered. As was said, it may be referred unto three heads: (1) grace of *acceptation* with God; (2) grace of *sanctification* from God; (3) grace of *privileges* with and before God.

GRACE OF ACCEPTATION WITH GOD

Of *acceptation* with God. Out of Christ, we are in a state of alienation from God,[1] accepted neither in our persons nor our services. Sin makes a separation between God and us: that state, with all its consequences and attendancies, is not my business to unfold. The first issue of purchased grace is to restore us into a state of acceptation. And this is done [in] two ways: (1) by a *removal* of that for which we are refused—the cause of the enmity; (2) by a *bestowing* of that for which we are accepted.

Not only all causes of quarrel were to be taken away, that so we should not be under displeasure, but also that was to be given unto us that makes us the objects of God's delight and pleasure, on the account of the want whereof we are distanced from God:

It gives a *removal* of that for which we are refused. This is *sin in the guilt*, and all the attendancies thereof. The first issue of purchased grace tends to the taking away of sin in its guilt, that it shall not bind over the soul to the wages of it, which is death.

---

1. John 3:36; Eph. 2:12–13.

How this is accomplished and brought about by Christ was evidenced in the close of the foregoing chapter. It is the fruit and effect of his death for us. Guilt of sin was the only cause of our separation and distance from God, as has been said. This made us obnoxious to wrath, punishment, and the whole displeasure of God; on the account hereof were we imprisoned under the curse of the law, and given up to the power of Satan. This is the state of our unacceptation.[2] By his death, Christ—bearing the curse, undergoing the punishment that was due to us, paying the ransom that was due for us—delivers us from this condition. And thus far the death of Christ is the sole cause of our acceptation with God—that all cause of quarrel and rejection of us is thereby taken away. And to that end are his sufferings reckoned to us; for, being "made sin for us" (2 Cor. 5:21), he is made "righteousness unto us" (1 Cor. 1:30).

But yet further; this will not *complete* our acceptation with God. The old quarrel may be laid aside, and yet no new friendship begun; we may be not sinners, and yet not be so far righteous as to have a right to the kingdom of heaven. Adam had no right to life because he was innocent; he must, moreover, "do this," and then he shall "live." He must not only have a *negative* righteousness—he was not guilty of anything; but also a *positive* righteousness—he must do all things.

This, then, is required, in the second place, to our complete acceptation, that we have not only the *not imputation of sin*, but also a *reckoning of righteousness*. Now, this we have in the obedience of the life of Christ. This also was discovered in the last chapter. The obedience of the life of Christ was for us, is imputed to us, and is our righteousness before God—by his obedience are we "made righteous" (Rom. 5:19). On what score the obedience of faith takes place, shall be afterward declared.

These two things, then, complete our grace of acceptation. Sin being removed, and righteousness bestowed, we have peace with God—are continually accepted before him. There is not any thing to charge us with: that which was, is taken out of the way by Christ, and nailed to his cross—made fast there; yea, publicly and legally cancelled, that it can never be admitted again as an evidence. What court among men would admit of evidence that has been publicly cancelled and nailed up for all to see it? So has Christ dealt with that which was against us; and not only so, but also he puts that upon us for which we are received into

---

2. state of being unaccepted; rejection.

favor. He makes us comely through his beauty; gives us white raiment to stand before the Lord. This is the first part of purchased grace wherein the saints have communion with Jesus Christ. In remission of sin and imputation of righteousness does it consist; from the death of Christ, as a price, sacrifice, and a punishment—from the life of Christ spent in obedience to the law, does it arise. The great product it is of the Father's righteousness, wisdom, love, and grace—the great and astonishable[3] fruit of the love and condescension of the Son—the great discovery of the Holy Ghost in the revelation of the mystery of the gospel.

Grace of Sanctification from God

The second is grace of *sanctification*. He makes us not only *accepted*, but also *acceptable*. He does not only purchase love for his saints, but also makes them lovely. He came not by blood only, but by water and blood. He does not only justify his saints from the *guilt* of sin, but also sanctify and wash them from the *filth* of sin. The first is from his life and death as a sacrifice of propitiation; this from his death as a purchase, and his life as an example. (So the apostle, Heb. 9:14; as also Eph. 5:26–27.) Two things are eminent in this issue of purchased grace: (1) the removal of *defilement*; (2) the bestowing of *cleanness* in actual grace.

For the first, it is also threefold:

First, the *habitual* cleansing of our nature. We are naturally unclean, defiled—habitually so; for "Who can bring a clean thing out of an unclean?" (Job 14:4); "That which is born of the flesh is flesh" (John 3:6). It is in the pollution of our blood that we are born (Ezekiel 16)—wholly defiled and polluted. The grace of sanctification, purchased by the blood of Christ, removes this defilement of our nature. "Such were some of you; but you are washed, you are sanctified" (1 Cor. 6:11). So also Titus 3:3–5, "He has saved us by the washing of regeneration, and the renewing of the Holy Ghost." How far this original, habitual pollution is removed, need not be disputed; it is certain the soul is made fair and beautiful in the sight of God. Though the sin that does defile remains, yet its habitual defilement is taken away. But the handling of this lies not in my aim.

Second, taking away the *pollutions of all our actual transgressions*. There is a defilement attending every actual sin. Our own clothes make us to be abhorred (Job 9:31). A spot, a stain, rust, wrinkle, filth, blood attends every sin. Now, "The blood of Jesus Christ cleanses us from all

---

3. measured to astonish and surprise

sin" (1 John 1:7). Besides the defilement of our natures which he purges (Titus 3:5), he takes away the defilement of our persons by actual follies. "By one offering he perfected forever them that are sanctified"; by himself he "purged our sins" before he sat down at the right hand of the Majesty on high (Heb. 1:3).

Third, in our best duties we have defilement (Isa. 64:6). Self, unbelief, form drop themselves into all that we do. We may be ashamed of our choicest performances. God has promised that the saints' good works shall follow them. Truly, were they to be measured by the rule as they come from us, and weighed in the balance of the sanctuary, it might be well for us that they might be buried forever: But the Lord Christ first, as our high priest, bears the iniquity, the guilt, and provocation, which in severe justice does attend them (Ex. 28:38); and not only so, but he washes away all their filth and defilements. He is as a refiner's fire, to purge both the sons of Levi and their offerings; adding, moreover, sweet incense to them, that they may be accepted. Whatever is of the *Spirit*, of *himself*, of *grace*—that remains; whatever is of *self*, *flesh*, *unbelief* (that is, hay and stubble [1 Cor. 3:12])—that he consumes, wastes, takes away. So that the saints' good works shall meet them one day with a changed countenance, that they shall scarce know them: that which seemed to them to be black, deformed, defiled, shall appear beautiful and glorious; they shall not be afraid of them, but rejoice to see and follow them.

And this cleansing of our natures, persons, and duties, has its whole foundation in the death of Christ. Hence our washing and purifying, our cleansing and purging, is ascribed to his blood and the sprinkling thereof meritoriously, this work is done, by the shedding of the blood of Christ; efficiently, by its sprinkling. The sprinkling of the blood of Christ proceeds from the communication of the Holy Ghost; which he promises to us, as purchased by him for us. He is the pure water, wherewith we are sprinkled from all our sins, that spirit of judgment and burning that takes away the filth and blood of the daughters of Zion [Isa. 4:4]. And this is the first thing in the grace of sanctification; of which more afterward.

By bestowing *cleanness* as to actual grace. The blood of Christ in this purchased grace does not only take away defilement, but also it gives purity; and that also in a threefold gradation:

First, it gives the *Spirit of holiness to dwell in us*. "He is made unto us sanctification" (1 Cor. 1:30), by procuring for us the Spirit of sanctification. Our renewing is of the Holy Ghost, who is shed on us through Christ alone (Titus 3:6). This the apostle mainly insists on [in] Romans 8—to wit, that the prime and principal gift of sanctification that we receive from Christ, is the indwelling of the Spirit, and our following after the guidance hereof. But what concerns the Spirit in any kind must be referred to that which I have to offer concerning our communion with him.

Second, he gives us *habitual grace*—a principle of grace, opposed to the principle of lust that is in us by nature. This is the grace that dwells in us, makes its abode with us; which, according to the distinct faculties of our souls wherein it is, or the distinct objects about which it is exercised, receives various appellations, being indeed all but one new principle of life. In the understanding, it is *light*; in the will, *obedience*; in the affections, *love*; in all, *faith*. So, also, it is differenced in respect of its operations. When it carries out the soul to rest on Christ, it is faith; when to delight in him, it is love; but still one and the same habit of grace. And this is the second thing.

Third, [there is an] *actual influence for the performance* of every spiritual duty whatever. After the saints have both the former, yet Christ tells them that without him "they can do nothing" (John 15:5). They are still in dependence upon him for new influences of grace, or supplies of the Spirit. They cannot live and spend upon the old stock; for every new act they must have new grace. He must "work in us to will and to do of his good pleasure" (Phil. 2:13). And in these three, thus briefly named, consists that purchased grace in the point of sanctification, as to the collating of purity and cleanness, wherein we have communion with Christ.

Grace of Privileges with and before God

This purchased grace consists in privileges to stand before God, and these are of two sorts—*primary* and *consequential*. Primary is *adoption*—the Spirit of adoption; consequential are all the *favors* of the gospel, which the saints alone have right unto. But of this I shall speak when I come to the last branch—of communion with the Holy Ghost.

These are the things wherein we have communion with Christ as to purchased grace in this life. Drive them up to perfection, and you have that which we call everlasting glory. Perfect acceptance, perfect holiness, perfect adoption, or inheritance of sons—that is glory.

Our process now, in the next place, is to what I mainly intend, even the manner how we hold communion with Christ in these things; and that in the order laid down; as—(1) how we hold communion with him

in the obedience of his *life and merit* of his death, as to acceptance with
God the Father;[4] (2) how we hold communion with Christ in his *blood*,
as to the Spirit of sanctification, the habits and acts of grace;[5] (3) how
we hold communion with him as to the privileges we enjoy.[6] Of which
in the ensuing chapters.

---

4. See chap. 8.
5. See chap. 9.
6. See chap. 10.

Chapter 8

How We Hold Communion with Christ in Purchased Grace

Communion with Christ unto Acceptance with God

Communion with Christ in purchased grace, as unto *acceptation with God*, from the obedience of his life and efficacy of his death, is the first thing we inquire into. The discovery of what on the part of Christ and what on our part is required thereunto (for our mutual actings, even his and ours, are necessary, that we may have fellowship and communion together herein) is that which herein I intend.

THE REQUIREMENTS OF CHRIST FOR THIS COMMUNION

First, on the part of Christ there is no more required but these two things: (1) That what he *did*, he did not for himself, but for us. (2) What he *suffered*, he suffered not for himself, but for us. That is, that his intention from eternity, and when he was in the world, was, that all that he did and suffered was and should be for us and our advantage, as to our acceptance with God; that he still continues making use of what he so did and suffered for that end and purpose, and that only. Now, this is most evident:

What he *did*, he did for us, and not for himself: "He was made under the law, that we might receive the adoption of sons" (Gal. 4:4–5). He was made under the law; that is, in that condition that he was obnoxious to the will and commands of it. And why was this? To what end? For himself? No; but to redeem us is the aim of all that he did—of all his obedience: and that he did. This very intention in what he did he acquaints us with: "For their sakes I sanctify myself, that they may be sanctified through the truth" (John 17:19). "I sanctify myself—dedicate and set myself apart to all that work I have to do. I came not to do my own will; I came to save that which was lost; to minister, not to be ministered unto; and to give my life a ransom"—it was the testimony he bore to all he did in the world. This intendment of his is especially to be eyed. From eternity he had thoughts of what he would do for us; and delighted himself therein. And when he was in the world, in all he went about, he had still this thought: "This is for them, and this is for them—my beloved." When he went to be baptized, says John, "I have need to be baptized of you, and come you to me?" (Matt. 3:14–15); as if he had said, "You have no need at all of it." But says Christ, "Suffer it to be so, now; for thus it becomes us to fulfill all righteousness"—"I do it for them who have none at all, and stand obliged unto all."

In what he *suffered*. This is more clear: "Messiah shall be cut off, but not for himself" (Dan. 9:26). And the apostle lays down this as a main difference between him and the high priests of the Jews, that when they made their solemn offerings, they offered first for themselves, and then for the people; but Jesus Christ offered only for others. He had no sin, and could make no sacrifice for his own sin, which he had not, but only for others. He "tasted death for every man" (Heb. 2:9)—"gave his life a ransom for many" (Matt. 20:28). The "iniquity of us all was made to meet on him" (Isa. 53: 6)—"He bore our sins in his own body on the tree" (1 Pet. 2:24)—"loved the church, and gave himself for it" (Eph. 5:25; Gal. 2:20; Rom. 4:25; Rev. 1:5–6; Titus 2:14; 1 Tim. 2:6; Isa. 53:12; John 17:19). But this is exceeding clear and confessed, that Christ in his suffering and oblation, had his intention only upon the good of his elect, and their acceptation with God; suffering for us, "the just for the unjust, that he might bring us to God" [1 Pet. 3:18].

Secondly, to complete this communion on the part of Christ, it is required—

That there be added to what he has done, *the gospel tenders* of that complete righteousness and acceptation with God which arises from his perfect obedience and sufferings. Now, they are twofold:

Declaratory, in the conditional promises of the gospel. Mark 16:15; Matthew 11:28; "He that believes shall be saved" (Mark 16:16); "Come unto me, and I will give you rest" (Matt. 11:28); "As Moses lifted up the serpent" [John 3:14], etc.; "Christ is the end of the law for righteousness to every one that believes" (Rom. 10:4); and innumerable others. Now, declaratory tenders are very precious, there is much kindness in them, and if they be rejected, they will be the "savor of death unto death" [2 Cor. 2:16]; but the Lord Christ knows that the outward letter, though never so effectually held out, will not enable any of his for that reception of his righteousness which is necessary to interest them therein; wherefore—

In this tender of acceptation with God, on the account of what he has done and suffered, a *law is established*, that whosoever receives it shall be so accepted. But Christ knows the condition and state of his in this world. This will not do; if he do [i.e., would] not effectually invest them with it, all is lost. Therefore—

He sends them *his Holy Spirit, to quicken them* (John 6:63), to cause them that are "dead to hear his voice" (John 5:25), and to work in them whatever is required of them, to make them partakers of his righteousness and accepted with God.

Thus does Christ deal with his: he lives and dies with an intention to work out and complete righteousness for them; their enjoying of it, to a perfect acceptation before God, is all that in the one and other he aimed at. Then he tenders it unto them, declares the usefulness and preciousness of it to their souls, stirring them up to a desire and valuation of it; and lastly, effectually bestows it upon them, reckons it unto them as theirs, that they should by it, for it, with it, be perfectly accepted with his Father.

Thus, for Our Acceptation with God, Two Things Are Required:

First, that *satisfaction be made for our disobedience*—for whatever we had done which might damage the justice and honor of God; and that God be atoned toward us: which could no otherwise be, but by undergoing the penalty of the law. This, I have showed abundantly, is done by the death of Christ. God "made him to be sin for us" (2 Cor. 5:21)—a "curse" (Gal. 3:13). On this account we have our absolution—our acquitment from the guilt of sin, the sentence of the law, the wrath of God (Rom. 8:33–34). We are justified, acquitted, freed from condemnation, because it was Christ that died; "he bore our sins in his own body on the tree" (1 Pet. 2:24).

Second, that *the righteousness of the law be fulfilled*, and the obedience performed that is required at our hands. And this is done by the life of Christ (Rom. 5:18–19). So that answerable hereunto, according to our state and the condition of our acceptance with God, there are two parts:

Our *absolution from the guilt of sin*, that our disobedience be not charged upon us. This we have by the death of Christ; our sins being imputed to him, shall not be imputed to us (2 Cor. 5:21; Rom. 4:25; Isa. 53:12).

Imputation of righteousness, that we may be accounted perfectly righteous before God; and this we have by the life of Christ. His righteousness in yielding obedience to the law is imputed to us. And thus is our acceptance with God completed. Being discharged from the guilt of our disobedience by the death of Christ, and having the righteousness of the life of Christ imputed to us, we have friendship and peace with God. And this is that which I call our grace of acceptance with God, wherein we have communion with Jesus Christ.

That which remains for me to do is to show how believers hold distinct communion with Christ in this grace of acceptance, and how thereby they keep alive a sense of it—the comfort and life of it being to be renewed every day. Without this, life is a hell; no peace, no joy can we be made partakers of, but what has its rise from hence. Look what grounded persuasion we have of our acceptance with God, that he is at peace with us; whereunto is the revenue of our peace, comfort, joy, yea, and holiness itself proportioned.

But yet, before I come in particular to handle our practical communion with the Lord Jesus in this thing, I must remove two considerable objections—the one of them lying against the first part of our acceptation with God, the other against the latter. I shall, God assisting, briefly remove these two objections, and then proceed to carry on the design in hand, about our communion with Christ.

OBJECTION AND ANSWER 1

Objection. For our absolution by and upon the death of Christ, it may be said that "if the elect have their absolution, reconciliation, and freedom by the death, blood, and cross of Christ, whence is it, then, that they were not *all actually absolved* at the death of Christ, or at least so soon as they are born, but that many of them live a long while under the wrath of God in this world, as being unbelievers, under the sentence and condemning power of the law? (John 3:36). Why are they not immediately freed, upon the payment of the price and making reconciliation for them?"

Answer. Jesus Christ, in his undertaking of the work of our reconciliation with God—for which cause he came into the world—and the accomplishment of it by his death, was constituted and considered as a *common, public person,* in the stead of them for whose reconciliation to God he suffered. Hence he is the "mediator between God and man" (1 Tim. 2:5)—that is, one who undertook to God for us, as the next words manifest, "Who gave himself a ransom for all" (1 Tim. 2:6)—and the "surety of the better covenant" (Heb. 7:22); undertaking for and on the behalf of them with whom that covenant was made. Hence he is said to be given "for a covenant of the people" (Isa. 42:6) and a "leader" (55:4). He was the second Adam (1 Cor. 15:45, 47), to all ends and purposes of righteousness, to his spiritual seed, as the first Adam was of sin to his natural seed (Rom. 5:15–19).

His being thus a *common person,* arose chiefly from these things:

In general, from *the covenant* entered into by himself with his Father to this purpose. (The terms of this covenant are at large insisted on [in] Isaiah 53, and summed up in Ps. 40:7–8; Heb. 10:8–10.) Hence the Father became to be his God; which is a covenant expression (Ps. 89:26; Heb. 1:5; Ps. 22:1; 40:8; 45:7; Rev. 3:12; Mic. 5:4). So was he by his Father on this account designed to this work (Isa. 42:1, 6; 49:9; Mal. 3:1; Zech. 13:7; John 3:16; 1 Tim. 1:15). Thus the "counsel of peace" became to be "between them both" (Zech. 6:13); that is, the Father and Son. And the Son rejoices from eternity in the thought of this undertaking (Prov. 8:22–30). The command given him to this purpose, the promises made to him thereon, the assistance afforded to him, I have elsewhere handled.

In the *sovereign grant,* appointment, and design of the Father, giving and delivering the elect to Jesus Christ in this covenant, to be redeemed and reconciled to himself. "Yours they were, and you gave them me" (John 17:6). They were God's by eternal designation and election, and he gave them to Christ to be redeemed. Hence, before their calling or believing, he calls them his "sheep" (John 10:15–16), laying down his life for them as such; and hence are we said to be "chosen in Christ" (Eph. 1:4), or designed to obtain all the fruits of the love of God by Christ, and committed into his hand for that end and purpose.

In his *undertaking to suffer* what was due to them, and to do what was to be done by them, that they might be delivered, reconciled, and accepted with God. And he undertakes to give in to the Father, without loss or miscarriage, what he had so received of the Father as above (John 17:2, 12; 6:37, 39); as Jacob did the cattle he received of Laban (Gen.

31:39–40). Of both these I have treated somewhat at large elsewhere, in handling the covenant between the Father and the Son; so that I shall not need to take it up here again.

They being *given* unto him, he undertaking for them to do and suffer what was on their part required, he received, *on their behalf and for them, all the promises* of all the mercies, grace, good things, and privileges, which they were to receive upon the account of his undertaking for them. On this account eternal life is said to be promised of God "before the world began" (Titus 1:2); that is, to the Son of God for us, on his undertaking on our behalf. And grace, also, is said to be given unto us "before the world began" (2 Tim. 1:9); that is, in Christ, our appointed head, mediator, and representative.

Christ being thus a common person, a mediator, surety, and representative of his church, upon his undertaking as to efficacy and merit, and upon his actual performance as *to solemn declaration*, was as such acquitted, absolved, justified, and freed from all and every thing that, on the behalf of the elect, as due to them, was charged upon him, or could so be; I say, as to all the efficacy and merit of his undertakings, he was immediately absolved upon his faithfulness, in his first engagement: and thereby all the saints of the Old Testament were saved by his blood no less than we. As to solemn declaration, he was so absolved when the "pains of death being loosed," he was "declared to be the Son of God with power, by the resurrection from the dead" (Rom. 1:4); God saying to him, "You are my Son; this day have I begotten you" (Ps. 2:7). And this his absolution does Christ express his confidence of (Isa. 50:5–9). And he was "justified" (1 Tim. 3:16). That which I intend by this absolution of Christ as a public person is this: God having made him under the law, for them who were so (Gal. 4:4); in their stead, obnoxious to the punishment due to sin, made him sin (2 Cor. 5:21); and so gave justice, and law, and all the consequents of the curse thereof, power against him (Isa. 53:6)—upon his undergoing of that which was required of him (Isa. 53:12), God looses the pains and power of death, accepts him, and is well pleased with him, as to the performance and discharge of his work (John 17:3–6); pronounces him free from the obligation that was on him (Acts 13); and gave him a promise of all good things he aimed at, and which his soul desired. Hereon are all the promises of God made to Christ, and their accomplishment—all the encouragements given him to ask and make demand of the things originally engaged for to him (Ps. 2:8) (which he did accordingly, John 17)—founded and built. And here lies the certain, stable foundation of our absolution and acceptation with

God. Christ in our stead, acting for us as our surety, being acquitted, absolved, solemnly declared to have answered the whole debt that was incumbent on him to pay, and made satisfaction for all the injury we had done, a general pardon is sealed for us all, to be sued out particularly in the way to be appointed. For—

Christ as a public person being thus absolved, it became righteous with God, a righteous thing, from the covenant, compact, and convention that was between him and the Mediator, that those in whose stead he was *should obtain, and have bestowed on them, all the fruits of his death*, in reconciliation with God (Rom. 5:8–11); that as Christ received the general acquittance for them all, so they should every one of them enjoy it respectively. This is everywhere manifested in those expressions which express a commutation[1] designed by God in this matter (as 2 Cor. 5:21; Gal. 3:13; 1 Pet. 2:21, 24—of which afterward).

Being thus acquitted in the covenant of the Mediator (whence they are said to be circumcised with him, to die with him, to be buried with him, to rise with him, to sit with him in heavenly places—namely, in the covenant of the Mediator), and it being righteous that they should be acquitted personally in the covenant of grace, it was determined by Father, Son, and Holy Ghost that the way of their actual personal deliverance from the sentence and curse of the law should be in and by such a way and dispensation as might lead to the *praise of the glorious grace of God* (Eph. 1:5–7). The appointment of God is that we shall have the adoption of children. The means of it is by Jesus Christ; the peculiar way of bringing it about is by the redemption that is in his blood; the end is the praise of his glorious grace. And thence it is—

That until the full time of their actual deliverance, determined and appointed to them in their several generations, be accomplished, they are *personally* under the curse of the law; and, on that account, are *legally* obnoxious to the wrath of God, from which they shall certainly be delivered—I say, they are thus personally obnoxious to the law, and the curse thereof; but not at all with its primitive intention of execution upon them, but as it is a means appointed to help forward their acquaintance with Christ, and acceptance with God, on his account. When this is accomplished, that whole obligation ceases, being continued on them in a design of love; their last condition being such as that they cannot without it be brought to a participation of Christ, to the praise of the glorious grace of God.

---

1. substitution, exchange.

The end of the dispensation of grace being to glorify the whole Trinity, the order fixed on and appointed wherein this is to be done, is by *ascending to the Father's love through the work of the Spirit and blood of the Son.* The emanation of divine love to us begins with the Father, is carried on by the Son, and then communicated by the Spirit; the Father designing, the Son purchasing, the Spirit effectually working: which is their order. Our participation is first by the work of the Spirit, to an actual interest in the blood of the Son; whence we have acceptation with the Father.

This, then, is the order whereby we are brought to acceptation with the Father, for the glory of God through Christ:

That the *Spirit may be glorified,* he is given unto us to quicken us, convert us, work faith in us (Rom. 8:11; Eph. 1:19–20); according to all the promises of the covenant (Isa. 4:4–5; Ezek. 11:19; 36:26).

This being wrought in us *for the glory of the Son,* we are actually interested, according to the tenor of the covenant, at the same instant of time, in the *blood of Christ,* as to the benefits which he has procured for us thereby; yea, this very work of the Spirit itself is a fruit and part of the purchase of Christ. But we speak of our sense of this thing, whereunto the communication of the Spirit is antecedent. And—

To the *glory of the Father,* we are accepted with him, justified, freed from guilt, pardoned, and have "peace with God" (Rom. 5:1). Thus, "through Christ we have access by one Spirit unto the Father" (Eph. 2:17). And thus are both Father and Son and the Holy Spirit glorified in our justification and acceptation with God; the Father in his free love, the Son in his full purchase, and the Holy Spirit in his effectual working.

All this, in all the parts of it, is no less fully procured for us, nor less freely bestowed on us, for Christ's sake, on his account, as part of his purchase and merits, than if all of us *immediately* upon his death had been translated into heaven; only this way of our deliverance and freedom is fixed on, that the whole Trinity may be glorified thereby. And this may suffice in answer to the first objection. Though our reconciliation with God be fully and completely procured by the death of Christ, and all the ways and means whereby it is accomplished; yet we are brought unto an actual enjoyment thereof, by the way and in the order mentioned, for the praise of the glorious grace of God.

OBJECTION AND ANSWER 2

Objection. "If the obedience of the life of Christ be imputed unto us, and that is our righteousness before God, then what *need we yield any obedience ourselves?* Is not all our praying, laboring, watching, fasting, giving alms—are not all fruits of holiness, in purity of heart and usefulness of conversation, all in vain and to no purpose? And who, then, will or need take care to be holy, humble, righteous, meek, temperate, patient, good, peaceable, or to abound in good works in the world?"

Answer. The second objection is, *"That if the righteousness and obedience of Christ to the law be imputed unto us, then what need we yield obedience ourselves?"* To this, also, I shall return [an] answer as briefly as I can in the ensuing observations:

The placing of our gospel obedience on the right foot of account (that it may neither be *exalted into a state,* condition, use, or end, not given it of God; nor any *reason,* cause, motive, end, necessity of it, on the other hand, taken away, weakened, or impaired) is a matter of great importance. Some make our obedience, the works of faith, our works the matter or cause of our justification; some, the condition of the imputation of the righteousness of Christ; some, the qualification of the person justified, on the one hand; some exclude all the necessity of them, and turn the grace of God into lasciviousness,[2] on the other. To debate these differences is not my present business; only, I say, on this and other accounts, the right stating of our obedience is of great importance as to our walking with God.

We do by no means assign the *same place,* condition, state, and use to the *obedience of Christ imputed* to us, and our *obedience performed* to God. If we did, they were really inconsistent. And therefore those who affirm that our obedience is the condition or cause of our justification, do all of them deny the imputation of the obedience of Christ unto us. The righteousness of Christ is imputed to us, as that on the account whereof we are accepted and esteemed righteous before God, and are really so, though not inherently. We are as truly righteous with the obedience of Christ imputed to us as Adam was, or could have been, by a complete righteousness of his own performance. So Romans 5:18: by his obedience we are made righteous—made so truly, and so accepted; as by the disobedience of Adam we are truly made trespassers, and so accounted. And this is that which the apostle desires to be found in, in opposition to his own righteousness (Phil. 3:9). But our own obedience is not the righteousness whereupon we are accepted and justified before God; although it be acceptable to God that we should abound therein. And this distinction the apostle does evidently deliver and confirm, so

---

2. inclination to lust, wantonness.

as nothing can be more clearly revealed: "For by grace are you saved through faith: and that not of yourselves: it is the gift of God: not of works, lest any man should boast. For we are his workmanship, created in Christ Jesus unto good works, which God has prepared that we should walk in them" (Eph. 2:8–10). We are saved, or justified (for that it is whereof the apostle treats), "by grace through faith," which receives Jesus Christ and his obedience; "not of works, lest any man should boast." "But what works are they that the apostle intends?" The works of believers, as in the very beginning of the next words is manifest: "'For we are,' we believers, with our obedience and our works, of whom I speak." "Yea; but what need, then, of works?" Need still there is: "We are his workmanship," etc.

Two things the apostle intimates in these words:

First, a reason why we cannot be saved by works—namely, because we do them not in or by *our own strength*; which is necessary we should do, if we will be saved by them, or justified by them. "But this is not so," says the apostle; "for we are the workmanship of God," etc.—all our works are wrought in us, by full and effectual undeserved grace.

Second, an assertion of the necessity of good works, notwithstanding that we are not saved by them; and that is, that God has *ordained* that we shall walk in them: which is a sufficient ground of our obedience, whatever be the use of it.

If you will say then, "What are the true and proper *gospel grounds, reasons*, uses, and motives of our obedience; whence the necessity thereof may be demonstrated, and our souls be stirred up to abound and be fruitful therein?" I say, they are so many, and lie so deep in the mystery of the gospel and dispensation of grace, spread themselves so throughout the whole revelation of the will of God unto us, that to handle them fully and distinctly, and to give them their due weight, is a thing that I cannot engage in, lest I should be turned aside from what I principally intend. I shall only give you some brief heads of what might at large be insisted on:

Our universal obedience and good works are indispensably necessary, from the *sovereign appointment* and *will of God*; Father, Son, and Holy Ghost.

In general. "This is the will of God, even your sanctification," or holiness (1 Thess. 4:3). This is that which God wills, which he requires of us—that we be holy, that we be obedient, that we do his will as the angels do in heaven. The equity, necessity, profit, and advantage of this ground of our obedience might at large be insisted on; and, were there no more, this might suffice alone—if it be the will of God, it is our duty:

The Father has ordained or appointed it. It is the will of the Father (Eph. 2:10). The Father is spoken of personally, Christ being mentioned as mediator.

The Son has ordained and appointed it as mediator. "'I have ordained you, that you should bring forth fruit' of obedience, and that it should remain" (John 15:16). And—

The Holy Ghost appoints and ordains believers to works of obedience and holiness, and to work holiness in others. So, in particular, he appoints and designs men to the great work of obedience in preaching the gospel (Acts 13:2). And in sinning, men sin against him.

Our holiness, our obedience, work of righteousness is one eminent and special end of the peculiar dispensation of Father, Son, and Spirit, in the business of exalting the glory of God in our salvation—of the electing love of the Father, the purchasing love of the Son, and the operative love of the Spirit:

It is a peculiar end of the *electing* love of the Father: "He has chosen us, that we should be holy and without blame" (Eph. 1:4; cf. Isa. 4:3–4). His aim and design in choosing of us was that we should be holy and unblameable before him in love. This he is to accomplish, and will bring about in them that are his. "He chooses us to salvation, through sanctification of the Spirit, and belief of the truth" (2 Thess. 2:13). This the Father designed as the first and immediate end of electing love; and proposes the consideration of that love as a motive to holiness (1 John 4:8–10).

It is so also of the *exceeding love* of the Son; whereof the testimonies are innumerable. I shall give but one or two: "Who gave himself for us, that he might redeem us from all iniquity, and purify unto himself a peculiar people, zealous of good works" (Titus 2:14). This was his aim, his design, in giving himself for us: "Christ loved the church, and gave himself for it; that he might sanctify and cleanse it with the washing of water by the word; that he might present it to himself a glorious church, not having spot, or wrinkle, or any such thing; but that it should be holy, and without blemish" (Eph. 5:25–27; cf. 2 Cor. 5:15; Rom. 6:11.)

It is the *very work of the love* of the Holy Ghost. His whole work upon us, in us, for us, consists in preparing of us for obedience; enabling of us thereunto, and bringing forth the fruits of it in us. And this he does in opposition to a righteousness of our own, either before it or to be made up by it (Titus 3:5). I need not insist on this. The fruits of the Spirit in us are known (Gal. 5:22–23).

And thus have we a twofold bottom of the necessity of our obedience and personal holiness: God has appointed it, he requires it; and it is an eminent immediate end of the distinct dispensation of Father, Son, and Holy Ghost, in the work of our salvation. If God's sovereignty over us is to be owned, if his love toward us be [i.e., is] to be regarded, if the whole work of the ever-blessed Trinity, for us, in us, be of any moment, [then] our obedience is necessary.

It is necessary in respect of the *end* thereof; and that whether you consider God, ourselves, or the world:

The end of our obedience, in respect of God, is his *glory and honor* (Mal. 1:6). This is God's honor—all that we give him. It is true, he will take his honor from the stoutest and proudest rebel in the world; but all we give him is in our obedience. The glorifying of God by our obedience is all that we are or can be. Particularly—

It is the glory of the *Father.* "Let your light so shine before men, that they may see your good works, and glorify your Father which is in heaven" (Matt. 5:16). By our walking in the light of faith does glory arise to the Father. The fruits of his love, of his grace, of his kindness, are seen upon us; and God is glorified in our behalf. And—

The *Son is glorified thereby.* It is the will of God that as all men honor the Father, so should they honor the Son (John 5:23). And how is this done? By believing in him (John 14:1); obeying of him. Hence, he says he is glorified in believers; and prays for an increase of grace and union for them, that he may yet be more glorified, and all might know that, as mediator, he was sent of God (John 17:10).

The *Spirit is glorified also by it.* He is grieved by our disobedience (Eph. 4:30); and therefore his glory is in our bringing forth fruit. He dwells in us, as in his temple; which is not to be defiled. Holiness becomes his habitation forever.

Now, if this that has been said be not sufficient to evince a necessity of our obedience, we must suppose ourselves to speak with a sort of men who regard neither the sovereignty, nor love, nor glory of God, Father, Son, or Holy Ghost. Let men say what they please, though our obedience should be all lost, and never regarded (which is impossible, for God is not unjust, to forget our labor of love), yet here is a sufficient bottom, ground, and reason of yielding more obedience unto God than ever we shall do while we live in this world. I speak also only of gospel grounds of obedience, and not of those that are natural and legal, which are indispensable to all mankind.

The end in respect of *ourselves* immediately is threefold: (1) honor; (2) peace; (3) usefulness.

Honor. It is by holiness that we are made like unto God, and his image is renewed again in us. This was our honor at our creation, this exalted us above all our fellow-creatures here below—we were made in the image of God. This we lost by sin, and became like the beasts that perish. To this honor, of conformity to God, of bearing his image, are we exalted again by holiness alone. "Be you holy," says God, "for I am holy" (1 Pet. 1:16); and, "Be you perfect" (that is, in doing good), "even as your Father which is in heaven is perfect" (Matt. 5:48)—in a likeness and conformity to him. And herein is the image of God renewed; therein we "put on the new man, which after God is created in righteousness and holiness of truth" (Eph. 4:23–24). This was that which originally was attended with power and dominion—is still all that is beautiful or comely in the world. How it makes men honorable and precious in the sight of God, of angels, of men; how alone it is that which is not despised, which is of price before the Lord; what contempt and scorn he has of them in whom it is not—in what abomination he has them and all their ways—might easily be evinced.

Peace. By it we have communion with God, wherein peace alone is to be enjoyed. "The wicked are like the troubled sea that cannot rest"; and, "There is no peace" to them, "says my God" (Isa. 57:20–21). There is no peace, rest, or quietness, in a distance, separation, or alienation from God. He is the rest of our souls. In the light of his countenance is life and peace. Now, "if we walk in the light, as he is in the light, we have fellowship one with another" (1 John 1:7); "and truly our fellowship is with the Father, and with his Son Jesus Christ" (1 John 1:3). He that walks in the light of new obedience, he has communion with God, and in his presence is fullness of joy forever; without it, there is nothing but darkness, and wandering, and confusion.

Usefulness. A man without holiness is good for nothing. "Ephraim," says the prophet, "is an empty vine that brings forth fruit to itself" [Hos. 10:1]. And what is such a vine good for? Nothing. Says another prophet, "A man cannot make so much as a pin of it, to hang a vessel on" [Ezek. 15:3]. A barren tree is good for nothing, but to be cut down for the fire. Notwithstanding the seeming usefulness of men who serve the providence of God in their generations, I could easily manifest that the world and the church might want them, and that, indeed, in themselves they are good for nothing. Only the holy man is *commune bonum*.[3]

The end of it in respect of *others* in the world is manifold:

It serves to the *conviction* and stopping the mouths of some of the enemies of God, both here and hereafter: *Here.* "Having a good conscience; that, wherein they speak evil of you, as of evildoers, they may be ashamed that falsely accuse your good conversation in Christ" (1 Pet. 3:16). By our keeping of a good conscience men will be made ashamed of their false accusations; that whereas their malice and hatred of the ways of God has provoked them to speak all manner of evil of the profession[4] of them, by the holiness and righteousness of the saints, they are convinced and made ashamed, as a thief is when he is taken, and be driven to acknowledge that God is amongst them, and that they are wicked themselves (John 17:23). *Hereafter.* It is said that the saints shall judge the world [1 Cor. 6:2]. It is on this, as well as upon other considerations: their good works, their righteousness, their holiness shall be brought forth and manifested to all the world; and the righteousness of God's judgments against wicked men be thence evinced. "See," says Christ, "these are they that I own, whom you so despised and abhorred; and see their works following them: this and that they have done, when you wallowed in your abominations" (Matt. 25:42–43).

The *conversion of others.* "Having your conversation honest among the Gentiles; that, wherein they speak against you as evildoers, they may, by your good works, which they shall behold, glorify God in the day of visitation" (1 Pet. 2:12; Matt. 5:16). Even revilers, persecutors, evil-speakers have been overcome by the constant holy walking of professors; and when their day of visitation has come, have glorified God on that account (1 Pet. 3:1–2).

The *benefit of all*; partly in keeping off judgments from the residue of men, as ten good men would have preserved Sodom (Gen. 18:32): partly by their real communication of good to them with whom they have to do in their generation. Holiness makes a man a good man, useful to all; and others eat of the fruits of the Spirit that he brings forth continually.

It is necessary in respect of the *state* and condition of *justified persons*; and that whether you consider their relative state of acceptation, or their state of sanctification:

---

3. common good
4. confession

First. They are *accepted* and received into friendship with a holy God—a God of purer eyes than to behold iniquity [Hab. 1:13]—who hates every unclean thing. And is it not necessary that they should be holy who are admitted into his presence, walk in his sight—yea, lie in his bosom? Should they not with all diligence cleanse themselves from all pollution of flesh and spirit, and perfect holiness in the fear of the Lord (2 Cor. 7:1)?

Secondly. In respect of *sanctification.* We have in us a new creature (2 Cor. 5:17). This new creature is fed, cherished, nourished, kept alive by the fruits of holiness. To what end has God given us new hearts and new natures? Is it that we should kill them? Stifle the creature that is found in us in the womb? That we should give him to the old man to be devoured?

It is necessary in respect of the *proper place of holiness* in the new covenant; and that is [three]fold:

First. Of the *means* unto the end. God has appointed that holiness shall be the means, the way to that eternal life, which, as in itself and originally is his gift by Jesus Christ, so, with regard to his constitution of our obedience, as the means of attaining it, is a reward, and God in bestowing of it a rewarder.[5] Though it be neither the cause, matter, nor condition of our justification, yet it is the way appointed of God for us to walk in for the obtaining of salvation. And therefore, he that has hope of eternal life purifies himself, as he is pure: and none shall ever come to that end who walks not in that way; for without holiness it is impossible to see God [Heb. 12:14].

Secondly. It is a *testimony* and pledge of adoption—a sign and evidence of grace; that is, of acceptation with God. And—

Thirdly. The whole *expression* of our thankfulness.

Now, there is not one of all these causes and reasons of the necessity, the indispensable necessity of our obedience, good works, and personal righteousness, but would require a more large discourse to unfold and explain than I have allotted to the proposal of them all; and innumerable others there are of the same import, that I cannot name. He that upon these accounts does not think universal holiness and obedience to be of indispensable necessity, unless also it be exalted into the room of the obedience and righteousness of Christ, let him be filthy still [cf. Isa. 64:6].

---

5. Rom. 6:23; Heb. 11:6; Gen. 17:1; Ps. 19:11; 58:11; Matt. 5:12; 10:41; Rom. 4:4; Col. 2:18; 3:24; Heb. 10:35; 11:26; 2 Pet. 2:13.

THE REQUIREMENTS OF BELIEVERS TO COMPLETE THIS COMMUNION

These objections being removed, and having, at the entrance of this chapter, declared what is done on the part of Christ, as to our fellowship with him in this purchased grace, as to our acceptance with God, it remains that I now show what also is required and performed on our part for the completing thereof. This, then, consists in the ensuing particulars:

The *saints cordially approve* of this righteousness, as that alone which is absolutely complete and able to make them acceptable before God. And this supposes six things:

Their clear and full *conviction* of the necessity of a righteousness wherewith to appear before God. This is always in their thoughts; this in their whole lives they take for granted. Many men spend their days in obstinacy and hardness, adding drunkenness unto thirst, never once inquiring what their condition shall be when they enter into eternity; others trifle away their time and their souls, sowing the wind of empty hopes, and preparing to reap a whirlwind of wrath; but this lies at the bottom of all the saints' communion with Christ—a deep, fixed, resolved persuasion of an absolute and indispensable necessity of a righteousness wherewith to appear before God. The holiness of God's nature, the righteousness of his government, the severity of his law, the terror of his wrath are always before them. They have been all convinced of sin, and have looked on themselves as ready to sink under the vengeance due to it. They have all cried, "Men and brethren, what shall we do to be saved?" "Wherewith shall we come before God?" and have all concluded, that it is in vain to flatter themselves with hopes of escaping as they are by nature. If God be holy and righteous, and of purer eyes than to behold iniquity [Hab. 1:13], they must have a righteousness to stand before him; and they know what will be the cry one day of those who now bear up themselves, as if they were otherwise minded (Isa. 53:1–5; Mic. 6:6–7).

They weigh their *own righteousness* in the balance, and find it wanting; and this [in] two ways:

In *general*, and upon the whole of the matter, at their first setting themselves before God. When men are convinced of the necessity of a righteousness, they catch[6] at every thing that presents itself to them for relief. Like men ready to sink in deep waters, [they] catch at that

---

6. eagerly grasp

which is next, to save them from drowning; which sometimes proves a rotten stick that sinks with them. So did the Jews (Rom. 9:31–32); they caught hold of the law, and it would not relieve them; and how they perished with it the apostle declares (Rom. 10:1–4). The law put them upon setting up a righteousness of their own. This kept them doing, and in hope; but kept them from submitting to the righteousness of God. Here many perish, and never get one step nearer God all their days. This the saints renounce; they have no confidence in the flesh: they know that all they can do, all that the law can do, which is weak through the flesh, will not avail them. See what judgment Paul makes of all a man's own righteousness (Phil. 3:8–10). This they bear in their minds daily, this they fill their thoughts with, that upon the account of what they have done, can do, ever shall do, they cannot be accepted with God, or justified thereby. This keeps their souls humble, full of a sense of their own vileness, all their days.

In *particular*. They daily weigh all their *particular actions* in the balance and find them wanting, as to any such completeness as, upon their own account, to be accepted with God. "Oh!" says a saint, "if I had nothing to commend me unto God but this prayer, this duty, this conquest of a temptation, wherein I myself see so many failings, so much imperfection, could I appear with any boldness before him? Shall I, then, piece up a garment of righteousness out of my best duties? Ah! it is all as a defiled cloth" (Isa. 64:6). These thoughts accompany them in all their duties, in their best and most choice performances: "Lord, what am I in my best estate? How little suitableness unto your holiness is in my best duties! O spare me,[7] in reference to the best thing that ever I did in my life!" When a man who lives upon convictions has got some enlargements in duties, some conquest over a sin or temptation, he hugs himself, like Micah when he had got a Levite to be his priest [Judg. 17:12–13]: now surely it shall be well with him, now God will bless him: his heart is now at ease; he has peace in what he has done. But he who has communion with Christ, when he is *highest in duties of sanctification and holiness is clearest in the apprehension of his own unprofitableness*, and rejects every thought that might arise in his heart of setting his peace in them, or upon them. He says to his soul, "Do these things seem something to you? Alas! you have to do with an infinitely righteous God, who looks through and through all that vanity,

---

7. Neh. 13:22.

which you are but little acquainted with; and should he deal with you according to your best works, you must perish."

They approve of, value, and rejoice in *this righteousness*, for their acceptation, *which the Lord Jesus has wrought out* and provided for them; this being discovered to them, they approve of it with all their hearts, and rest in it. "Surely, shall one say, in the LORD have I righteousness and strength" (Isa. 45:24). This is their voice and language, when once the righteousness of God in Christ is made known unto them: "Here is righteousness indeed; here have I rest for my soul. Like the merchant man in the gospel that finds the pearl of price (Matt. 13:45–46), I had been searching up and down; I looked this and that way for help, but it was far away; I spent my strength for that which was not bread: here is that, indeed, which makes me rich forever!" When first the righteousness of Christ, for acceptation with God, is revealed to a poor laboring soul, that has sought for rest and has found none, he is surprised and amazed, and is not able to contain himself: and such a one always in his heart approves this righteousness on a twofold account:

As full of *infinite wisdom*. "Unto them that believe," says the apostle, "Christ crucified is 'the wisdom of God'" (1 Cor. 1:24). They see infinite wisdom in this way of their acceptation with God. "In what darkness," says such a one, "in what straits,[8] in what entanglements, was my poor soul! How little able was I to look through the clouds and perplexities wherewith I was encompassed! I looked inward, and there was nothing but sin, horror, fear, tremblings; I looked upward and saw nothing but wrath, curses, and vengeance. I knew that God was a holy and righteous God, and that no unclean thing could abide before him; I knew that I was a poor, vile, unclean, and sinful creature; and how to bring these two together in peace, I knew not. But in the *righteousness of Christ* does a world of wisdom open itself, dispelling all difficulties and darkness, and manifesting a reconciliation of all this." "O the depth of the riches both of the wisdom and knowledge of God!" (Rom. 11:33; Col. 2:3). But of this before.

As *full of grace*. He knows that sin had shut up the whole way of grace toward him; and whereas God aims at nothing so much as the manifestation of his grace, he was utterly cut short of it. Now, to have a complete righteousness provided, and yet abundance of grace manifested, exceedingly delights the soul—to have God's dealing with his person all grace, and dealing with his righteousness all justice, takes

---

8. difficulties, distresses.

up his thoughts. God everywhere assures us that this righteousness is of grace. It is "by grace, and no more of works" (Rom. 11:6), as the apostle at large sets it out (Eph. 2:7–9). It is from riches of grace and kindness that the provision of this righteousness is made. It is of mere grace that it is bestowed on us, it is not at all of works; though it be in itself a righteousness of works, yet to us it is of mere grace. So Titus 3:4–7, "But after that the kindness and love of God our Savior toward man appeared, not by works of righteousness which we have done, but according to his mercy he saved us, by the washing of regeneration, and renewing of the Holy Ghost, which he shed on us abundantly through Jesus Christ our Savior, that being justified by his grace, we should be made heirs according to the hope of eternal life." The rise of all this dispensation is kindness and love; that is, *grace* (v. 4). The way of communication, negatively, is not by works of righteousness that we have done—positively, by the communication of the Holy Ghost (v. 5); the means of whose procurement is Jesus Christ (v. 6)—and the work itself is by grace (v. 7). Here is use made of every word almost, whereby the exceeding rich grace, kindness, mercy, and goodness of God may be expressed, all concurring in this work. As: (1) *Chrēstotēs*—his goodness, benignity, readiness to communicate of himself and his good things that may be profitable to us (2) *Philanthrōpia*—mercy, love, and propensity of mind to help, assist, relieve them of whom he speaks, toward whom he is so affected. (3) *Eleos*—mercy, forgiveness, compassion, tenderness, to them that suffer; and *charis*—free pardoning bounty, undeserved love. And all this is said to be *tou theou sōtēros*—he exercises all these properties and attributes of his nature toward us that he may save us; and in the bestowing of it, giving us the Holy Ghost, it is said, *execheen*—he poured him out as water out of a vessel, without stop and hesitation; and that not in a small measure, but *plousiōs*—richly and in abundance: whence, as to the work itself, it is emphatically said, *dikaiōthentes tē ekeinou* —justified by the grace of him who is such a one. And this do the saints of God, in their communion with Christ, exceedingly rejoice in before him, that the way of their acceptation before God is a way of grace, kindness, and mercy, that they might not boast in themselves, but in the Lord and his goodness, crying, "How great is your goodness! How great is your bounty!"

They approve of it, and rejoice in it, as *a way of great peace and security* to themselves and their own souls. They remember what was their state and condition while they went about to set up a righteousness of their own, and were not subject to the righteousness of Christ—how miserably they were tossed up and down with continual fluctuating thoughts. Sometimes they had hope, and sometimes were full of fear; sometimes they thought themselves in some good condition, and anon were at the very brink of hell, their consciences being racked and torn with sin and fear: but now, "being justified by faith, they have peace with God" (Rom. 5:1). All is *quiet and serene*; not only that *storm* is over, but they are in the *haven* where they would be. They have abiding peace with God. Hence is that description of Christ to a poor soul, "And a man shall be as a hiding place from the wind, and a covert from the tempest; as rivers of water in a dry place, as the shadow of a great rock in a weary land." (Isa. 32:2). Wind and tempest, and drought and weariness—nothing now troubles the soul that is in Christ; he has a hiding place, and a covert, and rivers of water, and the shadow of a great rock, for his security. This is the great mystery of faith in this business of our acceptation with God by Christ: that whereas the soul of a believer finds enough in him and upon him to rend the very caul[9] of the heart [Hos. 13:8], to fill him with fears, terror, disquietments all his days, yet through Christ he is at perfect peace with God (Isa. 26:3; Ps. 4:6–8). Hence do the souls of believers exceedingly magnify Jesus Christ, that they can behold the face of God with boldness, confidence, peace, joy, assurance—that they can call him Father, bear themselves on his love, walk up and down in quietness, and without fear. How glorious is the Son of God in this grace! They remember the wormwood and gall that they have eaten—the vinegar and tears they have drunk—the trembling of their souls, like an aspen leaf that is shaken with the wind. Whenever they thought of God, what contrivances have they had to hide, and fly, and escape! To be brought now to settlement and security, must needs greatly affect them.

They cordially *approve* of this righteousness, because it is a way and means of *exceeding exaltation* and honor of the Lord Jesus, whom their souls do love. Being once brought to an acquaintance with Jesus Christ, their hearts desire nothing more than that he may be honored and glorified to the utmost, and in all things have the preeminence. Now, what can more tend to the advancing and honoring of him in our hearts than to know that he is made of God unto us "wisdom and righteousness"? (1 Cor. 1:30). Not that he is this or that part of our acceptation with God; but he is all—he is the whole. They know that on the account of his working out their acceptation with God, he is—

---

9. membrane; the pericardium.

Honored of God *his Father*.

> He made himself of no reputation, and took upon him the form of a
> servant, and was made in the likeness of men: and being found in fashion
> as a man, he humbled himself, and became obedient unto death, even the
> death of the cross. *Wherefore* God also has highly exalted him, and given
> him a name which is above every name: that at the name of Jesus every
> knee should bow, of things in heaven, and things in earth, and things
> under the earth; and that every tongue should confess that Jesus Christ
> is Lord, to the glory of God the Father. (Phil. 2:7–11)

Whether that word "wherefore" denotes a connection of causality or only
a consequence, this is evident, that on the account of his suffering and
as the end of it, he was honored and exalted of God to an unspeakable
preeminence, dignity, and authority;[10] according as God had promised
him on the same account (Isa. 53:11–12; Acts 2:36; 5:30–31). And
therefore it is said, that when "he had by himself purged our sins, he
sat down at the right hand of the Majesty on high" (Heb. 1:3).

He is on this account honored of all *the angels in heaven*, even because of this great work of bringing sinners unto God; for they do not
only bow down and desire to look into the mystery of the cross (1 Pet.
1:12), but worship and praise him always on this account:

> I heard the voice of many angels round about the throne, and the living
> creatures and the elders: and the number of them was ten thousand times
> ten thousand, and thousands of thousands; saying with a loud voice,
> "Worthy is the Lamb that was slain to receive power, and riches, and
> wisdom, and strength, and honor, and glory, and blessing." And every
> creature which is in heaven and earth, and under the earth, and such as
> are in the sea, and all that are in them, heard I saying, "Blessing, and
> honor, and glory, and power, be unto him that sits upon the throne, and
> unto the Lamb forever and ever." And the living creatures said, "Amen."
> And the four and twenty elders fell down and worshipped him that lives
> forever and ever. (Rev. 5:11–14)

The reason given of this glorious and wonderful doxology, this attribu-
tion of honor and glory to Jesus Christ by the whole host of heaven is
because he was the Lamb that was slain; that is, because of the work
of our redemption and our bringing unto God. And it is not a little refreshment and rejoicing to the souls of the saints, to know that all the

---

10. Ps. 110:1, 5; 2:8–9; Zech. 9:10; Ps. 72:8; Rom. 14:11; Isa. 45:23; Phil. 2:10.

angels of God, the whole host of heaven, which never sinned, do yet continually rejoice and ascribe praise and honor to the Lord Jesus, for his bringing them to peace and favor with God.

He is honored *by his saints all the world over*; and indeed, if they do not, who should? If they honor him not as they honor the Father, they are, of all men, the most unworthy. But see what they do, "Unto him that loved us, and washed us from our sins in his own blood, and has made us kings and priests unto God and his Father; to him be glory and dominion forever and ever. Amen" (Rev. 1:5–6). "The four living creatures and four and twenty elders fell down before the Lamb, having every one of them harps, and golden vials full of odors, which are the prayers of saints. And they sung a new song, saying, you are worthy to take the book, and to open the seals thereof: for you were slain, and have redeemed us to God by your blood, out of every kindred, and tongue, and people, and nation; and have made us unto our God kings and priests: and we shall reign on the earth" (Rev. 5:8–10). The great, solemn worship of the Christian church consists in this assignation[11] of honor and glory to the Lord Jesus: therefore do they love him, honor him, delight in him; as Paul (Phil. 3:8); and so the spouse (Song 5:9–16). And this is on this account—

They cordially approve of this righteousness, this way of acceptation, as that which brings *glory to God as such*. When they were laboring under the guilt of sin, that which did most of all perplex their souls was that their safety was inconsistent with the glory and honor of the great God—with his justice, faithfulness, and truth, all which were engaged for the destruction of sin;[12] and how to come off from ruin without the loss of their honor [i.e., the honor of the aforementioned attributes] they saw not. But now by the revelation of this righteousness from faith to faith, they plainly see that all the properties of God are exceedingly glorified in the pardon, justification, and acceptance of poor sinners; as before was manifested.

And this is the first way whereby the saints hold daily communion with the Lord Jesus in this purchased grace of acceptation with God: they consider, approve of, and rejoice in the way, means, and thing itself.

They make an *actual commutation* with the Lord Jesus as to their sins and his righteousness. Of this there are also sundry parts:

---

11. assigning, assignment.
12. Rom. 1:17; 10:3–4.

They continually keep alive upon their hearts a *sense of the guilt* and evil of sin; even then when they are under some comfortable persuasions of their personal acceptance with God. Sense of pardon takes away the horror and fear, but not a due sense of the guilt of sin. It is the daily exercise of the saints of God, to consider the great provocation that is in sin—their sins, the sin of their nature and lives; to render themselves vile in their own hearts and thoughts on that account; to compare it with the terror of the Lord; and to judge themselves continually. This they do in general. "My sin is ever before me," says David [Ps. 51:3]. They set sin before them, not to terrify and affright their souls with it, but that a due sense of the evil of it may be kept alive upon their hearts.

They gather up in their thoughts the sins for which they have not made a *particular reckoning* with God in Christ; or if they have begun so to do, yet they have not made clear work of it, nor come to a clear and comfortable issue. There is nothing more dreadful than for a man to be able to digest his convictions—to have sin look him in the face, and speak perhaps some words of terror to him, and to be able, by any charms of diversions or delays, to put it off, without coming to a full trial as to state and condition in reference thereunto. This the saints do: they gather up their sins, lay them in the balance of the law, see and consider their weight and desert; and then—

They make this commutation I speak of with Jesus Christ; that is—

They seriously consider, and by faith *conquer*, all objections to the contrary, that Jesus Christ, by *the will and appointment* of the Father, has really undergone the punishment that was due to those sins that lie now under his eye and consideration.[13] He has as certainly and really answered the justice of God for them as, if he himself (the sinner) should at that instant be cast into hell, he could do.

They harken to the voice of Christ calling them to *him* with their burden, "Come unto me, all you that are weary and heavy laden" [Matt. 11:28]—"Come with your burdens; come, you poor soul, with your guilt of sin." Why? What to do? "Why, this is mine," says Christ; "this agreement I made with my Father, that I should come, and take your sins, and bear them away: they were my lot. Give me your *burden*, give me all your *sins*. You know not what to do with them; I know how to dispose of them well enough, so that God shall be glorified, and your soul delivered." Hereupon—

---

13. Isa. 53:6; 2 Cor. 5:21.

They lay down *their sins at the cross of Christ,* upon his shoulders. This is faith's great and bold venture upon the grace, faithfulness, and truth of God, to stand by the cross and say, "Ah! he is bruised for my sins, and wounded for my transgressions, and the chastisement of my peace is upon him. He is thus made sin for me. Here I give up my sins to him that is able to bear them, to undergo them. He requires it of my hands, that I should be content that he should undertake for them; and that I heartily consent unto." This is every day's work; I know not how any peace can be maintained with God without it. If it be the work of souls to receive Christ, as made sin for us, we must receive him as one that takes our sins upon him. Not as though he died any more, or suffered any more; but as the faith of the saints of old made that present and done before their eyes [which had] not yet come to pass (Heb. 11:1), so faith now makes that present which was accomplished and past many generations ago. This it is to know Christ crucified.

Having thus by faith given up their sins to Christ, and seen God laying them all on him, they draw nigh and *take from him that righteousness* which he has wrought out for them; so fulfilling the whole of that of the apostle, "He was made sin for us, that we might be made the righteousness of God in him" (2 Cor. 5:21). They consider him tendering himself and his righteousness, to be their righteousness before God; they take it, and accept of it, and complete this blessed bartering and exchange of faith. Anger, curse, wrath, death, sin as to its guilt, he took it all and takes it all away. With him we leave whatever of this nature belongs to us; and from him we receive love, life, righteousness, and peace.

Objection and Answer 1

Objection. But it may be said, "Surely this course of procedure can never be acceptable to Jesus Christ. What! shall we daily come to him with our filth, our guilt, our sins? May he not, will he not, bid us keep them to ourselves? They are our own. Shall we be always giving sins, and taking righteousness?"

Answer. There is not any thing that Jesus Christ is more delighted with, than that his saints should always hold communion with him as to this business of giving and receiving. For—

This *exceedingly honors* him, and gives him the glory that is his due. Many, indeed, cry "Lord, Lord" [Matt. 7:21] and make mention of him, but honor him not at all [Matt. 15:8]. How so? They take his work out of his hands, and ascribe it unto other things; their repentance, their duties, shall bear their iniquities. They do not say so; but they do so.

The commutation they make, if they make any, it is with themselves. All their bartering about sin is in and with their own souls. The work that Christ came to do in the world was to "bear our iniquities" [Isa. 53:11] and lay down his life a ransom for our sins [Mark 10:45]. The cup he had to drink of was filled with our sins, as to the punishment due to them. What greater dishonor, then, can be done to the Lord Jesus, than to ascribe this work to any thing else—to think to get rid of our sins [by] any other way or means? Herein, then, I say, is Christ honored indeed, when we go to him with our sins by faith, and say unto him, "Lord, this is your work; this is that for which you came into the world; this is that you have undertaken to do. You call for my burden, which is too heavy for me to bear; take it, blessed Redeemer, you tender your righteousness; that is my portion." Then is Christ honored, then is the glory of mediation ascribed to him, when we walk with him in this communion.

This *exceedingly endears the souls of the saints to him* and constrains them to put a due valuation upon him, his love, his righteousness, and grace. When they find, and have the daily use of it, then they do it. Who would not love him? "I have been with the Lord Jesus," may the poor soul say: "I have left my sins, my burden, with him; and he has given me his righteousness, wherewith I am going with boldness to God. I was *dead*, and am *alive*; for he *died* for me: I was *cursed*, and am *blessed*; for he was made a *curse for me*: I was *troubled*, but have *peace*; for the *chastisement of my peace* was upon him. I knew not what to do, nor whither to cause *my sorrow* to go; by him have I received *joy unspeakable and glorious*. If I do not love him, delight in him, obey him, live to him, die for him, I am worse than the devils in hell." Now the great aim of Christ in the world is to have a high place and esteem in the hearts of his people; to have there, as he has in himself, the preeminence in all things—not to be jostled up and down among other things—to be all, and in all [Col. 3:11]. And thus are the saints of God prepared to esteem him, upon the engaging themselves to this communion with him.

Objection and Answer 2

Objection. Yea, but you will say, "If this be so, what need we to *repent or amend our ways*? It is but going to Christ by faith, making this exchange with him: and so we may sin, that grace may abound."

Answer. I judge no man's person; but this I must needs say, that I do not understand how a man *that makes this objection in cold blood*, not under a temptation or accidental[14] darkness, can have any *true or real acquaintance with Jesus Christ*: however, this I am certain of, that this communion in itself produces quite other effects than those supposed. For—

For repentance; it is, I suppose, a *gospel repentance* that is intended. For a legal, bondage repentance, full of dread, amazement, terror, self-love, astonishment at the presence of God, I confess this communion takes it away, prevents it, casts it out with its bondage and fear; but for gospel repentance, whose nature consists in godly sorrow for sin, with its relinquishment, proceeding from faith, love, and abhorrence of sin, on accounts of Father, Son, and Spirit, both law and love—that this should be hindered by this communion, is not possible. I told you that the foundation of this communion is laid in a deep, serious, daily consideration of sin, its guilt, vileness, and abomination, and our own vileness on that account; that a sense hereof is to be kept alive in and upon the heart of every one that will enjoy this communion with Christ: without it Christ is of no value nor esteem to him. Now, is it possible that a man should daily fill his heart with the thoughts of the vileness of sin, on all considerations whatever—of law, love, grace, gospel, life, and death—and be filled with self-abhorrency on this account, and yet be a stranger to godly sorrow? Here is the mistake—the foundation of this communion is laid in that which they suppose it overthrows.

But what shall we say for *obedience*? "If Christ be so glorified and honored by taking our sins, the more we bring to him, the more will he be glorified." A man could not suppose that this objection would be made, but that the Holy Ghost, who knows what is in man and his heart, has made it for them and in their name (Rom. 6:1–3). The very same doctrine that I have insisted on being delivered (Rom. 5:18–20), the same objection is made to it: and for those who think it may have any weight, I refer them to the answer given in that chapter by the apostle; as also to what was said before to the necessity of our obedience, not-withstanding the imputation of the righteousness of Christ.

But you will say, "How should we address ourselves to the perfor-mance of this duty? What path are we to walk in?"

Faith exercises itself in it, especially three ways:

First, in *meditation*. The heart goes over, in its own thoughts, the part above insisted on, sometimes severally, sometimes jointly, sometimes fixing primarily on one thing, sometimes on another, and sometimes

---

14. nonessential, incidental.

going over the whole. At one time, perhaps, the soul is most upon consideration of its own sinfulness, and filling itself with shame and self-abhorrency on that account; sometimes it is filled with the thoughts of the righteousness of Christ, and with joy unspeakable and glorious on that account. Especially on great occasions, when grieved and burdened by negligence, or eruption of corruption, then the soul goes over the whole work, and so drives things to an issue with God, and takes up the peace that Christ has wrought out for him.

Second, in considering and *inquiring into the promises* of the gospel, which hold out all these things: the excellency, fullness, and suitableness of the righteousness of Christ, the rejection of all false righteousness, and the commutation made in the love of God; which was formerly insisted on.

Third, in *prayer*. Herein do their souls go through this work day by day; and this communion have all the saints with the Lord Jesus, as to their acceptation with God: which was the first thing proposed to consideration.

Chapter 9

Communion with Christ in the Grace of Sanctification

Our communion with the Lord Jesus as to that grace of *sanctification* and purification whereof we have made mention, in the several distinctions and degrees thereof, formerly, is next to be considered. And herein the former method must be observed; and we must show—(1) what are the peculiar *actings* of the Lord Christ as to this communion; and, (2) what is the *duty* of the saints herein. The sum is—How we hold communion with Christ in *holiness*, as well as in *righteousness*; and that very briefly.

The Actings of the Lord in This Communion

There are several acts ascribed unto the Lord Jesus in reference to this particular; as—

CHRIST'S INTERCESSION WITH THE FATHER

His *interceding* with the Father, by virtue of his oblation in the behalf of his, that he would bestow the Holy Spirit on them. Here I choose to enter, because of the oblation of Christ itself I have spoken before; otherwise, everything is to be run up to that head, that source and spring. There lies the foundation of all spiritual mercies whatever; as afterward also shall be manifested. Now the Spirit, as unto us a Spirit of grace, holiness, and consolation, is of the purchase of Christ. It is upon the matter, the great promise of the new covenant, "I will put a new spirit within you" (Ezek. 11:19; so also Ezek. 36:27; Jer. 32:39–40;

and in sundry other places, whereof afterward). Christ is the mediator and "surety of this new covenant." "Jesus was made surety of a better testament" (Heb. 7:22), or rather covenant—a testament needs no surety. He is the undertaker on the part of God and man also: of *man*, to give satisfaction; of *God*, to bestow the whole grace of the promise; "For this cause he is the mediator of the new testament, that by means of death, for the redemption of transgressions that were under the first testament, they which are called might receive the promise of eternal inheritance" (Heb. 9:15). He both satisfied for sin and procured the promise. He procures all the love and kindness which are the fruits of the covenant, being himself the original promise thereof (Gen. 3:15); the whole being so "ordered in all things, and made sure" (2 Sam. 23:5), that the residue of its effects should all be derived from him, depend upon him, and be procured by him—"that he in all things might have the preeminence" (Col. 1:18); according to the compact and agreement made with him (Isa. 53:12). They are all the purchase of his blood; and therefore the Spirit also, as promised in that covenant (1 Cor. 1:30). Now, the whole fruit and purchase of his death is made out from the Father upon his intercession. This he promises his disciples, that he will pursue the work which he has in hand in their behalf, and intercede with the Father for the Spirit, as a fruit of his purchase (John 14:16–18). Therefore he tells them that he will not pray the Father for his love unto them, because the eternal love of the Father is not the fruit but the fountain of his purchase: but the Spirit, that is a fruit; "That," says he, "I will pray the Father for," etc. And what Christ asks the Father as mediator to bestow on us, that is part of his purchase, being promised unto him, upon his undertaking to do the will of God.[1] And this is the first thing that is to be considered in the Lord Jesus, as to the communication of the Spirit of sanctification and purification, the first thing to be considered in this our communion with him—*he intercedes* with his Father, that he may be bestowed on us as a fruit of his death and blood shed in our behalf. This is the relation of the Spirit of holiness, as bestowed on us, unto the mediation of Christ. He is the great foundation of the covenant of grace;[2] being himself everlastingly destinated[3] and freely given to make a purchase of all the good things thereof. Receiving, according to promise,

---

1. Ps. 2:8; Isa. 53:12; Ps. 40:8–12.
2. Gen. 3:15; Isa. 42:6; 49:8; Dan. 9:24.
3. destined, ordained.

the Holy Ghost (Acts 2:33), he sheds him abroad on his own. This faith considers, fixes on, dwells upon. For—

CHRIST'S SENDING OF HIS SPIRIT

His prayer being granted, as the Father "hears him always" (John 11:42), he *actually sends his Spirit* into the hearts of his saints, there to dwell in his stead, and to do all things for them and in them which he himself has to do. This, secondly, is the Lord Christ by faith to be eyed in; and that not only in respect of the first enduing of our hearts with his Holy Spirit, but also of the continual supplies of it, drawing forth and exciting more effectual operations and actings[4] of that indwelling Spirit. Hence, though he says the Father will give them the Comforter (John 14:16), because the original and sovereign dispensation is in his hand, and it is by him made out, upon the intercession of Christ; yet, not being bestowed immediately on us, but, as it were, given into the hand of Christ for us, he affirms that (as to actual collation or bestowing) he sends him himself; "I will send the Comforter to you, from the Father" (John 15:26). He receives him from his Father, and actually sends him unto his saints. So, "I will send him" (John 16:7). And, he manifests how he will send him (John 16:14–15). He will furnish him with that which is his to bestow upon them: "He shall take of mine (of that which is properly and peculiarly so—mine, as mediator—the fruit of my life and death unto holiness) and give it unto you." But of these things more afterward. This, then, is the second thing that the Lord Christ does, and which is to be eyed in him: He sends his Holy Spirit into our hearts; which is the efficient cause of all holiness and sanctification[5]—quickening, enlightening, purifying the souls of his saints. How our union with him, with all the benefit thereon depending, flows from this his communication of the Spirit unto us, to abide with us, and to dwell in us, I have at large elsewhere declared;[6] where also this whole matter is more fully opened. And this is to be considered in him by faith, in reference to the Spirit itself.

CHRIST'S BESTOWAL OF HABITUAL GRACE

There is that which we call *habitual grace*; that is, the fruits of the Spirit—the spirit which is born of the Spirit (John 3:6). That which is

---

4. *Vicariam navare operam* ["To perform the work on his behalf." Cf. Tertullian, "De Praescriptionibus Haereticos (On Prescription Against Heretics)," ANF 3:249; PL 2, col. 26b]; Prov. 1:23.

5. Titus 3:5–6.

6. Owen, *Perseverance of the Saints* [*Works*, 11:329–65].

born of, or produced by, the Holy Ghost, in the heart or soul of a man
when he is regenerate, that which makes him so, is spirit; in opposition
to the flesh (Gal. 5:17), or that enmity which is in us by nature against
God. It is faith, love, joy, hope, and the rest of the graces of the gospel,
in their root or common principle, concerning which these two things
are to be observed:

That though many particular graces are mentioned, yet there are *not
different habits or qualities* in us—not several or distinct principles to
answer them; but only the same habit or spiritual principle[7] putting forth
itself in various operations or ways of working, according to the variety
of the objects which it goes forth unto, is their common principle: so
that it is called and distinguished, as above, rather in respect of *actual
exercise*, with relation to its objects, than habitual inherence; it being
one root which has these many branches.

This is that which I intend by this habit of grace—*a new,[8] gracious,
spiritual life,[9] or principle, created[10] and bestowed[11] on the soul, whereby
it is changed[12] in all its faculties and affections, fitted and enabled to go
forth in the way of obedience unto every divine object that is proposed
unto it, according to the mind of God.* For instance, the mind can discern
of spiritual things in a spiritual manner;[13] and therein it is light, *illumination*. The whole soul closes with Christ, as held forth in the promises
of the gospel for righteousness and salvation: that is *faith*; which being
the main and principal work of it, it often gives denomination unto
the whole. So when it rests in God, in Christ, with delight, desire, and
complacency, it is called *love*; being, indeed, the principle suiting all the
faculties of our souls for spiritual and living operations, according to
their natural use. Now it differs—

From the *Spirit dwelling* in the saints; for it is a *created quality*. The
Spirit dwells in us as a free agent in a holy habitation. This grace, as
a quality, remains in us, as in its own proper subject, that has not any
subsistence but therein, and is capable of being intended[14] or restrained
under great variety of degrees.

---

7. 2 Cor. 5:17.

8. 2 Cor. 5:17; Ezek. 11:19; 18:31; 36:26; Gal. 6:15; Eph. 2:15; 4:14; Col. 3:10; 1 Pet. 2:2;
John 3:6.

9. Col. 3:3–4; Eph. 2:1, 5; Rom. 8:11; John 5:21; 6:63.

10. Ps. 51:10; Eph. 2:10; 4:24; Col. 3:10; 2 Cor. 5:17.

11. 2 Cor. 3:5; 4:6; Acts. 5:31; Luke 1:79; John 4:14; 3:27; 1 Cor. 2:12; Eph. 4:7; Phil. 1:29.

12. Acts 26:18; Eph. 5:8; 2 Cor. 5:17; John 5:24.

13. 1 Cor. 2:12; Eph. 1:18; 2 Cor. 3:18; 4:6.

14. stretched, increased.

From *actual grace, which is transient*; this making its residence in the soul. *Actual grace is an illapse of divine influence and assistance, working in and by the soul any spiritual act or duty whatsoever, without any pre-existence unto that act or continuance after it,* "God working in us, both to will and to do."[15] But this habitual grace is always resident in us, causing the soul to be a meet principle for all those holy and spiritual operations which by actual grace are to be performed. And—

It is *capable of augmentation and diminution*, as was said. In some it is more large and more effectual than in others; yea, in some persons, more at one time than another. Hence are those dyings, decays, ruins, recoveries, complaints, and rejoicings, whereof so frequent mention is made in the Scripture.[16]

These things being premised as to the nature of it, let us now consider what we are to eye in the Lord Jesus in reference thereunto, to make an entrance into our communion with him therein, as things by him or on his part performed:

As I said of the Spirit, so, in the *first* place, I say of this, it is of the *purchase of Christ*, and is so to be looked on. "It is given unto us for his sake[17] to believe on him" (Phil. 1:29). The Lord, on the behalf of Christ, for his sake, because it is purchased and procured by him for us, bestows faith and (by same rule) all grace upon us. "We are blessed with all spiritual blessings in heavenly places in him" (Eph. 1:3). "In him" (1 John 2:1–2); that is, in and through his mediation for us. His oblation and intercession lie at the bottom of this dispensation. Were not grace by them procured, it would never by any one soul be enjoyed. All grace is from this fountain. In our receiving it from Christ, we must still consider what it cost him (Rom. 8:32). Want of this weakens faith in its proper workings. His whole intercession is founded on his oblation (1 John 2:1–2). What he purchased by his death, that—nor more nor less, as has been often said—he intercedes may be bestowed. And he prays that all his saints may have this grace whereof we speak (John 17:17). Did we continually consider all grace as the fruit of the purchase of Christ, it would be an exceeding endearment on our spirits: nor can we without this consideration, according to the tenor of the gospel, ask or expect any grace. It is no prejudice to the free grace of the Father, to look on anything as the purchase of the Son; it was from that grace

---

15. 2 Cor. 3:5; Ps. 119:36; Phil. 2:13.

16. Song 5:2; Rev. 2:5; 3:2–3, 17, 19; Hos. 14:4; Ps. 51, etc.

17. Gk. *huper Christou* ["for the sake of Christ"].

that he made that purchase: and in the receiving of grace from God, we have not communion with Christ, who is yet the treasury and store-house of it, unless we look upon it as his purchase. He has obtained that we should be sanctified throughout,[18] have life in us, be humble, holy, believing, dividing the spoil with the mighty, by destroying the works of the devil in us.

Secondly. The Lord Christ does *actually communicate* this grace unto his saints, and bestows it on them: "Of his fullness have all we received, and grace for grace" (John 1:16). For—

The Father *actually invests* him with all the grace whereof, by *compact* and agreement, he has made a purchase (as he received the promise of the Spirit); which is all that is of use for the bringing [of] his many sons to glory. "It pleased the Father that in him should all fullness dwell" (Col. 1:19)—that he should be invested with a fullness of that grace which is needful for his people. This [he] himself calls the "power of giving eternal life to his elect" (John 17:2); which power is not only his *ability* to do it, but also his *right* to do it. Hence this delivering of all things unto him by his Father, he lays as the bottom of his inviting sinners unto him for refreshment: "All things are delivered unto me of my Father" (Matt. 11:27). "Come unto me, all that labor and are heavy laden, and I will give you rest" (Matt. 11:28). This being the covenant of the Father with him, and his promise unto him, that upon the making "his soul an offering for sin, he should see his seed, and the pleasure of the LORD should prosper in his hand" (Isa. 53:10); in the verses following, the "pouring out of his soul unto death, and bearing the sins of many" [Isa. 53:12] is laid as the bottom and procuring cause of these things: (1) Of *justification*: "By his knowledge he shall justify many" [Isa. 53:11]. (2) Of *sanctification*; in "destroying the works of the devil" [1 John 3:8]. Thus comes our merciful high priest to be the great possessor of all grace, that he may give out to us according to his own pleasure, quickening whom he will. He has it in him really *as our head*, in that he received not that Spirit by measure (John 3:34) which is the bond of union between him and us (1 Cor. 6:17); whereby holding him, the head, we are filled with his fullness (Eph. 1:22–23; Col. 1:19). He has it *as a common person*, entrusted with it in our behalf (Rom. 5:14–17). "The last Adam is made" unto us "a quickening Spirit" (1 Cor. 15:45). He is also a treasury of this grace in a moral and law sense: not only as "it pleased the Father that in him should all fullness dwell"

---

18. Eph. 5:25–27; Titus 2:14; Rom. 6:4.

(Col. 1:19); but also because in his mediation, as has been declared, is founded the whole dispensation of grace.

Being thus actually vested with this power, and privilege, and fullness, he designs the Spirit to take of this fullness, and to give it unto us: "He shall take of mine, and shall show it unto you" (John 16:15). The Spirit takes of that fullness that is in Christ, and in the name of the Lord Jesus bestows it actually on them for whose sanctification he is sent. Concerning the manner and almighty efficacy of the Spirit of grace whereby this is done (I mean this actual collation of grace upon his peculiar ones), more will be spoken afterward.

For *actual grace*, or that influence or power whereby the saints are enabled to perform particular duties according to the mind of God, there is not any need of further enlargement about it. What concerns our communion with the Lord Christ therein, holds proportion with what was spoken before.

There remains only one thing more to be observed concerning those things whereof mention has been made, and I proceed to the way whereby we carry on communion with the Lord Jesus in all these; and that is, that these things may be considered two ways: (1) in respect of their *first collation*, or bestowing on the soul; (2) in respect of their *continuance and increase*, as unto the degrees of them.

In the first sense, as to the real communicating of the Spirit of grace unto the soul, so raising it from death unto life, the saints have no kind of communion with Christ therein but only what consists in a passive reception of that life-giving, quickening Spirit and power. They are but as the dead bones in the prophet; the wind blows on them, and they live—as Lazarus in the grave [John 11:43]; Christ calls, and they come forth, the call being accompanied with life and power. This, then, is not that whereof particularly I speak; but it is the second, in respect of further efficacy of the Spirit and increase of grace, both habitual and actual, whereby we become more holy, and to be more powerful in walking with God—have more fruit in obedience and success against temptations. And in this—

How Believers Hold Communion with the Lord Christ

They hold communion with the Lord Christ. And wherein and how they do it, shall now be declared.

They continually eye the Lord Jesus as the great Joseph, that has the disposal of all the granaries of the kingdom of heaven committed unto him; as one in whom it has pleased the Father to gather all things unto a head (Eph. 1:10), that from him all things might be dispensed unto them. All treasures, all fullness, the Spirit not by measure, are in him. And this fullness in this Joseph, in reference to their condition, they eye in these three particulars:

BELIEVERS LOOK TO THE PURIFYING EFFICACY OF CHRIST'S BLOOD

In the preparation unto the dispensation mentioned, in the *expiating, purging, purifying efficacy of his blood*. It was a sacrifice not only of atonement, as offered, but also of purification, as poured out. This the apostle eminently sets forth, "For if the blood of bulls and of goats, and the ashes of a heifer sprinkling the unclean, sanctifies to the purifying of the flesh: how much more shall the blood of Christ, who through the eternal Spirit offered himself without spot to God, purge your conscience from dead works to serve the living God?" (Heb. 9:13–14). This blood of his is that which answers all typical institutions for carnal purification; and therefore has a spiritually purifying, cleansing, sanctifying virtue in itself, as offered and poured out. Hence it is called, "A fountain for sin and for uncleanness" (Zech. 13:1); that is, for their washing and taking away—"A fountain opened"; ready prepared, virtuous, efficacious in itself, before any be put into it; because poured out, instituted, appointed to that purpose. The saints see that in themselves they are still exceedingly defiled; and, indeed, to have a sight of the defilements of sin is a more spiritual discovery than to have only a sense of the guilt of sin. *This* follows every conviction and is commensurate unto it; *that*, usually only such as reveal the purity and holiness of God and all his ways. Hereupon they cry with shame, within themselves, "Unclean, unclean"—unclean in their natures, unclean in their persons, unclean in their conversations; all rolled in the blood of their defilements;[19] their hearts by nature a very sink, and their lives a dung hill. They know, also, that no unclean thing shall enter into the kingdom of God [Eph. 5:5], or have place in the new Jerusalem; that God is of purer eyes than to behold iniquity [Hab. 1:13]. They cannot endure to look on themselves; and how shall they dare to appear in his presence? What remedies shall they now use? "Though they wash themselves with nitre,[20] and take them much soap, yet their

19. Ezek. 16:4, 6, etc; John 3:3, 5; Rev. 21:27, Gk. *pan koinoun* [Gk. "nothing unclean]; Hab. 1:13.
20. native sodium carbonate

iniquity will continue marked" (Jer. 2:22). Wherewith, then, shall they come before the Lord? For the removal of this, I say, they look, in the first place, to the purifying virtue of the blood of Christ, which is able to cleanse them from all their sins (1 John 1:7); being the spring from whence flows all the purifying virtue, which in the issue will take away all their spots and stains, "make them holy and without blemish, and in the end present them glorious unto himself" (Eph. 5:26–27). This they dwell upon with thoughts of faith; they roll it in their minds and spirits. Here faith obtains new life, new vigor, when a sense of vileness has even overwhelmed it. Here is a fountain opened: draw nigh, and see its beauty, purity, and efficacy. Here is a foundation laid of that work whose accomplishment we long for. One moment's communion with Christ by faith herein is more effectual to the purging of the soul, to the increasing of grace, than the utmost self-endeavors of a thousand ages.

BELIEVERS LOOK TO CHRIST'S BLOOD OF SPRINKLING

They eye the blood of Christ *as the blood of sprinkling*. Coming to "Jesus, the mediator of the new covenant," they come to the "blood of sprinkling"[21] (Heb. 12:24). The eyeing of the blood of Christ as shed will not of itself take away pollution. There is not only *haimatekchusia*—a "shedding of blood," without which there is no remission (Heb. 9:22); but there is also *haimatos rhantismos*—a "sprinkling of blood," without which there is no actual purification. This the apostle largely describes in Hebrews 9:19–23: "When Moses," says he, "had spoken every precept to all the people according to the law, he took the blood of calves and of goats, with water, and scarlet wool, and hyssop, and sprinkled both the book and all the people, saying, 'This is the blood of the testament which God has enjoined unto you.' Moreover he sprinkled likewise with blood both the tabernacle, and all the vessels of the ministry. And almost all things are by the law purged with blood. It was therefore necessary that the patterns of things in the heavens should be purified with these; but the heavenly things themselves with better sacrifices than these." He had formerly compared the blood of Christ to the blood of sacrifices, as offered, in respect of the impetration[22] and the purchase it made; now he does it unto that blood as sprinkled, in respect of its application unto purification and holiness. And he tells us how this sprinkling was performed: it was by dipping hyssop in the blood of the sacrifice, and so dashing it out upon the things and persons to be purified; as

---

21. *haima rhantismou*
22. act of obtaining by entreaty or petition

the institution also was with the *paschal*[23] lamb (Ex. 12:7). Hence, David, in a sense of the pollution of sin, prays that he may be "purged with hyssop" (Ps. 51:7). For that this peculiarly respected the uncleanness and defilement of sin is evident because there is no mention made, in the institution of any sacrifice (after that of the lamb before mentioned), of sprinkling blood with hyssop, but only in those which respected *purification* of uncleanness; as in the case of leprosy (Lev. 14:6); and all other defilements (Num. 19:18): which latter, indeed, is not of blood, but of the water of separation; this also being eminently typical of the blood of Christ, which is the fountain for separation for uncleanness (Zech. 13:1). Now, this *bunch* of hyssop, wherein the blood of purification was prepared for the sprinkling of the unclean, is (unto us) the free promises of Christ. The cleansing virtue of the blood of Christ lies in the promises, as the blood of sacrifices in the hyssop, ready to pass out unto them that draw nigh thereunto. Therefore the apostle argues from receiving of the promise unto universal *holiness and purity*: "Having therefore these promises, dearly beloved, let us cleanse ourselves from all filthiness of the flesh and spirit, perfecting holiness in the fear of God" (2 Cor. 7:1). This, then, the saints do: they eye the blood of Christ as it is in the promise, ready to issue out upon the soul, for the purification thereof; and thence is purging and cleansing virtue to be communicated unto them, and by the blood of Christ are they to be purged from all their sins (1 John 1:7). Thus far, as it were, this purifying blood, thus prepared and made ready, is at some distance to the soul. Though it be shed to this purpose, that it might purge, cleanse, and sanctify, though it be taken up with the bunch of hyssop in the promises, yet the soul may not partake of it. Wherefore—

BELIEVERS LOOK TO CHRIST AS THE DISPENSER OF THE SPIRIT AND OF ALL GRACE

They look upon him as, in his own Spirit, he is the only *dispenser of the Spirit and of all grace* of sanctification and holiness. They consider that upon his intercession it is granted to him that he shall make effectual all the fruits of his purchase, to the sanctification, the purifying and making glorious in holiness, of his whole people. They know that this is actually to be accomplished by the Spirit, according to the innumerable promises given to that purpose. He is to *sprinkle* that blood upon their souls; he is to *create* the holiness in them that they long after; he is to be himself in them a *well* of water springing up to everlasting life. In this state they

---

23. Passover

look to Jesus: here faith fixes itself, in expectation of his giving out the Spirit for all these ends and purposes; mixing the promises with faith, and so becoming actual partaker of all this grace. This is their way, this their communion with Christ; this is the life of faith, as to grace and holiness. Blessed is the soul that is exercised therein: "He shall be as a tree planted by the waters, and that spreads out her roots by the river, and shall not see when heat comes, but her leaf shall be green; and shall not be careful in the year of drought, neither shall cease from yielding fruit" (Jer. 17:8). Convinced persons who know not Christ, nor the fellowship of his sufferings, would spin a holiness out of their own bowels; they would work it out in their own strength. They begin it with trying endeavors (Rom. 10:1–4); and follow it with vows, duties, resolutions, engagements, sweating at it all the day long. Thus they continue for a season—their hypocrisy, for the most part, ending in *apostasy*. The saints of God do, in the very entrance of their walking with him, reckon upon it that they have a threefold want: (1) of the *Spirit of holiness* to dwell in them; (2) of a *habit of holiness* to be infused into them; (3) of *actual assistance* to work all their works for them; and that if these should continue to be wanting, they can never, with all their might, power, and endeavors perform any one act of holiness before the Lord. They know that of themselves they have no sufficiency—that without Christ they can do nothing (John 15:5): therefore they look to him, who is entrusted with a fullness of all these in their behalf; and thereupon by faith derive from him an increase of that whereof they stand in need. Thus, I say, have the saints communion with Christ, as to their *sanctification* and holiness. From him do they receive the Spirit to dwell in them; from him the new *principle* of life, which is the root of all their obedience; from him have they actual *assistance* for every duty they are called unto. In waiting for, expectation, and receiving of these blessings, on the accounts before mentioned, do they spend their lives and time with him. In vain is help looked for from other mountains; in vain do men spend their strength in following after righteousness, if this be wanting. Fix your soul here; you shall not tarry until you be ashamed. This is the way, the only way, to obtain full, effectual manifestations of the Spirit's dwelling in us; to have our hearts purified, our consciences purged, our sins mortified, our graces increased, our souls made humble, holy, zealous, believing—like to him; to have our lives fruitful, our deaths comfortable. Let us herein abide, eyeing Christ by faith, to attain that measure of conformity to him which is allotted unto us in this world, that when we shall see him as he is, we may be like unto him.

Chapter 10

Communion with Christ in the Grace of Privilege

The third thing wherein we have communion with Christ is grace of privilege before God; I mean, as the *third head* of purchased grace. The privileges we enjoy by Christ are great and innumerable; to insist on them in particular were work for a man's whole life, not a design to be wrapped up in a few sheets. I shall take a view of them only in the head, the spring and fountain whence they all arise and flow—this is *our adoption*: "Beloved, now are we the sons of God" (1 John 3:2). This is our great and fountain privilege. Whence is it that we are so? It is from the love of the Father. "Behold, what manner of love the Father has bestowed upon us, that we should be called the sons of God!" (1 John 3:1). But by whom immediately do we receive this honor? As many as believe on Christ, he gives them this power, to become the sons of God (John 1:12). [Christ] himself was appointed to be the firstborn among many brethren (Rom. 8:29); and his taking us to be brethren (Heb. 2:11) makes us become the children of God. Now, that God is our Father by being the Father of Christ, and we his children by being the brethren of Christ, being the head and sum of all the honor, privilege, right, and title we have, let us a little consider the nature of that act whereby we are invested with this state and title—namely, our adoption.

Now, *adoption is the authoritative translation of a believer, by Jesus Christ, from the family of the world and Satan into the family of God, with his investiture in all the privileges and advantages of that family.*

Requirements for Complete Adoption

To the complete adoption of any person, these five things are required:

FROM A FAMILY BY RIGHT

First, that he be *actually*, and of his own right, of another family than that whereinto he is adopted. He must be the son of one family or other, in his own right, as all persons are.

UNTO ANOTHER FAMILY WITHOUT A RIGHT

Second, that there be a *family* unto which of himself he has no right, whereinto he is to be grafted. If a man comes into a family upon a *personal* right, though originally at never so great a distance, that man is not adopted. If a man of a most remote consanguinity[1] do come into the inheritance of any family by the death of the nearer heirs, though his right before were little better than nothing, yet he is a born son of that family—he is not adopted. [In adoption] he is not to have the plea of the most remote *possibility* of succession.

AUTHORITATIVE, LEGAL TRANSLATION

Third, that there be an *authoritative, legal translation* of him, by some that have power thereinto, from one family into another. It was not, by the *law* of old, in the power of particular persons to adopt when and whom they would. It was to be done by the *authority* of the sovereign power.

FREED FROM ALL OBLIGATIONS

Fourth, that the adopted person be freed from all the obligations that be upon him unto the family from whence he is translated; otherwise he can be no way useful or serviceable unto the family whereinto he is engrafted. He cannot serve two masters, much less *two fathers*.

INVESTED IN NEW RIGHTS AND INHERITANCE

Fifth, that, by virtue of his adoption, he be invested in all the rights, *privileges*, advantages, and title to the whole inheritance of the family into which he is adopted, in as full and ample manner as if he had been born a son therein.

---

1. kinship; relationship by blood or common ancestor.

That Which Is Found in the Adoption of Believers

Now, all these things and circumstances do concur and are found in the adoption of believers:

From a Family by Right

First, they are, by their own *original right*, of another family than that whereinto they are adopted. They are "by nature the children of wrath" (Eph. 2:3)—sons of wrath—of that family whose inheritance is "wrath"—called "the power of darkness," for from thence does God "translate them into the kingdom of his dear Son" (Col. 1:13). This is the family of the world and of Satan, of which by nature believers are. Whatever is to be inherited in that family—as wrath, curse, death, hell—they have a right thereunto. Neither can they of themselves, or by themselves, get free of this family: a strong man armed keeps them in subjection. Their natural estate is a family condition, attended with all the circumstances of a family—family duties and services, rights and titles, relations and observances. They are of the black family of sin and Satan.

Unto Another Family without a Right

Second, there is another *family whereinto* they are to be translated, and whereunto of themselves they have neither right nor title. This is that family in heaven and earth which is called after the name of Christ (Eph. 3:15)—the great family of God. God has a house and family for his children; of whom some he maintains on the riches of his grace, and some he entertains with the fullness of his glory.[2] This is that house whereof the Lord Christ is the great dispenser, it having pleased the Father to "gather together in one all things in him, both which are in heaven, and which are on earth, even in him" (Eph. 1:10). Herein live all the sons and daughters of God, spending largely on the riches of his grace. Unto this family of themselves they have no right nor title; they are wholly alienated from it (Eph. 2:12), and can lay no claim to anything in it. God driving fallen Adam out of the garden, and shutting up all ways of return with a flaming sword [Gen. 3:24], ready to cut him off if he should attempt it, abundantly declares that he, and all in him, had lost all right of approaching unto God in any family relation.

---

2. Hab. 3:6.

Corrupted, cursed nature is not vested with the least right to anything of God. Therefore—

Authoritative, Legal Translation

Third, they have an *authoritative translation* from one of these families to another. It is not done in a *private*, underhand way, but in the way of authority. "As many as received him, to them gave he power to become the sons of God" (John 1:12)—power or authority. This investing them with the power, excellency, and right of the sons of God is a *forensical act* and has a legal proceeding in it. It is called the "making us meet to be partakers of the inheritance of the saints in light" (Col. 1:12)—a judicial exalting us into membership in that family, where God is the Father, Christ the elder brother,[3] all saints and angels brethren and fellow-children, and the inheritance a crown immortal and incorruptible, that fades not away.

Now, this authoritative translation of believers from one family into another consists of these two parts:

An *effectual proclamation* and declaration of such a person's immunity from all obligations to the former family, to which by nature he was related. And this declaration has a threefold object:

Angels. It is declared unto them: they are the sons of God. They are the sons of God,[4] and so of the family whereinto the adopted person is to be admitted; and therefore it concerns them to know who are invested with the rights of that family, that they may discharge their duty toward them. Unto them, then, it is declared that believers are freed from the family of sin and hell, to become fellow-sons and servants with them. And this is done [in] two ways:

1st. Generally, by *the doctrine of the gospel*. "Unto the principalities and powers in heavenly places is made known by the church the manifold wisdom of God" (Eph. 3:10).

By the church is this wisdom made known to the angels, either as the doctrine of the gospel is delivered unto it, or as it is gathered thereby. And what is this wisdom of God that is thus made known to principalities and powers? It is that "the Gentiles should be fellow-heirs and of the same body with us" (Eph. 3:6). The mystery of adopting sinners of the Gentiles, taking them from their slavery in the family of the world, that they might have a right of heirship, becoming sons in the family

---

3. Rom. 8:29; Heb. 2:12.
4. Job 1:6; 38:7; Heb. 12:22–24; Rev. 22:9.

of God, is this wisdom, thus made known. And how was it primitively made known? It was "revealed by the Spirit unto the prophets and apostles" (Eph. 3:5).

2dly. In particular, by *immediate revelation.* When any particular soul is freed from the family of this world, it is revealed to the angels. "There is joy in the presence of the angels of God" (that is, among the angels, and by them) "over one sinner that repents" (Luke 15:10). Now, the angels cannot of themselves absolutely know the true repentance of a sinner in itself; it is a work wrought in that cabinet which none has a key unto but Jesus Christ; by him it is revealed to the angels, when the peculiar care and charge of such a one is committed to them. These things have their transaction before the angels (Luke 12:8–9). Christ owns the names of his brethren before the angels (Rev. 3:5). When he gives them admittance into the family where they are (Heb. 12:22), he declares to them that they are sons, that they may discharge their duty toward them (Heb. 1:14).

It is denounced in a judicial way *unto Satan,* the great master of the family whereunto they were in subjection. When the Lord Christ delivers a soul from under the power of that strong armed one, he binds him—ties him from the exercise of that power and dominion which before he had over him. And by this means does he know that such a one is delivered from his family; and all his future attempts upon him are encroaching upon the possession and inheritance of the Lord Christ.

Unto *the conscience of the person adopted.* The Spirit of Christ testifies to the heart and conscience of a believer that he is freed from all engagements unto the family of Satan, and is become the son of God (Rom. 8:14–15); and enables him to cry, "Abba, Father" (Gal. 4:6). Of the particulars of this testification of the Spirit, and of its absolving the soul from its old alliance, I shall speak afterward. And herein consists the first thing mentioned.

There is *an authoritative engrafting* of a believer actually into the family of God, and investing him with the whole right of sonship. Now this, as unto us, has sundry acts:

The giving [of] a believer *a new name* in a white stone (Rev. 2:17). They that are adopted are to take new names; they change their names they had in their old families, to take the names of the families whereinto they are translated. This new name is, "A child of God." That is the new name given in adoption; and no man knows what is in that name, but only he that does receive it. And this new name is given and written in a white stone—that is the *tessera*[5] of our admission into the house of God. It is a stone of judicial acquittal. Our adoption by the Spirit is bottomed on our absolution in the blood of Jesus; and therefore is the new name in the white stone privilege grounded on discharge. The white stone quits[6] the claim of the old family; the new name gives entrance to the other.

An enrolling of his name in the catalogue of the household of God, admitting him thereby into fellowship therein. This is called the "writing of the house of Israel" (Ezek. 13:9); that is, the roll wherein all the names of the Israel, the family of God, are written. God has a catalogue of his household; Christ knows his sheep by name. When God writes up the people, he counts that "this man was born in Zion" (Ps. 87:6). This is an extract of the Lamb's book of life.

Testifying to his conscience [of] his acceptation with God, enabling him to behave himself as a child (Rom. 8:15; Gal. 4:5–6).

Freed from All Obligations, Invested in New Rights and Inheritance

Fourth, the two last things required to adoption are that the adopted person be freed from all *obligations* to the family from whence he is translated, and invested with the *rights and privileges* of that whereinto he is translated. Now, because these two comprise the whole issue of adoption, wherein the saints have communion with Christ, I shall handle them together, referring the concernments of them unto these four heads: (1) *liberty;* (2) *title,* or right; (3) *boldness;* (4) *correction.* These are the four things, in reference to the family of the adopted person, that he does receive by his adoption, wherein he holds communion with the Lord Jesus:

Liberty. The Spirit of the Lord, that was upon the Lord Jesus, did anoint him to proclaim liberty to the captives (Isa. 61:1); and "where the Spirit of the Lord is" (that is, the Spirit of Christ, given to us by him because we are sons), "there is liberty" (2 Cor. 3:17). All spiritual liberty is from the Spirit of adoption; whatever else is pretended, is licentiousness. So the apostle argues in Galatians 4:6–7, "He has sent forth his Spirit into their hearts, crying, 'Abba, Father.' Wherefore you are no more servants"—no more in bondage, but have the liberty of sons. And this liberty respects—

---

5. Gk./Lat. a small square tile of stone used in mosaic work.
6. discontinues, ceases.

In the first place, the family from whence the adopted person is translated. It is his setting free from all the obligations of that family. Now, in this sense, the liberty which the saints have by adoption is either from that which is *real* or that which is *pretended*:

That which is *real* respects a twofold issue of law and sin. The moral, unchangeable law of God, and sin, being in conjunction, meeting with reference to any persons, has, and has had, a twofold issue:

An *economical* institution of a new law of ordinances, keeping in bondage those to whom it was given (Col. 2:14).

A natural (if I may so call it) pressing of those persons with its power and efficacy against sin; whereof there are these parts: its *rigor* and terror in commanding; its *impossibility* for accomplishment, and so insufficiency for its primitively appointed end; the *issues* of its transgression; which are referred unto two heads: (1) curse, (2) death. I shall speak very briefly of these, because they are commonly handled and granted by all.

That which is *pretended* is the power of any whatever over *the conscience*, when once made free by Christ:

Believers are freed from *the instituted law of ordinances*, which, upon the testimony of the apostles, was a yoke which neither we nor our fathers (in the faith) could bear (Acts 15:10); wherefore Christ "blotted out this hand-writing of ordinances that was against them, which was contrary to them, and took it out of the way, nailing it to his cross" (Col. 2:14): and thereupon the apostle, after a long dispute concerning the liberty that we have from that law, concludes with this instruction: "Stand fast in the liberty wherewith Christ has made us free" (Gal. 5:1).

In reference to the *moral law*:

The first thing we have liberty from is its *rigor* and terror in commanding. "We are not come to the mount that might be touched, and that burned with fire, to the whirlwind, darkness, and tempest, to the sound of the trumpet, and the voice of words, which they that heard besought that they might hear it no more; but we are come to mount Sion," etc. (Heb. 12:18–22). As to that administration of the law wherein it was given out with dread and terror, and so exacted its obedience with rigor, we are freed from it, we are not called to that estate.

Its *impossibility* of accomplishment, and so insufficiency for its primitive end, by reason of sin; or, we are freed from the law as the instrument of righteousness, since, by the impossibility of its fulfilling as to us, it is become insufficient for any such purpose (Rom. 8:2–3; Gal. 3:21–23). There being an impossibility of obtaining life by the law, we are exempted from it as to any such end, and that by the righteousness of Christ (Rom. 8:3).

From *the issue of its transgression*:

Curse. There is a solemn curse enwrapping the whole wrath annexed to the law, with reference to the transgression thereof; and from this are we wholly at liberty. "Christ has redeemed us from the curse of the law by being made a curse for us" (Gal. 3:13).

Death (Heb. 2:15); and therewith from Satan (Heb. 2:14; Col. 1:13); and sin (Rom. 6:14, 1 Pet. 1:18); with the world (Gal. 1:4); with all the attendancies, advantages, and claims of them all (Gal. 4:3–5, Col. 2:20); without which we could not live one day.

That which is pretended and claimed by some (wherein in deed and in truth we were never in bondage, but are hereby eminently set free) is the power of binding conscience by any laws and constitutions not from God (Col. 2:20–22).

[In the second place,] there is a *liberty in* the family of God, as well as a *liberty from* the family of Satan. Sons are free. Their obedience is a free obedience; they have the Spirit of the Lord: and where he is, there is liberty (2 Cor. 3:17). As a Spirit of adoption, he is opposed to the spirit of bondage (Rom. 8:15). Now, this liberty of our Father's family, which we have as sons and children, being adopted by Christ through the Spirit, is a spiritual largeness of heart, whereby the children of God do freely, willingly, genuinely—without fear, terror, bondage, and constraint—go forth unto all holy obedience in Christ.

I say, this is our liberty in our Father's family: what we have liberty from, has been already declared.

There are *Gibeonites*[7] outwardly attending the family of God that do the service of his house as the *drudgery* of their lives. The principle they yield obedience upon, is a *spirit of bondage* unto fear (Rom. 8:15); the *rule* they do it by is the law in its dread and rigor, exacting it of them to the utmost, without mercy and mitigation; the *end* they do it for is to fly from the wrath to come, to pacify conscience, and seek righteousness as it were by the works of the law. Thus servilely,[8] painfully, fruitlessly they seek to serve their own conviction all their days.

The saints by adoption have a largeness of heart in all holy obedience. Says David, "I will walk at liberty, for I seek your precepts" (Ps. 119:45;

---

7. The Gibeonites were those who lied to Israel, saying they were from a far-off land and asking for a treaty. Without consulting God, the deceived Israelities accepted the treaty, and then found themselves forced to share the land with the Gibeonites. See Josh. 9:3–27.

8. submissively, cringingly, slavelike.

[cf.] Isa. 61:1; Luke 4:18; Rom. 8:2, 21; Gal. 4:7; 5:1, 13; James 1:25; John 8:32, 33, 36; Rom. 6:18; 1 Pet. 2:16). Now, this amplitude,[9] or son-like freedom of the Spirit in obedience, consists in sundry things:

In the principles of all spiritual service, which are *life* and *love*—the one respecting the *matter* of their obedience, giving them power; the other respecting the *manner* of their obedience, giving them joy and sweetness in it:

It is from *life*; that gives them power as to the matter of obedience. "The law of the Spirit of life in Christ Jesus sets them free from the law of sin and death" (Rom. 8:2). It frees them, it carries them out to all obedience freely; so that "they walk after the Spirit" (Rom. 8:1), that being the principle of their workings. "Christ lives in me; and the life which I now live in the flesh, I live by the faith of the Son of God" (Gal. 2:20)—"The life which I now live in the flesh (that is, the obedience which I yield unto God while I am in the flesh), it is from a principle of life, Christ living in me." There is, then, power for all living unto God, from Christ in them, the Spirit of life from Christ carrying them out thereto. The fruits of a dead root are but dead excrescences;[10] living acts are from a principle of life.

Hence you may see the difference between the liberty that slaves assume, and the liberty which is due to children:

Slaves take liberty *from* duty; children have liberty *in* duty. There is not a greater mistake in the world, than that the liberty of sons in the house of God consists in this—they can perform duties, or take the freedom to omit them; they can serve in the family of God (that is, they think they may if they will), and they can choose whether they will or no. This is a liberty stolen by slaves, not a liberty given by the Spirit unto sons.

The liberty of *sons* is in the inward spiritual freedom of their hearts, naturally and kindly going out in all the ways and worship of God. When they find themselves straitened and shut up in them, they wrestle with God for enlargement, and are never contented with the doing of a duty, unless it be done as in Christ, with free, genuine, and enlarged hearts. The liberty that servants have is *from duty*; the liberty given to sons is *in duty*.

The liberty of slaves or servants is from mistaken, *deceiving conclusions*; the liberty of sons is from the power of the indwelling Spirit of

---

9. largeness
10. abnormal growth on a plant (or animal)

grace. Or, the liberty of servants is from outward, dead conclusions; the liberty of sons, from an inward, living principle.

Love, as to the *manner* of their obedience, gives them delight and joy. "If you love me," says Christ, "keep my commandments" (John 14:15). Love is the bottom of all their duties; hence our Savior resolves all obedience into the love of God and our neighbor; and Paul, upon the same ground, tells us "that love is the fulfilling of the law" (Rom. 13:10). Where love is in any duty, it is complete in Christ. How often does David, even with admiration, express this principle of his walking with God! "O," says he, "how I love your commandments!" This gives saints delight, that the commandments of Christ are not grievous to them. Jacob's hard service was not grievous to him, because of his love to Rachel [Gen. 29:20]. No duty of a saint is grievous to him, because of his love to Christ. They do from hence all things with delight and complacency. Hence do they long for advantages of walking with God—pant after more ability; and this is a great share of their son-like freedom in obedience. It gives them joy in it. "There is no fear in love; but perfect love casts out fear" (1 John 4:18). When their soul is acted to obedience by love, it expels that fear which is the issue of bondage upon the spirit. Now, when there is a concurrence of these two (life and love), there is freedom, liberty, largeness of heart, exceedingly distanced from that strait and bondaged frame which many walk in all their days, that know not the adoption of sons.

The *object* of their obedience is represented to them as *desirable*, whereas to others it is *terrible*. In all their approaches to God, they eye him as a *Father*; they call him Father, not in the form of words, but in the spirit of sons (Gal. 4:6). God in Christ is continually before them; not only as one deserving all the honors and obedience which he requires, but also as one exceedingly to be delighted in, as being all-sufficient to satisfy and satiate all the desires of the soul. When others napkin[11] their talents, as having to deal with an austere master, they draw out their strength to the uttermost, as drawing nigh to a gracious rewarder. They go, from the principle of life and love, to the bosom of a living and loving Father; they do but return the strength they do receive unto the fountain, unto the ocean.

Their *motive* unto obedience is *love* (2 Cor. 5:14). From an apprehension of love, they are effectually carried out by love to give up themselves unto him who is love. What a freedom is this! What a largeness of spirit

---

11. To hide or to neglect through not using

is in them who walk according to this rule! Darkness, fear, bondage, conviction, hopes of righteousness accompany others in their ways; the sons, by the Spirit of adoption, have light, love, with complacency, in all their walkings with God. The world is a universal stranger unto the frame of children in their Father's house.

The *manner* of their obedience is *willingness*. "They yield themselves unto God, as those that are alive from the dead" (Rom. 6:13); they yield themselves—give up themselves willingly, cheerfully, freely. "With my whole heart," says David. Romans 12:1, "They present themselves a living sacrifice," and a willing sacrifice.

The *rule* of their walking with God is the law of liberty, as divested of all its terrifying, threatening, killing, condemning, cursing power; and rendered, in the blood of Jesus, sweet, tender, useful, directing—helpful as a rule of walking in the life they have received, not the way of working for the life they have not. I might give more instances. These may suffice to manifest that liberty of obedience in the family of God which his sons and daughters have, that the poor convinced Gibeonites are not acquainted with.

The second thing which the children of God have by adoption is *title*. They have title and right to all the privileges and advantages of the family whereinto they are translated. This is the *preeminence* of the true sons of any family. The ground on which Sarah pleaded the ejection of Ishmael was that he was the son of the bond woman (Gen. 21:10), and so no genuine child of the family; and therefore could have no right of heirship with Isaac. The apostle's arguing is, "We are no more servants, but sons; and if sons, then heirs" (Rom. 8:14–17)—"then have we right and title: and being not born hereunto (for by nature we are the children of wrath), we have this right by our adoption."

Now, the saints hereby have a double right and title: (1) *proper* and direct, in respect of spirituals; (2) *consequential*, in respect of temporals:

The first, also, or the title, as adopted sons, unto spirituals, is, in respect of the object of it, twofold: (1) unto a *present place*, name, and room, in the house of God, and all the privileges and administrations thereof; (2) to a *future fullness* of the great inheritance of glory—of a kingdom purchased for that whole family whereof they are by Jesus Christ:

They have a title unto, and an interest in, the whole *administration* of the family of God here.

The supreme administration of the house of God in the hand of the Lord Christ, as to the institution of ordinances and dispensation of the Spirit, to enliven and make effectual those ordinances for the end of their institution, is the prime notion of this administration. And hereof they are the prime objects; all this is for them and exercised toward them. God has given Jesus Christ to be the "head over all things unto the church, which is his body" (Eph. 1:22–23): he has made him the head over all these spiritual things, committed the authoritative administration of them all unto him, to the use and behoof[12] of the church; that is, the family of God. It is for the benefit and advantage of the many sons whom he will bring unto glory that he does all these things (Heb. 2:10; see Eph. 4:8–13). The aim of the Lord Jesus in establishing gospel administrations and administrators is "for the perfecting of the saints, the work of the ministry," etc. [Eph. 4:12]. All is for them, all is for the family. In that is the faithfulness of Christ exercised; he is faithful in all the house of God (Heb. 3:2). Hence the apostle tells the Corinthians, of all these gospel administrations and ordinances, they are all theirs and all for them (1 Cor. 3:22–23). Whatsoever benefit redounds[13] to the world by the things of the gospel (as much does every way), it is engaged for it to the children of this family. This, then, is the aim and intendment of the Lord Christ in the institution of all gospel ordinances and administrations—that they may be of use for the house and family of God, and all his children and servants therein.

It is true; the word is preached to all the world, to gather in the children of God's purpose that are scattered up and down in the world [John 11:52] and to leave the rest inexcusable; but the prime end and aim of the Lord Christ thereby is to gather in those heirs of salvation unto the enjoyment of that feast of fat things which he has prepared for them in his house.

Again: they, and they only, have right and title to gospel administrations, and the privileges of the family of God, as they are held out in his church according to his mind. The church is the "house of God" (1 Tim. 3:15; Heb. 3:6); herein he keeps and maintains his whole family, ordering them according to his mind and will. Now, who shall have any right in the house of God, but only his children? We will not allow a right to any but our own children in our houses: will God, think you, allow any right in his house but to his children? Is it meet to "take the children's bread and cast it unto the dogs?" [Matt. 15:26]. We shall see that none but children have any right or title to the privileges and advantages of the house of God, if we consider—

---

12. use, benefit, advantage.
13. results in some advantage

The *nature* of that house. It is made up of such persons as it is impossible that any but adopted children should have right unto a place in it. It is composed of "living stones" (1 Pet. 2:5)—a "chosen generation, a royal priesthood, a holy nation, a peculiar people" (1 Pet. 2:9)—"saints and faithful in Christ Jesus" (Eph. 1:1)—"saints and faithful brethren" (Col. 1:2)—a people that are "all righteous" (Isa. 60:21); and the whole fabric of it is glorious (Isa. 54:11–14)—the way of the house is "a way of holiness," which the unclean shall not pass through (Isa. 35:8); yea, expressly, they are the "sons and daughters of the Lord Almighty," and they only (2 Cor. 6:17–18); all others are excluded (Rev. 21:27). It is true that oftentimes, at unawares, other persons creep into the great house of God; and so there become in it "not only vessels of gold and silver, but also of wood and of earth," etc. (2 Tim. 2:20); but they only creep in, as Jude speaks (v. 4), they have no right nor title to it.

The *privileges* of the house are such as they will not suit nor profit any other. To what purpose is it to give food to a dead man? Will he grow strong by it? Will he increase upon it? The things of the family and house of God are food for living souls. Now, children only are alive; all others are dead in trespasses and sins [Eph. 2:1]. What will outward signs avail, if life and power be away? Look upon what particular you please of the saints' enjoyments in the family of God, you shall find them all suited unto believers; and being bestowed on the world, [they] would be a pearl in the snout of a swine.

It is, then, only the sons of the family that have this right; they have fellowship with one another, and *that* fellowship with the Father and the Son Jesus Christ; they set forth the Lord's death till he come; they are entrusted with all the ordinances of the house, and the administration of them. And who shall deny them the enjoyment of this right, or keep them from what Christ has purchased for them? And the Lord will in the end give them hearts everywhere to make use of this title accordingly, and not to wander on the mountains, forgetting their resting place.

They have a title to the future *fullness* of the inheritance that is purchased for this whole family by Jesus Christ. So the apostle argues, "If children, then heirs," etc. (Rom. 8:17). All God's children are "firstborn" (Heb. 12:23); and therefore are heirs: hence the whole weight of glory that is prepared for them is called the inheritance, "the inheritance of the saints in light" (Col. 1:12). "If you be Christ's, then are you Abraham's seed, and heirs according to the promise" (Gal. 3:29). Heirs of the promise; that is, of all things promised unto Abraham in and with Christ.

There are three things that in this regard the children of God are said to be heirs unto:

The *promise*, as in that place of Galatians 3:29 and Hebrews 6:17. God shows to "the heirs of the promise the immutability of his counsel," as Abraham, Isaac, and Jacob are said to be "heirs of the same promise" (Heb. 11:9). God had from the foundation of the world made a most excellent promise in Christ, containing a deliverance from all evil and an engagement for the bestowing of all good things upon them. It contains a deliverance from all the evil which the guilt of sin and dominion of Satan had brought upon them, with an investiture of them in all spiritual blessings in heavenly things in Christ Jesus. Hence the Holy Ghost calls it a "promise of the eternal inheritance" (Heb. 9:15). This, in the first place, are the adopted children of God heirs unto. Look, whatever is in the promise which God made at the beginning to fallen man, and has since solemnly renewed and confirmed by his oath; they are heirs of it, and are accepted in their claim for their inheritance in the courts of heaven.

They are heirs of *righteousness* (Heb. 11:7). Noah was an heir of the righteousness which is by faith; which Peter calls a being "heir of the grace of life" (1 Pet. 3:7). And James puts both these together, "Heirs of the kingdom which God has promised" (James 2:5); that is, of the kingdom of grace, and the righteousness thereof. And in this respect it is that the apostle tells us that "we have obtained an inheritance" (Eph. 1:11); which he also places with the righteousness of faith (Acts 26:18). Now, by this righteousness, grace, and inheritance is not only intended that righteousness which we are here actually made partakers of, but also the end and accomplishment of that righteousness in glory; which is also assured in the next place—

They are "heirs of *salvation*" (Heb. 1:14) and "heirs according to the hope of eternal life" (Titus 3:7); which Peter calls an "inheritance incorruptible" (1 Pet. 1:4) and Paul [calls] the "reward of the inheritance" (Col. 3:24)—that is, the issue of the inheritance of light and holiness, which they already enjoy. Thus, then, [they] distinguish the full salvation by Christ into the *foundation* of it, the promises; and the *means* of it, righteousness and holiness; and the *end* of it, eternal glory. The sons of God have a right and title to all, in that they are made heirs with Christ.

And this is that which is the main of the saints' title and right, which they have by adoption; which in sum is that the Lord is their portion and inheritance, and they are the inheritance of the Lord: and a large portion it is that they have; the lines are fallen to them in a goodly place [Ps. 16:6].

Besides this *principal [right]*, the adopted sons of God have a second *consequential* right—a right unto the things of this world; that is, unto all the portions of it which God is pleased to entrust them here with. Christ is the "heir of all things" (Heb. 1:2); all right and title to the things of the creation was lost and forfeited by sin. The Lord, by his sovereignty, had made an original grant of all things here below for man's use; he had appointed the residue of the works of his hands, in their several stations,[14] to be serviceable unto his behoof. Sin reversed this whole grant and institution—all things were set at liberty from this subjection unto him; yet that liberty, being a taking them off from the end to which they were originally appointed, is a part of their vanity and curse. It is evil to any thing to be laid aside as to the end to which it was primitively appointed. By this means the whole creation is turned loose from any subordinate ruler; and man, having lost the whole title whereby he held his dominion over and possession of the creatures, has not the least color of interest in any of them, nor can lay any claim unto them. But now the Lord, intending to take a portion to himself out of the lump of fallen mankind, whom he appointed heirs of salvation, he does not immediately destroy the works of creation, but reserve them for their use in their pilgrimage. To this end he invests the whole right and title of them in the second Adam, which the first had lost; he appoints him "heir of all things" [Heb. 1:2]. And thereupon his adopted ones, being "fellow-heirs with Christ" [Rom. 8:17], become also to have a right and title unto the things of this creation. To clear up this right, what it is, I must give some few observations:

The right they have is not as the right that Christ has; that is, sovereign and supreme, to do what he will with his own; but theirs is subordinate, and such as that they must be accountable for the use of those things whereunto they have a right and title. The right of Christ is the right of the *Lord* of the house; the right of the saints is the right of *servants*.

That the *whole number* of the children of God have a right unto the *whole earth*, which is the Lord's, and the fullness thereof, in these two regards:

First, he who is the sovereign Lord of it does preserve it merely for their use, and upon their account; all others whatever being *malæ fidei*

---

14. positions

possessores,[15] invading a portion of the Lord's territories, without grant or leave from him.

Second, in that Christ has promised to give them the kingdom and dominion of it, in such a way and manner as in his providence he shall dispose; that is, that the government of the earth shall be exercised to their advantage.

This right is a *spiritual right*, which does not give a civil interest, but only sanctifies the right and interest bestowed. God has providentially disposed of the civil bounds of the inheritance of men (Acts 17:26), suffering the men of the world to enjoy a portion here, and that oftentimes very full and plenteous; and that for his children's sake, that those beasts of the forest, which are made to be destroyed, may not break loose upon the whole possession. Hence—

No *one particular adopted person* has any right, by virtue thereof, to any portion of earthly things whereunto he has not right and title upon a *civil interest*, given him by the providence of God. But—

This they have by their adoption; that—

Look, whatever *portion* God is pleased to give them, they have a *right* unto it, as it is re-invested in Christ, and not as it lies wholly under the curse and vanity that is come upon the creation by sin; and therefore can never be called unto an account for usurping[16] that which they have no right unto, as shall all the sons of men who violently grasp those things which God has set at liberty from under their dominion because of sin.

By this their right, they are led unto a *sanctified use* of what thereby they do enjoy; inasmuch as the things themselves are to them *pledges* of the Father's love, washed in the blood of Christ, and endearments upon their spirits to live to his praise who gives them all things richly to enjoy [1 Tim. 6:7].

And this is a second thing we have by our adoption; and hence I dare say of unbelievers, they have no true right unto any thing, of what kind soever, that they do possess.

They have no true, unquestionable right, I say, even unto the temporal things they do possess; it is true they have a civil right in respect of others, but they have not a sanctified right in respect of their own souls. They have a right and title that will hold plea in the courts of men, but not a right that will hold in the court of God, and in their own conscience. It will one day be sad with them, when they shall come to

---

15. Lat. possessors of bad faith
16. seizing, taking control with power and force.

give an account of their enjoyments. They shall not only be reckoned with for the abuse of that they have possessed, that they have not used and laid it out for the glory of him whose it is; but also, that they have even laid their hands upon the creatures of God, and kept them from them for whose sakes alone they are preserved from destruction. When the God of glory shall come home to any of them, either in their consciences here, or in the judgment that is for to come, and speak with the terror of a revengeful judge, "I have suffered you to enjoy corn, wine, and oil—a great portion of my creatures; you have rolled yourselves in wealth and prosperity, when the right heirs of these things lived poor, and low, and mean, at the next doors—give in now an answer what and how you have used these things. What have you laid out for the service and advancement of the gospel? What have you given unto them for whom nothing was provided? What contribution have you made for the poor saints? Have you had a ready hand, and willing mind, to lay down all for my sake?"—when they shall be compelled to answer, as the truth is, "Lord, we had, indeed, a large portion in the world; but we took it to be our own, and thought we might have done what we would with our own. We have ate the fat, and drank the sweet, and left the rest of our substance for our babes: we have spent somewhat upon our lusts, somewhat upon our friends; but the truth is, we cannot say that we made friends of this unrighteous mammon—that we used it to the advancement of the gospel, or for ministering unto your poor saints: and now, behold, we must die," etc.: so also, when the Lord shall proceed further, and question not only the *use* of these things, but also their *title* to them, and tell them, "The earth is mine, and the fullness thereof [Ps. 24:1]. I did, indeed, make an original grant of these things to man; but that is lost by sin: I have restored it only for my saints. Why have you laid, then, your fingers of prey upon that which was not yours? Why have you compelled my creatures to serve you and your lusts, which I had set loose from under your dominion? Give me *my flax, my wine, and wool* [Hos. 2:9]; I will set you naked as in the day of your birth, and revenge upon you your rapine,[17] and unjust possession of that which was not yours."—I say, at such a time, what will men do?

Boldness with God by Christ is another privilege of our adoption. But hereof I have spoken at large before, in treating of the excellency of Christ in respect of our approach to God by him; so that I shall not re-assume the consideration of it.

---

17. pillage, robbery, plunder.

Affliction, also, as proceeding from love, as leading to spiritual advantages, as conforming unto Christ, as sweetened with his presence, is the privilege of children (Heb. 12:3–6); but on these particulars I must not insist.

This, I say, is the *head* and source of all the privileges which Christ has purchased for us, wherein also we have fellowship with him: fellowship in *name*; we are (as he is) sons of God: fellowship in *title* and right; we are heirs, co-heirs with Christ [Rom. 8:17]: fellowship in *likeness* and conformity; we are predestinated to be like the firstborn of the family [Rom. 8:29]: fellowship in *honor*; he is not ashamed to call us brethren [Heb. 2:11]: fellowship in *sufferings*; he learned obedience by what he suffered [Heb. 5:8], and every son is to be scourged that is received [Heb. 12:6]: fellowship in his *kingdom*; we shall reign with him [2 Tim. 2:12]. Of all which I must speak peculiarly in another place, and so shall not here draw out the discourse concerning them any further.

PART 3

OF COMMUNION WITH EACH PERSON DISTINCTLY—

OF COMMUNION WITH THE HOLY GHOST

Chapter 1

The foundation of all our communion with the Holy Ghost consisting in his *mission*, or sending to be our comforter, by Jesus Christ, the whole matter of that economy[1] or dispensation is firstly to be proposed and considered, that so we may have a right understanding of the truth inquired after. Now, the main promise hereof, and the chief considerations of it, with the good received and evil prevented thereby, being given and declared in the beginning of the 16th chapter of John, I shall take a view of the state of it as there proposed.

John 16:1–7

Our blessed Savior—being [about] to leave the world [and] having acquainted his disciples, among other things, with what entertainment in general they were likely to find in it and meet—gives the reason why he now gave them the doleful tidings of it, considering how sad and dispirited they were upon the mention of his departure from them. Verse 1, "These things have I spoken unto you, that you should not be offended."—"I have," says he, "given you an acquaintance with these things (that is, the things which will come upon you, which you are to suffer) beforehand, lest you who—poor souls!—have entertained expectations of another state of affairs, should be surprised so as to be offended at me and my doctrine, and fall away from me. You are now forewarned, and know what you have to look for. Yea," says he (v. 2), "having acquainted you in general that you shall be persecuted, I tell

---

1. *generally*: administration; *specifically*: the administration of the plan of salvation.

you plainly that there shall be a *combination* of all men against you, and all sorts of men will put forth their power for your ruin."—"They shall cast you out of the synagogues; yea, the time comes that whosoever kills you will think that he does God service."—"The *ecclesiastical* power shall *excommunicate* you—they shall put you out of their synagogues: and that you may not expect relief from the power of the *magistrate* against their perversity, they will *kill* you: and that you may know that they will do it to the purpose, without check or control, they will think that in killing you they do God good service; which will cause them to act rigorously, and to the utmost."

"But this is a shaking trial," might they reply: "is our condition such, that men, in killing us, will think to approve their consciences to God?" "Yea, they will," says our Savior; "but yet, that you be not mistaken, nor trouble your consciences about their confidences, know that their blind and desperate ignorance is the cause of their fury and persuasion," "These things will they do unto you, because they have not known the Father, nor me" (v. 3).

This, then, was to be the state with the disciples. But why did our Savior tell it them at this season to add fear and perplexities to their grief and sorrow? What advantage should they obtain thereby? says their blessed Master (v. 4), "There are *weighty reasons* why I should tell you these things; chiefly, that as you may be provided for them, so, when they do befall you, you may be supported with the consideration of my Deity and omniscience, who told you all these things before they came to pass." "But these things have I told you, that when the time shall come, you may remember that I told you of them." "But if they be so *necessary*, whence is it that you have not acquainted us with it all this while? Why not in the *beginning*—at our first *calling*?" "Even," says our Savior, "because there was no need of any such thing; for while I was with you, you had protection and direction at hand."—"'And these things I said not at the beginning, because I was present with you': but now the state of things is altered; I must leave you" (v. 4). "And for your parts, so are you astonished with sorrow, that you do not ask me 'whither I go;' the consideration whereof would certainly relieve you, seeing I go to take possession of my glory, and to carry on the work of your salvation: but your hearts are filled with sorrow and fears, and you do not so much as inquire after relief" (vv. 5–6). Whereupon he adjoins that wonderful assertion, "Nevertheless I tell you the truth: It is expedient for you that I go away, for if I go not away, the Comforter will not come unto you; but if I depart, I will send him unto you" (v. 7).

This verse, then, being *the peculiar foundation* of what shall afterward be declared, must particularly be considered, as to the words of it and their interpretation; and that both with respect to the preface of them and the asseveration in them, with the reason annexed thereunto.

The Preface

The preface to them:

The first word, *alla*, is an adversative, not excepting to anything of what himself had spoken before, but to their apprehension: "I know you have sad thoughts of these things; *but yet, nevertheless.*"

Egō tēn alētheian legō humin, "I tell you the truth." The words are exceedingly emphatical, and denote some great thing to be ushered in by them. First, *egō*—"*I* tell it you, this that shall now be spoken; I who love you, who take care of you, who am now about to lay down my life for you; they are my dying words, that you may believe me; I who am truth itself, I tell you." And—

Egō tēn alētheian legō—"I tell you *the truth*." "You have in your sad, misgiving hearts many misapprehensions of things. You think if I would abide with you, all these evils might be prevented; but, alas! you know not what is good for you, nor what is expedient. 'I tell you the truth'; this is truth itself; and quiet your hearts in it." There is need of a great deal of evidence of truth, to comfort their souls that are dejected and disconsolate under an apprehension of the absence of Christ from them, be the apprehension true or false.

And this is the first part of the words of our Savior, the preface to what he was to deliver to them, by way of a weighty, convincing asseveration, to disentangle thereby the thoughts of his disciples from prejudice and to prepare them for the receiving of that great truth which he was to deliver.

The Assertion

The assertion itself follows: *Sumpherei humin, hina egō apelthō*—"It is expedient for you that I go away."

There are two things in the words: Christ's *departure*; and the *usefulness* of it to his disciples:

For his *departure*, it is known what is intended by it—the withdrawing [of] his bodily presence from the earth after his resurrection, the "heaven being to receive him, until the times of the restitution of all things" (Acts 3:21); for in respect of his Deity, and the exercise of love and care toward them, he promised to be with them to the end of the world (Matt. 28:20). Of this, says he, *sumpherei humin*—"It conduces[2] to your good; it is *profitable* for you; it is for your advantage; it will answer the end that you aim at." That is the sense of the word which we have translated "expedient"—"it is for your profit and advantage." This, then, is that which our Savior asserts, and that with the earnestness before mentioned, desiring to convince his sorrowful followers of the truth of it—namely, that his departure, which they so much feared and were troubled to think of, would turn to their profit and advantage.

The Ground of the Truth

Now, although it might be expected that they should acquiesce in this asseveration of truth itself, yet because they were generally concerned in the *ground of the truth* of it, he acquaints them with that also; and, that we may confess it to be a great matter that gives certainty and evidence to that proposition, he expresses it negatively and positively: "If I go not away, he will not come; but if I depart, I will send him." Concerning the going away of Christ I have spoken before; of the Comforter, his coming and sending, I shall now treat, as being the thing aimed at.

Ho paraklētos: the word being of sundry significations, many translations have thought fit not to restrain it, but do retain the original word *paracletus*; so the Syriac also: and, as some think, it was a word before in use among the Jews (whence the Chaldee paraphrast makes use of it ([in] Job 16:20[3])); and amongst them it signifies one that so taught others as to delight them also in his teaching—that is, to be their comforter. In Scripture it has two eminent significations—an "advocate" and a "comforter"; in the first sense our Savior is called *paraklētos* (1 John 2:1). Whether it be better rendered here an advocate or a comforter may be doubted.

Look into the foregoing occasion of the words, which is the disciples' sorrow and trouble, and it seems to require the Comforter: "Sorrow has filled your hearts; but I will send you the Comforter"—look into the next words following, which contain his peculiar work for which he is now promised to be sent, and they require he should be an Advocate, to plead

---

2. leads, contributes.

3. William Goold, editor of the 1850s edition of Owen's works, writes: "*M^elitsay re'ay*, rendered in our translation, 'My friends scorn me,' is in the Targum, to which John Owen alludes, *p^raqelitay khaberay*, 'My advocates are my friends.' The word is the Greek *parakletoi* in Hebrew characters."

the cause of Christ against the world (John 16:8). I shall choose rather to interpret the promise by the occasion of it, which was the sorrow of his disciples, and to retain the name of the Comforter.

Who this Comforter is, our blessed Savior had before declared (John 15:26). He is *pneuma tēs alētheias*, "the Spirit of truth"; that is, the Holy Ghost, who reveals all truth to the sons of men. Now, of this Comforter two things are affirmed: (1) that he shall *come*; (2) that Christ shall *send* him.

The Comforter Shall Come

That he shall come. The affirmative of his coming on the performance of that condition of it, of Christ going away, is included in the negation of his coming without its accomplishment: "If I go not away, he will not come"—"If I do go (*eleusetai*), he will come." So that there is not only the mission of Christ, but the will of the Spirit, in his coming: "He will come"—his own will is in his work.

Christ Will Send the Comforter

Pempsō auton—"I will send him." The mystery of his sending the Spirit, our Savior instructs his disciples in by degrees. He says, "I will *pray the Father*, and he shall give you another Comforter" (John 14:16); in the progress of his discourse he gets one step more upon their faith, "But the Comforter, which is the Holy Ghost, *whom the Father will send in my name*" (John 14:26); but, he says, "*I will send him from the Father*" (John 15:26); and here, absolutely, "*I will send him.*" The business of sending the Holy Ghost by Christ—which argues his personal procession also from him, the Son—was a deep mystery, which at once they could not bear; and therefore he thus instructs them in it by degrees.

This is the sum: the presence of the Holy Ghost with believers as a comforter, sent by Christ for those ends and purposes for which he is promised, is better and more profitable for believers than any *corporeal* presence of Christ can be, now [that] he has fulfilled the one sacrifice for sin which he was to offer.

Now, the Holy Spirit is promised under a twofold consideration: (1) As a *Spirit of sanctification* to the elect, to convert them and make them believers. (2) As a *Spirit of consolation* to believers, to give them the privileges of the death and purchase of Christ: it is in the latter sense only wherein he is here spoken of. Now, as to his presence with us in this regard, and the end and purposes for which he is sent, for what is aimed at, observe—(1) the *rise* and fountain of it; (2) the *manner* of his being given; (3) our *manner of receiving him*; (4) his *abiding with us*; (5) his *acting in us*; (6) what are *the effects of his working* in us: and then how we hold communion with him will from all these appear.

What the Scripture speaks to these particulars shall briefly be considered:

For the fountain of his coming, it is mentioned in John 15:26, *para tou patros ekporeuetai*—"He proceeds from the Father"; this is the fountain of this dispensation, he proceeds from the Father. Now there is a twofold *ekporeusis*, or "procession," of the Spirit: (1) *phusikē*[4] or *hupostatikē*[5] in respect of *substance* and personality; (2) *oikonomikē*[6] or *dispensatory*, in respect of the work of grace.

Of the first—in which respect he is the Spirit of the Father and the Son, proceeding from both eternally, so receiving his substance and personality—I speak not: it is a business of another nature than that I have now in hand. Therein, indeed, lies the first and most remote foundation of all our distinct communion with him and our worship of him; but because abiding in the naked consideration hereof, we can make no other progress than the *bare acquiescence of faith* in the mystery revealed, with the performance of that which is due to the person solely on the account of his participation of the essence, I shall not at present dwell upon it.

His *ekporeusis* or *proceeding*, mentioned in the place insisted on, is his *economical* or dispensatory proceeding, for the carrying on of the work of grace. It is spoken of him in reference to his being sent by Christ after his ascension: "I will send him which proceeds"—namely, "then when I send him." As God is said to "come out of his place" (Isa. 26:21), not in regard of any mutation in him, but of the new work which he would effect; so it follows, the Lord comes out of his place "to punish the inhabitants of the earth." And it is in reference to a peculiar work that he is said to proceed—namely, to testify of Christ: which cannot be assigned to him in respect of his *eternal procession*, but of his *actual dispensation*; as it is said of Christ, "He came forth from God." The single mention of the Father in this place, and not of the Son, belongs to the gradation before mentioned, whereby our Savior discovers this mystery to his disciples. He speaks as much concerning himself (John

---

4. Gk. natural.
5. Gk. substantial.
6. Gk. administrative.

16:7). And this relation *ad extra*[7] (as they call it) of the Spirit unto the Father and the Son, in respect of operation, proves his relation *ad intra*,[8] in respect of personal procession; whereof I spake before.

Three things are considerable in the foundation of this dispensation, in reference to our communion with the Holy Ghost:

First, that the will of the Spirit is in the work: *Ekporeuetai*—"He comes forth himself." Frequent mention is made (as we shall see afterward) of his being sent, his being given, and poured out; [but] that it might not be thus apprehended, either that this Spirit were altogether an *inferior, created* spirit, a mere servant, as some have blasphemed, nor yet merely and principally, as to his personality, the virtue of God, as some have fancied, he has *idiōmata hupostatika*, personal properties, applied to him in this work, arguing his personality and liberty. *Ekporeuetai*—"He, of himself and of his own accord, proceeds."

Second, the *condescension* of the Holy Ghost in this order of working, this dispensation, to proceed from the Father and the Son, as to this work; to take upon him this work of a Comforter, as the Son did the work of a Redeemer: of which afterward.

Third, the *fountain* of the whole is discovered to be the Father, that we may know his works in the pursuit of electing love, which everywhere is ascribed to the Father. This is the order here intimated: First, there is the *prothesis* of the Father, or the *purpose* of his love, the fountain of all; then the *ephōtēsis*, the *asking* of the Son (John 14:16), which takes in his merit and purchase; whereunto follows *ekporeusis*, or willing *proceeding* of the Holy Ghost. And this gives testimony, also, to the foundation of this whole discourse—namely, our peculiar communion with the Father in love, the Son in grace, and the Holy Ghost in consolation. This is the door and entrance of that fellowship of the Holy Ghost whereunto we are called. His gracious and blessed will, his infinite and ineffable condescension, being eyed by faith as the foundation of all those effects which he works in us, and privileges whereof by him we are made partakers, our souls are peculiarly conversant with him, and their desires, affections, and thankfulness terminated on him: of which more afterward. This is the first thing considerable in our communion with the Holy Ghost.

---

7. Lat. external, outward, toward the outside (*opera Dei ad extra* means the outward or external acts of God).

8. Lat. internal, inward, toward the inside (*opera Dei ad intra* means the inward or internal acts of God).

The manner of his *collation* or bestowing, or the manner of his communication unto us from this fountain, is herein also considerable; and it is variously expressed, to denote three things:

First, the *freeness* of it: thus he is said to be *given*, "He shall give you another Comforter" (John 14:16). I need not multiply places to this purpose. The most frequent adjunct[9] of the communication of the Spirit is this, that he is given and received as of gift: "He will give his Holy Spirit to them that ask him" [Luke 11:13]. That which is of gift is free. The Spirit of grace is given of grace: and not only the Spirit of sanctification, or the Spirit to sanctify and convert us, is a gift of free grace, but in the sense whereof we speak, in respect of consolation, he is of gift also; he is promised to be given unto believers.[10] Hence the Spirit is said to be received by the gospel, not by the law (Gal. 3:2); that is, of *mere grace*, and not of *our own procuring*. And all his workings are called *charismata*—"free donations." He is freely bestowed, and freely works; and the different measures wherein he is received, for those ends and purposes of consolation which we shall consider, by believers, which are great, various, and inexpressible, arise from hence, that we have him by donation, or free gift. And this is the tenure whereby we hold and enjoy him, a tenure of *free donation*. So is he to be *eyed*, so to be *asked*, so to be *received*. And this, also, faith takes in and closes with, in our communion with the Comforter: the conjunction and accord of his will with the gift of Father and Son; the one respecting the distinct operation of the Deity in the person of the Holy Ghost; the other, the economy of the whole Trinity in the work of our salvation by Jesus Christ. Here the soul rejoices itself in the Comforter—that he is willing to come to him, that he is willing to be given him. And seeing all is will and gift, grace is magnified on this account.

Second, the *authority* of it. Thence he is said to be *sent*. "The Father will send him in my name" (John 14:26); and, "I will send him unto you from the Father" (John 15:26); and, "Him will I send unto you" (John 16:7). This mission of the Holy Ghost by the Father and the Son, as it answers the order of the persons' subsistence in the blessed Trinity, and his procession from them both, so the order voluntarily engaged in by them for the accomplishment, as was said, of the work of our salvation. There is in it, in a most special manner, the condescension of the

---

9. association, thing attached.
10. Neh. 9:20; John 14:16; 7:39; 20:22; Acts 2:38; 5:32; 8:15; 10:47; 15:8; 19:2; Rom. 5:5; 1 Cor. 2:12; 6:19; 12:7; 1 Thess. 4:8; 1 John 4:13.

Holy Ghost, in his love to us, to the authoritative delegation of Father and Son in this business; which argues not a disparity, dissimilitude, or inequality of *essence*, but of *office*, in this work. It is the office of the Holy Ghost to be an advocate for us, and a comforter to us; in which respect, not absolutely, he is thus sent authoritatively by Father and Son. It is a known maxim that *inæqualitas officii non tollit æqualitatem naturæ.*[11] This subjection (if I may so call it), or "inequality in respect of office," does [in] no way prejudice the equality of nature which he has with Father and Son; no more than the mission of the Son by the Father does his. And on this authoritative mission of the Spirit does the right apprehension of many mysteries in the gospel, and the ordering of our hearts in communion with him, depend.

Hence is the sin against the Holy Ghost (what it is I do not now dispute) unpardonable, and has that adjunct of rebellion put upon it that no other sin has—namely, because he comes not, he acts not, in his own name only, though in his own also, but in the name and authority of the Father and Son, from and by whom he is sent; and therefore, to sin against him is to sin against all the authority of God, all the love of the Trinity, and the utmost condescension of each person to the work of our salvation. It is, I say, from the authoritative mission of the Spirit that the sin against him is peculiarly unpardonable—it is a sin against the recapitulation of the love of the Father, Son, and Spirit. And from this consideration, were that our present business, might the true nature of the sin against the Holy Ghost be investigated. Certainly it must consist in the contempt of some operation of his, as acting in the name and authority of the whole Trinity, and that in their ineffable condescension to the work of grace. But this is of another consideration.

On this account we are to *pray the Father and the Son* to give the Spirit to us. "Your heavenly Father will give the Holy Spirit to them that ask him" (Luke 11:13). Now the Holy Ghost, being God, is no less to be invoked,[12] prayed to, and called on than the Father and Son; as elsewhere I have proved. How, then, do we ask the Father for him, as we do in all our supplications, seeing that we also pray that he himself would come to us, visit us, and abide with us? In our prayers that are directed to himself, we consider him as essentially God over all, blessed forevermore; we pray for him from the Father and Son, as under this mission and delegation

---

11. Lat. inequality with respect to office is not inequality with respect to nature Lit., Inequality of office does not remove (or destroy) inequality of nature.

12. invoked

from them. And, indeed, God having most plentifully revealed himself in the order of this dispensation to us, we are (as Christians generally do) in our communion to abound in answerable addresses; that is, not only to the person of the Holy Ghost himself, but properly to the Father and Son for him, which refers to this dispensation.

Hence is that great weight, in particular, laid upon our *not grieving the Spirit* (Eph. 4:30)—because he comes to us in the name, with the love, and upon the condescension of the whole blessed Trinity. To do that which might grieve him so sent, on such an account, for that end and purpose which shall afterward be mentioned, is a great aggravation of sin. He expects cheerful entertainment with us, and may do so justly, upon his own account and the account of the work which he comes about; but when this also is added, that he is sent of the Father and the Son, commissioned with their love and grace, to communicate them to their souls—this is that which is, or ought to be, of unspeakable esteem with believers. And this is that second thing expressed in the manner of his communication—he is sent by authority.

Third, he is said to be poured out or *shed* on us (Titus 3:6), *ou execheen eph hēmas plousiōs*—that Holy Ghost which he has "richly poured out upon us," or "shed on us abundantly." And this was the chief expression of his communication under the Old Testament; the mystery of the Father and the Son, and the matter of commission and delegation being then not so clearly discovered. "Until the Spirit be poured upon us from on high, and the wilderness be a fruitful field, and the fruitful field be counted for a forest" (Isa. 32:15); that is, till the Gentiles be called, and the Jews rejected. "I will pour my Spirit upon your seed, and my blessing upon your offspring" (Isa. 44:3). That eminent place of Zechariah 12:10 is always in our thoughts. Now, this expression, as is known, is taken from the allusion of the Spirit unto water; and that in relation to all the uses of water, both natural and typical. A particular relation of them I cannot now insist on; perhaps efficacy and plenty are chiefly intended.

Now, this threefold expression, of *giving*, *sending*, and *pouring* out of the Spirit, gives us the three great properties of the covenant of grace: *First*. That it is *free*; he is given. *Secondly*. That it is *orderly*, ordered in all things, and *sure*, from the love of the Father, by the procurement of the Son; and thence is that variety of expression, of the Father's sending him, and the Son's sending him from the Father, he being the gift of the Father's love, and purchase of the blood of the Son. *Thirdly*. The *efficacy* of it, as was last observed. And this is the second thing considerable.

The third, which is our *receiving* him, I shall speak more briefly of. That which I first proposed of the Spirit, considered as a Spirit of *sanctification* and a Spirit of *consolation*, is here to be minded. Our receiving of him as a Spirit of sanctification is a mere passive reception, as a vessel receives water. He comes as the wind on Ezekiel's dead bones [Ezek. 37:9–10] and makes them live; he comes into dead hearts and quickens them by an act of his almighty power: but now, as he is the Spirit of consolation, it is otherwise. In this sense our Savior tells us that the "world cannot receive him"—"The world receives him not, because it sees him not, neither knows him: but you know him, for he dwells with you, and shall be in you" (John 14:17). That it is the Spirit of consolation, or the Spirit for consolation, that here is promised, is evident from the close of the verse, where he is said then to be in them when he is promised to them. He was in them as a Spirit of quickening and sanctification when promised to them as a Spirit of comfort and consolation, to abide with them for that purpose. Now, the power that is here denied to be in the *world*, with the reason of it, that they cannot receive the Spirit, because they know him not, is ascribed to *believers*—they can receive him, because they know him. So that there is an active power to be put forth in his reception for consolation, though not in his reception for regeneration and sanctification. And this is the power of faith. So Galatians 3:2, they received the Spirit by the hearing of faith—the preaching of the gospel, begetting faith in them, enabled them to receive the Spirit. Hence, believing is put as the qualification of all our receiving the Holy Ghost. "This he spoke of the Spirit, which they that believe on him should receive" (John 7:39). It is believers that thus receive the Spirit; and they receive him by faith. Now, there are three special acts of faith, whereby it goes forth in the receiving of the Spirit. I shall but name them:

It considers the Spirit, in the *economy* before described, as promised. It is faith alone that makes profit of the benefit of the promises (Heb. 4:2). Now he is called the Spirit of that promise (Eph. 1:13)—the Spirit that in the covenant is promised; and we receive the promise of the Spirit through faith (Gal. 3:14): so that the receiving of the Spirit through faith is the receiving of him as promised. Faith eyes the promise of God and of Jesus Christ, of sending the Spirit for all those ends that he is desired; thus it depends, waits, mixing the promise with itself, until it receive him.

By *prayer*. He is given as a Spirit of supplication, that we may ask him as a Spirit of consolation (Luke 11:13); and, indeed, this asking of the Spirit of God, in the name of Christ, either directly or immediately, or under the name of some fruit and effect; of him, is the chief work of faith in this world.

It cherishes him, by *attending to his motions*, improving his actings according to his mind and will; which is all I shall say to this third thing, or our receiving of the Spirit, which is sent of Jesus Christ. We do it by faith, looking on him as purchased by Jesus Christ, and promised of the Father; we seek him at the hands of God, and do receive him.

The next considerable thing is his *abode* with us. Now this is two ways expressed in the Scripture:

In *general*. As to the thing itself, it is said he shall abide with us.

In *particular*. As to the manner of its abiding, it is by *inhabitation* or indwelling. Of the inhabitation of the Spirit I have spoken fully else-where,[13] nor shall I now insist on it. Only whereas the Spirit, as has been observed, is considered as a Spirit of sanctification, or a Spirit of consolation, he is said to dwell in us chiefly, or perhaps solely, as he is a Spirit of sanctification: which is evident from the work he does, as indwelling—he quickens and sanctifies (Rom. 8:11); and the manner of his indwelling—as in a temple, which he makes holy thereby (1 Cor. 6:19); and his permanency in his so doing—which, as is evident, relates to sanctification only: but yet the general notion of it in abiding is ascribed to him as a comforter: "He shall abide with you forever" (John 14:16). Now, all the difficulty of this promise lies in this, that whereas the Spirit of sanctification dwells in us always, and it is therefore impossible that we should lose utterly our holiness, whence is it that, if the *Comforter* abide with us forever, we may yet utterly lose *our comfort*? A little to clear this in our passage:

He is *promised* to abide with the disciples forever, in opposition to *the abode of Christ*. Christ, in the flesh, had been with them for a little while, and now was leaving them and going to his Father. He had been the comforter immediately himself for a season, but is now upon his departing; wherefore, promising them another comforter, they might fear that he would even but visit them for a little season also, and then their condition would be worse than ever. Nay, but says our Savior, "Fear it not: this is *the last dispensation*; there is to be no alteration. When I am gone, the Comforter is to do all the remaining work: there is not

---

13. Owen, *Perseverance of the Saints* [*Works*, 11:329–65].

another to be looked for, and I promise you him; nor shall he depart from you, but always abide with you."

The Comforter may always *abide* with us, though not always *comfort* us; he who is the Comforter may abide, though he do not always that work. For other ends and purposes he is always with us; as to sanctify and make us holy. So was the case with David, "Take not your Holy Spirit from me" (Ps. 51:11). The Holy Spirit of sanctification was still with David; but says he, "Restore unto me the joy of your salvation" (Ps. 51:12)—that is, the Spirit of consolation, that was lost, when the promise was made good in the abode of the other.

The Comforter may abide *as a comforter*, when he does not *actually comfort* the soul. In truth, as to the essence of holiness, he cannot dwell in us but withal he must make us holy; for the temple of God is holy—but as to his comforting, his actings therein are all of his sovereign will; so that he may abide, and yet not actually comfort us.

The Spirit often *works* for it, and *tenders* consolation to us, when we do not receive it; the well is nigh, and we see it not—we refuse to be comforted. I told you that the Spirit as a sanctifier comes with power, to conquer an unbelieving heart; the Spirit as a comforter comes with sweetness, to be received in a believing heart. He speaks, and we believe not that it is his voice; he tenders the things of consolation, and we receive them not. "My sore ran," says David, "and my soul refused to be comforted" [Ps. 77:2].

I deny that ever the Holy Spirit does *absolutely* and *universally* leave a believing soul *without consolation*. A man may be darkened, clouded, refuse comfort—actually find none, feel none; but radically he has a foundation of consolation, which in due time will be drawn forth: and therefore, when God promises that he will heal sinners and restore comfort to them (as Isa. 57:18), it is not that they were without any, but that they had not so much as they needed, that that promise is made. To insist on the several ways whereby men refuse comfort, and come short of the strong consolation which God is willing that we should receive, is not my purpose at present. Thus, then, the Spirit being sent and given, abides with the souls of believers—leaves them not, though he variously manifest himself in his operations: of which in the next place.

Chapter 2

Having thus declared from whence and how the Holy Ghost is given unto us as a Spirit of consolation, I come, in the next place—

To declare what are his *actings in us* and toward us, being so bestowed on us and received by us. Now, here are two general heads to be considered: first, the manner and kind of his actings in us, which are variously expressed; and, second, the particular products of his actings in our souls, wherein we have communion with him. The first is variously expressed; I shall pass through them briefly:

He is said "to work effectually" (*energein*): "All these work" (or effect) "that one and the self-same Spirit" (1 Cor. 12:11). It is spoken there, indeed, in respect of his distribution of gifts; but the way is the same for the communication of graces and privileges. He does it by working: which, as it evinces his personality, especially as considered with the words following, "Dividing to every man according to his will" (for to work according to will is the inseparable property of a person, and is spoken expressly of God, Eph. 1:11); so in relation to verse 6 [i.e., 1 Cor. 12:6], foregoing, it makes no less evident his Deity. What he is here said to do as the Spirit bestowed on us and given unto us, there is he said as God himself to do: "There are diversities of operations, but it is the same God which works all in all" [1 Cor. 12:4]; which here, in other words, is, "All these work that one and the self-same Spirit, dividing to every man severally as he will." What we have, then, from him, we have by the way of his energetical[1] working. It is not by propos-

---

1. emphatic, powerful.

ing this or that argument to us, persuading us by these or those moral motives or inducements alone, leaving us to make use of them as we can; but he works effectually himself, what he communicates of grace or consolation to us.

In the same verse, as to the manner of his operation, he is said *diairein*—he *divides* or distributes to *everyone as he will.* This of distribution adds to that of operation, choice, judgment, and freedom. He that distributes variously, does it with choice, and judgment, and freedom of will. Such are the proceedings of the Spirit in his dispensations: to one, he gives one thing eminently; to another, another—to one, in one degree; to another, in another. Thus are the saints, in his *sovereignty*, kept in a constant *dependence* on him. He distributes as he will. Who should not be content with his portion? What claim can any lay to that which he distributes as he will? Which is further manifested—

By his being said to *give* when and what he bestows. They "spoke with other tongues, as the Spirit gave them utterance" (Acts 2:4). He gave them to them; that is, freely: whatever he bestows upon us, is of his gift. And hence it is to be observed, that in the economy of our salvation, the acting of no one person does prejudice the freedom and liberty of any other: so the love of the Father in sending the Son is free, and his sending does [in] no ways prejudice the liberty and love of the Son, but that he lays down his life freely also; so the satisfaction and purchase made by the Son does [in] no way prejudice the freedom of the Father's grace in pardoning and accepting us thereupon; so the Father's and Son's sending of the Spirit does not derogate from his freedom in his workings, but he gives freely what he gives. And the reason of this is because the will of the Father, Son, and Holy Ghost is essentially the same; so that in the acting of one there is the counsel of all and each freely therein.

Thus, in general, is the manner and kind of his working in us and toward us, being bestowed upon us, described. Power, choice, freedom are evidently denoted in the expressions insisted on. It is not any peculiar work of his toward us that is hereby declared, but the manner how he does produce the *effects* that shall be insisted on.

That which remains, in the last place, for the explanation of the things proposed to be explained as the *foundation* of the communion which we have with the Holy Ghost, is—

The *effects* that, being thus sent and thus working, he does produce; which I shall do, not casting them into any artificial method, but taking them up as I find them lying scattered up and down in the Scripture, only descending from those which are more general to those which are more particular, neither aiming nor desiring to gather all the several, but insisting on those which do most obviously occur.

Only as formerly, so now you must observe, that I speak of the Spirit principally (if not only) as a *comforter*, and not as a *sanctifier*; and therefore the great work of the Spirit toward us all our days, in the constant and continual supplies of new light, power, vigor, as to our receiving of grace from him, belonging to that head of sanctification, must be omitted.

Nor shall I insist on those things which the Comforter does in believers effect toward others, in his testifying to them and convincing of the world, which are promised (John 15:26; 16:8), wherein he is properly their advocate; but only on those which as a comforter he works in and toward them on whom he is bestowed.

Chapter 3

The Things Wherein We Have Communion with the Holy Ghost

The things which, in the foregoing chapters, I called effects of the Holy Ghost in us, or toward us, are the subject matter of our communion with him, or the things wherein we hold peculiar fellowship with him as our comforter. These are now proposed to consideration:

The Spirit Brings to Mind the Things Spoken by Christ

The first and most general is that of John 14:26, "He shall teach you all things, and bring all things to your remembrance, whatsoever I have said unto you." There are two parts of this promise: (1) of *teaching*; (2) of *bringing to remembrance*.

OF HIS TEACHING

Of his teaching I shall speak afterward, when I come to treat of his anointing us.

OF HIS BRINGING TO REMEMBRANCE

His bringing the things to remembrance that Christ spake is the first general promise of him as a comforter: *hupomnēsi humas panta*—"he shall make you mind all these things." Now, this also may be considered two ways:

First, merely in respect of *the things spoken themselves*. So our Savior here promises his apostles that the Holy Ghost should bring to their minds, by an immediate efficacy, the things that he had spoken, that by

373

his inspiration they might be enabled to write and preach them for the good and benefit of his church. So Peter tells us, "Holy men of God spoke as they were moved by the Holy Ghost" (that is, in writing the Scripture) (2 Pet. 1:21); *hup Pneumatos hagiou pheromenoi*—borne up by him, carried beyond themselves, to speak his words, and what he indited to them. The apostles forgot much of what Christ had said to them, or might do so; and what they did retain, in a natural way of remembrance, was not a sufficient foundation to them to write what they so remembered for a rule of faith to the church. For the word of prophecy is not *idias epiluseōs*—from any man's proper impulse; it comes not from any private conception, understanding, or remembrance. Wherefore, Christ promises that the Holy Ghost shall do this work; that they might infallibly give out what he had delivered to them. Hence that expression in Luke 1:3, *purēkolouthēkoti anōthen*, is better rendered, "Having obtained perfect knowledge of things from above"—noting the rise and spring of his so understanding things as to be able infallibly to give them out in a rule of faith to the church, than the beginning of the things themselves spoken of; which the word itself will not easily allow of.

Second, in respect of the *comfort* of what he had spoken, which seems to be a great part of the intendment of this promise. He had been speaking to them things suited for their consolation; giving them precious promises of the supplies they should have from him in this life—of the love of the Father, of the glory he was providing for them, the sense and comfort whereof is unspeakable, and the joy arising from them full of glory. But says he, "I know how unable you are to make use of these things for your own consolation; the Spirit, therefore, shall recover them upon your minds, in their full strength and vigor, for that end for which I speak them." And this is one cause why it was expedient for believers that Christ's *bodily absence* should be supplied by the presence of the Spirit. While he was with them, how little efficacy on their hearts had any of the heavenly promises he gave them! When the Spirit came, how full of joy did he make all things to them! That which was his peculiar work, which belonged to him by virtue of his office, that he also might be glorified, was reserved for him. And this is his work to the end of the world—to bring the promises of Christ to our minds and hearts, to give us the comfort of them, the joy and sweetness of them, much beyond that which the disciples found in them, when Christ in person spoke them to them; their gracious influence being then restrained, that, as was said, the dispensation of the Spirit might be glorified. So are the next words to this promise: "Peace I leave with you. My peace

I give unto you" (John 14:27). The Comforter being sent to bring what Christ said to remembrance, the consequent of it is peace and freedom from trouble of heart—whatever peace, relief, comfort, joy, support-ment we have at any time received from any work, promise, or thing done by Christ, it all belongs to this dispensation of the Comforter. In vain should we apply our natural abilities to remember, call to mind, consider the promises of Christ; without success would it be—it is so daily: but when the Comforter does undertake the work, it is done to the purpose. How we have peculiar communion with him herein, in faith and obedience, in the consolation received in and by the promises of him brought to mind, shall be afterward declared. This, in general, is obtained: our Savior Jesus Christ, leaving the efficacy even of those promises which in person he gave to his apostles in their great distress, as to their consolation, unto the Holy Ghost, we may see the *immedi-ate spring* of all the spiritual comfort we have in this world, and the fellowship which we have with the Holy Ghost therein.

Only here, as in all the particulars following, the manner of the Spirit's working this thing is always to be borne in mind, and the interest of his power, will, and goodness in his working. He does this—(1) *powerfully*, or *effectually*; (2) *voluntarily*; (3) *freely*.

Powerfully: and therefore does comfort from the words and promises of Christ sometimes break in through all opposition into the saddest and darkest condition imaginable; it comes and makes men sing in a dungeon, rejoice in flames, glory in tribulation; it will [come] into pris-ons, racks, through temptations, and the greatest distresses imaginable. Whence is this? *To Pneuma energei*—the Spirit works effectually, his power is in it; he will work, and none shall let him. If he will bring to our remembrance the promises of Christ for our consolation, neither Satan nor man, sin nor world, nor death shall interrupt our comfort. This the saints, who have communion with the Holy Ghost, know to their advantage. Sometimes the heavens are black over them, and the earth trembles under them; public, personal calamities and distresses appear so full of horror and darkness that they are ready to faint with the apprehensions of them—hence is their great relief, and the retrieve-ment[1] of their spirits; their consolation or trouble depends not on any outward condition or inward frame of their own hearts, but on the powerful and effectual workings of the Holy Ghost, which by faith they give themselves up unto.

---

1. retrieval

Voluntarily—distributing to every one as he will; and therefore is this work done in so great variety, both as to the same person and diverse. For the same person, full of joy sometimes in a great distress, full of consolation—every promise brings sweetness when his pressures are great and heavy; another time, in the least trial [he] seeks for comfort, searches the promise, and it is far away. The reason is, *Pneuma diairei kathōs bouletai*—the Spirit distributes as he will. And so with diverse persons: to some each promise is full of life and comfort; others taste little all their days—all upon the same account. And this faith especially regards in the whole business of consolation: it depends on the sovereign will of the Holy Ghost; and so is not tied unto any rules or course of procedure. Therefore does it exercise itself in waiting upon him for the seasonable accomplishment of the good pleasure of his will.

Freely. Much of the variety of the dispensation of consolation by promises depends on this freedom of the Spirit's operation. Hence it is that comfort is given *unexpectedly*, when the heart has all the reasons in the world to look for distress and sorrow; thus sometimes it is the first means of recovering a backsliding soul, who might justly expect to be utterly cast off. And these considerations are to be carried on in all the other effects and fruits of the Comforter: of which afterward. And in this first general effect or work of the Holy Ghost toward us have we communion and fellowship with him. The life and soul of all our comforts lie treasured up in the promises of Christ. They are the breasts of all our consolation. Who knows not how powerless they are in the bare letter, even when improved to the uttermost by our considerations of them, and meditation on them? As also how unexpectedly they sometimes break upon the soul with a conquering, endearing life and vigor? Here faith deals peculiarly with the Holy Ghost. It considers the promises themselves; looks up to him, waits for him, considers his appearances in the word depended on—owns him in his work and efficacy. No sooner does the soul begin to feel the life of a promise warming his heart, relieving, cherishing, supporting, delivering from fear, entanglements, or troubles, but it may, it ought, to know that the Holy Ghost is there; which will add to his joy and lead him into fellowship with him.

The Spirit Glorifies Christ

The next general work seems to be that of John 16:14, "The Comforter shall glorify me; for he shall receive of mine, and shall show it unto you." The work of the Spirit is *to glorify Christ*: whence, by the way, we may see how far that spirit is from being the Comforter who sets up himself in the room of Christ; such a spirit as says he is all himself: "for as for him that suffered at Jerusalem, it is no matter that we trouble ourselves about him." This spirit is now all. This is not the Comforter. His work is to glorify Christ—him that sends him. And this is an evident sign of a false spirit, whatever its pretence be, if it glorify not that Christ who was now speaking to his apostles; and such are many that are gone abroad into the world. But what shall this Spirit do, that Christ may be glorified? "He shall," says he, "take of mine"—*ek tou emou lēpsetai.* What these things are is declared in the next verse: "All things that the Father has are mine; therefore I said he shall take of mine" [John 16:15]. It is not of the essence and essential properties of the Father and Son that our Savior speaks; but of the grace which is communicated to us by them. This Christ calls, "my things," being the fruit of his purchase and mediation: on which account he says all his Father's things are his; that is, the things that the Father, in his eternal love, has provided to be dispensed in the blood of his Son—all the fruits of election. "These," said he, "the Comforter shall receive; that is, they shall be committed unto him to dispose for your good and advantage, to the end before proposed." So it follows, *anaggelei*—"he shall show, or declare and make them known to you." Thus, then, is he a comforter. He reveals to the souls of sinners the good things of the covenant of grace, which the Father has provided, and the Son purchased. He shows to us mercy, grace, forgiveness, righteousness, acceptation with God; lets us know that these are the things of Christ, which he has procured for us; shows them to us for our comfort and establishment. These things, I say, he effectually declares to the souls of believers; and makes them know them for their own good—know them as originally the things of the Father, prepared from eternity in his love and goodwill; as purchased for them by Christ, and laid up in store in the covenant of grace for their use. Then is Christ magnified and glorified in their hearts; then they know what a Savior and Redeemer he is. A soul does never glorify or honor Christ upon a discovery or sense of the eternal redemption he has purchased for him, but it is in him a peculiar effect of the Holy Ghost as our comforter. "No man can say that Jesus is the Lord, but by the Holy Ghost" (1 Cor. 12:3).

The Spirit Sheds God's Love Abroad in Our Hearts

He "sheds the love of God abroad in our hearts" (Rom. 5:5). That it is the *love of God to us*, not *our love to God*, which is here intended, the context is so clear as nothing can be added thereunto. Now, the love of God is either of *ordination* or of *acceptation*—the love of his purpose to do us good, or the love of acceptation and approbation with him. Both these are called the love of God frequently in Scripture, as I have declared. Now, how can these be shed abroad in our hearts? Not in themselves, but in a sense of them—in a spiritual apprehension of them. *Ekkechutai* is "shed abroad"; the same word that is used concerning the Comforter being given us (Titus 3:6). God sheds him abundantly, or pours him on us; so he sheds abroad, or pours out the love of God in our hearts. Not to insist on the expression, which is metaphorical, the business is that the Comforter gives a sweet and plentiful evidence and persuasion of the love of God to us, such as the soul is taken, delighted, satiated with. This is his work, and he does it effectually. To give a poor sinful soul *a comfortable persuasion*, affecting it throughout, in all its faculties and affections, that God in Jesus Christ loves him, delights in him, is well pleased with him, has thoughts of tenderness and kindness toward him; to give, I say, a soul an overflowing sense hereof, is an inexpressible mercy.

This we have in a peculiar manner by the Holy Ghost; it is his peculiar work. As all his works are works of love and kindness, so this of communicating a sense of the love of the Father mixes itself with all the particulars of his actings. And as we have herein peculiar communion with himself, so by him we have communion with the Father, even in his love, which is thus shed abroad in our hearts: so not only do we rejoice in, and glorify the Holy Ghost, which does this work, but in him also whose love it is. Thus is it also in respect of the Son, in his taking of his, and showing of it unto us, as was declared. What we have of heaven in this world lies herein; and the manner of our fellowship with the Holy Ghost on this account falls in with what was spoken before.

The Spirit Bears Witness with Our Spirit That We Are the Children of God

Another effect we have of his: "The Spirit itself bears witness with our spirit, that we are the children of God" (Rom. 8:16). You know whose children we are by nature—children of Satan and of the curse, or of wrath. By the Spirit we are put into another capacity, and are *adopted to be the children of God*, inasmuch as by receiving the Spirit of our Father we become the children of our Father. Thence is he called "the Spirit of adoption" (Rom. 8:15). Now, sometimes the soul, because it has somewhat remaining in it of the principle that it had in its old condition, is put to question whether it be a child of God or no; and thereupon, as in a thing of the greatest importance, puts in its claim, with all the evidences that it has to make good its title. The Spirit comes and bears witness in this case. An allusion it is to judicial proceedings in point of titles and evidences. The judge being set, the person concerned lays his claim, produces his evidences, and pleads them; his adversaries endeavoring all that in them lies to invalidate them, and disannul his plea, and to cast him in his claim. In the midst of the trial, a person of known and approved integrity comes into the court, and gives testimony fully and directly on the behalf of the claimer; which stops the mouths of all his adversaries and fills the man that pleaded with joy and satisfaction. So is it in this case. The soul, by the power of its own conscience, is brought before the law of God. There a man puts in his plea—that he is a child of God, that he belongs to God's family; and for this end produces all his evidences, everything whereby faith gives him an interest in God. Satan, in the meantime, opposes with all his might; sin and law assist him; many flaws are found in his evidences; the truth of them all is questioned; and the soul hangs in suspense as to the issue. In the midst of the plea and contest the Comforter comes, and, by a word of promise or otherwise, overpowers the heart with a comfortable persuasion (and bears down all objections) that his plea is good, and that he is a child of God. And therefore it is said of him, *Summarturei tō pneumati hēmōn*[2] [Rom. 8:16]. When our spirits are pleading their right and title, he comes in and bears witness on our side; at the same time enabling us to put forth acts of filial[3] obedience, kind and childlike; which is called "crying, Abba, Father" (Gal. 4:6). Remember still the manner of the Spirit's working, before mentioned—that he does it effectually, voluntarily, and freely. Hence sometimes the dispute hangs long—the cause is pleading many years. The law seems sometimes to prevail, sin and Satan to rejoice; and the poor soul is filled with dread about its inheritance. Perhaps its own witness, from its faith, sanctification, former experience, keeps up the plea with some life and comfort; but the work is not done, the conquest

---

2. Gk. he [the Spirit] bears witness with our spirit.
3. pertaining to a son or daughter

is not fully obtained, until the Spirit, who works freely and effectually, when and how he will, comes in with his testimony also; clothing his power with a word of promise, he makes all parties concerned to attend unto him, and puts an end to the controversy.

Herein he gives us holy communion with himself. The soul knows his voice when he speaks, *Nec hominem sonat*.[4] There is something too great in it to be the effect of a created power. When the Lord Jesus Christ at one word stilled the raging of the sea and wind, all that were with him knew there was divine power at hand (Matt. 8:25–27). And when the Holy Ghost by one word stills the tumults and storms that are raised in the soul, giving it an immediate calm and security, it knows his divine power, and rejoices in his presence.

The Spirit Seals Us

"We are sealed by the Holy Spirit of promise" (Eph. 1:13); and, "grieve not the Holy Spirit, whereby you are sealed unto the day of redemption" (Eph. 4:30). I am not very clear in the certain peculiar intendment of this metaphor; what I am persuaded of the mind of God in it I shall briefly impart. In a seal two things are considered: (1) the *nature of it*; (2) the *use of it*.

The *nature* of sealing consists in the imparting of the image or character of the seal to the thing sealed. This is to seal a thing—to stamp the character of the seal on it. In this sense, the effectual communication of the image of God unto us should be our sealing. The Spirit in believers, really communicating the image of God, in righteousness and true holiness, unto the soul, seals us. To have this stamp of the Holy Ghost, so as to be an evidence unto the soul that it is accepted with God, is to be sealed by the Spirit; taking the metaphor from the nature of sealing (Rev. 7:4). And in this sense is our Savior said to be sealed of God (John 6:27), even from that impression of the power, wisdom, and majesty of God that he had upon him in the discharge of his office.

The *end* of sealing is twofold:

First, to *confirm or ratify* any grant or conveyance made in writing. In such cases men set their seals to make good and confirm their grants; and when this is done they are irrevocable. Or to confirm the testimony that is given by any one of the truth of any thing. Such was the manner among the Jews: when any one had given true witness unto any thing

---

4. "And he does not sound like a man" (cf. *Aeneid* I.328).

or matter, and it was received by the judges, they instantly set their seals to it, to confirm it in judgment. Hence it is said that he who receives the testimony of Christ "sets to his seal that God is true" (John 3:33). The promise is the great grant and conveyance of life and salvation in Christ to the souls of believers. That we may have full assurance of the truth and irrevocableness of the promise, God gives us the Spirit to satisfy our hearts of it; and thence is he said to seal us, by assuring our hearts of those promises and their stability. But, though many expositors go this way, I do not see how this can consist with the very meaning of the word. It is not said that the promise is sealed, but that we are sealed; and when we seal a deed or grant to any one, we do not say the man is sealed, but the deed or grant.

Second, to *appropriate, distinguish,* or *keep safe.* This is the end of sealing. Men set their seals on that which they appropriate and desire to keep safe for themselves. So, evidently, in this sense are the servants of God said to be sealed (Rev. 7:4); that is, marked with God's mark, as his peculiar ones—for this sealing answers to the setting of a mark (Ezek. 9:4). Then are believers sealed, when they are marked for God to be heirs of the purchased inheritance, and to be preserved to the day of redemption. Now, if this be the sealing intended, it denotes not an act of sense in the heart, but of security to the person. The Father gives the elect into the hands of Christ to be redeemed; having redeemed them, in due time they are called by the Spirit, and marked for God, and so give up themselves to the hands of the Father.

If you ask, now, "Which of these senses is chiefly intended in this expression of our being sealed by the Holy Ghost?" I answer: The first, not excluding the other. We are sealed to the day of redemption, when, from the stamp, image, and character of the Spirit upon our souls, we have a fresh sense of the love of God given to us, with a comfortable persuasion of our acceptation with him. But of this whole matter I have treated at large elsewhere.[5]

Thus, then, the Holy Ghost communicates unto us his own likeness; which is also the image of the Father and the Son. "We are changed into this image by the Lord the Spirit" (2 Cor. 3:18); and herein he brings us into fellowship with himself. Our likeness to him gives us boldness with him. His work we look for, his fruits we pray for; and when any effect of grace, any discovery of the image of Christ implanted in us,

---

5. Owen, *Perseverance of the Saints* [*Works,* 11:329–365].

gives us a persuasion of our being separated and set apart for God, we have a communion with him therein.

The Spirit Is an Earnest unto Us

He is an earnest⁶ unto us. He has "given the earnest of the Spirit in our hearts" (2 Cor. 1:22); "Who also has given unto us the earnest of the Spirit" (2 Cor. 5:5); as also, "you are sealed with that Holy Spirit of promise, which is the earnest of our inheritance" (Eph. 1:13–14). In the two former places we are said to have the earnest of the Spirit; in the latter, the Spirit is said to be our earnest: "of the Spirit," then, in the first place, is, as we say, *genitivus materiæ*;⁷ denoting not the cause, but the thing itself—not the author of the earnest, but the matter of it. The Spirit is our earnest; as in the last place is expressed. The consideration of what is meant by the "Spirit," here, and what is meant by an "earnest," will give some insight into this privilege, which we receive by the Comforter:

What *grace*, what gift of the Spirit, is intended by this earnest, some have made inquiry; I suppose to no purpose. It is the Spirit himself, *personally* considered, that is said to be this earnest (2 Cor. 1:22). It is God [who] has given the earnest of the Spirit in our hearts: an expression directly answering that of Galatians 4:6, "God has sent forth the Spirit of his Son into your hearts"—that is, the person of the Spirit; for nothing else can be called the Spirit of his Son: and in Ephesians 1:14, he has given the Spirit (*hos* for *ho*⁸), which is that earnest. The Spirit of promise himself is this earnest. In giving us this Spirit he gives us this earnest.

An earnest it is—*arrabōn*. Neither the Greek nor the Latin has any word to express directly what is here intended. The Latins have made words for it, from that expressed here in the Greek, *arrha* and *arrabo*. The Greek word is but the Hebrew *'erabon*; which, as some conceive, came amongst them by the Syrian merchants, being a word of trade. It is by some rendered, in Latin, *pignus*, a "pledge"; but this cannot be here intended. A *pledge* is that property which anyone gives or leaves in the custody of another, to assure him that he will give him, or pay

---

6. a payment, installment to secure a contract, a pledge.

7. Lat. genitive of material—a grammatical label indicating the material from which something came. Applied here, Owen is saying that the "earnest" is not produced *by* the Spirit, but *is* the Spirit.

8. Gk. *hos* is masculine singular (who); Gk. *ho* is neuter singular (which); *hos* is the preferred reading in Eph. 1:14.

him, some other thing; in the nature of that which we call a "pawn." Now, the thing that is here intended is a part of that which is to come, and but a part of it, according to the trade use of the word, whence the metaphor is taken; it is excellently rendered in our language, an "earnest." An earnest is part of the price of any thing, or part of any grant, given beforehand to assure the person to whom it is given that at the appointed season he shall receive the whole that is promised him.

That a thing be an earnest, it is required—

That it be part of the whole, *of the same kind* and nature with it; as we do give so much money in earnest to pay so much more.

That it be a *confirmation of a promise* and appointment; first the whole is promised, then the earnest is given for the good and true performance of that promise.

Thus the Spirit is this earnest. God gives us the promise of eternal life. To confirm this to us, he gives us his Spirit; which is, as the first part of the promise, to secure us of the whole. Hence he is said to be the earnest of the inheritance that is promised and purchased.

And it may be considered how it may be said to be an earnest on the part of God, who gives him; and on the part of believers, who receive him:

He is an earnest *on the part of God*, in that God gives him as a *choice part* of the inheritance itself, and of the same kind with the whole, as an earnest ought to be. The full inheritance promised is the fullness of the Spirit in the enjoyment of God. When that Spirit which is given us in this world shall have perfectly taken away all sin and sorrow, and shall have made us able to enjoy the glory of God in his presence, that is the full inheritance promised. So that the Spirit given us for the fitting of us for enjoyment of God in some measure, while we are here, is the earnest of the whole.

God does it to this purpose, to assure us and secure us of the inheritance. Having given us so many securities without us—his word, promises, covenant, oath, the revelation and discovery of his faithfulness and immutability in them all (Heb. 6:17–18)—he is pleased also graciously to give us one within us (Isa. 59:21), that we may have all the security we are capable of. What can more be done? He has given us of the Holy Spirit—in him the firstfruits of glory, the utmost pledge of his love, the earnest of all.

On *the part of believers* he is an earnest, in that he gives them an acquaintance with—

The *love of God*. Their acceptation with him makes known to them their favor in his sight—that he is their Father and will deal with them as with children; and consequently, that the inheritance shall be theirs. He sends his Spirit into our hearts, "crying, Abba, Father" (Gal. 4:6). And what is the inference of believers from hence? "Then we are not servants, but sons; and if sons, then heirs of God" (Gal. 4:7). The same apostle, again, "If children, then heirs; heirs of God, and joint heirs with Christ" (Rom. 8:17). On that persuasion of the Spirit that we are children, the inference is, "Then heirs, heirs of God, and joint heirs with Christ." We have, then, a right to an inheritance, and an eviction of it. This is the use, then, we have of it—even the Spirit persuading us of our sonship and acceptation with God our Father. And what is this inheritance of glory? "If we suffer with him, we shall be glorified together" [Rom. 8:17]. And that the Spirit is given for this end is attested, "Hereby we know that he abides in us, by the Spirit which he has given us" (1 John 3:24). The apostle is speaking of our union with God, which he expresses in the words foregoing: "He that keeps his commandments dwells in him, and he in him" [1 John 3:24]—of that union elsewhere. Now, this we know from hence, even by the Spirit which he has given us—the Spirit acquaints us with it. Not that we have such an acquaintance, but that the argument is good and conclusive in itself, "We have of the Spirit; therefore he dwells in us, and we in him": because, indeed, his dwelling in us is by that Spirit, and our interest in him is from thence. A sense of this he gives as he pleases.

The Spirit being given as an earnest, acquaints believers *with their inheritance* (1 Cor. 2:9–10.) As an earnest, being part of the whole, gives knowledge of it, so does the Spirit; as in sundry particulars might be demonstrated.

So is he in all respects completely an earnest—given of God, received by us, as the beginning of our inheritance, and the assurance of it. So much as we have of the Spirit, so much we have of heaven in perfect enjoyment, and so much evidence of its future fullness. Under this apprehension of him in the dispensation of grace do believers receive him and rejoice in him. Every gracious, self-evidencing act of his in their hearts they rejoice in, as a drop from heaven, and long for the ocean of it. Not to drive every effect of grace to this issue is to neglect the work of the Holy Ghost in us and toward us.

There remains only that a difference be, in a few words, assigned between believers receiving the Spirit as an earnest of the whole inheritance, and hypocrites "tasting of the powers of the world to come"

(Heb. 6:5). A taste of the powers of the world to come seems to be the same with the earnest of the inheritance. But—

That by "the powers of the world to come" in that place is intended the joys of heaven, there is, indeed, no ground to imagine. They are nowhere so called; nor does it suitably express the glory that shall be revealed, which we shall be made partakers of. It is, doubtless, the powerful ministry of the ordinances and dispensations of the times of the gospel (there called to the Hebrews according to their own idiom), the powers or great effectual things of the world to come, that is intended. But—

Suppose that by "the powers of the world to come" the glory of heaven is intended, [then] there is a wide difference between taking a *vanishing taste* of it ourselves, and receiving *an abiding earnest* from God. To take a taste of the things of heaven, and to have them assured of God as from his love, differ greatly. A hypocrite may have his thoughts raised to a great deal of joy and contentment in the consideration of the good things of the kingdom of God for a season, considering the things in themselves; but the Spirit, as he is an earnest, gives us a pledge of them as provided for us in the love of God and purchase of his Son Jesus Christ. This by the way.

The Spirit Anoints Believers

The Spirit *anoints believers*. We are "anointed" by the Spirit (2 Cor. 1:21). We have "an unction from the Holy One, and we know all things" (1 John 2:20, 27). I cannot intend to run this expression up into its rise and original; also, I have done it elsewhere. The use of unctions in the Judaical church, the meaning and intendment of the types attended therewith, the offices that men were consecrated unto thereby, are at the bottom of this expression; nearer the unction of Jesus Christ (from whence he is called Messiah, and the Christ, the whole performance of his office of mediatorship being called also his anointing, Dan. 9:24, as to his furnishment for it), concurs hereunto. Christ is said to be "anointed with the oil of gladness above his fellows" (Heb. 1:9); which is the same with that of John 3:34, "God gives not the Spirit by measure unto him." We, who have the Spirit by measure, are anointed with the "oil of gladness"; Christ has the fullness of the Spirit, whence our measure is communicated: so he is anointed above us, "that in all things he may have the preeminence" [Col. 1:18]. How Christ was anointed with the Spirit to his threefold office of king, priest, and prophet; how, by virtue of an unction, with the same Spirit dwelling in him and us, we become to be interested in these offices of his, and are made also kings, priests, and prophets to God, is known, and would be matter of a long discourse to handle; and my design is only to communicate the things treated of:

I shall only, therefore, fix on one place, where the communications of the Spirit in this unction of Christ are enumerated—of which, in our measure, from him and with him, by this unction, we are made partakers—and that is, "The Spirit of the LORD shall rest upon him, the Spirit of wisdom and understanding, the Spirit of counsel and might, the Spirit of knowledge, and of the fear of the LORD," etc. (Isa. 11:2–3). Many of *the endowments* of Christ, from the Spirit wherewith he was abundantly anointed, are here recounted. Principally those of wisdom, counsel, and understanding are insisted on; on the account whereof all the treasures of wisdom and knowledge are said to be in him (Col. 2:3). And though this be but some part of the furniture of Jesus Christ for the discharge of his office, yet it is such, as, where our anointing to the same purpose is mentioned, it is said peculiarly on effecting of such qualifications as these: so 1 John 2:20, 27, the work of the anointing is to teach us; the Spirit therein is a Spirit of wisdom and understanding, of counsel, knowledge, and quick understanding in the fear of the Lord. So was the great promise of the Comforter, that he should "teach us" (John 14:26)—that he should "guide us into all truth" (John 16:13). This of teaching us the mind and will of God, in the manner wherein we are taught it by the Spirit, our comforter, is an eminent part of our unction by him; which only I shall instance in. Give me leave to say, there is a threefold teaching by the Spirit.

A Teaching by the Spirit of Conviction and Illumination

A teaching by the Spirit of *conviction* and illumination. So the Spirit teaches the world (that is, many in it) by the preaching of the word; as he is promised to do (John 16:8).

A Teaching by the Spirit of Sanctification

A teaching by the Spirit of *sanctification*; opening blind eyes, giving a new understanding, shining into our hearts, to give us a knowledge of the glory of God in the face of Jesus Christ; enabling us to receive spiritual things in a spiritual light (1 Cor. 2:13); giving a saving knowledge of the mystery of the gospel: and this in several degrees is common to believers.

A Teaching by the Spirit of Consolation

A teaching by the Spirit of *consolation*—making sweet, useful, and joyful to the soul, the discoveries that are made of the mind and will of God in the light of the Spirit of sanctification. Here the oil of the Spirit is called the "oil of gladness"—that which brings joy and gladness with it; and the name of Christ thereby discovered is a sweet "ointment poured forth," that causes souls to run after him with joy and delight (Song 1:3). We see it by daily experience, that very many have little taste and sweetness and relish in their souls of those truths which yet they savingly know and believe; but when we are taught by this unction, oh, how sweet is every thing we know of God! As we may see in the place of John where mention is made of the teaching of this unction, it respects peculiarly the Spirit teaching of us the love of God in Christ, the shining of his countenance; which, as David speaks, puts gladness into our hearts (Ps. 4:6–7).

We have this, then, by the Spirit: he teaches us of the love of God in Christ; he makes every gospel truth as wine well refined to our souls, and the good things of it to be a feast of fat things—gives us joy and gladness of heart with all that we know of God; which is the great preservative of the soul to keep it close to truth. The apostle speaks of our teaching by this unction, as the means whereby we are preserved from seduction. Indeed, to know any truth in the power, sweetness, joy, and gladness of it, is that great security of the soul's constancy in the preservation and retaining of it. They will readily change truth for error, who find no more sweetness in the one than in the other. I must crave the reader's pardon for my brief passing over these great things of the gospel; my present design is rather to *enumerate* than to *unfold* them. This one work of the Holy Ghost, might it be pursued, would require a fuller discourse than I can allot unto the whole matter in hand. All the privileges we enjoy, all the dignity and honor we are invested with, our whole dedication unto God, our nobility and royalty, our interest in all church advantages and approaches to God in worship, our separation from the world, the name whereby we are called, the liberty we enjoy—all flow from this head, all are branches of this effect of the Holy Ghost. I have mentioned only our teaching by this unction—a teaching that brings joy and gladness with it, by giving the heart a sense of the truth wherein we are instructed. When we find any of the good truths of the gospel come home to our souls with life, vigor, and power, giving us gladness of heart, transforming us into the image and likeness of it—the Holy Ghost is then at his work, is pouring out of his oil.

He Is the Spirit of Adoption

We have *adoption also* by the Spirit; hence he is called the "Spirit of adoption"; that is, either he who is given to adopted ones, to secure them of it, to beget in their hearts a sense and persuasion of the Father's adopting love; or else to give them the privilege itself, as is intimated (John 1:12). Neither is that opposite hereunto which we have (Gal. 4:6); for God may send the Spirit of supplication into our hearts, because we are sons, and yet adopted by his Spirit. But of this elsewhere.

He Is the Spirit of Supplication

He is also called the "*Spirit of supplication*"; under which notion he is promised (Zech. 12:10); and how he effects that in us is declared (Rom. 8:26–27; Gal. 4:6); and we are thence said to "pray in the Holy Ghost" [Jude 20]. Our prayers may be considered two ways:

OUR PRAYERS AS A SPIRITUAL DUTY REQUIRED OF US BY GOD

First, as a *spiritual duty* required of us by God; and so they are wrought in us by the Spirit of sanctification, which helps us to perform all our duties, by exalting all the faculties of the soul for the spiritual discharge of their respective offices in them.

OUR PRAYERS AS A MEANS OF RETAINING COMMUNION WITH GOD

As *a means of retaining communion* with God, whereby we sweetly ease our hearts in the bosom of the Father, and receive in refreshing tastes of his love. The soul is never more raised with the love of God than when by the Spirit taken into intimate communion with him in the discharge of this duty; and therein it belongs to the Spirit of consolation, to the Spirit promised as a comforter. And this is the next thing to be considered in our communion with the Holy Ghost—namely, what are the peculiar effects which he works in us, and toward us, being so bestowed on us as was declared, and working in the way and manner insisted on. Now, these are: his bringing the promises of Christ to remembrance, glorifying him in our hearts, shedding abroad the love of God in us, witnessing with us as to our spiritual estate and condition, sealing us to the day of redemption (being the earnest of our inheritance), anointing us with privileges as to their consolation, confirming our adoption, and being present with us in our supplications. Here is the wisdom of faith: to find out and meet with the Comforter in all these things; not to lose their sweetness, by lying in the dark [as] to their author, nor coming short of the returns which are required of us.

Chapter 4

The General Consequences in Our Hearts of These Effects of the Holy Ghost

Having proceeded thus far in discovering the way of our communion with the Holy Ghost, and insisted on the most noble and known effects that he produces, it remains that it be declared what *general consequences* of these effects there are brought forth in the hearts of believers; and so we shall at least have made mention of the main heads of his dispensation and work in the economy of grace. Now, these (as with the former) I shall do little more than name; it being not at all in my design to handle the natures of them, but only to show what respects they bear to the business in hand.

Consolation

Consolation is the first of these: "The disciples walked in the fear of the Lord, and in the consolation of the Holy Ghost" (Acts 9:31), *Tē paraklēsei tou hagiou Pneumatos*. He is *ho paraklētos*[1] and he gives *paraklēsin*[2]: from his work toward us, and in us, we have comfort and consolation. This is the first general consequent of his dispensation and work. Whenever there is mention made of comfort and consolation in the Scripture given to the saints (as there is most frequently), it is the proper consequent of the work of the Holy Ghost toward them. Comfort, or consolation in general, is the setting and composing of

---

1. the helper/advocate.
2. consolation/comfort.

391

the soul in rest and contentedness in the midst of or from troubles, by the consideration or presence of some good, wherein it is interested, outweighing the evil, trouble, or perplexity that it has to wrestle with. Where mention is made of comfort and consolation, properly so called, there is relation to trouble or perplexity; so the apostle, "As the sufferings of Christ abound in us, so our consolation also abounds by Christ" (2 Cor. 1:5–6). Suffering and consolation are opposed, the latter being a relief against the former; so are all the promises of comfort, and all the expressions of it, in the Old and New Testament still proposed as relief against trouble.

And, as I said, consolation arises from the presence or consideration of a greater good that outbalances the evil or perplexity wherewith we are to contend. Now, in the effects or acts of the Holy Ghost before mentioned lie all the springs of our consolation. There is no comfort but from them; and there is no trouble that we may not have comfort in and against by them. That a man may have consolation in any condition, nothing is required but the presence of a good, rendering the evil wherewith he is pressed inconsiderable to him. Suppose a man under the greatest calamity that can possibly befall a child of God, or a confluence of all those evils numbered by Paul (Rom. 8:35, etc.); let this man have the Holy Ghost performing the works mentioned before toward him, and, in despite of all his evils, his consolations will abound. Suppose him to have a sense of the love of God all the while shed abroad in his heart, a clear witness within that he is a child of God, accepted with him, that he is sealed and marked of God for his own, that he is an heir of all the promises of God, and the like; it is impossible that man should not triumph in all his tribulations.

From this rise of all our consolation are those descriptions which we have of it in the Scripture, from its properties and adjuncts; as—

It Is Abiding

It is *abiding*. Thence it is called "everlasting consolation" (2 Thess. 2:16), "God, even our Father, which has loved us, and given us everlasting consolation"—that is, comfort that vanishes not; and that because it rises from everlasting things. There may be some perishing comfort given for a little season by perishing things; but abiding consolation, which we have by the Holy Ghost, is from things everlasting: everlasting love, eternal redemption, an everlasting inheritance.

It Is Strong

Strong. "That the heirs of the promise should receive strong consolation" (Heb. 6:18). As strong opposition lies sometimes against us, and trouble, whose bands are strong, so is our consolation strong; it abounds, and is unconquerable—*ischura paraklēsis.*[3] It is such as will make its way through all opposition; it confirms, corroborates, and strengthens the heart under any evil; it fortifies the soul, and makes it able cheerfully to undergo anything that it is called unto: and that because it is from him who is strong.

It Is Precious

It is *precious.* Hence the apostle makes it the great motive unto obedience, which he exhorts the Philippians unto: "If there be any consolation in Christ" (Phil. 2:1); "If you set any esteem and valuation upon this precious mercy of consolation in Christ, by those comforts, let it be so with you."

And this is the first general consequent in the hearts of believers of those great effects of the Holy Ghost before mentioned. Now, this is so large and comprehensive, comprising so many of our concernments in our walking with God, that the Holy Ghost receives his denomination, as to the whole work he has to perform for us, from hence—he is the Comforter; as Jesus Christ, from the work of redemption and salvation, is the Redeemer and Savior of his church. Now, as we have no consolation but from the Holy Ghost, so all his effects toward us have certainly this consequent more or less in us. Yea, I dare say, whatever we have in the kinds of the things before mentioned that brings not consolation with it, in the root at least, if not in the ripe fruit, is not of the Holy Ghost. The way whereby comfort issues out from those works of his, belongs to particular cases. The fellowship we have with him consists, in no small portion of it, in the consolation we receive from him. This gives us a valuation of his love; teaches whither to make applications in our distress—whom to pray for, to pray to—whom to wait upon, in perplexities.

Peace

Peace arises hence also. "The God of hope fill you with all peace in believing, that you may abound in hope through the power of the Holy Ghost" (Rom. 15:13). The power of the Holy Ghost is not only extended

---

3. Gk. strong consolation.

to hope, but to our peace also in believing. So is it in the connection of those promises, "I will give you the Comforter" (John 14:26)—and what then? What follows that grant? "Peace," says he, "I leave with you; my peace I give unto you" (John 14:27). Nor does Christ otherwise leave his peace, or give his peace unto them, but by bestowing the Comforter on them. The peace of Christ consists in the soul's sense of its acceptation with God in friendship. So is Christ said to be "our peace" (Eph. 2:14), by slaying the enmity between God and us, and in taking away the handwriting that was against us. "Being justified by faith, we have peace with God" (Rom. 5:1). A comfortable persuasion of our acceptation with God in Christ is the bottom of this peace; it enwraps deliverance from eternal wrath, hatred, curse, condemnation—all sweetly affecting the soul and conscience.

And this is a *branch* from the same *root* with that foregoing—a consequent of the effects of the Holy Ghost before mentioned. Suppose a man chosen in the eternal love of the Father, redeemed by the blood of the Son, and justified freely by the grace of God, so that he has a right to all the promises of the gospel; yet this person can by no reasoning nor arguments of his own heart, by no considerations of the promises themselves, nor of the love of God or grace of Christ in them, be brought to any establishment in peace, until it be produced in him as a fruit and consequent of the work of the Holy Ghost in him and toward him. "Peace" is the fruit of the Spirit (Gal. 5:22). The savor of the Spirit is "life and peace" (Rom. 8:6). All we have is from him and by him.

Joy

Joy, also, is of this number. The Spirit, as was showed, is called "the oil of gladness" (Heb. 1:9). His anointing brings gladness with it, "the oil of joy for mourning" (Isa. 61:3). "The kingdom of God is righteousness, and peace, and joy in the Holy Ghost" (Rom. 14:17); "received the word with joy in the Holy Ghost" (1 Thess. 1:6)—"with joy," as Peter tells believers, "unspeakable and full of glory" (1 Pet. 1:8). To give joy to the hearts of believers is eminently the work of the Comforter; and this he does by the particulars before instanced in. That "rejoicing in hope of the glory of God," mentioned [in] Romans 5:2, which carries the soul through any tribulation, even with glorying, has its rise in the Spirit's "shedding abroad the love of God in our hearts" (Rom. 5:5). Now, there are two ways whereby the Spirit works this joy in the hearts of believers:

He does it *immediately* by himself; without the consideration of any other acts or works of his, or the interposition of any reasonings, or deductions and conclusions. As in *sanctification* he is a well of water springing up in the soul, immediately exerting his efficacy and refreshment; so in *consolation*, he immediately works the soul and minds of men to a joyful, rejoicing, and spiritual frame, filling them with exultation and gladness—not that this arises from our reflex consideration of the love of God, but rather gives occasion thereunto. When he so sheds abroad the love of God in our hearts, and so fills them with gladness by an immediate act and operation (as he caused John Baptist to leap for joy in the womb upon the approach of the mother of Jesus [Luke 1:44])—then does the soul, even from hence, raise itself to a consideration of the love of God, whence joy and rejoicing does also flow. Of this joy there is no account to be given, but that the Spirit works it when and how he will. He secretly infuses and distils it into the soul, prevailing against all fears and sorrows, filling it with gladness, exultations; and sometimes with unspeakable raptures of mind.

Mediately. By his other works toward us, he gives a sense of the love of God, with our adoption and acceptation with him; and on the consideration thereof enables us to receive it. Let what has been spoken of his operations toward us be considered—what assurance he gives us of the love of God; what life, power, and security; what pledge of our eternal welfare—and it will be easily perceived that he lays a sufficient foundation of this joy and gladness. Not that we are able, upon any rational consideration, deduction, or conclusion, that we can make from the things mentioned, to affect our hearts with the joy and gladness intended; it is left no less the proper work of the Spirit to do it from hence, and by the intervenience[4] of these considerations, than to do it immediately without them. This process of producing joy in the heart, we have, "You anoint my head with oil" (Ps. 23:5–6). Hence is the conclusion, as in the way of exultation, "Surely goodness and mercy shall follow me." Of this effect of the Comforter, see Isaiah 35 throughout.

Hope

Hope, also, is an effect of those workings of the Holy Ghost in us and toward us (Rom. 15:13). These, I say, are the general consequents of the effects of the Holy Ghost upon the hearts of believers; which, if we might

---

4. intervention

consider them in their offspring, with all the branches that shoot out from them, in exultation, assurance, boldness, confidence, expectation, glorying, and the like, it would appear how far our whole communion with God is influenced by them. But I only name the heads of things, and hasten to what remains. It is the general and particular way of our communion with the Holy Ghost that should next ensue, but that some other considerations necessarily do here interpose themselves.

Chapter 5

Misunderstandings of the Dispensation of the Holy Ghost

This process being made, I should now show immediately how we hold the communion proposed with the Holy Ghost in the things laid down and manifested to contain his peculiar work toward us; but there are some miscarriages in the world in reference unto this *dispensation* of the Holy Ghost, both on the one hand and the other, in contempt of his true work and pretence of that which is not, that I cannot but remark in my passage: which to do shall be the business of this chapter.

Contempt for the Dispensation of the Spirit

Take a view, then, of the state and condition of them who, professing to believe the gospel of Jesus Christ, do yet contemn and despise his Spirit, as to all its operations, gifts, graces, and dispensations to his churches and saints. While Christ was in the world with his disciples, he made them no greater promise, neither in respect of their own good nor of carrying on the work which he had committed to them, than this of giving them the Holy Ghost. Him he instructs them to pray for of the Father, as that which is needful for them, as bread for children (Luke 11:13). Him he promises them, as a well of water springing up in them, for their refreshment, strengthening, and consolation unto everlasting life (John 7:37–39); as also to carry on and accomplish the whole work of the ministry to them committed (John 16:8–11); with all those eminent works and privileges before mentioned. And upon his ascension, this is laid as the bottom of that glorious communication of gifts and graces in his plentiful effusion mentioned (Eph. 4:8, 11, 12)—namely, that he had received of the Father the promise of the Holy Ghost (Acts 2:33); and that in such an eminent manner as thereby to make the greatest and most glorious difference between the administration of the new covenant and old. Especially does the whole work of the ministry relate to the Holy Ghost; though that be not my present business to evince. He calls men to that work, and they are separated unto him (Acts 13:2); he furnishes them with gifts and abilities for that employment (1 Cor. 12:7–10). So that the whole religion we profess, without this administration of the Spirit, is nothing; nor is there any fruit without it of the resurrection of Christ from the dead.

This being the state of things—that in our worship of and obedience to God, in our own consolation, sanctification, and ministerial employment, the Spirit is the principle, the life, soul, the all of the whole; yet so desperate has been the malice of Satan, and wickedness of men, that their great endeavor has been to shut him quite out of all gospel administrations.

THE PUBLIC CONTEMPT OF THE SPIRIT

First, his *gifts* and graces were not only decried, but almost *excluded* from the public worship of the church, by the imposition of an operose[1] form of service, to be read by the minister; which to do is neither a peculiar gift of the Holy Ghost to any, nor of the ministry at all. It is marvelous to consider what pleas and pretences were invented and used by learned men—from its *antiquity*, its *composure* and approbation by *martyrs*, the beauty of uniformity in the worship of God, established and pressed thereby, etc.—for the defense and maintenance of it. But the main argument they insisted on, and the chief field wherein they expatiated[2] and laid out all their eloquence, was the vain babbling repetitions and folly of men praying by the Spirit. When once this was fallen upon, all (at least as they supposed) was carried away before them, and their adversaries rendered sufficiently ridiculous: so great is the cunning of Satan, and so unsearchable are the follies of the hearts of men. The sum of all these reasonings amounts to no more but this—"Though the Lord Jesus Christ has promised the Holy Ghost to be with his church to the end of the world, to fit and furnish men with gifts and abilities for the carrying on of that worship which he requires and accepts at our hands, yet the

---

1. laborious, tedious from being elaborate.
2. to write at some length; to enlarge upon; extended discussion.

work is not done to the purpose; the gifts he bestows are not sufficient to that end, neither as to invocation nor doctrine: and, therefore, we will not only help men by our directions, but exclude them from their exercise." This, I say, was the sum of all, as I could undeniably evidence, were that my present business, what innumerable evils ensue on this principle, in a formal setting apart of men to the ministry who had never once "tasted of the powers of the world to come" [Heb. 6:5] nor received any gifts from the Holy Ghost to that purpose; of crying up and growing in an outside pompous worship, wholly foreign to the power and simplicity of the gospel; of silencing, destroying, banishing men whose ministry was accompanied with the evidence and demonstration of the Spirit—I shall not need to declare. This is that I aim at, to point out the public contempt of the Holy Ghost, his gifts and graces, with their administration in the church of God, that has been found even where the gospel has been professed.

The Private Contempt of the Spirit

Again: it is a thing of most sad consideration, once to call to mind the improvement of that principle of contempt of the Spirit in private men and their ways. The name of the Spirit was grown a term of reproach. To plead for, or pretend to pray by, the Spirit was enough to render a man the object of scorn and reproach from all sorts of men, from the pulpit to the stage. "What! you are full of the Spirit; you will pray by the Spirit; you have the gift: let us hear your nonsense"—and yet, perhaps, these men would think themselves wronged not to be accounted Christians. Christians! yea, have not some pretending themselves to be leaders of the flock—yea, mounted a story or two above their brethren, and claiming a rule and government over them—made it their business to scoff at and reproach the gifts of the Spirit of God? And if this were the frame of their spirit, what might be expected from others of professed profaneness? It is not imaginable to what height of blasphemy the process in this kind amounted. The Lord grant there be nothing of this cursed leaven still remaining amongst us! Some bleatings[3] of ill importance[4] are sometimes heard. Is this the fellowship of the Holy Ghost that believers are called unto? Is this the due entertainment of him whom our Savior promised to send for the supply of his bodily absence, so as we might be no losers thereby? Is it not enough that men should be contented with

---

3. cries, especially from a sheep.
4. import, meaning.

such a stupid blindness, as, being called Christians, to look no further for their comfort and consolation than moral considerations common to heathens would lead them, when one infinitely holy and blessed person of the Trinity has taken this office upon him to be our comforter, but they must oppose and despise him also? Nothing more discovers how few there are in the world that have interest in that blessed name whereby we are all called. But this is no place to pursue this discourse. The aim of this discourse is to evince the folly and madness of men in general who profess to own the gospel of Christ, and yet contemn and despise his Spirit, in whomsoever he is manifested. Let us be zealous of the gifts of the Spirit, not envious at them.

From what has been discoursed we may also *try the spirits* that are gone abroad in the world, and which have been exercising themselves, at several seasons, ever since the ascension of Christ. The iniquity of the generation that is past and passing away lay in open, cursed opposition to the Holy Ghost. God has been above them, wherein they behaved themselves presumptuously. Satan, whose design, as he is god of this world [2 Cor. 4:4], is to be uppermost, not to dwell wholly in any form cast down by the providence of God, has now transformed himself into an angel of light [2 Cor. 11:14]; and he will pretend the Spirit also and only. But there are "seducing spirits" (1 Tim. 4:1); and we have a "command not to believe every spirit, but try the spirits" (1 John 4:1); and the reason added is, "Because many false prophets are gone out into the world"—that is, men pretending to the revelation of new doctrines by the Spirit; whose deceits in the first church Paul intimates, calling on men not to be "shaken in mind by spirit" (2 Thess. 2:2). The truth is, the spirits of these days are so gross that a man of a very easy discerning may find them out, and yet their delusion so strong that not a few are deceived. This is one thing that lies evident to every eye—that, according to his wonted course, Satan, with his delusions, is run into an extreme to his former actings.

Not long since, his great design, as I manifested, was to cry up ordinances without the Spirit, casting all the reproach that he could upon him—now, to cry up a spirit without and against ordinances, casting all reproach and contempt possible upon them. Then, he would have a *ministry* without the *Spirit*—now, a *Spirit* without a *ministry*. Then, the *reading* of the word might suffice, without either preaching or praying by the Spirit—now, the *Spirit* is enough, without reading or studying the word at all. Then, he allowed a literal embracing of what Christ had done in the flesh—now, he talks of Christ in the Spirit only, and denies him to be come in the flesh—the proper character of the false spirit we are warned of (1 John 4:1). Now, because it is most certain that the Spirit which we are to hear and embrace is the Spirit promised by Christ (which is so clear that the Montanists' paraclete[5] and Mohammed himself pretended to be the Spirit, and those of our days affirm and pretend the same), let us briefly try them by some of the effects mentioned, which Christ has promised to give the Holy Ghost for:

Testing the Spirits by Comparing What Christ Promised to Effect through the Spirit

THE SPIRIT BRINGS TO MIND WHAT CHRIST SPOKE

The first general effect, as was observed, was this—that he should bring to remembrance the things that Christ spoke, for our guidance and consolation. This was to be the work of the Holy Ghost toward the apostles, who were to be the penmen of the Scriptures: this is to be his work toward believers to the end of the world. Now, the things that Christ has spoken and done are "written that we might believe, and believing, have life through his name" (John 20:31); they are written in the Scripture. This, then, is the work of the Spirit which Christ has promised—he shall bring to our remembrance, and give us understanding of the words of Christ in the Scripture, for our guidance and consolation. Is this, now, the work of the spirit which is abroad in the world, and perverts many? Nothing less. His business is to decry the things that Christ has spoken which are written in the word; to pretend *new revelations* of his own; to lead men from the written word, wherein the whole work of God and all the promises of Christ are recorded.

THE SPIRIT GLORIFIES CHRIST

Again: the work of the Spirit promised by Christ is to glorify him: "He shall glorify me; for he shall receive of mine, and shall show it unto you" (John 16:14). Him who was to suffer at Jerusalem, who then spoke to his disciples, it was to make him glorious, honorable, and of high esteem in the hearts of believers; and that by showing his things (his love, kindness, grace, and purchase) unto them. This is the work

---

5. Montanism was a sect founded in the middle of the second century AD by Montanus, who claimed to receive direct revelations from the Holy Spirit; he even claimed that that Spirit spoken of in John 14:6 and 16:7 "was now incarnate in him." See John Anthony McGuckin, *The Westminster Handbook to Patristic Theology*, The Westminster Handbooks to Christian Theology (Louisville, KY: Westminster John Knox Press, 2004), 230–32.

of the Spirit. The work of the spirit that is gone abroad is to glorify itself, to decry and render contemptible Christ that suffered for us, under the name of a Christ without us; which it slights and despises, and that professedly. Its own glory, its own honor, is all that it aims at; wholly inverting the order of the divine dispensations. The fountain of all being and lying in the Father's love, the Son came to glorify the Father. He still says, "I seek not mine own glory, but the glory of him that sent me." The Son having carried on the work of redemption, was now to be glorified with the Father. So he prays that it might be, "The hour is come, glorify your Son" (John 17:1); and that with the glory which he had before the world was, when his joint counsel was in the carrying on the Father's love. Wherefore the Holy Ghost is sent, and his work is to glorify the Son. But now, as I said, we have a spirit come forth whose whole business is to glorify himself; whereby we may easily know whence he is.

The Spirit Sheds Abroad the Love of God in the Hearts of Believers

Furthermore: the Holy Ghost sheds abroad the love of God in our hearts, as was declared [Rom. 5:5], and thence fills them with joy, peace, and hope [Rom. 15:13]; quieting and refreshing the hearts of them in whom he dwells; giving them liberty and rest, confidence, and the boldness of children. This spirit whereof men now boast is a spirit of bondage, whose utmost work is to make men quake and tremble; casting them into an un-son-like frame of spirit, driving them up and down with horror and bondage, and drinking up their *very natural spirits*, and making their whole man wither away. There is scarce any one thing that more evidently manifests the spirit whereby some are now acted not to be the Comforter promised by Christ, than this—that he is a spirit of bondage and slavery in them in whom he is, and a spirit of cruelty and reproach toward others; in a direct opposition to the Holy Ghost in believers, and all the ends and purposes for which, as a spirit of adoption and consolation, he is bestowed on them.

The Spirit Bestows on Believers a Spirit of Prayer and Supplication

To give one instance more: the Holy Ghost bestowed on believers is a Spirit of prayer and supplication; as was manifested. The spirit wherewith we have to do, pretends the carrying men above such low and contemptible means of communion with God.[6] In a word, it were a very easy and facile task to pass through all of the eminent effects of the Holy Ghost in and toward believers, and to manifest that the pretending spirit of our days comes in a direct opposition and contradiction to every one of them. Thus has Satan passed from one extreme to another—from a bitter, wretched opposition to the Spirit of Christ, unto a cursed pretending to the Spirit; still to the same end and purpose.

I might give sundry other instances of the contempt or abuse of the dispensation of the Spirit. Those mentioned are the extremes whereunto all other are or may be reduced; and I will not further divert from that which lies directly in my aim.

---

6. In other words, "The false spirit we have been discussing pretends to carry men above such low and contemptible means of communion with God (namely, the means of prayer)."

Chapter 6

The Comfort of the Holy Spirit

The way being thus made plain for us, I come to show how we hold particular communion with the Holy Ghost, as he is promised of Christ to be our comforter, and as working out our consolation by the means formerly insisted on. Now, the first thing I shall do herein, is the proposal of that which may be some preparation to the duty under consideration; and this by leading the souls of believers to a due valuation of this work of his toward us, whence he is called our Comforter.

To raise up our hearts to this frame, and fit us for the duty intended, let us consider these three things: (1) what it is he comforts us against; (2) wherewith he comforts us; (3) the principle of all his actings and operations in us for our consolation.

What the Spirit Comforts Us Against

There are but three things in the whole course of our pilgrimage that the consolations of the Holy Ghost are useful and necessary in:

COMFORT IN OUR AFFLICTIONS

In our *afflictions*. Affliction is part of the *provision* that God has made in his house for his children (Heb. 12:5–6). The great variety of its causes, means, uses, and effects is generally known. There is a measure of them appointed for every one. To be wholly without them is a temptation; and so in some measure an affliction. That which I am to speak unto is that in all our afflictions we need the consolations of the Holy Ghost.

It is the nature of man to relieve himself, when he is entangled, by all ways and means. According as men's natural spirits are, so do they manage themselves under pressures. "The spirit of a man will bear his infirmity" [Prov. 18:14]; at least, will struggle with it.

There are two great evils, one of which does generally seize on men under their afflictions, and keep them from a due management of them. The apostle mentions them both: *Mē oligōrei paideias Kuriou, mēde ekluou, hup autou elegchomenos*—"Despise not the chastisement of the Lord; neither faint when you are reproved" (Heb. 12:5). One of these extremes do men usually fall into; either they despise the Lord's correction, or sink under it.

Men *despise it*. They account that which befalls them to be *a light or common thing*; they take no notice of God in it; they can shift with it well enough: they look on instruments, second causes; provide for their own defense and vindication with little regard to God or his hand in their affliction. And the ground of this is, because they take in succors, in their trouble, that God will not mix his grace withal; they fix on other remedies than what he has appointed, and utterly lose all the benefits and advantage of their affliction. And so shall every man do that relieves himself from any thing but the consolations of the Holy Ghost.

Men *faint and sink* under their trials and afflictions; which the apostle further reproves (v. 12). The first despise the assistance of the Holy Ghost through pride of heart; the latter refuse it through dejectedness of spirit, and sink under the weight of their troubles. And who, almost, is there that offends not on one of these hands? Had we not learned to count light of the chastisements of the Lord, and to take little notice of his dealings with us, we should find the season of our afflictions to comprise no small portion of our pilgrimage.

Now, there is no due management of our souls under any affliction, so that God may have the glory of it, and ourselves any spiritual benefit or improvement thereby, but by the consolations of the Holy Ghost. All that our Savior promises his disciples, when he tells them of the great trials and tribulations they were to undergo, is, "I will send you the Spirit, the Comforter; he shall give you peace in me, when in the world you shall have trouble. He shall guide and direct, and keep you in all your trials." And so, the apostle tells us, it came to pass (2 Cor. 1:4–6); yea, and this, under the greatest afflictions, will carry the soul to the highest joy, peace, rest, and contentment. So the same apostle, "We glory in tribulations" (Rom. 5:3). It is a great expression. He had said before, "We rejoice in hope of the glory of God" (Rom. 5:2). Yea, but what if manifold afflictions and tribulations befall us? "Why, even in them also we glory," says he; "we glory in our tribulations." But whence is it that our spirits are so borne up to a due management of afflictions, as to glory in them in the Lord? He tells us, it is from the "shedding abroad of the love of God in our hearts by the Holy Ghost" (Rom. 5:5) And thence are believers said to "receive the word in much affliction, with joy of the Holy Ghost" (1 Thess. 1:6), and to "take joyfully the spoiling of their goods." This is that I aim at: there is no management nor improvement of any affliction, but merely and solely by the *consolations of the Holy Ghost*. Is it, then, of any esteem or value unto you that you lose not all your trials, temptations, and affliction? Learn to value that whereby alone they are rendered useful.

COMFORTS IN THE BURDEN OF OUR SIN

Sin is the *second burden* of our lives, and much the greatest. Unto this is this consolation peculiarly suited. So [in] Hebrews 6:17–18, an allusion is taken from the manslayer under the law, who, having killed a man unawares and brought the guilt of his blood upon himself, fled with speed for his deliverance to the city of refuge. Our great and only refuge from the guilt of sin is the Lord Jesus Christ; in our flying to him, does the Spirit administer consolation to us. *A sense of sin* fills the heart with troubles and disquietness; it is *the Holy Ghost* which gives us peace in Christ—that gives an apprehension of wrath; the Holy Ghost sheds abroad the love of God in our hearts—from thence does Satan and the law accuse us, as objects of God's hatred; the Spirit bears witness with our spirits that we are the children of God. There is not any one engine or instrument that sin uses or sets up against our peace, but one effect or other of the Holy Ghost toward us is suited and fitted to the casting of it down.

COMFORTS IN THE WHOLE COURSE OF OUR OBEDIENCE

In *the whole course of our obedience* are his consolations necessary also, that we may go through with it cheerfully, willingly, patiently to the end. This will afterward be more fully discovered, as to particulars, when I come to give directions for our communion with this blessed Comforter. In a word, in all the concerns of this life, and in our whole expectation of another, we stand in need of the consolations of the Holy Ghost.

- Without them, we shall either despise afflictions or faint under them, and God be neglected as to his intendments in them.
- Without them, *sin* will either harden us to a contempt of it, or cast us down to a neglect of the remedies graciously provided against it.
- Without them, *duties* will either puff us up with pride, or leave us without that sweetness which is in new obedience.
- Without them, *prosperity* will make us carnal, sensual, and to take up our contentment in these things, and utterly weaken us for the trials of adversity.
- Without them, the *comforts of our relations* will separate us from God, and the loss of them make our hearts as Nabal's [1 Samuel 25].
- Without them, the *calamity* of the church will overwhelm us, and the prosperity of the church will not concern us.
- Without them, we shall have *wisdom* for no work, *peace* in no condition, *strength* for no duty, *success* in no trial, *joy* in no state—no *comfort* in life, no *light* in death.

Now, our afflictions, our sins, and our obedience, with the attendancies of them respectively, are the great concernments of our lives. What we are in reference unto God is comprised in them, and the due management of them, with their contraries, which come under the same rule; through all these does there run a line of consolation from the Holy Ghost, that gives us a joyful issue throughout. How sad is the condition of poor souls destitute of these consolations. What poor shifts are they forced to betake themselves unto! What giants have they to encounter in their own strength! And whether they are conquered or seem to conquer, they have nothing but the misery of their trials!

Wherewith the Spirit Comforts Us

The second thing considerable, to teach us to put a due valuation on the consolations of the Holy Ghost, is the matter of them, or that wherewith he comforts us. Now, this may be referred to the two heads that I have formerly treated of—the love of the Father and the grace of the Son. All the consolations of the Holy Ghost consist in his acquainting us with, and communicating unto us, the love of the Father and the grace of the Son; nor is there anything in the one or the other but he makes it a matter of consolation to us: so that, indeed, we have our communion with the Father in his love, and the Son in his grace, by the operation of the Holy Ghost.

THE *Love* OF THE FATHER

He *communicates* to us, and acquaints us with, the *love* of the Father. Having informed his disciples with that ground and foundation of their consolation which by the Comforter they should receive, our blessed Savior shuts up all in this, "The Father himself loves you" (John 16:27). This is that which the Comforter is given to acquaint us with—even that God is the Father, and that he loves us. In particular, that the Father, the first person in the Trinity, considered so distinctly, loves us. On this account is he said so often to come forth from the Father, because he comes in pursuit of his love, and to acquaint the hearts of believers therewith, that they may be comforted and established. By persuading us of the eternal and unchangeable love of the Father, he fills us with consolation. And, indeed, all the effects of the Holy Ghost before mentioned have their tendency this way. Of this love and its transcendent excellency you heard at large before. Whatever is desirable in it is thus communicated to us by the Holy Ghost. A sense of this is able not only to relieve us, but to make us in every condition to rejoice with joy unspeakable and glorious [1 Pet. 1:8]. It is not with an increase of corn, and wine, and oil, but with the shining of the countenance of God upon us, that he comforts our souls (Ps. 4:6–7). "The *world* hates me," may such a soul as has the Spirit say; "but my *Father* loves me. Men despise me as a *hypocrite*; but my Father loves me as a *child*. I am *poor* in this world; but I have a *rich* inheritance in the love of my Father. I am *straitened* in all things; but there is *bread enough* in my Father's house. I *mourn* in secret under the power of my lusts and sin, where no eyes see me; but the Father sees me, and is full of compassion. With a sense of his kindness, which is better than life, I rejoice in tribulation, glory in affliction, triumph as a conqueror. Though I am killed all the day long, all my sorrows have a *bottom* that may be fathomed—my trials, *bounds* that may be compassed; but the *breadth*, and *depth*, and *height* of the love of the Father, who can express?" I might render glorious this way of the Spirit's comforting us with the love of the Father, by comparing it with all other causes and means of joy and consolation whatever; and so discover their emptiness, its fullness—their nothingness, its being all; as also by revealing the properties of it before rehearsed.

The *Grace* of Christ

Again: he does it by *communicating* to us, and acquainting us with, the *grace of Christ*—all the fruits of his purchase, all the desirableness of his person, as we are interested in him. The grace of Christ, as I formerly discoursed of at large, is referred to two heads—the grace of his person, and of his office and work. By both them does the Holy Ghost administer consolation to us (John 16:14). He glorifies Christ by revealing his excellencies and desirableness to believers, as the "chief of ten thousand—altogether lovely" [Song 5:10, 16] and then he shows them of the things of Christ—his love, grace, all the fruits of his death, suffering, resurrection, and intercession: and with these supports their hearts and souls. And here, whatever is of refreshment in the pardon of sin, deliverance from the curse, and wrath to come, in justification and adoption, with the innumerable privileges attending them in the hope of glory given unto us, comes in on this head of account.

The Principle and Fountain of All the Spirit's Actings for Our Consolation

Thirdly, the *principle* and fountain of all his actings for our consolation comes next under consideration, to the same end; and this leads us a little nearer to the communion intended to be directed in. Now, this is his own great love and infinite condescension. He willingly proceeds or comes forth from the Father to be our comforter. He knew what we were, and what we could do, and what would be our dealings with him—he knew we would grieve him, provoke him, quench his motions, defile his dwelling-place; and yet he would come to be our comforter. Want of a due consideration of this great love of the Holy Ghost weakens all the principles of our obedience. Did this dwell and abide upon our hearts, what a dear valuation must we needs put upon all his operations and actings toward us! Nothing, indeed, is valuable but what comes from love and goodwill. This is the way the Scripture takes to raise up our hearts to a right and due estimation of our redemption by Jesus Christ. It tells us that he did it freely; that of his own will he has laid down his life; that he did it out of love.[1] "In this was manifested the love of God, that he laid down his life for us"; "He loved us, and gave himself for us" [Gal. 2:20]; "He loved us, and washed us from our sins in his own blood." Hereunto it adds our state and condition, considered as he undertook for us—sinners, enemies,

---

1. 1 John 4:9; 3:16; Gal. 2:20; Rev. 1:5.

dead, alienated; then he loved us, and died for us, and washed us with his blood. May we not hence, also, have a valuation of the dispensation of the Spirit for our consolation? He proceeds to that end from the Father; he distributes as he will, works as he pleases. And what are we, toward whom he carries on this work? Froward, perverse, unthankful; grieving, vexing, provoking him. Yet in his love and tenderness does he continue to do us good. Let us by faith consider this love of the Holy Ghost. It is the head and source of all the communion we have with him in this life. This is, as I said, spoken only to prepare our hearts to the communion proposed; and what a little portion is it of what might be spoken! How might all these considerations be aggravated! What a numberless number might be added! It suffices that, from what is spoken, it appears that the work in hand is amongst the greatest duties and most excellent privileges of the gospel.

Chapter 7

General Directions for Communion with the Holy Spirit

As in the account given of the actings of the Holy Ghost in us, we manifested first the general adjuncts of his actings, or the manner thereof; so now, in the description of the returns of our souls to him, I shall, in the first place, propose the general actings of faith in reference to this work of the Holy Ghost, and then descend unto particulars. Now, there are three general ways of the soul's deportment in this communion, expressed all negatively in the Scripture, but all including positive duties. Now these are—First, *Not to grieve him*. Secondly, *Not to quench his motions*. Thirdly, *Not to resist him*.

There are three things considerable in the Holy Ghost: (1) his *person*, as dwelling in us; (2) his *actings by grace*, or his motions; (3) his *working in the ordinances* of the word, and the sacraments—all for the same end and purpose.

To these three are the three cautions before suited: (1) not to *grieve* him, in respect of his *person* dwelling in us. (2) Not to *quench* him, in respect of the *actings* and motions of his grace. (3) Not to *resist* him, in respect of the *ordinances* of Christ, and his gifts for their administration. Now, because the whole general duty of believers, in their communion with the Holy Ghost, is comprised in these three things, I shall handle them severally.

Do Not Grieve the Spirit because of His Person

The first *caution* concerns his *person* immediately, as dwelling in us. It is given [as] "Grieve not the Holy Spirit of God" (Eph. 4:30). There is a complaint (Isa. 63:10) of them who vexed or grieved the Spirit of God; and from thence does this caution seem to be taken. That it is the person of the Holy Ghost which is here intended, is evident—

THAT HOLY SPIRIT

From the *phrase*, or manner of expression, with a double article, *To Pneuma to hagion*—"That Holy Spirit"; and also—

THE WORK ASSIGNED TO HIM

From the *work* assigned to him in the following words, of "sealing to the day of redemption" [Eph. 4:30]; which, as has been manifested, is the work of the Holy Ghost. Now, whereas this may be understood of the Spirit in others, or in ourselves, it is evident that the apostle intends it in the latter sense, by his addition of that signal and eminent privilege which we ourselves enjoy by him: he seals us to the day of redemption.

Let us see, then, the tendency of this expression, as comprising the first general rule of our communion with the Holy Ghost—"Grieve not the Spirit."

The term of "grieving," or affecting with sorrow, may be considered either *actively*, in respect of the persons grieving; or *passively*, in respect of the persons grieved. In the latter sense the expression is metaphorical. The Spirit cannot be grieved, or affected with sorrow; which infers alteration, disappointment, weakness—all incompatible with his infinite perfections; yet men may actively do that which is fit and able to grieve anyone that stands affected toward them as does the Holy Ghost. If he be not grieved, it is no thanks to us, but to his own unchangeable nature. So that there are two things denoted in this expression:

First, that the Holy Ghost is affected toward us as one that is loving, careful, tender, *concerned in our good and well-doing*; and therefore upon our miscarriages is said to be grieved: as a good friend of a kind and loving nature is apt to be on the miscarriage of him whom he does affect. And this is that we are principally to regard in this caution, as the ground and foundation of it—the love, kindness, and tenderness of the Holy Ghost unto us. "Grieve him not."

Second, that we may do those things *that are proper to grieve him*, though he be not passively grieved; our sin being no less therein than if he were grieved as we are. Now, how this is done, how the Spirit is grieved, the apostle declares in the contexture[1] of that discourse (vv. 21–24). He presses to a progress in sanctification, and all the fruits of regeneration (vv. 25–29). He dehorts[2] from sundry particular evils that were contrary thereto, and then gives the general enforcement of the one and the other, "And grieve not the Holy Spirit of God"; that is, by coming short of that universal sanctification which our planting into Christ does require. The *positive duty* included in this caution, of not grieving the Holy Spirit, is this—that we pursue universal holiness with regard unto, and upon the account of, the love, kindness, and tenderness of the Holy Ghost. This is the foundation of our communion we have in general. When the soul considers the love, kindness, and tenderness of the Holy Ghost unto him; when he considers all the fruits and acts of his love and goodwill toward him; and on that account, and under that consideration, because he is so concerned in our ways and walkings, to abstain from evils, and to walk in all duties of holiness—this is to have communion with him. This consideration, that the Holy Ghost, who is our comforter, is delighted with our obedience, grieved at our evils and follies, being made a continual motive to, and reason of, our close walking with God in all holiness, is, I say, the first general way of our communion with him.

Here let us fix a little. We lose both the *power* and *pleasure* of our obedience for want of this consideration. We see on what account the Holy Ghost undertakes to be our comforter, by what ways and means he performs that office toward us; what an unworthy thing it is to grieve him who comes to us on purpose to give us consolation! Let the soul, in the whole course of its obedience, exercise itself by faith to thoughts hereof and lay due weight upon it: "The Holy Ghost, in his infinite love and kindness toward me, has condescended to be my comforter; he does it willingly, freely, powerfully. What have I received from him! In the multitude of my perplexities how has he refreshed my soul! Can I live one day without his consolations? And shall I be regardless[3] of him in that wherein he is concerned? Shall I grieve him by negligence, sin, and folly? Shall not his love constrain me to walk before him to all well-pleasing?" So have we in general fellowship with him.

---

1. structure, composition, texture, fabric.
2. exhorts in order to dissuade
3. disregarding

Do Not Quench the Spirit because of His Actings by Grace

The second is that of 1 Thessalonians 5:19, "Quench not the Spirit." There are various thoughts about the sense of these words. "The Spirit in others, that is, their spiritual gifts," say some; but then it falls in with what follows, "Despise not prophesying" (v. 20). "The light that God has set up in our hearts," say others; but where is that called absolutely *To Pneuma*—"The Spirit?" It is the Holy Ghost himself that is here intended, not immediately, in respect of his *person* (in which regard he is said to be grieved, which is a personal affection); but in respect of his *motions, actings, and operations*. The Holy Ghost was typified by the fire that was always kept alive on the altar. He is also called a "Spirit of burning" [Isa. 4:4]. The reasons of that allusion are manifold; not now to be insisted on. Now, the opposition that is made to fire in its actings is by quenching. Hence the opposition made to the actings of the Holy Ghost are called "quenching of the Spirit," as some kind of wet wood will do when it is cast into the fire. Thence are we said, in pursuance of the same metaphor, *anazōpurein*—to "stir up with new fire"—the gifts that are in us [2 Tim. 1:6]. The Holy Ghost is striving with us, acting in us, moving variously for our growth in grace, and bringing forth fruit meet for the principle he has endued[4] us with. "Take heed," says the apostle, "lest, by the power of your lusts and temptations, you attend not to his workings, but hinder him in his goodwill toward you; that is, what in you lies."

This, then, is the second general rule for our communion with the Holy Ghost. It respects his gracious *operations* in us and by us. There are several and various ways whereby the Holy Ghost is said to act, exert, and put forth his power in us; partly by moving upon and stirring up the grace we have received; partly by new supplies of grace from Jesus Christ, falling in with occasions for their exercise, raising good motions immediately or occasionally within us—all tending to our furtherance in obedience and walking with God. All these are we carefully to observe and take notice of—consider the fountain whence they come, and the end which they lead us unto. Hence have we communion with the Holy Ghost, when we can consider him by faith as the immediate author of all supplies, assistance, and the whole relief we have by grace; of all good actings, risings, motions in our hearts; of all strivings and contending against sin. When we consider, I say, all these his actings and workings

---

4. endowed

in their tendency to our consolation, and on that account are careful and watchful to improve them all to the end aimed at, as coming from him who is so loving, and kind, and tender to us, we have communion with him.

This is that which is intended—every gracious acting of the blessed Spirit in and toward our souls, is constantly by faith to be considered as coming from him in a peculiar manner; his mind, his goodwill is to be observed therein. Hence, care and diligence for the improvement of every motion of his will arise; thence reverence of his presence with us, with due spiritual regard to his holiness, does ensue, and our souls are wonted to intercourse with him.

Do Not Resist the Spirit because of the Ordinances of Christ

The third caution concerns him and his *work*, in the dispensation of that great *ordinance of the word*. Stephen tells the Jews that they "resisted the Holy Ghost" (Acts 7:51). How did they do it? Why, as their fathers did it: "As your fathers did, so do you." How did their fathers resist the Holy Ghost? "They persecuted the prophets, and slew them" (v. 52); their opposition to the prophets in preaching the gospel, or their showing of the coming of the Just One, was their resisting of the Holy Ghost. Now, the Holy Ghost is said to be resisted in the contempt of the preaching of the word; because the gift of preaching of it is from him. "The manifestation of the Spirit is given to profit" (1 Cor. 12:7). Hence, when our Savior promises the Spirit to his disciples, to be present with them for the conviction of the world, he tells them he will give them a mouth and wisdom, which their adversaries shall not be able to gainsay nor resist (Luke 21:15); concerning which, in the accomplishment of it in Stephen, it is said that they "were not able to resist the Spirit by which he spoke" (Acts 6:10). The Holy Ghost then setting up a ministry in the church, separating men thereto, furnishing them with gifts and abilities for the dispensation of the word; the not-obeying of that word, opposing of it, not falling down before it, is called resisting of the Holy Ghost. This, in the examples of the wickedness of others, are we cautioned against. And this enwraps the third general rule of our communion with the Holy Ghost: in the dispensation of the word of the gospel, the authority, wisdom, and goodness of the Holy Ghost, in furnishing men with gifts for that end and purpose, and his presence with them, as to the virtue thereof, is to be eyed, and subjection given unto it on that account. On this reason, I say, on this ground, is obedience to be yielded to the word, in the *ministerial dispensation thereof*—because the Holy Ghost, and he alone, does furnish with gifts to that end and purpose. When this consideration causes us to fall low before the word, then have we communion with the Holy Ghost in that ordinance. But this is commonly spoken unto.

Chapter 8

Particular Directions for Communion with the Holy Spirit

Before I name particular directions for our communion with the Holy Ghost, I must premise some *cautions*, as far as the *directions* to be given, concerning his worship.

In Worshiping One Person, We Worship the Whole Trinity

The *divine nature* is the reason and cause of all worship; so that it is impossible to *worship any one* person, and not worship the *whole* Trinity. It is, and that not without ground, denied by the schoolmen,[1] that the *formal reason* and object of divine worship is in the persons *precisely* considered; that is, under the formally constitutive reason of their personality, which is their relation to each other. But this belongs to the divine nature and essence, and to their *distinct* persons as they are *identified* with the essence itself. Hence is that way of praying to the Trinity, by the repetition of the same petition to the several persons (as in the Litany[2]), groundless, if not impious. It supposes that one person is worshiped, and not another, when each person is worshiped as God, and each person is so—as though we first should desire one thing of the Father, and be heard and granted by him, then ask the same thing of the Son, and so of the Holy Ghost; and so act as to the same thing three distinct acts of worship, and expect to be heard and have the same thing granted three times distinctly, when all the works of the Trinity, *ad extra*, are indivisible.

The proper and peculiar object of divine worship and invocation is *the essence of God*, in its infinite excellency, dignity, majesty, and its causality,

---

1. those scholars in the medieval Scholastic tradition
2. in the *Book of Common Prayer*

as the first sovereign cause of all things. Now, this is common to all the three persons, and is proper to each of them; not formally as a person, but as God blessed forever. All adoration respects that which is common to all; so that in each act of adoration and worship, all are adored and worshiped. The creatures worship their Creator; and a man, him in whose image he was created—namely, him "from whom descends every good and perfect gift" [James 1:17]: all this describing God as God. Hence—

In Praying to One Person, We Pray to the Whole Trinity

When we begin our *prayers* to God the Father, and end them in the name of Jesus Christ, yet the Son is no less invocated and worshiped in the beginning than the Father, though he be peculiarly mentioned as mediator in the close—not as Son to himself, but as *mediator to the whole Trinity*, or God in Trinity. But in the invocation of God the Father we invocate every person; because we invocate the Father as God, every person being so.

In Approaching God, We Worship the Whole Trinity

In that *heavenly directory* which we have (Eph. 2:18), this whole business is declared. Our access in our worship is said to be "to the Father"; and this "through Christ," or his mediation; "by the Spirit," or his assistance. Here is a distinction of the persons, as to their operations, but not at all as to their being the object of our worship. For the Son and the Holy Ghost are no less worshiped in our access to God than the Father himself; only, the grace of the Father, which we obtain by the mediation of the Son and the assistance of the Spirit, is that which we draw nigh to God for. So that when, by the distinct dispensation of the Trinity, and every person, we are led to worship (that is, to act faith on or invocate) any person, we do herein worship the whole Trinity; and every person, by whatsoever name, of Father, Son, or Holy Ghost, we invocate him. So that this is to be observed in this whole matter—that when any work of the Holy Ghost (or any other person), which is appropriated to him (we never exclude the concurrence of other persons), draws us to the worship of him, yet he is not worshiped exclusively, but the whole Godhead is worshiped.

We Are Distinctly to Worship the Spirit

These cautions being premised, I say that we are *distinctly to worship* the Holy Ghost. As it is in the case of faith in respect of the Father and the Son, "Believe in God, believe also in me" (John 14:1)—this extends itself no less to the Holy Ghost. Christ called the disciples for the acting of faith on him, he being upon the accomplishment of the great work of his mediation; and the Holy Ghost, now carrying on the work of his delegation, requires the same. And to the same purpose are their distinct operations mentioned: "My Father works hitherto, and I work" [John 5:17]. Now, as the formal reason of the worship of the Son is not his mediation, but his being God (his mediation being a powerful motive thereto), so the *formal reason* of our worshiping the Holy Ghost is not his *being our comforter*, but his *being God*; yet his being our comforter is a powerful motive thereunto.

This is the sum of the first direction: the grace, actings, love, effects of the Holy Ghost, as he is our comforter, ought to stir us up and provoke us to love, worship, believe in, and invocate him—though all this, being directed to him as God, is no less directed, on that account, to the other persons than to him. Only by the fruits of his love toward us are we stirred up unto it.

These things being presupposed, let the saints learn to act faith distinctly on the Holy Ghost, as the immediate efficient cause of all the good things mentioned—faith, I say, to believe in him; and faith in all things to believe him and to yield obedience to him; faith, not imagination. The distinction of the persons in the Trinity is not to be fancied, but believed. So, then, the Scripture so fully, frequently, clearly, distinctly ascribing the things we have been speaking of to the immediate efficiency of the Holy Ghost, faith closes with him in the truth revealed, and peculiarly regards him, worships him, serves him, waits for him, prays to him, praises him—all these things, I say, the saints do in faith. The person of the Holy Ghost, revealing itself in these operations and effects, is the peculiar object of our worship. Therefore, when he ought to be peculiarly honored, and is not, he is peculiarly sinned against. Ananias is said to lie to the Holy Ghost—not to God (Acts 5:3); which being taken essentially, would denote the whole Trinity, but peculiarly to the Holy Ghost. Him he was to have honored peculiarly in that special gift of his which he made profession of—not doing it, he sinned peculiarly against him. But this must be a little further branched into particulars:

Let us, then, lay weight on every effect of the Holy Ghost in any of the particulars before mentioned, on this account, that they are acts of his love and power toward us. This faith will do, that takes notice of his *kindness in all things*. Frequently he performs, in sundry particulars, the office of a comforter toward us, and we are not thoroughly comforted—we take no notice at all of what he does. Then is he grieved. Of those who do receive and own the consolation he tenders and administers, how few are there that consider him as the comforter, and rejoice in him as they ought! Upon every work of consolation that the believer receives, this ought his faith to resolve upon—"This is from the Holy Ghost; he is the Comforter, the God of all consolation; I know there is no joy, peace, hope, nor comfort, but what he works, gives, and bestows; and that he might give me this consolation, he has willingly condescended to this office of a comforter. His love was in it, and on that account does he continue it. Also, he is sent by the Father and Son for that end and purpose. By this means come I to be partaker of my joy—it is in the Holy Ghost; of consolation—he is the Comforter. What price, now, shall I set upon his love! How shall I value the mercy that I have received!"

This, I say, is applicable to every particular effect of the Holy Ghost toward us, and herein have we communion and fellowship with him, as was in part discovered in our handling the particulars. Does he shed abroad the love of God in our hearts? Does he witness unto our adoption? The soul considers his presence, ponders his love, his condescension, goodness, and kindness; is filled with reverence of him, and cares not to grieve him, and labors to preserve his temple, his habitation, pure and holy.

Again: our communion with him causes in us *returning praise*, and thanks, and honor, and glory, and blessing to him, on the account of the mercies and privileges which we receive from him; which are many. Herein consists our next direction. So do we with the Son of God on the account of our redemption: "Unto him that loved us, and washed us from our sins in his own blood, to him be glory and dominion forever and ever" (Rev. 1:5–6). And are not the like praises and blessings due to him by whom the work of redemption is made effectual to us? Who with no less infinite love undertook our consolation than the Son our redemption. When we feel our hearts warmed with joy, supported in peace, established in our obedience, let us ascribe to him the praise that is due to him, bless his name, and rejoice in him.

And this glorifying of the Holy Ghost in thanksgivings, *on a spiritual sense* of his consolations, is no small part of our communion with him. Considering his free engagement in this work, his coming forth from the Father to this purpose, his mission by the Son, and condescension therein, his love and kindness, the soul of a believer is poured out in thankful praises to him, and is sweetly affected with the duty. There is no duty that leaves a more heavenly savor in the soul than this does.

Also, in our prayers to him for the carrying on the work of our consolation, which he has undertaken, lies our communion with him.

John prays for grace and peace from the *seven Spirits* that are before the throne, or the Holy Ghost, whose operations are perfect and complete [Rev. 4:5]. This part of his worship is expressly mentioned frequently in Scripture; and all others do necessarily attend it. Let the saints consider what need they stand in of these effects of the Holy Ghost before mentioned, with many such others as might be insisted on; weigh all the privileges which we are made partakers of; remember that he distributes them as he will, that he has the sovereign disposal of them; and they will be prepared for this duty.

How and in what sense it is to be performed has been already declared: what is the *formal* reason of this worship, and *ultimate* object of it, I have also manifested. In the duty itself is put forth no small part of the life, efficacy, and vigor of faith; and we come short of that enlargedness[3] of spirit in dealing with God, and are straitened from walking in the breadth of his ways, which we are called unto, if we learn not ourselves to meet him with his worship in every way he is pleased to communicate himself unto us. In these things he does so in the person of the Holy Ghost. In that person do we meet him, his love, grace, and authority, by our prayers and supplications.

Again: consider him as he *condescends to this delegation* of the Father and the Son to be our comforter, and ask him daily of the Father in the name of Jesus Christ. This is the daily work of believers. They look upon, and by faith consider, the Holy Ghost as promised to be sent. In this promise, they know, lies all their grace, peace, mercy, joy, and hope. For by him so promised, and him alone, are these things communicated to them. If, therefore, our life to God, or the joy of that life, be considerable, in this we are to abound—to ask him of the Father, as children do of their parents daily bread. And as, in this asking and receiving of the Holy Ghost, we have communion with the Father in his love, whence he is sent; and with the Son in his grace, whereby he is obtained for us; so with himself, on the account of his voluntary condescension to this dispensation. Every request for the Holy Ghost implies our closing with all these. O the riches of the grace of God!

Humbling ourselves for our miscarriages in reference to him is another part of our communion with him. That we have *grieved* him as to his person, *quenched* him as to the motion of his grace, or *resisted* him in his ordinances, is to be mourned for; as has been declared. Let our souls be humbled before him on this account. This one considerable

---

3. liberation, freedom.

ingredient of godly sorrow, and the thoughts of it, are as suitable to the affecting of our hearts with humiliation, and indignation against sin, as any other whatever. I might proceed in the like considerations; as also make application of them to the particular effects of the Holy Ghost enumerated; but my design is only to point out the heads of things, and to leave them to the improvement of others.

The State of Those Not Interested in the Promise of the Spirit

I shall shut up this whole discourse with some considerations of the sad estate and condition of men not interested in this promise of the Spirit, nor made partakers of his consolation:

They Have No True Consolation or Comfort

They have no *true consolation* or comfort, be their estate and condition what it will. Are they under affliction or in trouble? They must bear their own burden; and how much too weak they are for it, if God be pleased to lay on his hand with more weight than ordinary, is easily known. Men may have stoutness of spirit, and put on great resolutions to wrestle with their troubles; but when this is merely from the natural spirit of a man—

IT IS OUTWARD ONLY

For the most part it is but an outside. It is done with respect to others, that they may not appear low-spirited or dejected. Their hearts are eaten up and devoured with troubles and anxiety of mind. Their thoughts are perplexed, and they are still striving, but never come to a conquest. Every new trouble, every little alteration in their trials, puts them to new vexation. It is an ungrounded resolution that bears them up, and they are easily shaken.

IT IS CONTENDING WITH GOD

What is the best of their resolves and enduring? It is but a contending with God, who has entangled them—the struggling of a flea under a mountain. Yea, though on outward considerations and principles they endeavor after patience and tolerance, yet all is but a contending with God—a striving to be quiet under that which God has sent on purpose to disturb them. God does not afflict men without the Spirit, to exercise their patience; but to disturb their peace and security. All their arming themselves with patience and resolution, is but to keep the hold that

God will cast them out of, or else make them the nearer to ruin. This is the best of their consolation in the time of their trouble.

It Is Illusory

If they do promise themselves anything of the care of God toward them, and relieve themselves thereby—as they often do, on one account or another, especially when they are driven from other holds—all their relief is but like the dreaming of a hungry man, who supposes that he eats and drinks, and is refreshed; but when he awakes, he is empty and disappointed. So are they as to all their relief that they promise to receive from God, and the support which they seem to have from him. When they are awaked at the latter day, and see all things clearly, they will find that God was their enemy, laughing at their calamity, and mocking when their fear was on them.

So is it with them in trouble. Is it any better with them in their prosperity? This, indeed, is often great, and is marvelously described in Scripture, as to their lives, and oftentimes quiet, peaceable end. But have they any true consolation all their days? They eat, drink, sleep, and make merry, and perhaps heap up to themselves; but how little do these things make them to differ from the beasts that perish! Solomon's advantage, to have the use and know the utmost of these things, much beyond any of the sons of men of our generation, is commonly taken notice of. The account also that he gives of them is known: "They are all vanity and vexation of spirit." This is their consolation: a crackling of thorns under the pot, a sudden flash and blaze, that begins but to perish. So that both adversity and prosperity slays them; and whether they are laughing or crying, they are still dying.

They Have No Peace

They have *no peace*—no peace with God, nor in their own souls. I know that many of them, upon false bottoms, grounds, and expectations, do make a shift to keep things in some quietness, neither is it my business at present to discover the falseness and unsoundness of it; but this is their state. True and solid peace being an effect of the Holy Ghost in the hearts of believers (as has been declared), they who are not made partakers of him have no such peace. They may cry, "Peace, peace," indeed, when sudden destruction is at hand. The *principles* of their peace (as may be easily evinced) are darkness or ignorance, treachery of conscience, self-righteousness, and vain hope. To these heads may all the principles of their peace be reduced; and what will these avail them in the day when the Lord shall deal with them?

They Have No Joy and Hope

I might say the same concerning their *joy* and *hope*—they are false and perishing. Let them, then, consider this, who have satisfied themselves with a persuasion of their interest in the good things of the gospel, and yet have despised the Spirit of Christ. I know there are many that may pretend to him, and yet are strangers from his grace; but if they perish who in profession use him kindly, and honor him, if he dwell not in them with power, where shall they appear who oppose and affront him? The Scripture tells us, that unless the Spirit of Christ be in us, we are dead, we are reprobates—we are none of Christ's. Without him you can have none of *those glorious effects* of his toward believers before mentioned; and you are so far from inquiring whether he be in you or no, as that you are ready to deride them in whom he is. Are there none who profess the gospel, who have never once seriously inquired whether they are made partakers of the Holy Ghost or no? You that almost account it a ridiculous thing to be put upon any such question, who look on all men as vain pretenders that talk of the Spirit, the Lord awake such men to a sight of their condition before it be too late! If the Spirit dwells not in you, if he be not your Comforter, neither is God your Father, nor the Son your Advocate, nor have you any portion in the gospel. Oh, that God would awake some poor soul to the consideration of this thing, before the neglect and contempt of the Holy Ghost come to that despising of him from which there is no recovery! That the Lord would spread before them all the folly of their hearts, that they may be *ashamed* and confounded, and do no more presumptuously!

GLOSSARY

accidental. Nonessential, incidental.

acquitment. Aquittal, discharge, release.

adjudged. Sentenced, judged, settled judicially.

adjunct. Association, thing attached.

affiance. Trust.

afford. Supply.

aggravates. Adds to the weight of.

amplitude. Largeness

annexed. Joined, added, united, attached.

anon (1). Presently, soon.

anon (2). Again.

appellations. Names, designations.

approbation. Praise, approval, commendation.

appurtenances. Apparatus, instruments.

asseveration. Solemn and emphatic assertion, declaration.

assignation. Assigning, assignment.

astonishable. Measured to astonish and surprise.

aversation. A moral turning away; estrangement.

becomes. Suits; is fitting.

behoof. Use, benefit, advantage.

betroth. Commit to marriage.

bewail. Wail, cry out, lament.

bleatings. Cries, especially from a sheep.

bottom. Basis.

bottomed. Grounded.

brake. Past participle of *broke*.

breach. Gap.

catch. Eagerly grasp.

caul. Membrane; the pericardium.

cause. Action or person who brings about the desired result.

chimera. Vain, fanciful illusion.

close. Unite, settle, consummate.

closer. Union.

coincident. Matching point for point; in exact agreement.

comeliness. Attractiveness.

comminations. Denunciations, threats.

commutation. Substitution, exchange.

compass. Delimitation, measure.

compassing. Attaining, achieving.

conduces. Leads, contributes.

conjoin. Join together, unite.

conjugal. Marital.

consanguinity. Kinship, relationship by blood or common ancestor.

contemn. Despise with contempt, scorn, disdain.

contexture. Structure, composition, texture, fabric.

conversation. Way of life.

covert. Shelter.

cross. In contradiction, against.

cruciate. Torment, torture.

dainties. That which is sweet, delicious.

days-man. Arbiter, mediator, umpire.

dehorts. Exhorts in order to dissuade.

denomination. Name, designation.

deportment. Conduct, behavior, demeanor.

desert. That which it deserves, punishment.

destinated. Destined, ordained.

determinate. Determined, resolved, settled.

disannul. Annul, cancel, make void.

discover. Reveal, uncover.

discovery. Revelation.

dispensation. Arrangement, provision, ordering.

disquietment. Disturbance, uneasiness, anxiety, unrest.

earnest. A payment, installment to secure a contract, a pledge.

economy. *Generally*: administration; *specifically*: the administration of the plan of salvation.

efficient cause. The means or agency by which something comes into being.

endued. Endowed.

energetical. Emphatic, powerful.

enlargedness. Liberation, freedom.

ensue. Follow.

entertainment. Act of upholding, maintaining, receiving; providing for; spending time with.

espousals. Wedding, wedding feast.

evince. Prove, evidence, make manifest.

excrescences. abnormal growth on a plant (or animal)

exinanition. Abasement, humiliation.

expatiate. Write at some length; enlarge upon; extended discussion.

expostulate. Reason earnestly with someone so as to dissuade them.

exurgency. Urgent force

eye. Look, Gaze upon.

facile. Effortless.

fain. Eager, well-disposed; be delighted to.

flagon. A large, spouted vessel for holding and pouring liquids, usually wine.

filial. Pertaining to a son or daughter.

froward. Stubbornly contrary, obstinate.

furniture. Endowments, qualities, capacities.

galleries. Tresses, long hair.

giddiness. Incapable of serious thought or attention, akin to intoxication.

haply. Perhaps, perchance.

illapses. Permeations, descents.

illatively. Inferentially.

impetration. Act of obtaining by entreaty or petition.

import. Signify.

importance. Import, meaning.

improvement. Good or profitable enhancement, completion.

incumbent. Obligatory.

indigent. Lacking, impoverished, deficient.

indisposedness. Disinclination, unwillingness.

inlet. Entrance.

inquest. Inquiry, investigation.

insensible. Imperceptible; barely able to be perceived.

instantly. Insistently.

intended. Stretched, increased.

intendment. Intention.

intercourse. Communication.

interest. Share in, claim of.

interposition. Interjection, intervention.

intervenience. Intervention.

intimate. Communicate, make known.

invocated. Invoked.

iota. The ninth letter of the Greek alphabet, referring to a tiny portion.

issues. Proceedings.

Judaical. Jewish.

lasciviousness. Inclination to lust, wantonness.

lees. Wine that has been laid down for a significant period of time so that it ages properly.

malefactor. Criminal.

manuduction. Guidance (by the hand).

mean. Despicable, vile, lowly.

meanest. Lowliest, most debased.

meet. Fitting, appropriate.

metathesis. Transposition of letters, sounds, or syllables within a word.

metonymy (metonymical). A figure of speech whereby one term is substituted for another term which is closely associated with it.

mind. Remind.

napkin. To hide or to neglect through not using.

nigh. Near.

nitre. Native sodium carbonate.

obdurate. Hardened, unyielding, obstinate.

obediential. Obedient.

oblation. Offering, sacrifice.

obnoxious. Liable, subject to, exposed, made susceptible to harm.

odoriferous. Fragrant.

offscouring. Refuse, filth scoured off and cast away.

operose. Laborious, tedious from being elaborate.

ornament. Adornment.

owning. Admitting, acknowledging, confessing to be true.

papists. Negative label for Roman Catholics, due to their belief in papal supremacy.

paraphrast. Paraphraser.

paschal. Passover.

pathetical. Affecting, moving.

peculiar. Particular, characteristic, in its own way.

pitch. Level, degree.

popish. Negative label for Roman Catholicism, relating to belief in papal supremacy.

procured. Gained, obtained.

procuring cause. Action or person who brings about the desired result.

profession. Confession.

professors. Ones who make a religious confession.

progenitors. Ancestors.

promiscuously. Indiscriminately.

quickening. Giving life to.

quits. Discontinues, ceases.

raiment. Garments, clothing.

rapine. Pillage, robbery, plunder.

rectitude. Uprightness.

redounds. Results in some advantage.

regardless. Disregarding.

repining. Discontentment, fretting, grumbling.

reposes. Brings relief, respite.

retirements. Privacy and seclusion, usually leisure.

retrievement. Retrieval.

satiated. Satisfied.

scholiast. Scholar who writes explanatory notes.

servilely. Submissively, cringingly, slavelike.

shed. Poured forth.

signal. Significant, striking, remarkable, notably out of the ordinary.

stations. Positions.

stay. Sustain.

stead. Place.

straitenings. Constrictions.

straits. Difficulties, distresses.

subduct. Remove from use, influence.

subservient. Subject.

subsistence. Mode or quality of existence.

succor. Assist, relieve.

suffered. Allowed, permitted, tolerated.

suffices. Satisfies, is enough for.

sullied. Polluted, soiled.

sundry. Various, particular, distinct.

sup. Eat, have supper.

supererogation. Roman Catholic doctrine that actions going beyond the call of duty and the requirements for salvation produce a superabundance of merit deposited in a spiritual treasury of the church and are used by ordinary sinners for the remittance of their sins.

susception. Reception.

temper. Character, constitution, quality.

tempered. Balanced.

tender. Careful.

tenders. Offers.

tergiversations. Evasions, falsifications.

tittle. A small distinguishing mark, such as a diacritic, accent, or the dot over an *i*.

tumultuating. Agitation, disturbing, stirring up.

unacceptation. Unacceptability.

unction. Anointing.

unctions. Ointments.

usurping. Seizing, taking control with power and force.

variance. Dissent, discord.

velleity. Inclination, mere desire, wish.

vesture. Garment, covering, robe.

vexation. Annoyance.

want. Lack.

wantonness. Unrestrained rebelliousness.

wax. Grow, become.

well-head. Source, spring, fountain.

without. Outside, external to.

wonted. Accustomed.

wroth. Wrathful.

Subject Index

Name Index

SCRIPTURE INDEX

New Testament